Young People's Attitudes to Religious Diversity

Investigating the hitherto unexplored topic of how young people understand and relate to religious diversity in the social context in which they are growing up, this volume makes a significant contribution to the existing body of literature on religious diversity and multiculturalism. It closes a gap in knowledge about young people's attitudes to religious diversity, and reports data gathered across the whole of the UK as well as comparative chapters on Canada, the United States and continental Europe. Reporting findings from both qualitative and quantitative research which reveal, for example, the importance of the particular social and geographical context within which young people are embedded, the volume addresses young people's attitudes towards the range of 'world religions' as well as non-religious stances and offers an interdisciplinary approach through the different analytical perspectives of the contributors.

Elisabeth Arweck is Principal Research Fellow in the Warwick Religions and Education Research Unit (WRERU), Centre for Education Studies, University of Warwick, and the Editor of the Journal of Contemporary Religion. Her recent research has focused on young people's attitudes to religious diversity and the religious socialisation and nurture of young people. Recent publications include a number of co-authored articles (with Eleanor Nesbitt) and (co-edited) volumes, such as *Religion and Knowledge* (with Mathew Guest, Ashgate 2013), *Exploring Religion and the Sacred in a Media Age* (with Chris Deacy, Ashgate 2009) and *Reading Religion in Text and Context* (with Peter Collins, Ashgate 2006). She is the author of several book chapters and of *Researching New Religious Movements in the West* (Routledge 2007) and co-author (with Peter Clarke) of *New Religious Movements in Western Europe: An Annotated Bibliography* (Greenwood Press 1997).

AHRC/ESRC Religion and Society Series
Series Editors: Linda Woodhead and Rebecca Catto

This book series emanates from the largest research programme on religion in Europe today – the AHRC/ESRC Religion and Society Programme which has invested in over seventy-five research projects. Thirty-two separate disciplines are represented looking at religion across the world, many with a contemporary and some with an historical focus. This international, multi-disciplinary and interdisciplinary book series includes monographs, paperback textbooks and edited research collections drawn from this leading research programme.

Other titles in the series include:

Everyday Lived Islam in Europe
Edited by Nathal M. Dessing, Nadia Jeldtoft and Linda Woodhead

Religion Italian Style
Continuities and Changes in a Catholic Country
Franco Garelli

Exploring New Monastic Communities
The (Re)invention of Tradition
Stefania Palmisano

Religion and Legal Pluralism
Edited by Russell Sandberg

A Sociology of Prayer
Edited by Giuseppe Giordan and Linda Woodhead

Young People's Attitudes to Religious Diversity

Edited by Elisabeth Arweck

Routledge
Taylor & Francis Group

LONDON AND NEW YORK

First published 2017
by Routledge
2 Park Square, Milton Park, Abingdon, Oxon OX14 4RN

and by Routledge
711 Third Avenue, New York, NY 10017

Routledge is an imprint of the Taylor & Francis Group, an informa business

British Library Cataloguing in Publication Data
A catalogue record for this book is available from the British Library

Library of Congress Cataloging-in-Publication Data
Names: Arweck, Elisabeth, editor.
Title: Young people's attitudes to religious diversity / edited by Elisabeth Arweck.
Description: New York : Routledge, 2016. | Includes bibliographical references and index.
Identifiers: LCCN 2016025437 | ISBN 9781472444301 (hardback) | ISBN 9781315546032 (ebook)
Subjects: LCSH: Religious pluralism—Public opinion. | Multiculturalism—Religious aspects—Public opinion. | Young adults—Attitudes.
Classification: LCC BL85 .Y675 2016 | DDC 201/.5—dc23
LC record available at https://lccn.loc.gov/2016025437

ISBN: 978-1-4724-4430-1 (hbk)
ISBN: 978-1-315-54603-2 (ebk)

Typeset in Bembo
by Apex CoVantage, LLC

Printed in the United Kingdom
by Henry Ling Limited

Contents

Preface	ix
List of figures	xii
List of tables	xiii
Acknowledgements	xv

PART ONE
Setting the context — 1

1 **The Young People's Attitudes to Religious Diversity project in the context of Warwick Religions and Education Research Unit (WRERU) research** — 3
ROBERT JACKSON AND URSULA MCKENNA

2 **The qualitative strand: listening in depth** — 19
ELISABETH ARWECK AND JULIA IPGRAVE

3 **The quantitative strand: an individual differences approach** — 31
LESLIE J. FRANCIS, GEMMA PENNY AND MANDY ROBBINS

PART TWO
Qualitative perspectives — 43

4 **Sources of knowledge and authority: religious education for young Muslims in a Birmingham comprehensive school** — 45
JULIA IPGRAVE

5 **Uniting two communities or creating a third community? Research in a Northern Irish integrated school** — 61
JULIA IPGRAVE

6 Cradling Catholics in secular Scotland: research in
a Scottish Roman Catholic high school   77
JULIA IPGRAVE

7 The matter of context: the case of two community schools
in Wales   97
ELISABETH ARWECK

8 Religious diversity as a personal and social value:
impressions from a multicultural school in London   125
ELISABETH ARWECK

PART THREE
Quantitative perspectives   151

9 Does RE work and contribute to the common good
in England?   153
LESLIE J. FRANCIS, GEMMA PENNY AND URSULA McKENNA

10 Testing the 'worlds apart' thesis: Catholic and
Protestant schools in Northern Ireland   170
LESLIE J. FRANCIS, GEMMA PENNY AND PHILIP BARNES

11 Growing up Catholic in Scotland: not one Catholic
community but three   186
LESLIE J. FRANCIS, GEMMA PENNY AND PETER NEIL

12 Schools with a religious character and community
cohesion in Wales   204
LESLIE J. FRANCIS, GEMMA PENNY AND TANIA AP SIÔN

13 The personal and social significance of diverse
religious affiliation in multi-faith London   222
LESLIE J. FRANCIS AND GEMMA PENNY

PART FOUR
International engagement   243

14 Young people and religious diversity: a Canadian perspective   245
LORI G. BEAMAN, PETER BEYER AND CHRISTINE L. CUSACK

15 **A collage of contexts: young people and religious
    diversity in the United States**   263
    MARY ELIZABETH MOORE

16 **Young people and religious diversity: a European
    perspective, with particular reference to Germany**   275
    ALEXANDER YENDELL

    List of contributors   291
    Index   296

Preface

Although many of the pupils at the state-funded grammar school for boys that I attended in North London were from Jewish or Catholic backgrounds, its daily act of religious worship and its compulsory lessons in Religious Instruction were unmistakably Protestant. The school also boasted an annual ceremony in Westminster Abbey to honour the memory of the Duchess of Somerset, a benefactor of the school who died in 1692 (Robinson 1840, 234). And the Religious Instruction teacher presented a copy of *The Sectional New Testament* and a hand-written letter to the one hundred or so pupils who left the school each year. The letter addressed to 'Dear Beckford' in July 1961 explained that 'The great objective of the Book is to lead us to a personal act of commitment, when we definitely trust Jesus Christ our Lord & Saviour and yield our lives to Him, & to receive His eternal life'. In other words, Protestant Christianity was the default position not only for me but, I suspect, for millions of other products of British schools in the nineteenth and twentieth centuries.

It was only when I began studying the history of French thought as an undergraduate in the early 1960s that questions about religious difference, religious diversity, religious tolerance and religious freedom made their first inroads into my mind. The writings of Michel de Montaigne, Blaise Pascal, Denis Diderot and Voltaire were the first catalysts for the sociological studies that I eventually conducted of sectarian movements, religious minorities, public policies for 'managing' religions, prison chaplaincies and, most recently, migration and religion. Each of these studies reflects the fact that diversity has become a major feature of everything that counts as 'religion' nowadays in the UK and many other parts of the world. The reasons for the growth of religious diversity may differ from country to country; and the implications of religious diversity for other aspects of social and cultural life may also be varied. But there is no doubt that – with the exception of a small number of countries where diversity is deliberately suppressed – the label of 'religion' can be applied to an increasing number of different phenomena in the early twenty-first century.

Studies of religious heresy, dissidence, sectarianism, tolerance and intolerance have a long history, but it is only since the 1980s that research has been firmly focused on patterns of interactions within and between religions as social and cultural entities. To some extent, questions about religious diversity were previously implicit in topics as varied as 'race', ethnicities, multiculturalism, multi-faith and interfaith dialogues or migration. But studies of relations within and between majorities and minorities framed as 'religious' have now become more common, more important and more urgent. The reasons for the attention increasingly paid to these relations reflect a wide range of factors that include the acceleration of global communications, the geographical mobility of migrants, refugees and asylum seekers, the sophistication of mechanisms for making claims in the name of religions, the readiness of state agencies to recognize and interpellate religious groups as partners, the activation of international treaties protecting the right to hold religious beliefs and the force of legal doctrines, either making it illegal to discriminate on the grounds of 'religion or belief' or asserting the equality of all religions or beliefs.

These changes throw religious diversity into sharp relief at international, national and local levels. It is no longer enough to think merely in terms of the differences between religions. Indeed, any focus on religious differences alone runs the risk of exaggerating the extent to which religions can be usefully considered as unitary, homogeneous or unchanging entities. It can also give the misleading impression that differences can be readily measured against a fixed norm. And it tends to accentuate points of disagreement or tension between religions. By contrast, a focus on religious diversity brings to light the overall variety of religious expressions in any given territory without neglecting the legacy of historical patterns of majorities and minorities, dominance and sub-mission or legitimation and disqualification. The focus on diversity brings to light not only the variety and the concentrations of religious expressions but also, and most importantly, their interactions.

The number of scholarly publications about religious diversity has increased significantly since 2000, but the chapters that follow make three distinctive and important contributions to the stock of knowledge. The first is that this book is one of the very few in-depth investigations of religious diversity which focus specifically on schools and young people. The second is that it examines both quantitative *and* qualitative data about the attitudes expressed by large numbers of pupils towards religious diversity in their schools. And the third is that data from schools in England, Wales, Scotland and Northern Ireland are comple-mented by insights into the situation in Canada, the USA and Germany.

This study of young people's attitudes towards religious diversity could hardly be timelier or more necessary. In 2015 alone, no fewer than three substantial reports were published on research into religious education and collective wor-ship in British schools (Clarke and Woodhead 2015; Dinham and Shaw 2015; Cumper and Mawhinnie 2015). A fourth report in 2015 also considered these topics in the broader context of religion and belief in British public life (see Commission on Religion and Belief in British Public Life 2015). The driv-ing force behind all this research is the realization that the current relationship between religion and education, which was 'settled' in legislation in 1944 and revised in 1988, may no longer be appropriate in Britain today. The main reason for this is that religious diversity, coupled with the spread of outlooks and ways of life that owe little or nothing to religion, has advanced to the point where disagreements and disputes about how best – if at all – to make space for religion in schools are growing louder in public debates.

This volume makes particularly valuable and original contributions to the public debate about religious diversity not only because it tackles such a 'hot button' topic but also because its approach foregrounds young people's own opinions and attitudes. Contributors are also careful to clarify the theoretical debates in which their empirical investigations are grounded and the methods that they used to collect information. Readers will appreciate the book's extensive scope as well as its intensive drilling down into robust findings about young people and their attitudes to religious diversity.

James A. Beckford

References

Clarke, Charles, and Linda Woodhead. 2015. *A New Settlement: Religion and Belief in Schools*. London, Westminster Faith Debates.

Commission on Religion and Belief in British Public Life. 2015. *Living with Difference: Community, Diversity and the Common Good*. Cambridge: The Woolf Institute.

Cumper, Peter, and Alison Mawhinnie. 2015. *Collective Worship and Religious Observance in Schools: An Evaluation of Law and Policy in the UK*. Leicester: University of Leicester.

Dinham, Adam, and Martha Shaw. 2015. *RE for Real: The Future of Teaching and Learning about Religion and Belief*. London: Goldsmiths College, University of London.

Robinson, William. 1840. *The History and Antiquities of the Parish of Tottenham in the County of Middlesex*. Vol. II. 2nd ed. London: Nicholls and Son.

Figures

16.1   Respect for all religions by country and age groups   277
16.2   Support of freedom of religious belief by country and
          age groups   278
16.3   Granting rights for all religious groups by country and
          age groups   279
16.4   Religious diversity as cultural enrichment by country
          and age groups   279
16.5   Support for building mosques by country and age groups   280
16.6   Restriction of Islamic faith by country and age groups   281
16.7   Positive attitudes towards Muslims by country and age groups   281
16.8   Contact with Muslims by age groups   282
16.9   Rejection of Muslims as neighbours   287

Tables

9.1	Religious beliefs	159
9.2	Religious affect	160
9.3	Religious environment	160
9.4	Religious discussion	161
9.5	Main influences	162
9.6	Studying religions at school	163
9.7	Understanding religious and cultural difference	163
9.8	Attitudes towards religions	164
9.9	Attitudes towards religious plurality	165
9.10	Attitude towards cultural diversity	166
9.11	Attitudes towards religious distinctiveness	166
10.1	Attitudes towards religion	176
10.2	Attitudes towards Protestants	177
10.3	Attitudes towards Catholics	177
10.4	Shaping views about Protestants	178
10.5	Shaping views about Catholics	179
10.6	Accepting religious plurality	179
10.7	Living with religious plurality	180
10.8	Living with cultural diversity	181
10.9	Studying religion in school	182
10.10	Accepting religious clothing	183
11.1	Religious identity	191
11.2	Religious conversation	192
11.3	Religion and life	193
11.4	Christian beliefs	193
11.5	Religious affect	194
11.6	Non-conventional beliefs	195
11.7	Religion and education	195
11.8	Religion and society	196
11.9	Accepting religious plurality	197
11.10	Living with religious plurality	198
11.11	Living with cultural diversity	199
11.12	Accepting religious differences	200

12.1	Religious identity	211
12.2	Religious discussion	211
12.3	Religious self-assessment	212
12.4	Religious beliefs	212
12.5	Religion in schools	213
12.6	Attitudes towards religions	214
12.7	Accepting religious plurality	215
12.8	Living with religious plurality	215
12.9	Living with cultural diversity	216
12.10	Accepting religious clothing	217
12.11	Sources of influence	218
12.12	Studying religion in school	219
13.1	Religious identity	229
13.2	Religious importance	230
13.3	Religious self-assessment	230
13.4	Religious conversation	231
13.5	Religious influence	232
13.6	Religious beliefs	232
13.7	Personal wellbeing	233
13.8	Social wellbeing	234
13.9	Attitudes towards religions	235
13.10	Attitudes towards religious plurality	235
13.11	Living with religious plurality	236
13.12	Living with cultural diversity	237
13.13	Living with religious differences	238
16.1	Results of the structural equation model: attitudes towards Muslims	283
16.2	Frequency of contacts with Muslims	286

Acknowledgements

WRERU staff involved in this project gratefully acknowledge funding from the Religion and Society Programme of the Arts and Humanities Research Council (AHRC) and the Economic and Social Research Council (ESRC). They greatly appreciate the assistance of the staff of the schools visited and value the participation of the young people who took part in the discussion groups or completed the survey questionnaires. They are also grateful to Associate Fellows of the Warwick Religions and Education Research Unit (WRERU), University of Warwick, and other colleagues (e.g. religious education advisors, teachers, lecturers) who facilitated some school visits or completion of questionnaires in some schools.

Part One

Setting the context

1 The Young People's Attitudes to Religious Diversity project in the context of Warwick Religions and Education Research Unit (WRERU) research

Robert Jackson and Ursula McKenna

WRERU's studies of religious diversity and education

Warwick Religions and Education Research Unit (WRERU) has undertaken externally funded empirical research on various aspects of religions and education since its foundation in 1994. From 1994 to 2013, WRERU was based in the Institute of Education at the University of Warwick. Since October 2013, WRERU has been part of the University of Warwick's newly formed interdisciplinary Centre for Education Studies.

The Young People's Attitudes to Religious Diversity project continued a tradition of WRERU studies concerned with religious diversity in the UK. Most of these studies have been variously concerned with the experience of children and young people from a range of religious and cultural backgrounds. They have built on earlier ethnographic studies, such as Warwick's Religious Education and Community Project, involving children in Britain from Christian, Jewish, Muslim and Sikh backgrounds, and the first UK project on religion and education to be funded by the Economic and Social Research Council (ESRC) (Jackson and Nesbitt 1992; Nesbitt and Jackson 1992, 1995; Woodward and Jackson 1993), together with studies of children from a Hindu background funded from various sources, including the Leverhulme Trust (e.g. Jackson and Nesbitt 1993).

These early ethnographic studies were inspired by listening to the personal stories of children in schools and homes, and through meeting, spending much time with and interviewing their parents and members of their wider communities. Reflection on academic issues related to the study of religions 'on the ground' and methodological issues concerned with understanding, portraying and responding at a personal level to another's religious life, together with issues related to the 'transmission' of religious culture, inspired the interpretive approach to religious education. This drew eclectically on methods and ideas from a range of sources and disciplines, including ethnography, social psychology, literary theory, religious studies and hermeneutical theory. Its key concepts of representation, interpretation and reflexivity provided a research framework which was also used pedagogically, as a basis for teaching and learning in other contexts: the learner's challenges of comprehension mirrored those of the researcher (Jackson 1997, 2012c). This period also included experiments in producing texts for use in schools drawing on research material collected during ethnographic studies (e.g. Barratt 1994a, 1994b, 1994c, 1994d, 1994e; Barratt and Price 1996; Jackson and Nesbitt 1990; Mercier 1996; Robson 1995; Wayne et al. 1996).

WRERU's subsequent wide-ranging qualitative research extended to school-based as well as family- and community-based studies. These included a longitudinal study of young people from a Hindu background (e.g. Nesbitt 1991; Nesbitt and Jackson 1992), research on the life histories of teachers and students of religious education (e.g. Sikes and Everington 2001), studies of pupil-to-pupil dialogue in the classroom (e.g. Ipgrave 2001, 2013; McKenna, Ipgrave and Jackson 2008) and religious education for children with special educational needs (e.g. McKenna 2002). The Arts and Humanities Research Council (AHRC) funded research on the religious identity formation of young people in mixed-faith families (e.g. Arweck 2013; Arweck and Nesbitt 2010, 2012) and on the influence of Hindu-related 'religious movements' on classroom practice in various contexts (e.g. Arweck, Nesbitt and Jackson 2005, 2008). This period also saw further development of theory and pedagogy in religious education (e.g. Jackson 2004).[1]

In 2006, WRERU had the opportunity to broaden its research perspective in two ways: to work collaboratively with teams of researchers from across Europe interested in themes connected with diversity, and to extend its repertoire of research techniques, for example introducing a mixed-method approach to research (e.g. Jackson 2012a). Thus WRERU participated in a large European project, the REDCo (Religion, Education, Dialogue, Conflict) project, involving researchers from eight European countries (see later in this chapter).

Expansion of WRERU and the UK government DCSF project

In 2007, considerable expertise in quantitative research was added to WRERU's team, when Prof. Leslie Francis and other colleagues (Dr Mandy Robbins, Dr Emyr Williams, Dr Tania ap Siôn and Prof. David Lankshear) joined. As well as bringing huge knowledge and experience of quantitative methodologies, Prof. Francis's deep experience in psychology (especially individual differences psychology) and practical and empirical theology complemented existing WRERU competence in fields such as ethnography, sociology, interfaith dialogue, religious studies and religious education, making large-scale collaborative mixed-methods research feasible.

The first major opportunity to use the new research team came in 2008, when WRERU won a competitive bid from the UK Government's then Department for Children, Schools and Families (DCSF) to investigate 'materials used in schools to teach world religions'. The project employed 29 staff, including WRERU researchers and associate fellows, experts in academic studies of religions, information and communications technology (ICT) and primary and secondary religious education as well as consultants from faith communities. The research included three strands: in strand 1, a sample of published materials (identified in strands 2 and 3) was reviewed by a panel of experts consisting of members of faith groups, academic experts and professional religious education (RE) experts. Strand 2 was a quantitative survey of materials used in schools, in which subject leaders were asked to identify materials which were used by teachers in the preparation of lessons, by both teachers and pupils during lessons, and by pupils during their own independent researches. Strand 3 consisted of qualitative case studies conducted in 10 primary and 10 secondary schools, selected from maintained and independent schools of all types. Case study research included: documentary analysis (e.g. the RE syllabus used by the school); visual ethnography (e.g. observation of visual images in the school relating to religion, religious diversity and community cohesion); lesson observations (e.g. to see how materials were used); semi-structured interviews with key staff and pupils; and focus group interviews with pupils. Throughout the project, there was consultation between the research groups involved in the three strands, the schools involved in the case studies and the experts from the different faith communities. Project publications included the main report to the DCSF (Jackson et al. 2010). However, the key significance of the project for WRERU was its leap forward in terms of capacity to design and conduct large-scale mixed-methods research in religious education.

The REDCo project

WRERU's participation in the European Commission Framework 6 REDCo project produced a body of research on young people in eight European nations, including WRERU's studies in England. These consisted of qualitative (e.g. Ipgrave and McKenna 2008) and quantitative (e.g. McKenna, Neill and Jackson 2009) studies of the views of 14- to 16-year-olds as well as qualitative studies of classroom interaction (e.g. O'Grady 2009). One of WRERU's distinctive contributions to REDCo was an experiment in using key principles from the interpretive approach (Jackson 1997) in a series of school-based action research studies conducted through the ongoing work of a collaborative community of practice, including teachers, teacher trainers and a religious education adviser (Ipgrave, Jackson and O'Grady 2009). The key concepts of the interpretive approach were used not as a formal theoretical framework but as a theoretical stimulus and the basis for a checklist for researchers working in the field (Jackson 2011, 2012b).[2]

The REDCo project set out to explore whether religious education in Europe was a factor contributing positively to religious dialogue or, on the contrary, a potential source of conflict. The main aim was to establish and compare the potentials and limitations of religion in the educational fields of the selected European countries and regions (England, Estonia, France, Germany, the Netherlands, Norway, the Russian Federation and Spain). Another aim was to identify approaches and policies that might make religion in education a factor which promotes dialogue. Qualitative, quantitative and classroom interaction studies were carried out in the eight nations and various complementary studies were conducted.

The REDCo project was innovative in that, while it was a cross-European project, data analysis was enabled at both the national and European levels. Its data can be viewed nationally or as part of the wider dataset from the eight European countries, providing collections of examples of religion in education in a variety of northern, southern, western and eastern European countries (e.g. Knauth et al. 2008; ter Avest et al. 2009; Valk et al. 2009). Moreover, because qualitative and quantitative studies across participating nations used the same research methods, comparisons, such as between the English and the Dutch data (Bertram-Troost and O'Grady 2008), could be made between countries of diverse historical and socio-cultural backgrounds, including different histories of religion and state. Reports of a cross-section of the REDCo studies can be found in Jackson (2012a), while detailed findings of different project strands are presented in particular collections (e.g. qualitative studies in Knauth et al. 2008, quantitative findings in Valk et al. 2009 and classroom interaction studies in ter Avest et al. 2009).

Despite contextual differences between and within the participant countries, the main findings of the REDCo project included the following (based on information at http://www.redco.uni-hamburg.de/cosmea/core/corebase/mediabase/awr/redco/research_findings/REDCo_policy_rec_eng.pdf):

- The majority of pupils appreciated the religious heterogeneity in their societies, although a range of prejudices was expressed.
- The most important source of information about religions and worldviews was generally the family, followed by the school.
- The school population included a sizeable group of pupils for whom religion was important in their lives, a sizeable group for whom religion was not important and a sizeable group who held a variety of occasionally fluctuating positions between these two poles.
- Irrespective of their religious positions, a majority of pupils were interested in learning about religions in school.
- Pupils were well aware of and experienced religious diversity mostly in, but also outside, school.
- Pupils were generally open towards peers of different religious backgrounds. At the same time they tended to socialize with peers from the same background as themselves, even when they lived in areas characterized by religious diversity.
- Pupils often expressed a tolerant attitude at an abstract rather than practical level. The tolerance expressed in classroom discussion was not always replicated in their daily life-worlds.
- Those who learnt about religious diversity in school were more willing to enter into conversations about religions and worldviews with pupils from other backgrounds, compared to those who did not have this opportunity for learning.

- Pupils desired peaceful coexistence across religious differences and believed that this was possible.
- Pupils believed that the main preconditions for peaceful coexistence between people of different religions were knowledge about each other's religions and worldviews, shared interests and joint activities.
- In most countries pupils supported the right of adherents to a moderate expression of religious faith in school. For example, they did not oppose in school the wearing of unobtrusive religious symbols or did not object to voluntary acts of worship for pupils who were adherents of a particular religion.
- Pupils for whom religion was important in their lives were more likely to respect the religious backgrounds of others and valued the role of religion in the world.
- Most pupils wanted to see school dedicated more to teaching about different religions than to guiding them towards a particular religious belief or worldview; however, pupils tended to favour the model of education about religion with which they were most familiar.
- Pupils wanted learning about religions to take place in a safe classroom environment governed by agreed procedures for expression and discussion.
- Pupils generally wished to avoid conflict on religious issues and some of the religiously committed pupils felt especially vulnerable.
- Dialogue was a favoured strategy for teachers to cope with diversity in the classroom, but pupils were more ambivalent about its value since, in practice, not all pupils were comfortable with the way diversity was managed in schools.

Many of these findings are reinforced by the Young People's Attitudes to Religious Diversity project, but this project is able to provide more nuanced findings because it is based on bigger samples (see later).

Critical feedback on the REDCo project

Some criticisms have been advanced against REDCo, some of which could equally have been directed at the Young People's Attitudes to Religious Diversity project (see later). Two criticisms, in particular, have been made by Liam Gearon (2013).

The first criticism is the assertion that research using theory and method grounded in the social sciences and psychology is inherently secularist and therefore exhibits an anti-religious bias. The basis of this criticism is the association of such disciplines with the European Enlightenment and its legacy, especially the association of disciplines with 'founding' intellectuals whose work, in effect, attempted to explain religion away. Sociology is associated by Gearon with Durkheim, while psychology is linked to its Freudian ancestry. Thus, Francis's work is placed in a vague and cover-all 'psychological-experiential paradigm', along with that of others who make a strong use of psychology, regardless of the type of psychology they employ or the nature of its use in their research or pedagogy (Gearon 2013, 115–122). Jackson's work (coupled with that of WRERU colleagues Nesbitt and Arweck) is seen to occupy its own distinctive 'socio-cultural paradigm'. Regarding Jackson's interpretive approach, Gearon claims that

> the origins of this approach lie in the founding sociological work of Emile Durkheim and especially *The Elementary Forms of the Religious Life* . . . From Durkheim's analysis of what were then regarded as religion's primitive origins, it was surmised that religion itself originated in society's self deification.
>
> (ibid., 127)

But Jackson's work *never* refers to Durkheim as an influence; the only reference to Durkheim in *Religious Education: An Interpretive Approach* is a critical one (Jackson 1997, 31). Jackson's interpretive approach has multiple influences from a variety of disciplines (see earlier), including the use or adaptation of *methods* associated with certain strands of social or cultural anthropology. The resultant, eclectically sourced methodology (Jackson 2012c) aims to help researchers and learners (whatever their own religious or cultural backgrounds) to *understand* and *reflect upon* (partly through processes of 'participation' and 'distanciation') the *religious* meanings of others. Similarly, Francis's psychological research is grounded in a specific mix of psychological theory and dovetails with his work in practical and empirical theology. To claim that all of such work is inherently secularist because of the origins of the family of disciplines it uses ignores theoretical diversity within the subjects concerned, including ongoing debates by those actually working in the fields about their nature and assumptions (e.g. Evans-Pritchard 1962; Jackson 1997, 30–32; Jackson 2012d).

The second criticism is the claim that participation in any *research* relating to religious education having an instrumental social or political aim (for example, being concerned with the contribution that studies of religion might make to social cohesion or addressing issues of dialogue and conflict) implies that those researchers and the users of their research regard the *process* of religious education as having a single 'political' aim (e.g. Gearon 2013, 132–134). This claim is linked to others. The argument can be summarized as follows: democratic states, in response to increasing cultural and religious diversity, have an interest in promoting tolerance (through promoting democratic values or human rights, for example) and therefore develop policies to support it. In accepting funding from sources such as the European Commission to conduct research related to tolerance, researchers collude with such agencies (ibid., 36). REDCo researchers, says Gearon, focused entirely on issues raised by young people, developing a religious education pedagogy aiming to increase tolerance through classroom 'dialogue' (ibid., 133). In the research itself, and in pedagogy that relates to it, conflict is filtered out, profound differences are not taken seriously and truth claims are not considered. Furthermore, an underlying pluralistic theology is assumed – 'a theological notion of religious pluralism in which all religions represent cultural variations of one ultimate reality' (ibid., 134).

Gearon's claims are very much open to question. First, it does not follow from the fact that a piece of research focuses on a 'social' issue, in this case dealing with the topic of religion in pluralistic classrooms, that the researchers involved in this must adhere to a single 'historical-political' aim for religious education. For example, social aims (such as increasing tolerance) are closely interrelated with personal views, which also connect with the wider teachings of religious groups and traditions in the case of those with religious commitments. Moreover, participants in research might also support other aims, such as regarding the study of religion and values as an intrinsic element of liberal education.

Second, Gearon claims a dubious relationship between the agendas of political bodies (e.g. national governments or the European Commission) and funding for particular research projects, such as REDCo: the political body provides the funding on their terms; the researchers apply for it (e.g. Gearon 2013, 36). However, why should not the priorities of a political body accurately reflect actual social need? Researchers (like any other citizens) might share some current governmental concerns, such as community cohesion, in increasingly diverse and complex democratic societies.

Third, it does not follow that research findings concerned with young people's views and experiences engender a type of religious education that is entirely based upon young people's views and experience. REDCo researchers were interested in issues surrounding pupil-to-pupil dialogue, but there was no assumption that such dialogue should *constitute* religious education. The goal of having well-informed teachers, able to provide authoritative information about religions and beliefs, was regarded as essential (e.g. von der Lippe 2010). Teacher competence in this field requires both subject knowledge and skills enabling civil interaction among students (Jackson 2014).

Fourth, there was no agenda to play down or 'filter out' conflict in pupil exchanges in the REDCo project. REDCo research argues explicitly, and in a variety of research reports and discussions, for the constructive use of 'conflict' in teaching and learning (e.g. Knauth 2009; Skeie 2008; von der Lippe 2011), while accounts of classroom interaction give concrete examples of such use (e.g. Kozyrev 2009; O'Grady 2013).

Fifth, no universalist or pluralistic theology was assumed in the REDCo project and there was no expectation that students should be encouraged to adopt such a theology. Many pupils with conservative religious theologies participated in REDCo research and showed no signs of changing their views. REDCo researchers came from a variety of religious (including Christian and Muslim) and non-religious backgrounds and did not share a common theological viewpoint.[3]

Where REDCo could have been criticized legitimately was in the limited scale of the studies within particular nations; however, they were never intended as *national* indicators. WRERU researchers were thus keen to follow up REDCo with a larger scale and more representative study in the United Kingdom.

The Religion and Society Programme:
Young People's Attitudes to Religious Diversity

An opportunity to design such a large-scale mixed-methods research project came through the Religion and Society Programme. This strategic research initiative, funded by two UK Government–funded research bodies, the AHRC and the ESRC, ran from 2007 to 2012. The programme funded 75 projects across UK universities, investigating various aspects of the complex relationships between religion and society, both historical and contemporary. The programme was coordinated by Prof. Linda Woodhead of Lancaster University and supported by a Steering Committee, on which Jackson was invited to serve.

WRERU's project Young People's Attitudes to Religious Diversity (AH/G014035/1) or 'the Diversity project' was conducted between October 2009 and December 2012. It sought to extend and expand the earlier English REDCo study across the UK. Thus it combined findings from qualitative focus group interviews among 13- to 16-year-old pupils with a large-scale quantitative survey of nearly 12,000 pupils aged 13–15 years attending different types of schools (with and without a religious character). Both qualitative and quantitative studies were conducted across all four nations of the UK and in London. London was treated separately because its population is considerably larger than that of each of Scotland, Wales and Northern Ireland, and it presents a different pattern of diversity from England as a whole. The strategy also allowed due attention to English regions outside London. The project thus aimed to provide empirical evidence of the attitudes of young people towards religious diversity across the whole of the United Kingdom.

Project proposal

The project proposal was drafted by Jackson and Francis in consultation with other WRERU colleagues who became members of the project team. The proposed research was intended to build on the earlier REDCo studies in a variety of ways, including the following:

- Extending the research to all four UK nations and adding London as a distinctive case.
- Using the pupils' own perspectives to frame the expanded research questions.
- Checking the findings against much larger UK samples.
- Giving greater visibility to the different attitudes of members of minority religious groups.
- Exploring the influences of a variety of contextual factors on pupils' patterns of thought.
- Contributing to research by European partners.
- Providing stakeholders/end users with information relevant to policy, practice and academic debate on religious education and community cohesion issues.

The proposed project also connected closely with aspects of two themes in the Religion and Society Programme's 'youth call': Education, Socialization and

Identity; Community, Welfare and Prosperity. It responded to significant developments in the personal, social and cultural landscapes of the UK, including the following:

- Growing visibility of religious plurality in both conventional and unconventional forms.
- Changes to traditional patterns of religious socialization through home, school and faith community.
- Growth of certain forms of religious intransigence.
- Increasing public recognition of religion's social significance.
- Increasing attention to international research on that significance.

The proposed project was relevant to developments at the interface between religious education and citizenship education (DfES 2007; Jackson 2003a) and to debates about separate faith schooling (Jackson 2003b). It was argued that more detailed knowledge and understanding of young people's attitudes to religious diversity would provide reliable information relevant to the development of policy and important data to inform academic discussion.

The proposal included interrelated research questions to be addressed by qualitative fieldwork and a quantitative survey informed by the findings of the qualitative study. The main research questions were:

1 Using qualitative methods, what are the key issues 13- to 16-year-old pupils identify with religious diversity and how do they respond to these? (The plan was to use pupils' own experiences and perspectives to frame and expand the following research questions.)
2 Using quantitative methods, how widespread are the responses identified by the qualitative methods?
3 Drawing on insights from individual differences psychology, how far can quantitative approaches, using recognized measures of personality and other individual-level variables (emotional intelligence, self-concept, empathy), explain attitudes towards religious diversity?
4 Drawing on insights from social psychology, how far can social and contextual factors (school, family, media, local neighbourhood) explain individual differences in attitudes towards religious diversity?
5 Drawing on insights from empirical theology, how far can religious affiliation, beliefs, practices and views of transcendence explain individual differences in attitudes towards religious diversity?
6 Drawing on insights from qualitative research, how can attitudes towards religious diversity be more adequately operationalized in quantitative studies?

Once WRERU researchers were informed that their proposal had been successful, steps were taken to establish a research team and begin work. The main project team consisted of Prof. Robert Jackson (Principal Investigator), Prof. Leslie

Francis (Co-investigator), Dr Elisabeth Arweck and Dr Julia Ipgrave (qualitative research), Dr Mandy Robbins (2009–2010) and Jennifer Croft (2011–2012) (quantitative research), Dr Ursula McKenna (processing qualitative and quantitative data) and Alice Pyke (PhD student working on both quantitative and qualitative aspects of the project). Regular team meetings were held throughout the project period. More colleagues were brought in later to assist with the analysis and interpretation of quantitative data.

From the start, the project team worked with local education advisers, education inspectors and colleagues in teacher education from across the UK in order to identify schools to participate in the project in both qualitative and quantitative strands. In some cases these contacts assisted in the initial approaches to the schools. In addition, school managers and religious education teachers were actively involved in the research helping to identify groups of pupils to take part in the qualitative and quantitative research and taking on the organization and time-tabling of the research days.

Qualitative strand

Qualitative research took place in 21 schools spread across the four nations of the UK and London, capturing for each a diversity of localized patterns of religion and religious plurality. The schools selected covered various religious, cultural, ethnic and socio-economic contexts to accommodate a variety of experiences and perspectives. The selection included schools of a designated religious character. The diversity of local contexts covered in the research is reflected in Chapters 4–8.

Semi-structured group interviews (in effect focus groups) were used with three to six groups of around six pupils in each of the participating schools. These groups were selected from each school to ensure as far as possible a range of ages in the 13–16 age bracket and sufficient flexibility about the mix of gender, religious affiliation/no religious affiliation and ethnicity to access a wide diversity of views. Group interviews gave greater agency to the pupils as they responded to each other's views on their shared contexts. Pupils were asked for their views on experiences of religious diversity in their own localities and awareness of religious diversity in the national and international context and to express their predictions of the role religion would have in shaping society in the future. The group interviews created detailed pictures of young people's thinking about religious diversity in their different settings. They were used to identify themes and to generate hypotheses in order to inform the design and focus of the quantitative research. Thus young people had a voice in the research questions that guided the rest of the project.

Quantitative strand

The quantitative survey was informed by two components. First, insights from the qualitative study provided information from which psychometrically sound measures of attitudes towards religious diversity could be generated, reflecting the ideas, language and themes of young people themselves. The qualitative survey also posed theories and hypotheses to be tested by quantitative methods. Second, the quantitative study drew on established measures and theories within empirical theology and psychology relevant for exploring individual differences in attitudes towards religious diversity. Thus, the questionnaire covered themes directly arising from the initial qualitative studies (many of them dealing with issues similar to the earlier REDCo studies), together with themes related to Francis's earlier quantitative studies.

The quantitative survey was UK-wide, intending to establish a representative sample of 10,000 pupils from state-maintained, independent and faith-based schools, building on Francis's previous studies, such as the Teenage Religion and Values project (Francis and Robbins 2005), with large samples in order to give minorities reliable visibility. The survey employed established psychometric instruments and specially originated scales, thus enabling creative use of various statistical techniques to facilitate the development and testing of multivariate models.

The survey explored topics such as: pupils' contact with different religions; whether they had friends/family members belonging to different religions; their views on the discussion of religious issues in class; school visits to places of worship; and the wearing of religious symbols and celebration of religious festivals in school. Other questions emerged from the qualitative studies and elicited factors related to pupils' attitudes. The original target of 10,000 pupils was exceeded, resulting in a database of around 12,000, and data were entered on computer for analysis. Interim analyses were undertaken to provide material for presentations at specific conferences and to prepare the project's first publications.

Synergy of REDCo and the Diversity project

As previously indicated, many findings from the Diversity project reinforce the generic REDCo findings summarized earlier, but employ a wider and more detailed selection of qualitative studies and draw on much bigger samples in the quantitative research. Moreover, more diverse educational settings across the UK are covered in the Diversity project than in the English contributions to the REDCo project. As later chapters in this volume show, the qualitative studies in the former reveal the high importance and relevance of *context*, especially in schools with a dominant religious tradition or sub-tradition, while the quantitative findings, drawing on large samples, are able to present a more detailed and nuanced picture than the REDCo findings.

For example, REDCo found that, generally speaking, in the participant countries, pupils for whom religion is important in their lives were more likely to respect the religious backgrounds of others and value the role of religion in the world. The Diversity project provides a more nuanced picture for the UK. For example, in a preliminary analysis of 5,000 questionnaires from 13- to 15-year-old pupils attending state-maintained schools without a religious character across England, Northern Ireland, Scotland and Wales, 70 per cent who described themselves as having no religion agreed that 'studying religion at school helps me to understand people from other religions.' These proportions rose to 82 per cent among pupils self-identifying as Christian, 84 per cent among pupils with a Sikh background, 85 per cent among Muslim pupils and 92 per cent among Hindu pupils.

In a second example, REDCo found that pupils in the participant countries generally wished to avoid conflict on religious issues, with some religiously committed pupils feeling especially vulnerable. The Diversity project provides a more refined picture for the UK. In the same preliminary analysis, 11 per cent of the pupils who described themselves as Christians said that at school 'I am bullied because of my religion,' with the proportions rising to 18 per cent among Hindu pupils, 23 per cent among Muslim pupils, 32 per cent among Jewish pupils and 42 per cent among Sikh pupils (WRERU 2013).

The Diversity project can also give a more sophisticated picture of the internal diversity of religious traditions than was possible in the REDCo project, as exemplified in Chapter 10 in this volume, reporting research on young people in Catholic and Protestant schools in Northern Ireland, and Chapter 11 illustrating the internal diversity of the Catholic community.

Conclusion

The Young People's Attitudes to Religious Diversity project marks a significant recent development in WRERU's work. It continues a tradition of empirical research concerned with religious diversity and education going back over 20 years that is relevant to educational policy and practice, building on the earlier work of the Warwick Religious Education and Community Project. WRERU's early ethnographic studies concentrated on religion in the life-world of children and young people, including the context of family, especially young people from a variety of minority religious backgrounds. WRERU's participation in the REDCo project enabled international research collaboration, capacity building (especially through the participation of research students) and the introduction of mixed-methods research.

WRERU's use of combined qualitative and quantitative methods was extended through the appointment of new staff, enabling the design of a project for the UK Government on 'materials used to teach about world religions in schools in England'. Finally, the Diversity project enabled the strengthened WRERU team to undertake a major study of young people's attitudes across the UK using an integrated mixed-methods approach. WRERU staff are pleased to present some of the findings of the research in this volume. Further publications from the Diversity project will appear and from the follow-up of the REDCo project (McKenna et al. 2014). WRERU's work continues in new directions through involvement with further international projects, for example, with the Council of Europe and the European Wergeland Centre (e.g. Jackson 2014); a range of European universities, including the Religion and Dialogue in Modern Societies (ReDi) project with the Academy of World Religions at the University of

Hamburg; the Religious Education at Schools in Europe (REL-EDU) project with the University of Vienna (e.g. Rothgangel, Jackson and Jäggle 2014); the Life Skills project with the University of Stockholm; and the Religion Educators: Stress and Work-Related Psychological Health project. WRERU also maintains a range of partnerships with colleagues in countries such as Australia, the United States and South Africa.

Notes

1 Further discussion and applications of the interpretive approach by WRERU research students and Associate Fellows are collected in Miller et al. 2013.
2 The theoretical background to the issues different European countries faced in the field is in Jackson et al. 2007.
3 Liam Gearon's arguments are replied to in detail in Jackson (2015a, 2015b).

References

Arweck, Elisabeth. 2013. 'The Role of Emotion and Identity in Mixed-Faith Families.' In *Emotions and Religious Dynamic: Interdisciplinary Perspectives*, ed. Douglas Davies, 9–25. Farnham: Ashgate.

Arweck, Elisabeth, and Eleanor Nesbitt. 2010. 'Young People's Identity Formation in Mixed-Faith Families: Continuity or Discontinuity of Religious Traditions?' *Journal of Contemporary Religion* 25 (1): 67–87.

———. 2012. 'Young People in Mixed Faith Families: A Case of Knowledge and Experience of Two Traditions?' In *Religion and Knowledge*, ed. Mathew Guest and Elisabeth Arweck, 57–75. Farnham: Ashgate.

Arweck, Elisabeth, Eleanor Nesbitt, and Robert Jackson. 2005. 'Common Values for the Common School? Using Two Values Education Programmes to Promote "Spiritual and Moral Development,"' *Journal of Moral Education* 34 (3): 325–342.

———. 2008. 'Educating the Next Generation in Universal Values? Hindu-related New Religious Movements and Values Education in the Common School.' *Journal of Religious Education* (Australia) 56 (3): 33–41.

Avest, Ina ter, Dan-Paul Jozsa, Thorsten Knauth, Javier Rosón, and Geir Skeie, eds. 2009. *Dialogue and Conflict on Religion: Studies of Classroom Interaction on European Countries.* Münster: Waxmann.

Barratt, Margaret. 1994a, b, c, d, e. *An Egg for Babcha, Lucy's Sunday, Something to Share, The Buddha's Birthday, The Seventh Day Is Shabbat.* Bridges to Religions series. The Warwick RE Project. Oxford: Heinemann.

Barratt, Margaret, and Jo Price. 1996. *Meeting Christians: Book One.* Bridges to Religions series. The Warwick RE Project. Oxford: Heinemann.

Bertram-Troost, Gerdien, and Kevin O'Grady. 2008. 'Religion and Education in England and the Netherlands: A Comparative Account of Young People's Views and Experiences.' In *Encountering Religious Pluralism in School and Society: A Qualitative Study of Teenage Perspectives in Europe*, ed. Thorsten Knauth, Dan-Paul Jozsa, Gerdien Bertram-Troost, and Julia Ipgrave, 339–355. Münster: Waxmann.

DfES. 2007. *Living Together in the UK: Diversity and Citizenship Curriculum Review.* London: DfES.

Evans-Pritchard, Edward E. 1962. 'Religion and the Anthropologists.' In *Social Anthropology and Other Essays*, ed. Edward Evans-Pritchard, 155–171. Glencoe, IL: Free Press.

Francis, Leslie J., and Mandy Robbins. 2005. *Urban Hope and Spiritual Health: The Adolescent Voice*. Peterborough: Epworth.

Gearon, Liam. 2013. *Master Class in Religious Education: Transforming Teaching and Learning*. London: Bloomsbury.

Ipgrave, Julia. 2001. 'Pupil-to-Pupil Dialogue in the Classroom as a Tool for Religious Education.' Warwick Religions and Education Research Unit, Working Paper 2. Coventry: Institute of Education, University of Warwick.

———. 2013. 'The Language of Inter Faith Encounter among Inner City Primary School Children.' *Religion and Education* 40 (1): 35–49.

Ipgrave, Julia, and Ursula McKenna. 2008. 'Diverse Experiences and Common Vision: English Students' Perspectives on Religion and Religious Education.' In *Encountering Religious Pluralism in School and Society: A Qualitative Study of Teenage Perspectives in Europe*, ed. Thorsten Knauth, Dan-Paul Jozsa, Gerdien Bertram-Troost, and Julia Ipgrave, 133–147. Münster: Waxmann.

Ipgrave, Julia, Robert Jackson, and Kevin O'Grady, eds. 2009. *Religious Education Research through a Community of Practice: Action Research and the Interpretive Approach*. Münster: Waxmann.

Jackson, Robert. 1997. *Religious Education: An Interpretive Approach*. London: Hodder and Stoughton.

———. ed. 2003a. *International Perspectives on Citizenship, Education and Religious Diversity*. London: RoutledgeFalmer.

———. 2003b. 'Should the State Fund Faith Based Schools? A Review of the Arguments.' *British Journal of Religious Education* 25 (2): 89–102.

———. 2004. *Rethinking Religious Education and Plurality: Issues in Diversity and Pedagogy*. London: RoutledgeFalmer.

———. 2011. 'The Interpretive Approach as a Research Tool: Inside the REDCo Project.' *British Journal of Religious Education* 33 (2): 189–208.

———. ed. 2012a. *Religion, Education, Dialogue and Conflict: Perspectives on Religious Education Research*. London: Routledge.

———. 2012b. 'The Interpretive Approach as a Research Tool: Inside the REDCo Project.' In *Religion, Education, Dialogue and Conflict: Perspectives on Religious Education Research*, ed. Robert Jackson, 84–102. London: Routledge.

———. 2012c. 'Religious Education and the Arts of Interpretation Revisited.' In *On the Edge: (Auto)Biography and Pedagogical Theories on Religious Education*, ed. Ina ter Avest, 57–68. Rotterdam: Sense.

———. 2012d. 'The Interpretive Approach to Religious Education: Challenging Thompson's Interpretation.' *Journal of Beliefs and Values* 33 (1): 1–9.

———. 2014. *Signposts: Policy and Practice for Teaching about Religions and Non-religious Worldviews in Intercultural Education*. Strasbourg: Council of Europe.

———. (2015a) 'Misrepresenting Religious Education's Past and Present in Looking Forward: Gearon Using Kuhn's Concepts of Paradigm, Paradigm Shift and Incommensurability.' *Journal of Beliefs and Values* 36 (1): 64–78.

———. (2015b) 'The Politicisation and Securitisation of Religious Education? A Rejoinder.' *British Journal of Educational Studies, Special Issue on Education, Security and Intelligence Studies* 63 (3): 345–366.

Jackson, Robert, and Eleanor Nesbitt. 1990. *Listening to Hindus*. London: Unwin Hyman.

———. 1992. 'The Diversity of Experience in the Religious Upbringing of Children from Christian Families in Britain.' *British Journal of Religious Education* 15 (1): 19–28.

———. 1993. *Hindu Children in Britain*. Stoke-on-Trent: Trentham.

Jackson, Robert, Julia Ipgrave, Mary Hayward, Paul Hopkins, Nigel Fancourt, Mandy Robbins, Leslie J. Francis and Ursula McKenna. 2010. *Materials Used to Teach about World Religions in Schools in England*. London: Department for Children, Schools and Families.

Jackson, Robert, Siebren Miedema, Wolfram Weisse, and Jean-Paul Willaime, eds. 2007. *Religion and Education in Europe: Developments, Contexts and Debates*. Münster: Waxmann.

Knauth, Thorsten. 2009. 'Dialogue on a Grassroots-level: Analysing Dialogue-oriented Classroom Interaction in Hamburg RE.' In *Dialogue and Conflict on Religion: Studies of Classroom Interaction on European Countries*, ed. Ina ter Avest, Dan-Paul Jozsa, Thorsten Knauth, Javier Rosón, and Geir Skeie, 17–27. Münster: Waxmann.

Knauth, Thorsten, Dan Paul Jozsa, Gerdien Bertram-Troost, and Julia Ipgrave, eds. 2008. *Encountering Religious Pluralism in School and Society: A Qualitative Study of Teenage Perspectives in Europe*. Religious Diversity and Education in Europe series. Münster: Waxmann.

Kozyrev, Fedor. 2009. 'Dialogue about Religion: Incident Analysis of Classroom Interaction in St Petersburg.' In *Dialogue and Conflict on Religion: Studies of Classroom Interaction in European Countries*, ed. Ina ter Avest, Dan-Paul Jozsa, Thorsten Knauth, and Javier Rosón, 194–224. Waxmann: Münster.

McKenna, Ursula. 2002. 'Towards an Inclusive Pedagogy for Religious Education in Primary Schools.' Warwick Religions and Education Research Unit Occasional Papers 3. Coventry: Institute of Education, University of Warwick.

McKenna, Ursula, Leslie J. Francis, Sean Neill, and Robert Jackson. 2014. 'The Role of Personal Religiosity in Predicting Attitude toward Religious Education and Attitude toward Religious Diversity among 14- to 16-year-old Students in England.' *Religious Education Journal of Australia* 30 (2): 16–24.

McKenna, Ursula, Julia Ipgrave, and Robert Jackson. 2008. *Interfaith Dialogue By Email in Primary Schools: An Evaluation of the Building E-Bridges Project*. Münster: Waxmann.

McKenna, Ursula, Sean Neill, and Robert Jackson. 2009. 'Personal Worldviews, Dialogue and Tolerance: Students' Views on Religious Education in England.' In *Teenagers' Perspectives on the Role of Religion in their Lives, Schools and Societies: A European Quantitative Study*, ed. Pille Valk, Gerdien Bertram-Troost, Markus Friederici, and Céline Beraud, 49–70. Religious Diversity and Education in Europe series. Münster: Waxmann.

Mercier, S. Carrie. 1996. *Interpreting Religions: Muslims*. Oxford: Heinemann.

Miller, Joyce, Kevin O'Grady, and Ursula McKenna, eds. 2013. *Religion in Education: Innovation in International Research*. New York and London: Routledge.

Nesbitt, Eleanor. 1991. ' "My Dad's Hindu, my Mum's Side Are Sikhs": Issues in Religious Identity.' Arts, Culture, Education, Research and Curriculum Paper. Charlbury: National Foundation for Arts Education. Online at: http://www.casas.org.uk/papers/pdfpapers/identity.pdf

Nesbitt, Eleanor, and Robert Jackson. 1992. 'Christian and Hindu Children: Their Perceptions of their Own and Each Other's Religious Traditions.' *Journal of Empirical Theology* 5 (2): 39–62.

———. 1995. 'Sikh Children's Use of "God": Ethnographic Fieldwork and Religious Education.' *British Journal of Religious Education* 17 (2): 108–120.

O'Grady, Kevin. 2009. 'Brainwashing? An Example of Dialogue and Conflict from Religious Education in England.' In *Dialogue and Conflict on Religion: Studies of Classroom Interaction in European Countries*, ed. Ina ter Avest, Dan-Paul Jozsa, Thorsten Knauth, and Javier Rosón, 41–61. Münster: Waxmann.

———. 2013. 'Action Research and the Interpretive Approach to Religious Education.' *Religion & Education* 40 (1): 62–77. Also in *Religion in Education: Innovation in International Research*, ed. Joyce Miller, Kevin O'Grady, and Ursula McKenna, 134–148. London: Routledge.

Robson, Geoff. 1995. *Christians.* Interpreting Religions series. The Warwick RE Project. Oxford: Heinemann.

Rothgangel, Martin, Robert Jackson, and Martin Jäggle, eds. 2014. *Religious Education at Schools in Europe. Vol. 2: Western Europe.* Wiener Forum für Theologie und Religionswissenschaft, Band 10.2. Göttingen: Vienna University Press/V&R Unipress.

Sikes, Pat, and Judith Everington. 2001. 'Becoming an RE Teacher: A Life History Approach.' *British Journal of Religious Education* 24 (1): 8–20.

Skeie, Geir. 2008. 'Dialogue and Conflict in the Religious Education Classroom: Some Intermediate Reflections from a Research Project.' In *Lived Religion: Conceptual, Empirical and Practical-theological Approaches. Essays in Honour of Hans-Günther Heimbrock*, ed. Heinz Streib, Astrid Dinter, and Kerstin Söderblom, 337–348. Leiden: Brill.

Valk, Pille, Gerdien Bertram-Troost, Markus Friederici, and Céline Beraud, eds. 2009. *Teenagers' Perspectives on the Role of Religion in their Lives, Schools and Societies: A European Quantitative Study.* Religious Diversity and Education in Europe Series. Münster: Waxmann.

von der Lippe, Marie. 2010. ' "I have my Own Religion": A Qualitative Study of Young People's Constructions of Religion and Identity in a Norwegian Context.' In 'Youth, Religion and Diversity: A Qualitative Study of Young People's Talk about Religion in a Secular and Plural Society. A Norwegian Case', Marie von der Lippe, 1–13 (Art. 4). Unpublished PhD thesis. Norway: University of Stavanger.

———. 2011. 'Reality Can Bite: The Perspectives of Young People on the Role of Religion in their World.' *Nordidactica: Journal of Humanities and Social Science Education* 2011 (2): 15–34.

Wayne, Elizabeth, Judith Everington, Dilip Kadodwala, and Eleanor Nesbitt. 1996. *Hindus.* Interpreting Religions series. The Warwick RE Project. Oxford: Heinemann.

Woodward, Peter, and Robert Jackson. 1993. 'RECP: An Outline of an Ethnographic Study of the Religious Nurture of Jewish Children in an English City.' *Australian Journal of Jewish Studies* 7 (1): 153–160.

WRERU (Warwick Religions and Education Research Unit). 2013. 'Young People's Attitudes to Diversity: A Research Project.' Internal Report. Coventry: WRERU, Institute of Education, University of Warwick.

2 The qualitative strand

Listening in depth

Elisabeth Arweck and Julia Ipgrave

Introduction

This chapter discusses the design of the qualitative component of the Young People's Attitudes to Religious Diversity project and draws attention to published work resulting from these data before the publication of the present volume. The qualitative component preceded the quantitative component within the mixed-method design of the project so that the latter could build on the former. Although the emphasis here is on the qualitative part of the project – the focus group discussions (both the method and data arising from them) – there are references to the quantitative phase of the project and the ways in which the data arising from the research can be brought in dialogue with theory. This chapter comprises six main sections. The first two sections describe the way in which the qualitative part of the project was conceived in the research design, also in relation to the quantitative part. The third and fourth sections present some of the overarching themes emerging from the qualitative data and their implications for actors involved in education at the policy and school levels. The final section sets out the rationale of the chapters in this volume and how they relate to the chapters reporting quantitative data. The contributions by the authors of the present chapter report qualitative data with reference to particular geographic and school contexts as well as specific themes which represent related strands which are interwoven in the fabric of the volume.

The qualitative phase within the project

The project on Young People's Attitudes to Religious Diversity aimed to extend research on young people's attitudes towards religious diversity and the factors which influence the formation of young people's attitudes by using a mixed-method approach involving interviews with pupils (the qualitative study) and a large-scale questionnaire (the quantitative study). In the first stage of the project, focus group discussions were conducted in a range of schools across the UK: in England, Wales, Scotland and Northern Ireland as well as in London. (A special case was made for London because of the size of its population; its particular – and constantly changing – demographic and its position in the religious landscape of the UK as a place where communal religion is growing not only in the multiplying migrant congregations and churches, but also in more traditional, established churches. The project sought to capture this and also do justice to England outside the metropolis.) Themes from the discussions were then included in the design of a questionnaire which was distributed in schools across the UK and London in the second stage of the project.

Qualitative research took place in 21 secondary schools spread across the four nations of the UK and London. The schools were chosen in such a way that as wide a range as possible would be covered – in terms of composition, location, social context and type of school. The selected schools were also intended to cover various religious, cultural, ethnic and socio-economic contexts to accommodate a variety of young people's experiences and perspectives. Contexts included areas with long-established communities of migration background and with new migrant communities; areas where the population is relatively homogeneous culturally and religiously; areas with a history of sectarian divisions; areas of socio-economic difficulty and more prosperous districts; and urban and rural regions. Thus the schools the authors of this chapter visited ranged from inner-city Birmingham to the Scottish Islands; from urban, semi-urban and rural locations in Wales to the industrial North East; from County Tyrone in Northern Ireland to South London. The number of schools visited in the different nations breaks down as follows:

- Four schools in Scotland
- Four schools in Northern Ireland
- Three schools in Wales
- Seven schools in England (outside London)
- Three schools in London.

As indicated earlier, the schools were deliberately chosen to present a variety of social and geographical contexts in relation to religion. Some models of community religious context found in the qualitative part of the project can be characterized as follows:

- 'Mono-religious' local culture, levels of religious activity high;
- Religiously active and religiously plural;
- Religiously plural, including a sizeable non-religious element;
- Low levels of religious activity;
- Low levels of religious activity but separate, clearly defined religious groups in proximity;
- Some religious diversity/activity and a sizeable non-religious/not religiously active element (e.g. area in a multicultural city).

In this way the research acknowledged from the outset the sheer diversity of patterns of religion within the United Kingdom that exists in tension with any attempts to present an overarching narrative or sociological trajectory such as secularization or the fragmentation or individualization of religion. While remaining alert to the shared discourses of the national media, educational philosophy and teenage culture to which the young people of this research were exposed, the research was interested in investigating the impact on young people's outlook on the profile of religion in their immediate socio-geographical context.

Julia Ipgrave (2012) discusses in further detail the relationships between local patterns of religious practice and young people's attitudes to the religiosity of their peers. Ensuring a variety of social and geographical contexts in relation to religion involved pupils from a variety of religious backgrounds (different faith traditions, different degrees of participation and familiarity) so that some of the diversities beyond the standard differences of identity (e.g. being a practising Christian in a minority or majority context) can be teased out. Elisabeth Arweck and Gemma Penny (2015) examined the socializing agents and factors emerging from the data, addressing religious socialization in the home, with active participation in religious communities, and across generations. They also examined whether/how religious socialization (or its lack) differs between and within religions and between particular localities, and also sought to identify factors which facilitate or impede socializing processes.

The schools were asked to put together groups of pupils who either identified as 'religious' or 'non-religious'. When such groups were provided, we explored, as much as possible, what these labels meant to the pupils in the respective groups. Arweck (2013) explores how young people articulated their religious and non-religious identities and their perceptions of belief or lack of belief.

The qualitative part of the project was exploratory in nature in that the research team sought to get a sense of young people's attitudes to religion, non-religion and religious diversity by conducting semi-structured discussions with small pupil groups (typically six pupils per group). Thus this stage of the research was flexible, allowing new themes to emerge in the course of the discussions. These themes, together with questions and hypotheses, were drawn from the data gathered in this phase and passed on to team members who worked on the quantitative aspect of the project.

It needs to be taken into account that the qualitative research was to be the *exploratory* stage of the project, identifying key issues that could be investigated further. The questions used did not address attitudes to diversity directly but were scoping questions to explore different factors and contexts that might have an impact on attitude and so could be included in the quantitative survey. Further, regarding the theoretical background of this phase of the project, in particular working definitions of religious diversity, the research team decided not to unpick this particular concept and what is or might be meant by it at the outset. The young people, whatever or however strong their faith or belief, are living in contexts where there are recognized alternatives to their own positions; their contexts can thus be understood broadly in terms of Charles Taylor's society that is secular 'in a third sense'. This 'consists, among other things, of a move from a society where belief in God is unchallenged and indeed unproblematic to one in which it is understood to be one option among others, and frequently not the easiest to embrace' (Taylor 2007, 3). Beyond this there was no determining theoretical framework for the project at that point. Instead, the findings that emerged during the course of this phase of the research were to be related to and fro in dialogue to a variety of empirical and theoretical literature in the areas of religious diversity, interreligious understanding and young people's religion. Thus, what the qualitative data yield is not a set of definitive or representative qualitative findings on attitudes to diversity and a set of quantitative findings on attitudes to diversity, which could be compared with each other as analogous sets of data. What the qualitative findings usefully do is offer a more sophisticated understanding of the complexities involved in some of the categories commonly employed in relation to young people's religious identities and contexts so that these categories can be used more advisedly when they are related to attitudes to religious diversity. They also provide some hypotheses for further investigation and question some assumptions of research and pedagogies in this field through the use of living examples. For example, Ipgrave (2012) attempts to do this last by way of the following:

1   demonstrating that multi-faith religious education (RE) does not necessarily lead to greater tolerance of other's religion;
2   questioning a too ready pairing of religious and diversity – do young people's attitudes to diversity and diversity identity raise a wider question more suited to citizenship education?
3   noting that attitudes towards and tolerance of *religiosity* are issues that need exploring and addressing;
4   giving some indication of how knowledge about religions (as perceived and understood by the pupils) relates to their views of religion or other religions, depending on their respective standpoints.

The qualitative research also helped the team to consider that there are attitudes to *diversity* and attitudes to *religiosity*. Therefore, if the purpose of the research was to understand better how young people relate to the religiously 'other', both need attention but may act very differently from each other – for example, pupils who are quite happy for other people to have different religious identities as long as their religion does not have too big an impact on their behaviour, dress, engagement in 'teenage' activities and so forth. Arweck (2016) reports young people's perceptions and attitudes towards material expressions of religious belonging or adherence, including dress and religious symbols, examining how young people related to individuals' clothing in terms of what it suggests about religious belonging; what they thought of fellow pupils wearing religious symbols in school; young people's stances towards observance of particular religious disciplines, such as fasting during Ramadan; and how young people deal with different dietary requirements. Also, perceptions of those who do not identify with religion (or with a religion) with regard to those who have a religion and practise their religion can be drawn from the focus group interviews (see Arweck 2013).

Contextualizations: where qualitative and quantitative meet

The design of the project specified three contextualizations of the key research questions. In order for the different elements of the project to work together in a way that maximized the potential of each and enabled them to support each other, the qualitative research needed to be able to explore these contextualizations in ways that helped the formulation of the quantitative study.

The first contextualization was concerned with individual differences, with individual differences psychology coming into play regarding well-established measures such as self-concept, empathy and emotional intelligence. However, for our theme, individual differences are more concerned with the values network within which attitudes towards religious diversity are situated. Thus a broad range of values needed to be examined by the qualitative study. Since the research took place, values have been given a new prominence in educational discourse and policy, with the promotion of 'British Values' as a strategy for countering 'extremist' influences on young people (see also Jackson 2014). In the light of this increased emphasis it is interesting to note that, in research discussions, the young people found questions about values the most difficult questions to answer.

The second contextualization was concerned with social context – hence sociology and social psychology coming to bear with standard items such as school, family, media and local neighbourhood. However, social context differences are more concerned with the religious environment, which is why a broad range of different religious contexts needed to be included in the identification of the schools chosen for the qualitative study.

The third contextualization referred to the power of religious beliefs, frameworks and assumptions to shape the view of the (familiar) self and the view of the (strange) other. This is the domain of empirical theology with established notions like religious affiliation, beliefs, practices and views of transcendence. However, theological context needs to get inside the young person's formulation of the implications of his/her personal faith/worldview for the way in which empirical reality is interpreted. This required in-depth discussion within the qualitative strand, engaging young people for whom faith matters in order to identify, understand and interpret the impact of faith positions on responding to religious diversity.

Given the location of the qualitative study across the four nations and London, it was crucial that the pupils selected reflected on all three contextual issues. This was achieved by listening with care and in depth to the young people in the schools visited during this part of the project. As indicated earlier, while the qualitative phase was of an exploratory nature and thus did not result in a set of representative data, we shall now sketch some of the emerging themes in order to convey some of the indicative findings.

Some overarching themes

The data gathered during the qualitative phase of the project provide interesting insights into the way different aspects converge in young people's views of religious diversity and (non)religion. The particular social/community context, the ethos of their school, the place of RE in their school, the content of RE and how it is taught, their own religious practice or lack of it, their families and upbringing – all these are important factors which influence young people's stances (see also Arweck and Penny 2015). Thus the data collected are rich in that they allow for nuanced pictures to emerge, even if these pictures are snapshots taken at a particular time and place. The following sections set out some of the influences and insights which emerged from the discussions with pupils across the schools.

School influence

There was a commonly expressed view among pupils that knowledge about other religions increases sympathy towards and understanding of the religiously 'other'. However, there were reports from pupils showing this was not necessarily the case – instances where a multi-faith RE had not obviously increased tolerance and where knowledge about religions provided fodder for religious teasing. Usually, schools were not seen by pupils to have a major impact on their values, at least not relative to the influence of parents and friends. Some young people (in two Scottish schools) suggested that teachers were confined by a 'PC' (politically correct) ethos and thus were not able to give moral guidance to young people. The question was raised about how a shared morality might be achieved.

Media influence

Although young people recognized media bias, they still admitted to being influenced by media reports, often even against their own better judgement. Media influence included the simplistic science versus religion debate and negativity about religion (especially Islam). Several of the young people admitted that media influence meant that there was an association between Islam and extremism in their minds, even when their own knowledge of or friendship with Muslims worked against this view.

(Religious) diversity

Across the different locations of research there was a wide range of experiences of diversity and different degrees of comfort or discomfort with it. Young people's comments indicated that their approach to diversity was an acquired skill and arose from direct knowledge of practitioners of religion, thus through direct contact and interaction with 'the other', whatever the other might be or however it might be conceived. Such knowledge mitigated stereotypical (mis)representation (e.g. in the media), although it did not completely negate its influence. The fact of religious diversity was rarely viewed as a negative or a problem in itself, although young people realized that it might present challenges. Non-religious young people used 'respect' for people's right to be different and had their own opinions as regulatory principles for relating to religious diversity. Religious young people added religious imperatives to 'love' all people whatever their differences and reference to God's unconditional love – whatever their notion of 'God' in other respects. The pupils often had more difficulty with other people's religiosity than with their religious identity. In several cases young people were more concerned about, or reported more problems with, diversity of more recent European migration to the UK than with longer standing religious diversity. Ethnic, racial and linguistic diversity were all raised as points of tension in the community and sometimes in school.

Community

The young people's responses to religion and religiosity – their own or that of other people – varied considerably between the locations, depending on the prominence, the public or private nature of religion within the different local communities. In communities where religion was more practised and public (for example, in South London, inner-city Birmingham, Northern Irish and Scottish Island schools), there was more respect for the religious among the non-religious or less religious and greater confidence among young people about expressing their religion in the school context. Where there was a trend away from public expression of religion in the local community, there was more evidence of teasing and discrimination against a practising minority. In a couple of locations, the schools were situated in proximity to a small close-knit religious community (an alternative religious community in Scotland, a Haredi Jewish community in North East England). In these places, such religious communities were viewed as 'weird' and stories and myths were developing about their practices.

Young people with little experience of practising religion reported generational changes in religious engagement, with grandparents often more likely to be involved than their parents' generation. Some reported situations where parents had periodically tried to re-establish a link with religion but had not managed to maintain it, leading to sporadic influences in the lives of their children. Several of the religious young people described their faith as a communal faith involving a communal identity, relationship to a tradition, the importance of family and of faith community leadership. This was the case with several Hindus and Roman Catholics; Protestants and Muslims often spoke of an individual path of faith supported by communal tradition. Many of the young people had assimilated the discourse in education of freedom of choice and individual autonomy, which is in some tension with that of some forms of communal religion.

Own religion and others' (non)religion

There were more difficulties with those of a non-religious perspective under-standing a religious perspective and vice versa than with understanding across religions. Religious young people noted epistemological differences between them and their non-religious peers which posed barriers to understanding. There was a feeling expressed by several religious pupils that the lives of those who did not have a faith were seriously lacking. Non-religious pupils who had positive attitudes towards differences of religious identity had more negative attitudes towards expressions of religious commitment, especially where these seemed to be in tension with what was deemed to be 'normal' teenage behaviour. Stereotypes about religious people included views that they were stupid, 'close-minded', prejudiced (especially against homosexuals), 'killjoys' and 'uncool'. In some schools young people reported peer pressure against forming friendships with people who were obviously religious (e.g. went to church). In some schools there were 'hidden' Christians who kept quiet about their religious commitment for fear of being 'viewed differently', of being teased or ostracized. Some young Muslims indicated that their religious identity receded somewhat when they were outside their homes. All these themes appear in the chapters in this volume that present qualitative findings from particular research sites in more detail.

Implications

Consideration of the overarching themes allows us to draw out some implica-tions for policy makers and school managers, for RE teachers and departments. These are outlined in the following sections.

For policy makers and school managers

Those with a faith of their own tended to demonstrate greater interest in and higher levels of tolerance for the religions and religious practices of others: debates around the religious character of schools should recognize that educa-tion that supports the nurture of pupils' own faith can have a positive impact on their receptivity to people of other faiths.

The character of the neighbourhoods where the young people lived and the nature and prominence of religious practice there had a marked influence on their knowledge of and attitudes to religion and to the religion of others, whether or not they were themselves religiously practising. Therefore, there needs to be flexibility in the curriculum and possibilities for differentiation in the content and delivery of religious education according to the local context of the schools.

There was widespread agreement among the young people that religious edu-cation or RE can help increase understanding of people of other religions. This is one reason for supporting (well-taught) religious education: it has an impor-tant part to play in developing young people's understanding of other people in a religiously plural society. However, the issue of attitudes towards diversity was found to be wider than attitudes to religious diversity, with a number of other areas of diversity (ethnicity, language) raising concern: education for diversity needs to be more widely spread than the religious education curriculum and other important and potentially problematic areas of difference tackled through educational programmes.

The number of young people who reported being bullied or teased because of their religion and the admission of some that they kept their religious identity hidden for fear of being teased emerged as being unacceptably high: policies designed to protect pupils' wellbeing and to prevent discrimination against minorities in schools need to take into account the likelihood of religious discrimination and seek to address this issue.

For Religious Education teachers and departments

In general, the study found a gap between those who have no religion and those who have a religion in terms of interest in religion and tolerance of religious expression: a burden is placed on the RE teacher and RE department to encourage an interest in understanding religion and religious lives among the non-religious. Pupils (religious and non-religious) were found to be more tolerant of religion and religious diversity in contexts where there was an awareness of religion in the community and less so where there was ignorance about and disconnection from local and family religious and cultural history. Thus encouraging pupils' interest in their family, community and local religious narratives and cultures could be a way of increasing tolerance for religion more generally.

While learning about different religions may increase understanding at one level, findings indicate that it does not necessarily increase understanding at the levels of attitudes, of respect or of empathy: teachers need to be aware that other approaches and strategies are needed beyond information about other religions to encourage positive attitudes. The young people showed more tolerance towards and respect for diversity of religious identity than towards religiosity and religious expression: attention towards religiosity and what it means for a person of religion to have his/her life framed by personal and communal faith needs to be an important part of religious education. This is particularly the case when concerns about 'extremism' in media, politics and educational policy mean that religious practice more than religious identity has become an object of scrutiny and suspicion.

Understanding (or lack of understanding) between young people of religious and non-religious perspectives has been influenced by popular and simplistic science versus religion and reason versus faith discourses. A move away from interpreting religion and non-religion predominantly in terms of propositional belief could help increase understanding between these different perspectives.

Young people from minority religious positions (including practising Christians in largely non-practising schools) reported being teased for their religion. In the short term teachers need to be aware that requiring individual pupils to talk about their religion in class might make them vulnerable to such teasing and in the longer term teachers need to create an ethos where this is not the case.

The chapters in this volume

In identifying overarching themes and implications for policy makers, we have sought to draw attention to the local dynamics that are so often lost in the broader picture. In order to convey the significance of localized factors for a more nuanced understanding of young people's experience of and attitudes to religion and religious diversity, we have chosen in this volume to present some of the outcomes of our qualitative study in the form of micro-studies of research carried out in particular schools. In each case the individual school study shows the interplay of contextual factors on young people's understanding within that particular setting and suggests how the particular instance can be used to interrogate broader theoretical frames in the field, such as theories of 'cultural competences' and 'plural identities' (Deardorff 2009; Østberg 2000) or 'validation regimes' (Hervieu-Léger 2001).

Similar to the quantitative chapters, the subjects of the qualitative chapters have been carefully selected to make sure that the four nations of the UK and London each have one chapter in the collection of studies and that particular national (or metropolitan) factors are considered in the presentation and analysis of findings from each school. The themes of the chapters – both quantitative and qualitative – were also carefully chosen so that they would be in dialogue with one another, addressing related themes but shedding light on different aspects with the help of the data which emerged from the respective methodological approach. They are thus companion pieces which not only provide findings and insights from all the four nations of the UK and London, but also reflect on themes to which both quantitative and qualitative data can speak. For example, Chapter 13 (The Personal and Social Significance of Diverse Religious Affiliation in Multi-faith London) resumes the topic of Chapter 8 (Religious Diversity as a Personal and Social Value: Impressions from a Multicultural School in London) by focusing on pupils in London and on their attitudes and values that are of personal and social importance.

The studies cannot be understood to be representative of each of the nations, however, nor can the differences between the six schools given this attention be taken as indicative of national differences, for the wide variety of experience and perspective within each nation has also been a theme of our study. Indeed, far from being typical, the Northern Irish school presented in this study (Ipgrave's Chapter 5, Uniting Two Communities or Creating a Third Community? Research in a Northern Irish Integrated School) is one of a small minority of 'integrated schools' in the province and, in its structures and (as it transpired) in the outlook of its students, stood out as different from the other three more traditional Northern Irish schools involved in the research. (These receive more attention in Ipgrave 2012.) Nevertheless, a school of this character could only have emerged from the Northern Irish context.

The selection of subjects for the qualitative elements in this volume thus move beyond representations of the different UK nations and London to ensure the inclusion of other variables in keeping with some of the contextual settings identified earlier in this chapter. Arweck's Chapter 7 (The Matter of Context: The Case of Two Community Schools in Wales) makes a detailed and deliberate comparison between a rural and an urban school in Wales. The Birmingham school that is the focus of Ipgrave's Chapter 4 (Sources of Knowledge and Authority: Religious Education for Young Muslims in a Birmingham Comprehensive School) is embedded in a 'mono-religious' local culture where levels of religious activity are high. The context of the London school in Arweck's Chapter 8 can be described as religiously active and religiously plural. The urban Welsh school in Chapter 7 has a religiously plural setting with a sizeable non-religious element, while the rural school is in an area with low levels of religious activity. The Scottish school in Ipgrave's Chapter 6 (Cradling Catholics in Secular Scotland: Research in a Scottish Roman Catholic High School) was situated in an area that could be described as having some religious diversity and activity but a sizeable non-religious or not religiously active element. The case of this school is special, however, for as a Roman Catholic school it is a religious enclave in a predominantly secular location, a position of which the pupils themselves were aware. In several of the research schools the students themselves warned against a too ready correlation of urban and rural with particular patterns of religious practice, speaking instead of different areas of the towns where they lived where different patterns could be found.

The case of the Scottish school points to another variation between the selected schools: the character of the school and the role of religion within it. Thus there are included among the six schools presented a school of designated religious character, an integrated (Catholic and Protestant) school, an academy and several comprehensive schools. All the schools chosen include teaching about other religions as part of their religious education but, as the chapters indicate, the prominence given to this aspect of religious learning and that given to learning about the pupils' own religion varies between the schools.

From the outset, the qualitative strand of the Young People's Attitudes to Religious Diversity project aimed to capture young people's articulation of their experiences and perspectives and to feed these to the quantitative strand in the language of the young people themselves so as to capture the nuances of their thought and the relationships between ideas. At this stage in the process the analysis was effected through the organization of the data, the identification of key themes and initial hypotheses. The expectation was that familiarity with the young people's own wording and expressions would aid the formulation of a questionnaire that was meaningful to them. In accordance with this ethos, the qualitative studies presented in this volume make extensive use of the pupils' own words through frequent and in some cases extended quotations. While the authors have employed them to present a case-by-case analysis and argument in the chapters, it is hoped that these quotations will speak to readers directly and that they may find resonances across the cases and with other research into the field of young people and religion leading to continuing conversations with our material. These conversations begin in the final chapters of this volume in which colleagues from North America (Canada and the United States) and Europe (Germany) have been invited to comment on our findings as presented in this volume and relate them to a wider conception of the field against the background of their own work and knowledge of the research done in the respective countries.

References

Arweck, Elisabeth. 2013. ' "I've been Christened, but I don't Really Believe in It": How Young People Articulate their (Non)Religious Identities and Perceptions of (Non)Belief.' In *Social Identities between the Scared and the Secular*, ed. Abby Day, Christopher R. Cotter, and Giselle Vincett, 103–125. Farnham: Ashgate.

———. 2016. 'Religion Materialized in the Everyday: Young People's Attitudes towards Material Expressions of Religion.' In *Religion and Material Culture*, ed. Tim Hutchings and Joanne McKenzie. Farnham: Ashgate. (forthcoming)

Arweck, Elisabeth, and Gemma Penny. 2015. 'Young People's Attitudes to Religious Diversity: Socialising Agents and Factors Emerging from Qualitative and Quantitative Data of a Nation-Wide Project in the UK.' 36 (3 June): 255–273. Special issue of *Journal of Intercultural Studies* on 'Education about Religions and Worldviews: Promoting Intercultural and Interreligious Understanding in Secular Societies', ed. Anna Halafoff, Elisabeth Arweck, and Donald Boisvert.

Deardorff, Darla K., ed. 2009. *The Sage Handbook of Intercultural Competence.* Thousand Oaks, CA: Sage.

Hervieu-Léger, Danièle. 2001. 'Individualism, the Validation of Faith, and the Social Nature of Religion in Modernity.' In *The Blackwell Companion to the Sociology of Religion*, ed. Richard K. Fenn, 161–175. Oxford: Blackwell.

Ipgrave, Julia. 2012. 'Relationships between Local Patterns of Religious Practice and Young People's Attitudes to the Religiosity of their Peers.' *Journal of Beliefs and Values* 33 (3): 261–274.

Jackson, Robert. 2014. ' "Tolerating Difference"? British Values or Universal Human Values?' Unpublished paper. Coventry: University of Warwick, WRERU.

Østberg, Sissel. 2000. 'Islamic Nurture and Identity Management: The Lifeworld of Pakistani Children in Norway.' *British Journal of Religious Education* 22 (2): 91–103.

Taylor, Charles. 2007. *A Secular Age.* Cambridge, MA: Belknap Press/Harvard University Press.

3 The quantitative strand

An individual differences approach

Leslie J. Francis, Gemma Penny and Mandy Robbins

Introduction

The Young People's Attitudes to Religious Diversity project (from now on the 'Diversity project'), conceived and directed by Prof. Robert Jackson within the Warwick Religions and Education Research Unit (WRERU), was designed to draw on insights of both qualitative and quantitative research methods. Within a three-year period, the project began with qualitative research so that the findings from this qualitative approach could inform aspects of the quantitative approach. The aims of the present chapter are to consider the design of the quantitative study and to draw attention to some of the studies that have already been published from the data. The discussion will be advanced in six steps: introducing the major sources of theory on which the quantitative approach builds; locating the empirical traditions of research among young people that have shaped the study; clarifying the notions and levels of measurement employed in the study; discussing some of the established measures incorporated in the survey; defining the ways in which the sample was structured; and introducing the five relevant chapters in this volume.

Sources of theory

The rich and thick data generated by the qualitative study raised a number of key issues about how young people expressed their attitudes towards religious diversity and about the factors that helped to shape those attitudes. Such influences included sociological factors (e.g. family), personal factors (e.g. sex), psychological factors (e.g. personality) and theological factors (e.g. ideas about God). These key issues resonated with work already well established within various quantitative research traditions. Two particularly relevant quantitative research traditions are provided by the psychology of religion and by empirical theology.

Quantitative research in the psychology of religion has its roots in the late-nineteenth and early twentieth centuries, but it was not until the mid-1950s that sufficient independent studies had been conducted to provide the basis for beginning to coordinate evidence and to draw useful conclusions. Michael

Argyle's (1958) pioneering book *Religious Behaviour* clearly demonstrated that a body of empirically based knowledge was emerging in the psychology of religion. Argyle provided significant updates of his original review of the literature in the mid-1970s and the mid-1990s (see Argyle and Beit-Hallahmi 1975; Beit-Hallahmi and Argyle 1997).

Essentially Argyle's work stands within the individual differences tradition of psychology. In the 1950s Argyle concluded that the major individual difference associated with religion was that of sex difference. Routinely empirical studies showed women to be more religious than men, at least when religion is defined in terms of Christian beliefs, practices, attitudes and values. By the 1990s Argyle concluded that the connection between religion and personality was a second secure finding, drawing on the growing number of studies that had concentrated on testing this association from the early 1980s (see Francis et al. 1981a, 1981b; Francis, Pearson and Kay 1982). The trends charted by Argyle have been brought further up to date (from an American perspective) by Ralph Hood, Peter Hill and Bernard Spilka (2009).

The quantitative component of the Diversity project drew on theories developed within the individual differences approach to the psychology of religion, including theories concerned with the influence of sex and the influence of personality. By taking such theories into account, findings from the study can be integrated within and inform current debates featured in journals like *Archive for the Psychology of Religion, International Journal for the Psychology of Religion, Mental Health, Religion and Culture*, and *Psychology of Religion and Spirituality*.

Quantitative research in empirical theology has its roots in the 1970s and was shaped by theologians working with methods and theories informed by the social sciences. Empirical theology was established in the Netherlands by Hans van der Ven as an intradisciplinary activity, whereby the tools of the social sciences could be taken into theology and tested by the theological academy. Empirical theology was established in England and Wales by Leslie Francis as an intradisciplinary activity, whereby the practitioners of empirical theology sought to have their work tested both by the theological academy and by social scientists. The debate between these two perspectives was well captured by Mark Cartledge (1999) in the *Journal of Beliefs and Values*.

As a relatively new and emerging discipline, it is too early for major reviews to have drawn together key findings within the field of empirical theology, although clear patterns are emerging through the *Journal of Empirical Theology*; the conferences of the International Society for Empirical Research in Theology; and the series of essays published by Brill, including *Religion Inside and Outside Traditional Institutions* (Streib 2007), *Empirical Theology in Texts and Tables: Qualitative, Quantitative and Comparative Perspectives* (Francis, Robbins and Astley 2009), *The Public Significance of Religion* (Francis and Ziebertz 2011), and *Religious Identity and National Heritage* (Anthony and Ziebertz 2012).

Empirical theology is concerned to conceptualize and to operationalize constructs informed by theological debate rather than by sociological or psychological debate. One good example of such constructs is provided by the notion of God images as displayed by Hans-Georg Ziebertz (2001) in the collection of essays *Imagining God* and by Pierre Hegy (2007) in the collection of essays *What Do We Imagine God to Be?* God images may be concerned with key theological concepts like the debate between the God of mercy and the God of justice. A second good example of such constructs is provided by the notion of the theology of individual differences as displayed by Francis (2005) and Francis and Andrew Village (2008). Drawing on a strong doctrine of creation shaped by Genesis 1:27, the theology of individual differences posits fundamental human differences (e.g. sex, ethnicity, psychological type) as theologically informed constructs reflecting the image of the divine creator.

The quantitative component of the Diversity project drew on theories developed within the individual differences approach to empirical theology, including theories concerned with the influence of God images. By taking such theories into account, findings from the study can be integrated within and inform the current debates featured in journals like *Practical Theology*, *Journal of Empirical Theology*, *Review of Religious Research*, and *Journal of Psychology and Theology*.

Empirical traditions

The quantitative phase of the Diversity project was not developed within an intellectual vacuum, but built on three traditions of empirical research already established by colleagues within WRERU, namely the Teenage Religion and Values project, the Attitudes toward Religion project, and the Outgroup Prejudice project.

The Teenage Religion and Values project had its roots in a series of studies published during the 1980s and 1990s, including *Youth in Transit* (Francis 1982), *Teenagers and the Church* (Francis 1984) and *Teenage Religion and Values* (Francis and Kay 1995), all concerned with modelling the association between (on the one hand) religion and spirituality and (on the other hand) social and personal values and attitudes. During the 1990s, the Teenage Religion and Values project set out to compile a database of 34,000 Year 9 and Year 10 students (13–15 years of age), reflecting the distribution of young people within state-maintained and independent schools, including schools with a religious character and schools without a religious foundation, from across England and Wales. Findings from this project were published in two major books, *The Values Debate* (Francis 2001) and *Urban Hope and Spiritual Health* (Francis and Robbins 2005), and in a wide range of journal articles.

The Teenage Religion and Values project brought to the quantitative component of the Diversity project a number of strengths, including experience in the design and administration of questionnaires among a large number of young people, sets of well-tested items and a secure platform of empirical evidence against which findings from the new survey could be located. In particular, this project offered a helpful recognition of the multi-dimensional nature of religion operationalized by social scientific empirical research, distinguishing between five dimensions. These five dimensions were included in the quantitative component of the Diversity project.

The first dimension is self-assigned religious affiliation. This is the dimension of religiosity routinely gathered in many countries within the context of the national census and included for the first time in 2001 in the census for England and Wales and for Scotland (see Sherif 2011). In England and Wales the census distinguished between the six main faith traditions (Buddhism, Christianity, Hinduism, Islam, Judaism, Sikhism). In Scotland the census also distinguished between denominational strands within Christianity. Recognizing the importance of the denominational differences within Christianity, the Teenage Religion and Values project made fine distinctions between different groups.

The second dimension is self-reported attendance at public centres of worship (including churches, synagogues and mosques). Public religious practice accesses an extrinsic aspect of religiosity, where the personal and social faces of religion meet.

The third dimension is self-reported personal prayer and self-reported reading of scripture. Personal religious practice accesses an intrinsic aspect of religiosity, properly shielded from the public gaze.

The fourth dimension is religious belief. Belief in God may operate independently of self-assigned religious affiliation and of self-reported public and personal religious practice.

The fifth dimension is God images. Alongside a well-established research tradition concerned with assessing the social significance of belief in God, a second research tradition has examined the importance of the *kind* of God in whom people believe (their image of God). The Teenage Religion and Values project included items concerned both with belief in God and with the *kind* of God in whom individuals believe.

Alongside these indicators of conventional religiosity, the Teenage Religion and Values project also included a range of markers tapping aspects of alternative spiritualities. One key aspect of this area focused on paranormal and supernatural beliefs.

The Diversity project had its roots in a study published in the late 1970s by Francis (1978) that argued for the primacy of the attitudinal dimension of religion in building a coordinated approach to the psychology of religion. Initially this body of research was shaped entirely within the Christian tradition, drawing on the Francis Scale of Attitude toward Christianity, and by the mid-1990s William Kay and Francis (1996) were able to integrate the findings from the first hundred studies to use that instrument.

The scope of the Diversity project was subsequently extended to include other faith traditions through the Katz-Francis Scale of Attitude toward Judaism (Francis and Katz 2007), the Sahin-Francis Scale of Attitude toward Islam (Francis, Sahin and Al-Failakawi 2008; Sahin and Francis 2002) and the Santosh-Francis Scale of Attitude toward Hinduism (Francis et al. 2008). More recently, the Astley-Francis Scale of Attitude toward Theistic Faith allows comparable studies to employ the same instrument within Christian, Islamic and Jewish contexts as well as secular contexts (Astley, Francis and Robbins 2012). In order to locate its findings alongside the growing body of empirical evidence organized by the Diversity project, the quantitative component of the Diversity project included the Astley-Francis Scale of Attitude toward Theistic Faith.

The Outgroup Prejudice project has its roots in collaborative work with Adrian Brockett and Village at York St John University. The first database developed by this project was employed by Brockett, Village and Francis (2009) to develop the Attitude toward Muslim Proximity Index by analyzing attitudes among 1,777 non-Muslim secondary school students in northern England. The scale was based on physical and social distance, using items related to the idea of having Muslims living at various distances from the respondent, to having Muslims marry into the family and to mixing with Muslims wearing cultural dress (the hijab). The study showed that the notion of proximity could be used effectively to measure prejudice towards Muslims among non-Muslim secondary school students. The advantage of the scale was that it was based on a range of notions surrounding 'proximity' of the outgroup, including different levels of proximity. One limitation of the scale was that it was applicable to non-Muslim attitudes towards Muslims and not vice versa.

The second database developed by the Outgroup Prejudice project was designed to develop a scale using concepts related to the Attitude toward Muslim Proximity Index, but one that could be generalized across ethnic or religious groups. This second database, comprising 930 pupils from Blackburn, 1,376 pupils from Kirklees and 2,116 pupils from York was employed by Brockett, Village and Francis (2010) and by Village (2011) to develop and test the Outgroup Prejudice Index as a reliable and valid scale that was comparable in measuring attitudes towards outgroups among Christians, Muslims and those of no religious affiliation.

Drawing on the Outgroup Prejudice project, the quantitative component of the Diversity project included a wide range of proximity measures.

Levels of measurement

At the design stage, a quantitative survey needs to be clear about the levels of measurement to be achieved by the data, since this in turn shapes the statistical techniques that can be employed to interrogate the data at a later stage. The quantitative component of the Diversity project was designed to be amenable to a range of statistical analyses, including multilevel linear models. Different parts of the survey included nominal, ordinal, interval and scaled levels of measurement.

Nominal levels of measurement include the question concerning religious affiliation, for example. Such questions allow individuals to be placed within categories, but there is no natural progression within and between these categories. The question concerning sex is also a nominal variable, but since there are only two categories, this is a nominal variable that can conventionally be employed in linear models as a dummy variable.

Ordinal levels of measurement allow individuals to be placed in rank order without making assumptions about the equality of distances between the points within the ranking. The question concerning frequency of praying may fall into this category when individuals are invited to check one of the five options: nearly every day, at least once a week, at least once a month, occasionally, never. Although the intervals between the points are clearly not equal, such variables may be employed in linear models.

Interval levels of measurement allow assumptions about the equality of distances between the points. Within the social sciences this assumption is conventionally made with Likert scaling, following Rensis Likert (1932). The form of Likert scaling employed in the quantitative component of the Diversity project invited students to assess clear well-focused statements on the conventional 5-point scale: agree strongly, agree, not certain, disagree, disagree strongly.

Scaled levels of measurement go one stage further and combine a set of items to assess a broader underlying construct. There are three main benefits from this process of scaling. The first is that it is possible to build a more complex theoretical understanding of what is being measured. For example, the notion of *extraversion* is more complex than something that can be captured by a single item, but may be more adequately captured by a set of items. The second benefit is that, while the individual's responses to a single item may fluctuate from day to day, the overall pattern of responses to a set of items remains more stable. Scales access a deeper level of personal stability. The third benefit is that when multiple items are brought together, the range of scores is expanded. For example, on the Likert scale, each item has a range of just 5 points (1 through 5), but when 10 Likert items are combined, the range expands (10 through 50). This provides greater differentiation between individuals. To be effective, scales require careful development and testing.

Instruments of measurement

Along with providing an opportunity for the development of new scales, the quantitative component of the Diversity project included a range of recognized and established instruments in order to link the findings from this study into established and developing fields of enquiry. Such established scales include measures of attitude towards religion, God images, self-esteem, empathy and personality. This aspect of measurement will be illustrated by reference to the Eysenckian dimensional model of personality and the family of instruments designed to access and assess these dimensions.

Hans Eysenck's dimensional model of personality was selected for inclusion in the quantitative component of the Diversity project for three reasons. First, the model proposes an economical and robust account of individual differences in terms of three higher order factors that have been shown to be stable across cultures and across the age range. Moreover, the model proposes a continuum from normal to abnormal personality that in turn may function as an index of individual differences in psychological health. Second, as Ben Beit-Hallahmi and Argyle (1997) demonstrated, since the 1980s there has been a concerted research interest in establishing both the theoretical and the empirical connection between this model of personality and individual differences in religiosity. Third, the model has played a key role in the three earlier projects on which the Diversity project builds, namely the Teenage Religion and Values project, the Attitudes toward Religion project and the Outgroup Prejudice project.

Eysenck's three higher order dimensions of personality are all named by the high scoring pole of the continuum: extraversion, neuroticism, psychoticism. Eysenck's choice of terms such as 'neuroticism' and 'psychoticism' to describe aspects of normal personality is both illuminating and unhelpful. It is illuminating in the sense of underscoring the Eysenckian view that neurotic and psychotic disorders are not discrete categories discontinuous from normal personality. It is unhelpful in the sense of describing perfectly healthy aspects of normal personality with terms redolent of poor psychological health. These three dimensions have been measured among adults by the Eysenck Personality Questionnaire (Eysenck and Eysenck 1975) and by the Eysenck Personality Questionnaire Revised (Eysenck, Eysenck and Barrett 1985). They have been measured among young people by the Junior Eysenck Personality Questionnaire (Eysenck and Eysenck 1975) and by the Junior Eysenck Personality Questionnaire Revised (Corulla 1990). These instruments also routinely include a lie scale. Alongside the full versions of these measures, abbreviated forms have been produced for use among adults (Francis, Brown and Philipchalk 1992) and among young people (Francis 1996). It is the abbreviated form of the Junior Eysenck Personality Questionnaire Revised that has been included in the quantitative component of the Diversity project.

The first dimension assesses introversion, through ambiversion, to extraversion. Eysenck's extraversion scales measure sociability and impulsivity. The opposite of extraversion is introversion. The middle range between extraversion and introversion is often termed 'ambiversion'. The high scorer on the extraversion scale is characterized by the test manual (Eysenck and Eysenck 1975) as a sociable individual who likes parties, has many friends, needs to have people to talk to and prefers meeting people to reading or studying alone. In the survey, extraversion is accessed by items like 'Do you like going out a lot?' and 'Would you rather be alone instead of being with other people?'

The second dimension assesses emotional stability, through emotional lability, to neurotic disorder. Eysenck's neuroticism scales identify the underlying personality traits which at one extreme define neurotic disorders, including emotional lability and over-reactivity. The opposite of neuroticism is emotional stability. The high scorer on the neuroticism scale is characterized by the test manual as an anxious, worrying individual who is moody and frequently depressed, likely to sleep badly and to suffer from various psychosomatic disorders (Eysenck and Eysenck 1975). In the survey, neuroticism is accessed by items like 'Are your feelings easily hurt?' and 'Do you often feel "fed up"?'

The third dimension assesses tendermindedness, through toughmindedness, to psychotic disorder. Eysenck's psychoticism scales identify the underlying personality traits which at one extreme define psychotic disorders. The opposite of psychoticism is normal personality. The high scorer on the psychoticism scale is characterized by Eysenck and Eysenck (1976) as being cold, impersonal, hostile, lacking in sympathy, unfriendly, untrustful, odd, unemotional, unhelpful, lacking in insight, strange and paranoid. In the survey, psychoticism is accessed by items like 'Do you enjoy hurting people you like?' and 'Would you enjoy practical jokes that could sometimes hurt people?'

The lie scale was originally introduced to personality tests to identify individuals who were trying to create a good impression, but subsequently scores recorded on the lie scale have been interpreted more broadly to reflect a form of social conformity or social acquiescence. In the survey, this construct is accessed by items like 'Have you ever said anything bad or nasty about anyone?' and 'Have you ever taken anything (even a sweet) that belonged to someone else?'

Designing and conducting the survey

As in all good quantitative studies, the first step is to design a pilot survey. At this stage a long questionnaire is devised in order to test various options from which the best could be included in the final survey. For the Diversity project, the long questionnaire was administered throughout one school that was particularly interested in working on the project. This pilot study involved both cognitive testing and quantitative testing in order to check how the sections worked and to select the better performing components.

The main project was designed to collect data from at least 2,000 students between the ages of 13 and 15 years from each of the nations of the UK (England, Northern Ireland, Scotland, Wales) and London (as a special case in light of London's distinctive profile of religious diversity). Within each area, half the pupils were recruited from state-maintained schools with a religious character and half from state-maintained schools without a religious foundation.

In each of the five areas, key colleagues helped us to identify schools that were likely to be interested in supporting the research and could be seen to be typical schools within the area. In this connection the core research team has particularly appreciated the help of Philip Barnes in Northern Ireland, Peter Neil in Scotland, and Tania ap Siôn in Wales. The number of schools involved is too small to sustain the claim that we have a representative sample of students, although we are confident that we have a robust sample of typical students. Participating schools were assured that they would not be named in the findings and were asked to include within the survey all students within the two relevant year groups covering the age span between 13 and 15 years.

Students themselves were also guaranteed confidentiality and anonymity and given the choice not to participate in the survey. The level of interest shown in the project meant that very few students decided not to participate. All submitted questionnaires were individually checked by the research group before being coded for statistical analysis. After rejecting incomplete or carelessly completed questionnaires, thoroughly completed questionnaires were available from:

- 2,398 students in England
- 1,988 students in Northern Ireland

- 2,724 students in Scotland
- 2,319 students in Wales
- 2,296 students in London.

Planning this volume

Responses from nearly 12,000 young people (from the four nations and London) offering detailed data across a range of issues hold enormous potential. Initial publications drawing on these data have explored the development of a scale to measure attitudes towards religious diversity and proposed the Attitude toward Religious Diversity Index (Francis et al. 2012); the linkage between God images and individual differences in empathy (Francis, Croft and Pyke 2012); the social phenomenon of religious diversity through the eyes of young male atheists (Francis, Penny and Pyke 2013); belief in God as a matter of public concern in contemporary Wales (Francis, ap Siôn and Penny 2014); the comparative effects of personal, psychological, religious and school factors in shaping attitudes towards religious diversity (Francis and Village 2014); and the connection between religious affect and self-esteem (Penny and Francis 2014).

Building on these earlier studies, the intention in planning the present volume was to identify one research question with particular relevance to each of the five geographical areas included in the survey and to address those questions in ways that would be accessible to colleagues who may not possess professional skills and expertise in complex statistical procedures. Each of the five chapters therefore begins by defining the specific research question and situating that question within the relevant literature. In each case the research question is focused and shaped in a way that can be addressed by comparing findings for two or more groups. The statistical test employed to check the difference between the groups is chi square, set against the three conventional probability levels of .05, .01 and .001. The .05 level claims that there is 95 per cent confidence that the differences between the groups could not have occurred by chance. The .001 level claims that there is 99.9 per cent confidence that differences between the groups could not have occurred by chance.

Using the data from England, the research questionnaire was stimulated by Jim Conroy's project to ask: 'Does RE [religious education] work and contribute to the common good?' (see Conroy et al. 2013). This question is addressed from the perspective of ethos theory, comparing the overall ethos generated by one group of students (in this case, those taking RE examination classes) with the overall ethos generated by a second group of students (those not taking RE examination classes).

Using the data from Northern Ireland, the research question was stimulated by Dominic Murray's study (1985) that formulated the notion that students educated in Catholic schools and students educated in Protestant schools were 'worlds apart'. This question is addressed by comparing attitudes towards religion and attitudes towards religious diversity among students attending the two types of schools.

Using the data from Scotland, the research question was stimulated by Francis's earlier study (2002) that suggested that the Catholic community of Great Britain needs to be conceptualized not as an homogeneous community (united around one common set of values and beliefs) but as three overlapping communities all differentiated from the religiously unaffiliated, but in varying degrees. This question is addressed by taking self-assigned religious affiliation as identifying the Catholic community and then by distinguishing within the community according to three levels of religious practice: those who never attend church, those who attend church but less often than weekly and those who attend church weekly.

Using data from Wales, the research question was stimulated by the thesis proposed by the Runnymede Trust's report *Right to Divide?* (Berkeley 2008), that schools with a religious character fail to prepare students for life in a religiously and ethnically diverse society and consequently fail to promote community cohesion. This question is addressed by comparing attitudes towards religious diversity recorded by students attending schools with a religious character in Wales and attitudes towards religious diversity recorded by students attending schools without a religious foundation.

Using data from London, the research question was stimulated by the debate flowing from the introduction in 2001 of the religious affiliation question into the national census for England and Wales. The controversy concerns the power of self-assigned religious affiliation to predict matters of personal and social significance (see Francis 2003). This question is addressed by comparing a range of personal and social attitudes and values (relevant both to the wellbeing of young people themselves and to the wellbeing of society as a whole) recorded by four groups of students: Christians, Hindus, Muslims and those claiming no self-assigned religious affiliation.

References

Anthony, F.-V., and H.-G. Ziebertz, eds. 2012. *Religious Identity and National Heritage.* Leiden: Brill.

Argyle, M. 1958. *Religious Behaviour.* London: Routledge and Kegan Paul.

Argyle, M., and B. Beit-Hallahmi. 1975. *The Social Psychology of Religion.* London: Routledge and Kegan Paul.

Astley, J., L. J. Francis, and M. Robbins. 2012. 'Assessing Attitude towards Religion: The Astley-Francis Scale of Attitude toward Theistic Belief.' *British Journal of Religious Education* 34 (2): 183–193.

Beit-Hallahmi, B., and M. Argyle. 1997. *The Psychology of Religious Behaviour, Belief and Experience.* London: Routledge.

Berkeley, R. 2008. *Right to Divide? Faith Schools and Community Cohesion.* London: Runnymede.

Brockett, A., A. Village, and L. J. Francis. 2009. 'Internal Consistency Reliability and Construct Validity of the Attitude toward Muslim Proximity Index (AMPI): A Measure of Social Distance.' *British Journal of Religious Education* 31 (3): 241–249.

———. 2010. 'Assessing Outgroup Prejudice among Secondary Pupils in Northern England: Introducing the Outgroup Prejudice Index (OPI).' *Research in Education* 83 (1): 67–77.

Cartledge, Mark J. 1999. 'Empirical Theology: Inter- or Intra-disciplinary?' *Journal of Beliefs and Values* 20 (1): 98–104.

Conroy, J. C., D. Lundie, R. A. Davis, V. Baumfield, L. P. Barnes, T. Gallagher, K. Lowden, N. Bourque, and K. Wenell. 2013. *Does Religious Education Work? A Multidimensional Investigation.* London: Bloomsbury.

Corulla, W. J. 1990. 'A Revised Version of the Psychoticism Scale for Children.' *Personality and Individual Differences* 11 (1): 65–76.

Cronbach, L. J. 1951. 'Coefficient alpha and the Internal Structure of Tests.' *Psychometrika* 16 (3): 297–334.

DeVellis, R. F. 2003. *Scale Development: Theory and Applications.* London: Sage.

Eysenck, H. J., and S.B.G. Eysenck. 1975. *Manual of the Eysenck Personality Questionnaire (Adult and Junior).* London: Hodder and Stoughton.

———. 1976. *Psychoticism as a Dimension of Personality.* London: Hodder and Stoughton.

Eysenck, S.B.G., H. J. Eysenck, and P. Barrett. 1985. 'A Revised Version of the Psychoticism Scale.' *Personality and Individual Differences* 6 (1): 21–29.

Francis, L. J. 1978. 'Measurement Reapplied: Research into the Child's Attitude towards Religion.' *British Journal of Religious Education* 1 (2): 45–51.

———. 1982. *Youth in Transit: A Profile of 16–25 Year Olds.* Aldershot: Gower.

———. 1984. *Teenagers and the Church: A Profile of Church-going Youth in the 1980s.* London: Collins Liturgical.

———. 1996. 'The Development of an Abbreviated Form of the Revised Eysenck Personality Questionnaire (JEPQR-A) among 13- to 15-Year-Olds.' *Personality and Individual Differences* 21 (6): 835–844.

———. 2001. *The Values Debate: A Voice from the Pupils.* London: Woburn Press.

———. 2002. 'Catholic Schools and Catholic Values: A Study of Moral and Religious Values among 13–15 Year Old Pupils Attending Non-denominational and Catholic Schools in England and Wales.' *International Journal of Education and Religion* 3 (1): 69–84.

———. 2003. 'Religion and Social Capital: The Flaw in the 2001 Census in England and Wales.' In *Public Faith: The State of Religious Belief and Practice in Britain*, ed. P. Avis, 45–64. London: SPCK.

———. 2005. *Faith and Psychology: Personality, Religion and the Individual.* London: Darton, Longman and Todd.

Francis, L. J., T. ap Siôn, and G. Penny. 2014. 'Is Belief in God a Matter of Public Concern in Contemporary Wales? An Empirical Enquiry concerning Religious Diversity among 13- to 15-year-old Males.' *Contemporary Wales* 27 (1): 40–57.

Francis, L. J., L. B. Brown, and R. Philipchalk. 1992. 'The Development of an Abbreviated Form of the Revised Eysenck Personality Questionnaire (EPQR-A): Its Use among Students in England, Canada, the USA and Australia.' *Personality and Individual Differences* 13 (4): 443–449.

Francis, L. J., J. Croft, and A. Pyke. 2012. 'Religious Diversity, Empathy and God Images: Perspectives from the Psychology of Religion and Empirical Theology Shaping a Study among Adolescents in the UK.' *Journal of Beliefs and Values* 33 (3): 293–307.

Francis, L. J., J. Croft, A. Pyke, and M. Robbins. 2012. 'Young People's Attitudes to Religious Diversity: Quantitative Approaches from Social Psychology and Empirical Theology.' *Journal of Beliefs and Values* 33 (3): 279–292.

Francis, L. J., and Y. J. Katz. 2007. 'Measuring Attitude toward Judaism: The Internal Consistency Reliability of the Katz-Francis Scale of Attitude toward Judaism.' *Mental Health, Religion and Culture* 10 (4): 309–324.

Francis, L. J., and W. K. Kay. 1995. *Teenage Religion and Values.* Leominster: Gracewing.

Francis, L. J., P. R. Pearson, M. Carter, and W. K. Kay. 1981a. 'Are Introverts More Religious?' *British Journal of Social Psychology* 20 (2): 101–104.

———. 1981b. 'The Relationship between Neuroticism and Religiosity among English 15- and 16-Year Olds. *Journal of Social Psychology* 114 (1): 99–102.

Francis, L. J., P. R. Pearson, and W. K. Kay. 1982. 'Eysenck's Personality Quadrants and Religiosity.' *British Journal of Social Psychology* 21 (3): 262–264.

Francis, L. J., G. Penny, and A. Pyke. 2013. 'Young Atheists' Attitudes toward Religious Diversity: A Study among 13- to 15-year-old Males in the UK.' *Theo-web: Zeitschrift für Religionspädagogik* 12 (1): 57–78.

Francis, L. J., and M. Robbins. 2005. *Urban Hope and Spiritual Health: The Adolescent Voice.* Peterborough: Epworth.

Francis, L. J., M. Robbins, and J. Astley, eds. 2009. *Empirical Theology in Texts and Tables: Qualitative, Quantitative and Comparative Perspectives.* Leiden: Brill.

Francis, L. J., A. Sahin, and F. Al-Failakawi. 2008. 'Psychometric Properties of Two Islamic Measures among Young Adults in Kuwait: The Sahin-Francis Scale of Attitude toward Islam and the Sahin Index of Islamic Moral Values.' *Journal of Muslim Mental Health* 3 (1): 9–34.

Francis, L. J., Y. R. Santosh, M. Robbins, and S. Vij. 2008. 'Assessing Attitude toward Hinduism: The Santosh-Francis Scale.' *Mental Health, Religion and Culture* 11 (6): 609–621.

Francis, L. J., and A. Village. 2008. *Preaching with All Our Souls.* London: Continuum.

———. 2014. 'Church Schools Preparing Adolescents for Living in a Religiously Diverse Society: An Empirical Enquiry in England and Wales.' *Religious Education* 109 (3): 264–283.

Francis, L. J., and H.-G. Ziebertz, eds. 2011. *The Public Significance of Religion.* Leiden: Brill.

Hegy, P., ed. 2007. *What do We Imagine God to Be? The Function of 'God Images' in Our Lives.* Lewiston, New York: Edwin Mellen.

Hood, R. W. Jr., P. C. Hill, and B. Spilka. 2009. *The Psychology of Religion: An Empirical Approach* (4th ed.). New York: Guilford Press.

Kay, W. K., and L. J. Francis. 1996. *Drift from the Churches: Attitude toward Christianity during Childhood and Adolescence.* Cardiff: University of Wales Press.

Likert, R. 1932. 'A Technique for the Measurement of Attitudes.' *Archives of Psychology* 22 (140): 1–55.

Murray, D. 1985. *Worlds Apart: Segregated Schools in Northern Ireland.* Belfast: Appletree Press.

Penny, G., and L. J. Francis. 2014. 'Religion and Self-esteem: A Study among 13- to 15-year-old Students in the UK.' In *Handbook on the Psychology of Self-esteem*, ed. J. H. Borders, 19–45. New York: Nova Science.

Sahin, A., and L. J. Francis. 2002. 'Assessing Attitude toward Islam among Muslim Adolescents: The Psychometric Properties of the Sahin-Francis Scale.' *Muslim Education Quarterly* 19 (4): 35–47.

Sherif, J. 2011. 'A Census Chronicle: Reflections on the Campaign for a Religious Question in the 2001 Census for England and Wales.' *Journal of Beliefs and Values* 32 (1): 1–18.

Streib, H., ed. 2007. *Religion Inside and Outside Traditional Institutions.* Leiden: Brill.

Village, A. 2011. 'Outgroup Prejudice, Personality and Religiosity: Disentangling a Complex Web of Relationships among Adolescents in the UK.' *Psychology of Religion and Spirituality* 3 (4): 269–284.

Ziebertz, H.-G., ed. 2001. *Imagining God: Empirical Explanations from an International Perspective.* Münster: LIT Verlag.

Part Two

Qualitative perspectives

4 Sources of knowledge and authority

Religious education for young Muslims in a Birmingham comprehensive school

Julia Ipgrave

Religion, modernity and authority

The subject of this chapter is the attitude to religion of young Muslims in the city of Birmingham. It is a subject that has received a great deal of unwelcome attention since the research was carried out, as a number of schools in the city were accused of complicity in a coordinated programme of Islamic radicalization (the so-called Trojan Horse affair of 2014) – an accusation that provoked national controversy and won international notoriety. Birmingham has struggled against negative perceptions and stereotypes; the purported plot was found to be a misrepresentation of the truth, and the city itself earned the distinction of receiving a public apology from the US Fox News Network for having described Birmingham as a 'totally Muslim city' (Muslims account for around 22 per cent of the population) and a no-go area for non-Muslims.[1] Heath Wood School (not the school's real name) that provides the case study for this chapter was not one of those named in the controversy, but its context as a state comprehensive school serving mainly Muslim families in a predominantly Muslim area of inner-city Birmingham[2] makes it an object of interest in the current climate of suspicion. This chapter does not delve into the 'Trojan Horse' questions of school governance or 'extremist' infiltration, but seeks to contribute to a better understanding of the young people themselves, of their relationship to their own religion and to the religions of others.

The chapter is based on findings from group discussions with pupils of Heath Wood School. All pupils were Muslim, predominantly of Pakistani or Bangladeshi origin, with one Somali and one Turkish pupil. Their experiences of being brought up in a fairly mono-religious environment (Muslim, predominantly Sunni) and being both a majority in their locality and a minority nationally mean that they had a particular perspective on religion to offer to the wider project. As occasionally happens with research in schools, various changes in the school programme meant that fieldwork arrangements were altered on the day. Instead of coming from parallel forms, the students participating came from two quite different age groups, Group B being from the lower end of the project's 13–16 age range and Group A being six formers aged 17–18. The gap of about four years between the two groups set up some interesting contrasts and points of comparison, possibly reflecting a development of religious experience and thinking over these teenage years. The trends of these changes, however, do not fit the pattern of rejection of traditional religious forms (such as adherence to doctrine or deference to leaders) observed in some other research into young people's religion (Woodhead 2010, 240). The findings indicate a keen respect among the young people for religious authority and concern to conform their thoughts and actions to its guidance.

Other chapters in this volume (e.g. Chapter 6) refer to the use, in a number of studies, of concepts of autonomy to interpret young people's religiosity and spirituality – the imperative towards 'doing your own thing' and the individualization of religion. The case of the young people of Heath Wood School challenges this concept of modern religion by presenting an example of a contrasting trend, one that places value on authority over autonomy, where religion is experienced as given rather than constructed and where preference and choice give way to obedience and duty. The demographic context of the school in an enclave of predominantly Muslim and Pakistani heritage might lead some observers to view the pupils' religious lives and outlook as conservative remainders of another world, out of step with modern British or Western society. This seems to be the tenor of some school inspection assessments which, in the wake of the Trojan Horse affair, have been required to make judgements on whether pupils are acquiring the values necessary 'for life in modern Britain' (Ipgrave 2015) – opportunities to encounter religious diversity, the degree of social mingling between girls and boys, pupils' awareness of and attitudes to homosexual relationships and pupils' views on gender roles have all been subjects of inspection. There are other examples of young people in the Young People's Attitudes to Religious Diversity project who, like the pupils of Heath Wood, locate their religion in external authority and communal tradition: Christian pupils of African heritage in inner-city London and Protestant pupils in rural Northern Ireland and the Scottish Isles, for example. However to classify them as 'unmodern', as representatives of a passing form of religion, would be to risk binding sociological analysis to predictions about an uncertain future and making normative claims about what 'modern' religion is or should be (Jakelić 2010, 193–194).

There is something of a struggle between forms of religion – specifically between forms of Islam and the normative claims of liberalism – in educational discourse and policy that dates back beyond the Trojan Horse affair. Liberal theologies and pedagogies combined in the early years of multicultural education to suggest that personal choice between religious (and non-religious) options was the approach for a modern and plural age. Religious educationalist John Hull, always an outspoken opponent of the authority of so-called religionists, proposed that school assemblies should be used from time to time to impart knowledge about different religions in order to 'deepen understanding and facilitate choice' (Hull 1984, 15), while the influential Swann Report spoke of the role of religious education (RE) as broadening the horizon of all pupils to a greater understanding of the nature of belief, the religious dimension of human existence and the diverse life stances, 'thus enabling them to determine (and justify) their own religious position' (Swann Report 1985, 475). The idea of RE as a space where young people formulate or revise their own religious position is more common now, with discursive approaches and the sharing of pupils' own views and opinions dominating many RE lessons, the 'democratic classroom' which James Conroy interprets as 'a subject trying to compensate for its inherited associations with hierarchy, power and sacred authority – influences proverbially linked to the estrangement of most modern young people from the subject (and from religion generally)' (Conroy et al. 2013, 9). Added to this – and of particular relevance to the Muslim identity of the pupils of Heath Wood – is the significance given to liberal critiques of religion in the post-9/11 political discourse and educational policy. The 2007 Ofsted report on RE spoke of the need for the subject to respond effectively to 'the changing social reality of religion post-9/11' by adopting a more critical evaluative approach to religion (Ofsted 2007, 39–40). Several policy and guidance documents relevant to RE have made strong links between the development of young people's thinking skills and protection from extremism (DCSF 2008, 29; DCSF 2010, 8). In its guidance for community cohesion, the Religious Education Council (REC) states that 'it is a fundamental characteristic of a liberal democracy, that every individual, including every child has the right to have a critical view of their own and others' beliefs and values' (REC 2009, 4). In the same document, the REC acknowledges that it is promoting one form of religion above another by recognizing that 'for some young people and their parents, particularly those with a strong religious faith or from a strong religious background, this might feel alien, even dangerous' (ibid.) and that 'critical engagement with beliefs sits comfortably with western, secular world views but less so with others' (ibid.,10).

What we see here is a divergence of understanding between a 'Western', 'secular' and 'liberal' framing of religion promoted through public education and the religion of the 'strongly religious' as represented in this chapter by the pupils of Heath Wood. The danger of this divergence and the accompanying marginalization of the latter form of religion in the public space (risking disengagement and disaffection) were recognized even before the events of the new millennium. The basis of Adam Seligman's critique of the normative assumptions of modernity is its hostility – in politics, epistemologies and economies – to authority and its inability to understand its persistence: 'We ignore the phenomenon of authority at our peril, for by so doing we fail to recognize the import of the re-emergence of ethnic, religious and primordial identities in today's culture' (Seligman 2000, 1).

A self-understanding that relates to authority rather than autonomy is not a surrender to the past – indeed, the findings show a dynamic, forward-moving relationship with authority among some of the young people at Heath Wood. The religion of these students from this 'conservative' Muslim community in inner-city Birmingham will be presented as an expression of modern religion and their words will be analyzed to identify its main characteristics and challenges. It is a religion that (to use Michel Sandel's distinctions) can be characterized as 'discovered', not 'chosen' – hence the importance to the young people of the acquisition of knowledge, as 'constitutive' rather than 'attributive', and therefore integral to their identity (Sandel 1998, 150–151). The deference to authority and reliance on authoritative sources rather than one's own opinion to determine truth and right practice inevitably has some impact on attitudes towards other religions; this will also be considered.

Constitutive religion

The young people interviewed at Heath Wood School were all agreed that religion was of great significance to their lives and self-understanding. It is commonplace for Muslims to describe Islam as a 'way of life' rather than (just) a religion, and this sense of the faith as the overarching framework of their living was evident in the words of some of the young people:

> Religion is your identity and basically it applies to every aspect of your life – your family life, school life, social life – all the way from beginning to end.
>
> (Group A)

> I think religion is important like you have an identity and it's also the fact that it gives some structure to your life.
>
> (Group A)

But their comments revealed their religion to be more than a structure for their living; it was also a joy and a reassurance. This affective relationship with Islam is evident in one boy's delight in learning more about his faith, the 'spiritual feeling' of closeness to God, his sense that it is in that relationship and in that knowledge that he finds himself:

> Religion is like you actually want to know and when you learn one thing it lasts for hours and it gives you that spiritual feeling and you actually feel that you're close to God and you feel you are close to something and you know who you are.
>
> (Group A)

The idea of Islam as constitutive of their being – that it is their faith that makes them who they are – was expressed by others. Two sixth-form girls linked their sense of self to the comfort they received during the stressful times of end-of-school examinations when it is easy to lose oneself under the pressure:

> It makes you feel you know who you are . . . Like because I'm in the middle of all my exams . . . and it really got to me at one point and it just got on top of me and I really got upset about it but I found myself when I was praying afterwards and I was asking for guidance and I was looking for a

way to resolve it, I found that I found it in a sense and it was like – it's hard to explain but I felt kind of reassurance in myself.

(Group A)

God is able at such times to restore one to oneself:

You know if you're helpless and you're down that it's reassuring to know there's someone to get you back up to where you're supposed to be and I guess it's that reassuring feeling that you get.

(Group A)

The sense of finding oneself in closeness to God is crucial, as that God is also the ultimate source of authority for these young people, so there is acceptance of authority as part of self rather than denial of self. This is different from the understanding of some young people interviewed in other schools who found objectionable the idea of religiously imposed commands that restrict free exercise of our own reason and judgement, but it has strong parallels with Northern Irish Protestant girls discussing the common perception of religion as just 'rules and regulations':

They fall into place, like if you love God it's not just doing what God says, if you love Him, you'll want to be like Him.

(Pupil in Enniskillen)

The Heath Wood pupils and the girls from Enniskillen are presenting a position at odds with visions of the radical autonomy of the individual. It has relevance, however, to a volume concerned with mutual understanding across diverse presentations of religion. As Seligman argues, analysis of this connection between authority and self-identity is needed for a more sophisticated enquiry into the re-emergent religious consciousness of the modern age (Seligman 2000, 7).

Obedience

The young people interviewed at Heath Wood were conscious of the difference between their authority-bound lives and the preference-and-choice discourse often associated with modern living. They found divisive the dominant discourse of 'secular society' and the media that 'there's not much importance of religion and I can live my life the way I want to and I don't want anyone to dictate it for me,' and contrasted this with their own religion:

Sometimes people don't understand – it's only 'I want to do this' and 'I want to do that' – but Islam isn't about wanting, you have to do these things and it's our religion and there's no question about it.

(Group A)

These pupils' desire to please God and their obedience to His authority had outward expression in their adherence to various Islamic practices within school as well as outside:

> In terms of like rules and guidance and what we should or shouldn't do in a sense like we're not allowed to eat *haram* food like pork or drink alcohol or something like that and so we'll bring that into our school life and in doing so we're kind of pleasing God because we're basically obeying Him and we're putting it into our own life and we're doing it the right way rather than the wrong way.
>
> (Group A)

This rooting of motivation and action in God's will relates to Charles Taylor's distinction between strong and weak evaluations of desires. What the young people are putting into their lives is not evaluated by the weaker desire of what is desirable to them, but the stronger desire to do what is pleasing to God (Taylor 1985, 14–15).

The two groups reported conversations with their peers about Islamic rules. Both boys and girls discussed rules of women's dress:

> We have debates like because it says in the Qur'an that women have to cover themselves and not show their shape.
>
> (Group B)

The conviction that there is a 'right way' – the keen interest in orthopraxy – contrasts sharply with the 'no right or wrong answers' approach to ethical issues common in secondary RE (Thompson 2004, 126). Obedience to an ultimate authority that overrides social norms and human authority is not an easy position to hold in relations with friends or with parents. The young people risk appearing pompous and 'holier than thou'; one girl observed of her family, 'Like sometimes you're too religious or sometimes they feel you're imposing this on them.' There is some evidence of young people's strategic use of the language of choice when it is more likely to help them win an argument. For example, a female pupil who explained that she wore the hijab to conform to Islamic strictures on modesty and to avoid committing a sin by leaving her hair uncovered told her parents, 'I want to, it's my personal choice' when they questioned the rigour of her observance.

The conviction that there is a 'right' determined by external authority rather than internal conviction and that it is thus possible to be 'wrong' poses a challenge for these young people in a context where there is a plurality of practice – a challenge that is increased by the consciousness articulated by the older pupils that, where practically possible, they have a religious obligation to oppose error in others, not just in themselves. These young people cited the authorities (Qur'an and Hadith) for this responsibility:

> It says in the Qur'an you should do what is good and shun what is evil and the Prophet Muhammad SAW said that if you see someone doing

something wrong then try to stop him with your hand and if you can't then speak out against it and if you can't speak out against it then disapprove of it in your heart.

(Group A)

How this might be done without causing ill feeling and offence was another question discussed by the group. They agreed that criticism should be given 'nicely' and 'gently' in acknowledgement of the fact that 'people make mistakes all the time' and in keeping with a religion that is 'really soft . . . about peace . . . not about anger':

Because mainly they're your friends, so you'll kind of guide them like, 'ah, do you know, maybe you're doing something wrong' and 'is there anything we can help you with?'

(Group A)

Reports from Group B of arguments between peers about the wearing of headscarves or clothes that show off a girl's figure show that this soft tone was not always easy to maintain.

Obedience is costly and difficult for those trying to abide by the commands of their faith, particularly given the distractions of Western culture. Group B spoke of the 'weaker desires' that were in conflict with their religious obligations – computers, PlayStations. Group A spoke of TV programmes, meeting up with friends, going to the cinema, of school work and school routines that clash with Islamic prayer times; as they expressed it, 'Our Western modern society kind of gets in the way.'

Other divine commands by which the young people feel bound to obey appear less problematic. The Qur'anic diktat (presented by the students as 'a command of God') 'to seek knowledge, to constantly seek knowledge' fits neatly within the ethos and purposes of the school, and the expansion of knowledge, in the oft-quoted reference to China, encourages positive attitudes towards difference by supporting interreligious learning:

[The Prophet Muhammad] said you have to learn even if you go to China and basically what he meant was we have to learn about other religions as well as our religion.

(Group B)

More precious to these young people, however, was their learning about their own religion.

Discovery

In their accounts of their exploration of Islam, the difference between their religious outlook and the concept of religion as individual construction is particularly marked, even though they might use some of the same means of exploration (digital media, for example) as young people who select between a variety of religious offerings to construct a religious identity of their own. The words of the young people at Heath Wood suggest that they are not constructing something new, but rather seeking to discover (or uncover) something that is there eternally, in which they already believe, though they may not yet know or understand – it is Anselm's *fides quaerens intellectum*. One boy pronounced that 'Islam is all about education – the key is education,' and the imperative to learn is underpinned by a strong realism, a sense that there is what is and you need to know it and why it is so:

> You should know about your religion completely up until you learn it to a point about why this is and why this is so.
>
> (Group B)

The concern with obedience and correct practice is closely linked to the pursuit of knowledge, as greater knowledge of Islam enables closer conformity to God's wishes:

> [As teenagers] you haven't got a good understanding of your religion and you need a really good understanding to get more religious.
>
> (Group B)

The idea that learning about one's religion is also a journey of self-discovery within that religion is very strong in the words of the pupil already cited: 'You feel you are close to something, you know who you are.' Getting close to the source of being and authority involved more than understanding and obeying divine teaching; the sacred character of the Qur'an meant that being able to pronounce God's words correctly was a key element of the knowledge sought.

When discussing their Islamic learning, the young people in Group A made use of the language of 'freedom'. The kind of freedom that they reported and valued in their religious development was not the freedom to choose belief and practice but a freedom of opportunity to learn what beliefs and practices were required of them as Muslims ('to go out and go to these classes and learn from these sheikhs') that they felt had not been available to their parents when they were young and that they understood to be a condition of their living in the West. This freedom, it was suggested, was experienced by the boys in particular. Girls also reported attending separate Islamic classes after school – a contrast, one noted, with her mother who had learnt all she knew of Islam from her grandmother.

> Because we are living here in the West and we've got like more freedom and stuff – the guys especially – we can go out and seek knowledge and find out that – for example, I've been studying Islam studies for three years now and the more I learn the more I feel like a beginner – I've been learning with a Sheikh.
>
> (Group A)

The young people valued and exercised this autonomy from their parents, in pursuit of what they perceived to be Islamic orthodoxy. One example was given of tension between a girl and her family around this freedom to learn, initially with her mother but also with her father and brothers. The dialogue reported here combines the particular language of Islamic learning with the common language of teenager/parent negotiation:

> With regards to [Qur'an classes] I had this little argument with my mum when I was talking about them to her, I was like 'I want to learn more about the Qur'an, I want to learn how to pronounce it properly' . . . and when I asked her, it was like winter time and she wasn't happy about it because I had to walk quite a bit and she was like 'No, because it's dark then'. She was coming up with all of these excuses and I was like 'I want you to be happy for me, I want you to be happy for the fact that I'm taking an interest in our religion and wanting to learn it', but I didn't get that support even though she knew where I was coming from, she saw my safety came first, she saw what my Dad would say first, she saw what my brothers would say before my religion, and I think that's a big problem in a lot of families.
>
> (Group A)

Just as it matters to the young people if fellow Muslims do not live their lives in obedience to God, so it matters if they have false understanding; it is the false understanding of parents that those in Group A noted in particular:

> When you start learning and then your Mum says something and you're, 'What, how can you believe that? – that's wrong!'
>
> (Group A)

This interest in what is 'right' and the perception that parents sometimes get it 'wrong' raises the question of sources of religious authority in the lives of the young people: which authorities are to be trusted to represent correctly the eternal truths of Islam?

Authority

Pupils in both groups indicated their reliance on external authority in the framing of their thoughts and actions. The repeated use by a pupil in Group B of the phrase 'It is said . . .' is indicative of this. Both groups spoke of doing what 'Islam teaches' or 'our religion teaches' and accepted doctrinal and moral guidance from the Qur'an: 'from the Qur'an'; 'what the Qur'an wants you to'; 'It says in the Qur'an'; '[You should do] what the Qur'an wants you to.' They spoke of following the teachings of the Prophet: 'The Prophet Muhammad said . . .'; 'The Prophet Muhammad SAW said. . . .' The authority of the Qur'an or Prophet was not in question; what was less certain was which secondary authorities might be the most trusted interpreters of these primary sources. There was a marked difference between the younger and older pupils in their views on their parents' ability to translate this authority correctly to them. The religious authority of fathers in particular was respected by members of the younger group: 'I always listen to my father . . . because I trust him.' One remarked on the special authority Islam accorded to fathers as being closer to God:

> It's said that one of the signs of the Day of Judgement is that children will listen to their friends before their fathers and it says that friends should follow your father and your father is higher and you should consider your father's opinion because he is closer to Allah and you know that your father knows more – is wiser than children.
>
> (Group B)

As discussed earlier, the older pupils had less confidence in the correctness of their parents' interpretation of Islam and so gave them less credence as authorities on right belief and practice. In particular, they were conscious of cultural accretions that obscured the pure and true Islam they themselves were seeking – something their parents had acquired in their countries of origin but that had less influence over their own generation:

> A lot of our parents emigrated from Pakistan or Bangladesh and so on and they were really cultured [*sic*] and the fact that they came here and there was nothing here and they hung on to that culture and I guess as the generations grow up we're becoming less cultured and we question our culture really . . . and I think it's harder for them to distinguish between the two [culture and religion] because that's how they've grown up, it's what they know.
>
> (Group A)

In some cases there is evidence of a reversal of the relationship so that the young people, through their learning outside the family, are becoming interpreters of Islam to their own parents:

> I start questioning my mum, I go home from Islamic classes and say to Mum, 'I learned this but what you're doing, that's culture, that's not Islam' and then I'm slowly getting my mum round now.
>
> (Group A)

The authorities whom these older pupils trust are the 'pious teachers' who have knowledge of Islam beyond that of their parents:

> They have pious teachers out there that actually know what they're talking about – they know about Islam, they know the basics and they can reach you and Mum didn't have the opportunity – apart from her granny – that obviously we have had.
>
> (Group A)

They spoke of their sheikhs and their Islamic classes after school and on Sundays where they learnt Arabic and Islamic knowledge, 'like the belief in God and our religion and what are the basics we have to know'.

These evening and weekend classes were not the only contexts for formal learning about Islam, however. As pupils at a community comprehensive school they also learnt about Islam within their multi-faith RE, the predominantly Muslim demographic of the school being a reason why the RE department had chosen options that give particular prominence to the pupils' Islamic religion. The authority of the non-Muslim RE teachers to teach about Islam was a point of discussion in both interview groups with different conclusions drawn. The younger pupils expressed more misgivings about this arrangement. The school teachers 'know a different language'; they cannot read the Qur'an or Islamic texts 'so they can totally misunderstand'. The RE teacher who 'has to know about all the religions' is compared with the mosque teacher who 'knows a lot about one', and the former's knowledge is found wanting. Pupils in Group B remarked that the teacher was actually finding out about Islam from them ('like we teach her because there are things you don't find in books'). They reported occasions on which they had told the teacher that their textbooks were wrong in what they said about Islamic customs. These younger pupils, more bound by their home culture, accepted an Islam that was closely interwoven with ethnicity and they deemed the teacher's understanding of this relationship to be deficient:

> I think it's hard for the teacher to understand our Islam because, you know, when you are at home, sometimes religion and ethnicity are mixed but here it's just from the book, but at home – like say a teacher says 'do you have to wear *shalwar kameez?*' – it doesn't say that you have to wear it in the Qur'an as long as you're covered, but at home you have to wear it because you come from the background of it.
>
> (Group B)

In these cases the young people were dealing with questions and practices with which they were familiar, where they themselves were the authorities. More troubling for them were occasions when the RE teacher was telling them things about Islam about which they themselves did not have knowledge, whether what she said could be taken as authoritative and correct when she was not a Muslim herself:

> We have a Christian teacher who teaches us Islam and sometimes it doesn't feel right what she's teaching us and you don't know if it's true because she's not in Islam. It's hard to believe it because she might think it's true, but you never know, she could've got it wrong somehow.
>
> (Group B)

By contrast the older pupils, less bound by their parents' Islam, seemed more prepared to trust the teacher's word and accept that she might know things about Islam that they themselves did not know:

> And [our teacher] knows things and she kind of makes us understand it and we say, 'Oh, you've got a lot of knowledge, you've got even more knowledge than us and you're not a Muslim.'
>
> (Group A)

Although the two groups came to different conclusions about the veracity of their teacher's teaching, they both showed a strong realism in their religion, a concern with knowledge and with what is true. This concern influences their relationship with other religions as well as with 'erroneous' interpretations of their own.

Relating to 'the other'

One factor in the students' relations with other religions is their situation of living and learning in contexts where Muslims are very much in the majority, and interaction with those of other faiths – or no faith – is limited. They admitted to feeling secure cocooned in their own community and expressed some nervousness of the wider society outside. As one girl said:

> You feel comfortable round people who – like if you're a Muslim with Muslims – because you feel you have something in common with them.
>
> (Group A)

A classmate expressed the same view and then said that she would find it very challenging to be in a minority among people of a different faith:

> I think we're lucky in the sense that we've been brought up in such a solid society. Our school is predominantly Muslim and because we're surrounded with the same people . . . if I were a Muslim in a predominantly Christian school, I'd find that incredibly difficult.
>
> (Group A)

Reasons given for being nervous of a more mixed or minority context were the lack of understanding they might encounter ('like the way I wear my *hijab*, I think that would cause a big problem within school and they'd be questioning me why'), fear of prejudice ('you don't want to come across people who are kind of horrible and judge your religion') and anxiety about the temptations they would face among people who did not share their moral code. In a school where everyone is Muslim and everyone is 'like you', one boy in Group B claimed, 'No one does things you shouldn't do, so you wouldn't be tempted to do it.' Greater exposure to the influences of 'the West' would make it harder to lead one's life according to Qur'anic principles; as another pupil explained, 'It's easy to do what you're not supposed to do because people around us do it so it's hard.'

Weighed against these fears is the consciousness that a more mixed school and community would give them and their non-Muslim neighbours a chance to get to know each other better and so reduce prejudice, both theirs and other people's, so that 'you'll feel more comfortable in time' and 'you'd learn how to get on with them,' and a recognition that it would be a better reflection of the plural society beyond their immediate environment:

> If you're like in a mixed school with a lot of faiths and people who don't have a religion and people who do have a religion, I guess it's more easy for people to socialize, I guess it's an idea of how society is really and I guess it all comes down to education and people know that even like a small minority of that religion, it makes people more tolerant to each other and not just believe what people are told in the media and stuff.
>
> (Group A)

Although they may have little opportunity for face-to-face encounter with people of other religions (apart from teachers), the young people do encounter other faith traditions in their RE lessons. Conviction that there is a right and wrong in religion and confidence in the truth of Islam necessarily have an impact on the way the young people approach these other religions. Some similarities between religions were recognized, 'the basic values that you shouldn't kill people, the 10 Commandments and so on'; however, the young people were generally keen to maintain the distinctiveness between them and stressed their commitment to their own. Although learning different religions was the policy within the school, some students were unconvinced about its value. For one boy there was no point learning about religions that you did not yourself believe in:

> I don't get why you have to learn about other religions when you're not following them, but I want to learn about my own.
>
> (Group B)

Another was concerned that learning about other religions might confuse his own faith and lead him astray:

> If you learn about their religion and you begin to agree with something and to think, 'yeah, I do feel this is right', then it will completely mess up your own thoughts and it would be bad for your religion.
>
> (Group B)

In his thinking there was no room for the idea that he might have anything to learn from another faith. Rather the idea that personal faith might be destabilized by an encounter with different religions means that the believer has to be firm in his/her own religion before engaging with others. What is needed, according to one pupil, is not just thoughts and inclinations towards Islam but secure and full knowledge of its truth:

> Before you learn about other religions you should know your own religion completely up until you learn it to a point about why this is and why this is so that when you come to the other religion you can compare it. And it's not just that you *think* this is right and this is wrong, you don't just think it but you *know*, so you need to know your religion fully first.
>
> (Group B)

Those who were approving of multi-faith RE saw its value in terms of greater understanding of other people from those faith traditions, not in anything it might contribute to their own religious development – the idea that it might facilitate choice was very far from their thinking. Maintaining the purity of one's own religion and the 'otherness' of the other was important but did not exclude interaction across these differences. For some, interreligious learning was about learning the etiquette of interreligious encounter. Knowing how to behave with people of different religions, 'how to act and what you must say or do', was viewed as the important outcome of multi-faith RE:

> It's good to learn about other religions in case at any time in your life you need to deal with people with different religions or to talk with people with different religions.
>
> (Group B)

A girl in Group A argued for learning about other faiths ('the Christian faith, the Jews, the Hindus, the Sikhs') even from primary age, on the grounds that 'from an early age to make us aware of what's around us is really important'. A segregated existence, though it might be more comfortable, was seen as neither possible nor ultimately desirable given the need to prepare themselves for the diversity they were likely to encounter in their adult lives.

Conclusion

In their book *The Faith of Generation Y*, Sylvia Collins-Mayo and colleagues pose the question, 'What do late modern young people believe and trust which gives them a sense of ontological security?' (Collins-Mayo and Pink Dandelion 2010, 32). This chapter answers that question for a group of young Muslim people in inner-city Birmingham. Their ontological security, and indeed their ontological selves, rest in Islam. Their religion and their religious values do not stand apart from the self, but are, in an essential sense, constitutive of the self (Seligman 2000, 24). Finding out who they are is finding out the truth of Islam, hence prime importance is given to correct knowledge and legitimate authority.

This Islam is not a direct import from their ancestral homes in Pakistan, Bangladesh and Somalia; it is experienced differently in their Western setting. It would be misleading, however, to attempt to view the religion of these modern young people through the Western liberal prism of individualization, autonomy and choice. Their words indicate that what they value in their Western context is not freedom *from* the authority of Islam but freedom *for* it. The older pupils, including the girls, appreciate the greater freedom they have from family and cultural conventions to seek out those who (stripping away the accumulation of ethnic culture and local custom) are able to interpret for them with more surety the truths of their faith and, because that faith constitutes self, to increase their knowledge of who they already are as Muslims. What interests them is clarity and authority rather than personal opinion, rational calculation and autonomous choice. It is this authority that challenges them to put aside the 'weaker desires' of modern teenage culture and focus on the 'stronger desire' to conform to God's will. It also, less comfortably, gives them a set of standards against which they evaluate the rightness or wrongness of the beliefs and actions of others.

The power the hunger for Islamic learning gives to those whom they accept as authorities potentially makes the young people vulnerable (a cause of concern in the current climate of the securitization of Islam), but it can also provide them with a strong sense of purpose and motivation to good action. This is evident in the concern for moral conduct and the seriousness with which the pupils in Group A approached their studies and future plans. As they prepared to leave school for the life of work and university, these plans acknowledged that their adult lives might be lived out beyond the familiar environment of Heath Wood.

In their discussions about social encounter with people of other faiths and learning about other religions in RE, the young people interviewed conceived of themselves as a distinct and bounded group within a wider context of diversity, with a religion sufficient to their needs and aspirations. The young people offered varying opinions on whether it was better to maintain a separateness from wider society or to engage with it, whether non-Islamic religions and lifestyles were irrelevant to their ways of being, whether they were a threat to them or of interest to enhanced understanding of 'the other' and improved relations between communities. Where the young people expressed willingness to meet with religious difference, their engagement was not about negotiating their identities – they seemed secure in these as constituted by Islam and obedience to God – but about negotiating their relations with others and a place for them as observant Muslims in a plural world.

Notes

1 BBC News, 'Apology for Muslim Birmingham Fox News Claim' (http://www.bbc. co.uk/news/uk-england-30773297, access date: 12 February 2015).

2 According to 2007 figures, the white British population counted 22 per cent, residents of Pakistani origin 51 per cent and those of Bangladeshi origin 9 per cent.

References

Collins-Mayo, Sylvia, and Pink Dandelion. 2010. *The Faith of Generation Y*. Farnham: Ashgate.

Conroy, James, David Lundie, Robert Davis, Vivienne Baumfield, L. Philip Barnes, Tony Gallagher, Kevin Lowden, Nicole Bourque, and Karen Wenell. 2013. *Does Religious Education Work? A Multidimensional Approach*. London: Bloomsbury.

DCSF (Department for Children, Schools and Families). 2008. *Learning Together to Be Safe: A Toolkit to Support Schools in Preventing Violent Extremism*. Nottingham: DCSF.

———. 2010. *Religious Education in English Schools: Non-statutory Guidance*. Nottingham: DCSF.

Hull, John. 1984. *Studies in Religion and Education*. Lewes: Falmer Press.

Ipgrave, Julia. 2015. 'Trojan Horse', 'British Values' and Education for Modern Britain. *RE Today*, 32 (3): 57–60.

Jakelić, Slavica. 2010. *Collectivistic Religions: Religion, Choice and Identity in Late Modernity*. Farnham: Ashgate.

Ofsted. 2007. *Making Sense of Religion: A Report on Religious Education in Schools and the Impact of Locally Agreed Syllabuses*. London: Ofsted.

REC (Religious Education Research Council of England and Wales). 2009. *Religious Education and Community Cohesion*. London: REC. Available at: http://www.religiouseducationcouncil.org/content/blogcategory/49/78/, access date: 4 July 2012.

Sandel, Michel J. 1998. *Liberalism and the Limits of Justice* (2nd ed.). Cambridge: Cambridge University Press.

Seligman, Adam B. 2000. *Modernity's Wager: Authority, the Self, and Transcendence*. Princeton, NJ: Princeton University Press.

Swann Report. 1985. *Education for All*. London: HMSO.

Taylor, Charles. 1985. *Philosophical Papers. Vol. 1. Human Agency and Language*. Cambridge: Cambridge University Press.

Thompson, Penny. 2004. *Whatever Happened to Religious Education?* Cambridge: Lutterworth Press.

Woodhead, Linda. 2010. 'Epilogue.' In *Religion and Youth*, ed. Sylvia Collins-Mayo and Pink Dandelion, 239–241. Farnham: Ashgate.

5 Uniting two communities or creating a third community?

Research in a Northern Irish integrated school

Julia Ipgrave

Integrated education in context

From the four Northern Irish schools that participated in the Young People's Attitudes to Religious Diversity project (the 'Diversity project'), Woodside Integrated College[1] has been selected as the focus of this chapter because of the particular perspective it has to offer on our central theme. Woodside was established in 1992 as part of the Northern Ireland Council for Integrated Education (NICIE) movement whose explicit intention was to encourage attitudinal change among young people and within society. This movement, by bringing together Catholics and Protestants in the same (non-denominational Christian) schools, aims at 'the promotion of equality and good relations . . . to everyone in the school and to their families regardless of their religious, cultural or social background' (NICIE 2008, 1) and at the empowerment of pupils as they grow and mature 'to affect [*sic*] positive change in the shared society we live in' (ibid., 2).[2] It is part of a broader international trend that sees education not just as a mirror of society but as an agent for positive change. This trend was evident in the landmark US Supreme Court decision (*Brown v Board of Education*) in which the educational system was legally identified as the institution that could initiate social change – in this case in the transformation of race relations (Hayes, McAllister and Dowds 2007, 475). More recently, post 9/11, this trend was further evident in concerns for the promotion of interreligious understanding through education expressed in policy documents and guidance produced at European level, including the *Toledo Guiding Principles*, from the Office of Democratic Institutions and Human Rights (ODHIR 2007), and the Council of Europe's *Signposts* (Jackson 2014). There are also numerous smaller scale initiatives at a more local level, such as intercultural partnerships between schools of contrasting pupil populations.[3] These initiatives have been strongly influenced by the contact hypothesis as elaborated by Gordon Allport (1954) and others. One of the assumptions underlying the contact hypothesis is that conflict arises from lack of information about the other group and lack of opportunities to obtain this information, in particular by meeting with 'the other'. In schools, what children learn and whom they meet becomes important. Curriculum and contact are both included in the affirmations of the NICIE that children and young people have a right to an education that gives 'opportunities for them to explore the diversity of the world in which they live' and that 'in an inherently segregated and contested society, children and young people can learn to respect difference more effectively when they are afforded the opportunity to have meaningful and sustained engagement with those who are different from themselves' (NICIE 2008, 2).

Northern Ireland has been accorded a particular place in discussions about education's role in effecting social changes, as the traditional system of the province (whereby 90 per cent of pupils attend Catholic-maintained schools or de facto Protestant-controlled schools) is widely perceived to be a major contributing factor to the well-known divisions of that society. US President Obama himself used his presence in Northern Ireland for the G8 summit of June 2013 to deliver a controversial speech that targeted 'segregated schools' as divisive and generative of conflict:

> If towns remain divided – if Catholics have their schools and buildings, and Protestants have theirs – if we can't see ourselves in one another, if fear and resentment are allowed to harden, that encourages division.
>
> (Jeffrey 2013)

Ultimately it all comes down to 'attitudes'. In 2010, Northern Ireland's First Minister Peter Robinson himself described the province's education system as 'a benign form of apartheid, which is fundamentally damaging to our society' (*Belfast Telegraph* 2010). Across the Irish Sea, campaigners against faith schools have long used the divisions in Northern Ireland as warnings of what might happen, should the faith sector in England continue to grow (BHA 2006, 3), although the validity of extrapolations from Northern Ireland to other contexts is highly questionable. Here the situation cannot be understood simply in terms of religious difference but also has to be understood in terms of territorial allegiances, or what have been described as 'religiously-based ethnonationalist identities': Protestants who wish to remain part of the United Kingdom and Catholics who want unification with the rest of Ireland (Hayes and McAllister 2001, 455).

Separate, religiously based education is not a uniquely Northern Irish phenomenon; what makes it a particular focus of concern is the wider lack of intercommunal contact in a country that is deeply divided residentially – more than 70 per cent of social housing estates are occupied by 90 per cent who have a single identity – and in the workplace (Borooah and Knox 2013, 925). That such separation hinders the healing process and can lead to a renewal of civil unrest and violence is a perennial anxiety. The Northern Irish peace process and the political agreements (leading to a power-sharing coalition in a devolved government) have produced a period of welcome stability. Nevertheless, the history of the Troubles continues to haunt the province's community relations and the residue of sectarian tension still occasionally bubbles up to the surface. There were several bombing attempts during the months when fieldwork was carried out for the Diversity project. The fact that the core principles of

Integrated Education include the aim that pupils 'understand and engage with the use of non-violent means of conflict resolution' implies a context where violence is an ever-present threat (see NICIE website: http://www.nicie.org). Northern Ireland is described as 'an inherently segregated and contested society' (NICIE 2008, 2).

History has made it easy for the Protestant-Catholic duality to dominate thinking on diversity in Northern Ireland, but it is important to recognize beyond this divide the increasing ethnic and religious diversity through new migration (an upward trend since the end of large-scale violence). The Department of Education's 2012–2013 school census data reveal that the number of 'newcomer' children in Northern Irish schools has risen from 0.5 per cent of the population in the 2001–2002 school year to 3 per cent in 2012–2013 (Torney 2013). These demographic changes are acknowledged in NICIE's thinking and viewed there as a hopeful sign for a new Northern Ireland:

> At the same time the influx of newcomers from other parts of the world brings with it the challenge of enhanced ethnic diversity, demonstrating that Northern Ireland cannot afford to remain isolated and trapped in time. The 21st century therefore brings hope for the future, despite being burdened by the legacy of the past.
>
> (NICIE 2008, 2)

The NICIE website (http://www.nicie.org) presents Integrated Education as the model of education for this new world, 'a positive choice for the future of our country', 'the way forward'. NICIE's stated principles for integrated schools acknowledge and value different religious identities in the pupil body: '[the integrated school] aspires to create an environment where those of all faiths and none are acknowledged, respected and accepted as valued members of the school community' (NICIE 2008, 48), though at many schools the management admit to finding it a challenge to maintain the essentially Christian character, which is officially part of the Integrated School ethos, within an increasingly diverse society and a context of growing secularism and atheism (Macaulay 2009, 46).

Since the movement began, the number of pupils educated in integrated schools has risen from 28 pupils in one school in Lagan in 1981 to nearly 22,000 in 2013–2014 (see NICIE website: http://www.nicie.org), but these figures still amount to a very small proportion of the province's school population (6 per cent). The sector has attracted widespread attention and research interest disproportionate to its size. Integrated Education in Northern Ireland has been investigated by aspiration, by experience and by impact. In the first area of interest, aspiration, a 2008 survey by Millward Brown found that 82 per cent of adults believed integrated education was either very or fairly important to peace and reconciliation. An Ipsos Mori survey of 1,007 adults in 2011 found 88 per cent to be in favour of integrated schools. Such statistics are used by the Integrated Education Fund to argue for the need for their schools and more like them

(Integrated Education Fund 2014). A 2003 survey exploring the experience of different members of integrated school communities found that parents particularly valued the attitudes of mutual respect promoted by integrated education – it was described as 'an island of normality in a sea of abnormality'; several pupils also acknowledged the benefits of being 'mixed' and 'able to learn with other traditions', although in their generally positive response to their schooling the majority identified the same 'favourite things about school' as their peers in other education sectors (Montgomery et al. 2003, 11). One angle taken by this study was an interest in stability or fluidity of identity. There were a variety of pupil responses to the question whether attending an integrated school made them feel less or more Catholic or Protestant, and a variety of interpretations of the impact of integrated schooling on pre-existing social identity and personal identity, but there was also evidence of the development of other identities. The majority felt they had taken on an 'integrated' identity ('integrated schools churn out people with a particular identity') defined mainly in terms of shared values: being 'broadminded and understanding'; 'better informed, more rounded, probably more positive' (ibid., 43–44). One former pupil described difficulties relating as an 'integrated' person to the more 'close-minded' attitudes of her fellow students at university: 'I think they got sick of me because I was too "integrated" if you like' (ibid., 39).

To investigate the impact of integrated education on community relations, Bernadette Hayes and Ian McAllister analyzed a pooled sample of surveys conducted among the adult population of Northern Ireland between 1998 and 2006. Their study found that those who attended a 'formally integrated' school[4] are significantly more likely to have friends and neighbours from across the religious divide (Hayes and McAllister 2009). A later study by Hayes, McAllister and Lizanne Dowds (using 2005–2009 data) examined attitudes and found that those who attended 'formally integrated' schools were more likely to claim understanding of and respect for other religious communities (Hayes, McAllister and Dowds 2013). These research findings are not conclusive, however. The statistical data show that, while levels of respect and understanding may be higher for past pupils of integrated schools, the number of respondents who show respect *without* the experience of Integrated Education suggests there may be factors other than schooling involved. It has not been possible to distinguish between school environment and parental influence in the results: parents who send their children to integrated schools might be expected to be more open-minded.

Despite a widespread enthusiasm for the principle, Integrated Education has also been subjected to criticism. Some of the criticism is that Integrated Education fails to live up to the claims made for it. Despite NICIE directives about the ideal balance of Catholics and Protestants in the population of an integrated school (40 per cent of each group), few schools are achieving this. To take the case of one school, Priory Integrated College[5] found itself with a pupil body that was 77 per cent Protestant and a staff that was 70 per cent Protestant. In order to raise the confidence and self-esteem of its own Catholic minority, Priory entered into a partnership with another integrated school that was majority Catholic (McCreadie 2013). Critics have also suggested an overemphasis on contact, as opposed to curricular work, in integrated schools, hindering the development of deep understanding of 'the other' (Hayes, McAllister and Dowds 2007, 458). A failure to explore cultural differences in schools and a tendency to minimize differences 'are likely to impede rather than facilitate good community relations' (Donnelly 2008, 187). The avoidance of controversial issues in mixed company – the 'social grammar' of Northern Ireland – means young people can engage in cross-community contact yet remain largely ignorant of the views of the 'other side' on fundamental issues that cause division (Gallagher 2004, 119–120). Another issue concerns identity and the perceived threat to community and individual identity that these schools pose. Some view loss of identity as the sine qua non of integrated education (Borooah and Knox 2013, 944.) Others offer a more nuanced analysis of the impact of contact with 'the other': Hayes, McAllister and Dowds conclude that identity preferences and the persistence or transformation of traditional viewpoints depend on the nature of the contact situation, on the numerical composition of the groups involved and their relative status. There is a difference, they point out, between trying to reduce intergroup conflict through 'a shared compromise between the aspirations of two traditions' and a reduction in division through 'acceptance of the dominant view' (Hayes, McAllister and Dowds 2007, 477).

Sectarian conflict is not the only problem in the province; the community is divided on socio-economic, not just religious 'ethnonationalist' lines – divisions which appear to be reflected in the selective education system. In addition, the decline in pupil population presents the education sector with practical and financial challenges: integrated education becomes yet another sector competing for a diminishing number of pupils. These and other issues were explored in an independent strategic review of education in 2006, *Schools for the Future: Funding, Strategy, Sharing* (Bain 2006), which recommended collaboration, sharing of resources and specialisms and the development of mutual understanding through regular interschool engagement. *The Shared Education Programme* (SEP) was launched in the province in 2007 to support schools from different sectors as they work in cross-community partnerships and deliver shared classes and activities to improve education outcomes.[6] A research paper for the Northern Ireland Assembly Research and Information Service of 2011 found that, despite the largely positive attitudes to shared education, collaboration is often hindered by practical and cultural challenges (Perry 2011).

Although several integrated schools have worked to build up links with local churches, relations can be difficult: the churches have tended to prioritize the protection of existing schools (maintained and controlled schools) in which they have governance, over support for or involvement in the development of integrated education in Northern Ireland (Macaulay 2009, 4). The Roman Catholic Church in Northern Ireland has been a vocal critic of Integrated Education which it sees as undermining the ethos of the maintained (Catholic) sector. It has also objected to the directive approach taken by the education department in advancing school reforms, given that, with responsibility for 45 per cent of pupils, the Church is in fact the major stakeholder in Northern Ireland's education system.[7] There is a barely disguised hint of irritation in the Catholic bishops' response to the Independent Strategic Review:

> It would be unfortunate if the Review were to give credence to the trite assumption that a Catholic school was just a school for Catholics, merely a place where Catholic religious teaching was communicated to pupils, in the Religious Education classes and elsewhere.
>
> (Catholic Bishops of Northern Ireland 2006, 5)

Catholic education, it argues, is motivated by a particular educational philosophy and committed to transmitting a particular *Weltanschauung* of which solidarity, justice and human dignity are core elements. While the bishops recognize in the education system 'the scars of our turbulent and painful history', they argue forcefully that 'no contribution is made to a genuinely pluralist society by someone who imagines that all those who are out of step with his/her "enlightened" educational and political vision have somehow capriciously chosen to indulge themselves as recidivist segregationists' (ibid., 5). The bishops are also able to point out the relatively diverse nature of the Catholic maintained school population. The 2011 school census found that 59 per cent of newcomers were educated in the Catholic maintained schools, 29 per cent in controlled schools and 7 per cent in integrated schools. The Catholic school that was the focus for another case study in the Diversity project had a significant number of Muslim pupils – it was the school used to obtain the views of Muslim young people in Northern Ireland – and 22 per cent of pupils had English as an additional language.

Amid the debates that surround Integrated Education it is clear that the sector carries a heavy burden of expectation in what is a very complex situation. Ultimately the key questions gather around identities and attitudes and the relationship between them. In the next section I examine how these play out in the case of one particular integrated secondary school.

Perspectives from the pupils of Woodside Integrated College

Woodside Integrated College is situated on the edge of a Northern Irish city[8] which has a troubled history of sectarian conflict. Located in an open park and woodland area, the school does not serve an obvious local community; pupils are bused in from different parts of the city. There is, therefore, a degree of physical separation from the rest of the city, which was reflected to some degree in the pupils' discussions where they commented on their city but at a remove. The time of the focus groups coincided with the publication of the Bloody Sunday Report following a lengthy inquiry into one of the most controversial events of the Troubles: in 1972, 26 civilian protestors and bystanders were shot by British soldiers; 13 of those who were shot were killed. The inquiry found, among other things, that the responsibility for the deaths and injuries lay with the soldiers whose firing had been 'unjustifiable' (Saville 2010). The coincidence of timing had some impact on the research in terms of both the organization of the focus groups and the content of their discussions.

The pupil population of the school is predominantly Catholic, Protestants being in the minority; those who do not profess to a particular religion constitute a still smaller minority. These groupings were all represented among the 24 pupils participating in the focus groups; the Catholic participants were the largest grouping. The actual constitution of the three groups differed from that originally planned for the research. Initially the idea had been that, as with other schools in the Diversity project, religious identity would be a key factor in deciding which pupils would participate in the different groups. In the pre-research planning meeting, the principal had welcomed the opportunity this project would afford: to explore in more detail the perspectives of the Protestant pupils in particular by giving them a platform to express their views unrestrained by the presence of the majority. The position of the Protestant minority in the school was a cause of concern for the principal (himself a Roman Catholic). He made reference to recent research and reports that drew attention to the insecurity of the city's Protestant population who, reports suggested, felt themselves to be 'the underdog' in the face of demographic, political and cultural change, of external indifference and deficient internal leadership (Shirlow et al. 2006, 14). The principal gave as an illustration the increasing number of republican flags flying in the local cemetery – a situation, he said, many found provocative and distasteful. Once it became clear that the research and the Bloody Sunday Report would coincide, however, the principal decided that it would be better to interview pupils in mixed groups, because of the heightened sensitivity of questions of intercommunity relations and because separate religious identity-based groupings would be contrary to 'the integrated ethos of the school'. Thus, even before the focus groups began, a number of interesting issues had been raised: awareness of the school management that minority groups might feel at a disadvantage within the school; a reluctance to delve into issues that might prove painful; and the idea that such deep-delving was contrary to the integrated ethos. The mixed groupings also had an impact on the research events and resulting data. They meant that generally accepted discourse was likely to dominate over particular concerns of individuals or groups of pupils; this situation had its own value for the light it could throw on the school ethos.

When prompted in the group interviews, the pupils showed a readiness to talk about the Bloody Sunday Inquiry and the historical experiences and feelings that it revived. Interestingly their comments related to conversations in their homes with members of their family rather than to any school input: 'My parents they told me . . .'; 'My gran told me . . .'; 'Our parents told us . . . .' Although the discussions were amicable, Catholic perspectives tended to dominate both in explanations of the start of the Troubles – '[It was] a protest for rights because they couldn't get jobs . . . and it all comes from that . . . because they wanted jobs and they wanted the rights'; 'People don't want others living in our country. They believe that the British came over and took over our country and they don't want them here' – and in interpretations of the significance of the inquiry to people of the city:

> they remember they were told that their siblings and stuff were guilty and they were killed for a reason, whereas on Tuesday when they found they were innocent, there was so much joy throughout Derry and it was so happy . . . it's such a relief for all the families and stuff.

Religious identity, its continuity and fluidity, is one of the areas that has interested research on integrated schools, as described earlier. The group discussions for the Diversity project explored the identity of the pupils as they discussed influences on their religious practice and thinking. The picture that emerged was mixed. The majority of Woodside pupils taking part in the focus groups had some religious faith: most had some personal and family religious involvement, most had a church link of some kind and some were regular attenders; in this regard they were comparable with young people in other Northern Irish schools who took part in the project. The young people's engagement with religion, or lack of it, was frequently linked to their parents' practice. Where parents were regularly involved, young people also tended to be; where parents were more casual about religion, so were the young people, even though the given religious identity (Catholic or Protestant) might persist: '[my family] have got a religion, but we don't really go by it. We are Catholic, but we don't go to chapel or anything.' Atheist as well as religious identities were passed on by parents; one boy reported how his atheist father, starting with the Bible, had argued him out of believing anything. Alongside this intergenerational transmission and continuity were signs of fluidity, with young people reporting going through a 'phase' or 'stage': 'a phase when I think I'm going to change my religion because other religions do seem interesting'; 'a sort of agnostic stage' when 'I just didn't know what I believed in.' As one said, 'Everybody has the potential to swing.'

In the discussions the young people showed themselves to be positive about religious diversity beyond the familiar Protestant-Catholic distinction, but less positive about religion as such, especially insofar as it related to them or to their community. For them, part of the ethic of Integrated Education was that it was novel and different from the familiar; religious education in their school broadened their minds by introducing them to new, previously unexplored territory, so it is 'not just focused on Catholic and Protestant but like all religions' and 'so it makes you think that there's more than just one religion in the world and not just Protestants and Catholics'. The concept of equality was also important to their understanding of the school's ethos and this was another reason why they valued a multi-faith Religious Education (RE): '[RE] is based on every religion, not focused on one more than another because it's unfair.' Pupils spoke approvingly of the school's acknowledgement of a diversity of traditions: 'our school mixes cultures and religions.' They reported how in assemblies they celebrated different occasions for different religions, mentioning Jewish New Year and Islamic festivals. They recalled a school visit to a Sikh gurdwara which had evidently been a positive experience for them. Different pupils spoke in favourable terms of religions they had studied:

> Islam was such an interesting religion, I mean I was reading up on it and it was so interesting and it was so different that it was interesting and that was the same with every other religion that we've ever covered in school in RE, I've just, you know, I always find myself attached to religions because it's a different way of thinking, it's putting yourself into a different perspective.

Pupils recognized an ethic of diversity and also an ethic of commonalty. One explained that learning about a range of religions 'just shows you that people aren't that different'; another remarked that 'Jews believe the same as us' and a third stated how, although they may differ now, Christians and Muslims 'started off the same'. But above all it was in relation to Catholics and Protestants that pupils wanted to stress an underlying sameness that renders foolish the sectarian distinctions that cause such damage to community relations in their city: 'There's not even that big a difference between Protestant and Catholic . . . nothing to fight about'; 'They're basically nearly the same.' The young people did not suggest that Catholicism and Protestantism and the relations between them should be included within the school curriculum – indeed, one declared that to learn about Christianity in RE would be boring as 'you've already like grown up with it and stuff' – but rather they suggested that the awareness of commonalty and closeness was something that would result from contact:

> [Divisions exist] because they're not given the opportunity to actually talk to people from the other side, like if they were Catholic to actually talk to a Protestant, and then I think if they were to mix, then they'd realize that they're all the same.

In the young people's view, their school was able to effect this mixing: 'it brings different religions together and they see that there's no point fighting, it's just stupid.' One pupil gave a concrete illustration of the kind of cross-cultural friendships that integrated education made possible:

> I've been at an integrated school my whole life and I think it's like – you know, like go back to the Troubles, you know there's still that divide there, but there's people on my bus – we pick people up from X, which is a typically Catholic area and just down the road there's Y, which is a typically Protestant area, and there's two people on my bus and they're the best of friends though they're from both X and Y.

Despite their professed enthusiasm for learning about other faiths, it emerged from the discussion that many pupils preferred to wear their own religion lightly. Some expressed concern not to be labelled as belonging to a particular religion – a concern intensified by apprehension that there might be unpleasant consequences if their religious identity was too obvious, because of tensions between communities and because in certain areas of the city 'Someone would just come over and jump you if you belong to a certain religion.' For some it seemed better not to care about religion. The following comment includes the concern about religion's conflict potential, but it also suggests that a move from the maintained to the integrated sector has made a significant difference to this young person's attitude to and engagement with religion:

> I used to go to a Catholic school and I always used to go to church with the school and confirmation and communion, but once I came to this school, I haven't seen church since primary 7. I don't see the point now. It's just there's no point in it; I don't really care about religion and what religion is and stuff, I just don't. I don't really think about it – it's pointless having fights about religion.

In distancing themselves from open expression of religion, pupils pointed to the private nature of religion: 'I think religion does matter . . . but only to you'; 'I do follow a religion, but I don't think it's necessary for you to follow a religion – I just feel the need to myself.' Another theme was the rejection of organized religion, its authority and rules: one Christian pupil claimed to feel closer to atheists than to people of other faiths 'because they don't have any rules or anything like that', and another declared:

> I don't believe in organized religion. I don't believe in sitting around and just sort of bowing down to somebody – like I don't believe in going to church, I think you don't need to go to church if you're religious.

These themes were common in the focus groups at several schools in other parts of the United Kingdom, but were less common at the other Northern Irish schools where the pupils showed more acceptance of the authority of the church (or Islamic religion) with which they identified. It is hard to find a definitive answer to the question whether the attitudes expressed by Woodside pupils were the product of an integrated education or whether they reflect the character of the school intake. There are indications of both in the young people's comments. According to one group, the school adopts a neutrality that prefers to downplay pupils' religious identity: 'I'd say it's neutral'; 'I'd say it's fairly neutral'; 'It'd be like the majority of it is fairly Christian and then there's a smaller group of different religions. But the school wouldn't like show it and make it obvious.'

While pupils at other schools might be 'very strong on religion', this school 'influences you not to care about stuff like that'. Other comments described the school as a preferred destination for 'people in the middle' whose religious identity is already weak: 'Well, where I live, there's like nobody cares about religion and my parents wanted to see what it was like [at this school]'; 'There are some people who are Protestant or Catholic and then there are people in the middle and they would choose to come here.' The school ethos described by the young people differs from the Christian character intended in the initial establishment of the integrated sector and reflects a lack of interest in, or disenchantment with, religion.

While there is little recognition of a specifically Christian character, the young people had assimilated other explicit messages from the school about inclusion, equality, the commonalty of human beings across divisions of religion and ethnicity, and respect for different groups in society: 'At the end of the day there's just humans and . . . we go back to equality'; 'We're all people and we all breathe and all'; 'Respect is the key moral.' They claimed that 'we learn that everybody's equal, no matter what religion they're normal.' In their discussions about education and wider society they made much of the school's and their own integrated identity; they made frequent use of the word 'integrated': 'They want us now to integrate with each other'; 'It's gotten better the more people are integrated'; 'We've come to an integrated school'; 'I came because it was integrated.' They described the school's 'integration week', where all the form classes are mixed up for different activities. They gave definitions of what an integrated education means – 'It [is] integrated because it's not that kind of one-sided religion and thinking you know this is the best religion but it's accepting people for who they are' – and of what its effects might be – 'I think it's going to an integrated school that's opened their eyes'; 'It means more people learn about different people'; 'You're more aware of what's going on'; 'It makes you more open and you talk to people.' One described the school's purposes in terms of nurture, acculturation of the young into a new mindset that would ultimately have a major impact on Northern Irish society:

> I think when we start teaching integrated education in schools from a young age, we will eventually get rid of the problem of religion causing a divide because what you learn from a young age. It's a fact that children as young as three in Northern Ireland know how to be sectarian without knowing why they're doing it, which tells you that these are children who in their family life are learning to be sectarian without knowing they are – so if we tackle sectarianism at a younger age and get rid of sectarianism before it has a chance to develop.

Although it remains true that the pupil intake of many controlled and maintained schools is quite homogeneous, the idea that the integrated sector is the *only* sector where pupils are likely to encounter people of different religious backgrounds is, as we have seen, a false one. Developments in religious education in Northern Ireland mean that controlled and maintained schools now include some teaching about other religions and traditions, although the bias may be towards their own. This was the case in the other three Northern Irish schools (all from different sectors) in the Diversity project. However, as Woodside pupils set up a shared integrated identity (broad-minded, tolerant and fair) for themselves, they often did so by positioning their integrated identity against negative assessments of what is happening in other education sectors; other schools were portrayed as limited and close-minded. In particular they compared Woodside with the maintained (Catholic) schools; perhaps, for the Catholics in the groups, this was a defensive response to some disapproval for integrated education among people in their own community. The distinctions they drew between the different sectors were in curriculum and contact: '[An integrated school] is just better than going to like an all Catholic school, say, where you're just focusing on one thing and everybody's a Catholic'; 'In a Catholic school you'd only be able to do what's considered like a Catholic sport'; 'If you went to a one-faith school, you would only learn about that faith'; 'that kind of one-sided religion'. There was also a hint of superiority in the comments: 'I've got some friends in Catholic schools and . . . they don't say anything, but we're more confident here'; 'more confident to talk to like other people of different religions'.

These young people were eager to differentiate themselves in experience and attitude from their peers in other education sectors; they were also (ironically, for an 'integrated' school) adopting a position separated from the wider community of their city. The sense that Woodside was a 'school apart' has its geographical expression in its location away from the areas where people live; the young people have to be bused to the school, taken out of their neighbourhoods, in order to attend. The young people did comment on their city and described it as one where there had been marked improvements in community relations since their parents were young, but where there were still divisions. They shared some of their direct experiences of intercommunal tension in their city as well as their strategies for dealing with it:

> A lot of people only shout out at you because you give a reaction to them and they get fun out of your reaction and if you just go along whatever they say and just shrug it off your shoulder, they'll soon get bored of it.

In several comments, however, there was a feeling of being at a remove from this scene: some lived in areas where 'no one has fights . . . about religion'; 'It's just everybody's from different religions and all'; 'Nobody cares about religion.' Others lived closer (but still on the edges) to areas where tensions between religiously based identities might erupt: 'If I lived a bit closer, [religion] might be part of my life because I'm like a field away and it doesn't really play a part.' In another case a pupil reported how his choice to attend an integrated school was a conscious decision not to get involved:

> Where I live, usually it's a mainly Protestant area and it's like waving the Union Jack and all that – I don't support it, I just live on the edge of it and

I really wouldn't like to get involved in that so that's why I came here –
I don't want to have a label for what school I go to.

Like others of his peers he resisted being categorized by religious identity. In
general, whatever the young people's personal religious affiliation, the 'strong
Protestant' or 'strong Catholic' identity was something held by other people
who lived in other areas of the city; the young people were able to name these
pockets of sectarianism and which 'side' was dominant there. Added to the 'othering' of the Protestant or Catholic identity was a social class element. The
neighbourhoods they identified as having a strong sectarian identity were several
times described as being 'rough' areas of the city: 'It's a very rough area'; 'There
would be a lot of Catholic areas and a lot of Protestant areas and you know
there would be a roughness around that, depending on where they are'; 'like a
rough part of town where there's murals and flags and things like that and there's
always people standing on street corners and it can be sort of intimidating'.
From their attendance at an integrated school, it seems, the young people were
not learning to feel more positive about the Catholic and Protestant identities
in their city, but were rather feeling themselves reassuringly separate from the
threats they posed.

Conclusion

What can be concluded from this study of pupil perspectives at Woodside, and
how do these findings relate to wider discussions about Integrated Education?
It has already been suggested that questions of numerical dominance and status
affect the outcomes of contact between different groups. Within the religiously
mixed context of the research discussions (one can only conjecture what might
have been the case if the groups had not been mixed in this way), the Catholic or
Protestant identities of the participants do appear to have been subordinated to
another identity and set of views. Apart from the discussion of Bloody Sunday,
which was conducted in terms acquired from outside the school discourse, it
was not the Catholic identity of the majority that dominated; this was perhaps
because the Roman Catholic pupils had to some degree separated themselves
from the traditions of the Catholic community by coming to an integrated
school rather than to a maintained school. The identity that expressed itself
most clearly was an integrated identity; as in the analysis by Hayes, McAllister
and Dowds (2007), for these pupils, too, potential divisions had been reduced by
shared acceptance of a dominant (integrated) view. One way of aligning themselves with an integrated ethic was to distance themselves from education in
non-integrated sectors. Their negative interpretations of non-integrated education fitted the Catholic bishops' criticism of those who labelled as 'segregationists' all who did not accept their 'enlightened' vision of education.

Although Integrated Education was initially envisaged as having a Christian ethos, the young people's comments reflected a more secular viewpoint.
The common representation of religion was of something private, individual,

autonomous (characterized by the kind of enlightenment philosophy identified by Catholic bishops in new educational trends). The pupils' interpretations of religion matched those found in many English schools promoted by an RE that combines the presentation of variety within religion with an emphasis on the value of one's own opinion and choice. It could be argued that young people for whom religion is not very important might want a school environment where they can feel comfortable in their secularity, but there is at the same time the danger of a widening gap of understanding, similar to that found in other parts of the United Kingdom, between young people from localities and schools where religion is not the norm and those where it is an accepted and significant part of life (Ipgrave 2012).

An encouraging finding was that the young people expressed very positive attitudes towards other religions. This positivity was part of the integrated ethos. The language used related to an ethic of diversity, respect, broad-mindedness and equality. While they found other religions interesting and valued them because they were different, pupils tended to dismiss differences that might really have an impact on them or their community and, in the context of Catholic and Protestant relations, to see 'strong' religious identity as an obstacle. This view contrasts with some of the project's findings in other sectors of the Northern Irish school system, where pupils sought to relate from their religious commitment to the religious commitment of others and use it as a basis for engagement and understanding. For example, 'strongly' Protestant pupils who recognized that many Catholics like them loved God, or Christian pupils who found similarities with Muslims because they, too, tried to lead their lives according to the rules of their religion or were seeking to find God in their religion (Ipgrave 2012, 271). The position adopted by these pupils was more in line with the ethic of shared education, whereby young people are secure in their own identity and meeting others in theirs.

There was a discernible difference between the Woodside pupils' approaches to other, non-Christian religions and their approach to Catholic/Protestant distinctions. They viewed the former in curriculum terms – increasing respect by learning more about them – but viewed the latter in terms of contact. Several times pupils expressed the rather simplistic view that 'if we have opportunities to meet, then we will get on'; at the same time it was evident that in this context they experienced strong Catholic or Protestant identities as a threatening presence. The school was not a meeting place between strong identities but rather an escape from them. The desire for distance is problematic for an education system intended to have an impact on community relations. The title of this chapter poses the question whether the integrated school brings together two communities or creates a third. Evidence from the pupils' discussions implies that, despite the high hopes for its contribution to the unification of a divided society, what is being created is indeed not 'a shared compromise between the aspirations of two traditions' but something new. That 'something new' involves much that is positive in its readiness to respect and be open to a range of diversities, nevertheless its separateness limits the contribution it can make to building bridges between communities.

Notes

1 In order to preserve the school's anonymity, its real name is not used here.
2 See NICIE website (http://www.nicie.org/about-us/integrated-education/what-is-integrated-education/, access date: 6 May 2015).
3 For example, school link partnerships organized by the Three Faiths Forum in London and Bradford's Schools Linking Network.
4 The term 'formally integrated' is used to distinguish integrated schools from schools in other education sectors, which nevertheless have fairly mixed pupil populations.
5 The name of this school is anonymized as it is discussed in detail by name in a chapter in McGlynn, Zembylas and Bekerman (2013).
6 The programme is supported by external funding from Atlantic Philanthropies and the International Fund for Ireland.
7 The figure applies to 2006. Only 43 per cent of pupils attend 'controlled' schools, of which the state is the legal owner (Catholic Bishops of Northern Ireland 2006).
8 Attempts have been made to anonymize the details about the school, but it has not been possible to avoid all clues about the school's identity without withholding information needed to make sense of the data.

References

Allport, Gordon W. 1954. *The Nature of Prejudice.* Cambridge, MA: Addison Wesley.
Bain, George. 2006. *Schools for the Future: Funding, Strategy, Sharing.* Bangor: Department of Education.
Belfast Telegraph. 2010. 'Peter Robinson calls for an End to School Segregation.' *Belfast Telegraph,* 16 October 2010. Available at: http://www.belfasttelegraph.co.uk/news/education/peter-robinson-calls-for-end-to-school-segregation-28565048.html, access date: 24 August 2014.
BHA (British Humanist Association). 2006. *BHA Briefing 2006/4: Faith Schools.* London: BHA.
Borooah, Vani, and Colin Knox. 2013. 'The Contribution of 'Shared Education' to Catholic-Protestant Reconciliation in Northern Ireland: A Third Way?' *British Educational Research Journal* 39 (5): 925–946.
Catholic Bishops of Northern Ireland. 2006. *Independent Strategic Review of Education: A Paper Prepared for Consultation June 2006. A Response from the Catholic Bishops of Northern Ireland.* Available at: http://www.deni.gov.United Kingdom/bishops__response.pdf, access date: 28 August 2014.
Donnelly, Caitlin. 2008. 'The Integrated School in a Conflict Society: A Comparative Analysis of Two Integrated Primary Schools in Northern Ireland.' *Cambridge Journal of Education* 38 (2): 187–198.
Gallagher, Tony. 2004. *Education in Divided Societies.* Basingstoke: Palgrave.
Hayes, Bernadette C., and Ian McAllister. 2009. 'Education as a Mechanism for Conflict Resolution in Northern Ireland.' *Oxford Review of Education* 35 (4): 437–450.
Hayes, Bernadette C., Ian McAllister, and Lizanne Dowds. 2007. 'Integrated Education, Intergroup Relations, and Political Identities in Northern Ireland.' *Social Problems* 54 (4): 454–482.
———. 2013. 'Integrated Schooling and Religious Tolerance.' *Journal of Contemporary Religion* 28 (1): 67–78.
Integrated Education Fund. 2014. *Why We Need Support.* Available at: http://www.ief.org. United Kingdom/get-involved/why-we-need-your-support/, access date: 26 August 2014.
Ipgrave, Julia. 2012. 'Relationships between Local Patterns of Religious Practice and Young People's Attitudes to the Religiosity of their Peers.' *Journal of Beliefs and Values* 33 (3): 261–274.

Ipsos Mori. 2011. *Attitudinal Survey on Integrated Education.* London: Ipsos Mori.

Jackson, Robert. 2014. *Signposts: Policy and Practice for Teaching about Religions and Non-religious World Views in Intercultural Education.* Strasbourg: Council of Europe.

Jeffrey, Terence P. 2013. 'Obama: "If Catholics Have their Schools and Buildings and Protestants Have theirs . . . that Encourages Division".' CNSNews. Available at: http://cnsnews.com/news/article/obama-if-catholics-have-their-schools-and-buildings-and-protestants-have-theirs, access date: 23 August 2014.

Macaulay, Tony. 2009. *Churches and Christian Ethos in Integrated Schools.* Belfast: Macaulay Associates. Available at: http://cain.ulst.ac.United Kingdom/issues/education/docs/macaulay270109.pdf, access date: 26 August 2014.

McCreadie, Peter. 2013. 'Priory Integrated College: A Transformed College – A College Transformed.' In *Integrated Education and Conflicted Societies*, ed. Claire McGlynn, Michalinos Zembylas, and Zvi Bekerman, 107–120. New York: Palgrave Macmillan.

McGlynn, Claire, Michalinos Zembylas, and Zvi Bekerman, eds. 2013. *Integrated Education and Conflicted Societies.* New York: Palgrave Macmillan.

Montgomery, Alison, Grace Fraser, Claire McGlynn, Alan Smith, and Tony Gallagher. 2003. *Integrated Education in Northern Ireland: Participation, Profile and Performance.* Research Report. Coleraine: The Nuffield Foundation. UNESCO Centre, University of Ulster.

NICIE (Northern Ireland Council for Integrated Education). 2008. *Statement of Principles.* Belfast: NICIE.

———. 'Educating Children Together.' Available at: http://www.nicie.org, access date: 24 August 2014.

ODHIR (Office of Democratic Institutions and Human Rights). 2007. *Toledo Guiding Principles on Teaching about Religions and Beliefs in Public Schools.* Brussels: OSCE.

Perry, Caroline. 2011. *Sharing and Collaborating in Education.* Belfast: Northern Irish Assembly Research and Information Service.

Saville, Lord. 2010. *Report of the Bloody Sunday Inquiry.* Open Government Licence. Available at: https://www.gov.United Kingdom/government/publications/report-of-the-bloody-sunday-inquiry, access date: 6 May 2015.

Shirlow, Peter, Brian Graham, Amanda McMullan, Brendan Murtagh, Gillian Robinson, and Neil Southern. 2006. *Population Change and Social Inclusion Study Derry/Londonderry.* Available at: http://cain.ulst.ac.United Kingdom/issues/population/popchangederry05.pdf, access date: 6 May 2015.

Torney, Kathryn. 2013. 'Dramatic Increase in Newcomer Pupils Attending NI's schools.' *Legacy.* Community Relations Council. Available at: http://www.thedetail.tv/issues/304/newcomer-pupils/dramatic-increase-in-newcomer-pupils-attending-nis-schools, access date: 26 August 2014.

6 Cradling Catholics in secular Scotland

Research in a Scottish Roman Catholic high school

Julia Ipgrave

Context: Scotland, young people and religious memory

This chapter was written in 2014, a year when a referendum on independence from the rest of the UK meant that Scotland and the identity of the Scottish people received a good deal of attention in public, political and media discourse. In September, a proposal for full Scottish independence was defeated with 55.3 per cent voting against it and 44.7 per cent in favour of it. The day after the results, the former UK prime minister Gordon Brown made a speech in his Fife constituency on the state of Scotland. He considered reasons for the surge of nationalism reflected in the recent campaigning and debates and linked it to an identity problem in Scottish society – organizations and institutions that had given Scots a sense of identity in the past no longer had the same hold on the population. Brown mentioned the Trade Union movement and slump in its membership; he also mentioned the Church, and, in reference to the younger generation, spoke of a decline in Sunday school attendance from the 60 per cent in his youth to the 5 per cent of today.[1] The idea of a disconnect between individuals and collective tradition embedded in Brown's speech has resonances with Danièle Hervieu-Léger's theory of rupture in the chain of collective memory in religion as well as in other aspects of modern society (Hervieu-Léger 2000). When Brown suggested that the nationalist identity as manifested in the referendum campaign was an isolated rather than integrated identity, his interpretation was in keeping with the differentiation and fragmentation of memory – into family memory, religious memory, national memory, class memory and so on – that Hervieu-Léger posits as a characteristic of modernity. For her this fragmentation is preliminary to the disintegration of collective memory before the forces of globalization, democratization, mass societies and media encroachment (ibid., 127–128). If these are such influential trends in the contemporary world, they have relevance to the Young People's Attitudes to Religious Diversity project (from here on the 'Diversity project') as the context of young people's religious and attitudinal formation.

Memory and identity are closely linked and, in this respect, young people face a particular challenge. Hervieu-Léger notes the difficulties entailed in processing the mass of information and impressions with which young people are continuously bombarded: 'What is at issue is whether young people have the ability to organize this mass of information by relating it to a lineage to which they spontaneously see themselves as belonging' (Hervieu-Léger 2000, 129–130). The concept of 'belonging' is a prominent theme of sociological and psychological studies of religion in the UK as well as in Hervieu-Léger's France, whether it is Grace Davie's 'believing without belonging' (Davie 1994), Leslie Francis and Mandy Robbins's 'belonging without believing' (Francis and Robbins 2004) or Abby Day's 'believing in belonging' (Day 2009, 2011), the latter two formulae having been developed through empirical studies with young people. A second theme, building on Charles Taylor's work, is that of 'authenticity' – the importance of achieving, self-understanding and of living by what you believe (Taylor 1991, 473–474; Collins-Mayo and Dandelion 2010, 81). A third is that of 'validation' linked to the challenge of finding one's bearings amid the confusions of the present religious landscape as well as the need for the assurance to stand by one's beliefs, practices and religious (or non-religious) identities and for a sense of 'ontological security' (Collins-Mayo et al. 2010, 32). Again, Hervieu-Léger's theory has been influential, offering a model of four 'validation regimes' ranging from 'self-validation' (IV), whereby individuals determine for themselves the truth and correctness of their own beliefs and practices, drawing on a range of resources and based on subjective experience and judgement, to 'institutional validation' (I), where the institutional authorities define the rules and norms which are the hallmarks of the faith and to which individuals are invited to conform (Hervieu-Léger 2001, 165–166). The regimes in between these poles are 'communal validation' (II), applying to smaller, egalitarian groups which work out together a shared truth and set of values; and 'mutual validation' (III), whereby security of faith and identity is found in sharing one's ideas and experiences through social interaction with others and recognizing the authenticity of their beliefs as well as one's own without having to come to an agreement about what constitutes the truth. Again, these models are found to have particular pertinence to young people, as in Sylvia Collins-Mayo's study where the four regimes are applied – as a 'continuum of strength of group validation' – to the religion of 8- to 23-year-olds participating in Christian youth and community outreach projects (Collins-Mayo et al. 2010, 60–61). They will provide a starting point for the analysis of the young people's perspectives that forms the main body of this chapter.

   Collins-Mayo et al.'s study is one of a number of qualitative studies exploring the disconnection of young people from traditional religion, the nature of their religiosity or spirituality outside the parameters of organized and inherited religion and their sources of validation (Collins-Mayo et al. 2010). Such studies have noted an imperative towards autonomy for young people, an injunction to 'do your own thing' (Woodhead 2010, 239) rather than follow what has been handed down through generations and by the authority of religious institutions. The drift of younger generations away from traditional organized religion is mirrored in the decline over the years of those identifying as Christian in national census statistics and a corresponding increase in those who identify with the 'non-religion' category. The relationship may be closer than a mirror image if, as David Voas writes, society is changing religiously, not because individuals are changing but because old people are being replaced by young people with different characteristics (Voas 2010, 32). The census statistics have in fact acted as stimulus and rationale for further investigation of young people's religious and non-religious perspectives (Wallis 2014). At the same time, however, the variety of positions on religion among the young people in the Diversity project cautions against a too ready 'lumping together' of young people under a Generation Y (or, as new birth cohorts reach their teenage years, Generation Z) label, distinguished by shared experiences and therefore common characteristics (Ipgrave 2012).

Returning to Scotland, we find the same trend away from organized religion in the 2011 census,[2] with 54 per cent claiming to belong to Christianity or a Christian church (a decrease of 11 per cent since 2001) and 37 per cent (an increase of 9 per cent) stating that they have 'no religion'. In different regions of the country, however, the picture is very different, with around 75 per cent of the population reporting as Christians in the Western Isles (the location of one of the Diversity project's case study schools) and less than 50 per cent (similar to the proportion of 'no religion') as Christian in Edinburgh (the site of the school that forms the focus of this chapter).

Within the Christian category, there was also divergence in the experience of the different denominations with the national church, the Church of Scotland, suffering steeper decline (10 percentage points between 2001 and 2011)[3] than others. Roman Catholic figures remained roughly the same at 18 per cent of the population (the Church of Scotland figure for 2011 was 32 per cent). As the son of a Church of Scotland minister, it may well be the experience of this church in particular that Gordon Brown had in mind in his speech. There are a number of reasons for this disparity in the fortunes of the Church of Scotland and the Roman Catholic Church in Scotland, including the role of migration in maintaining the numbers of the Roman Catholic community – Polish, Italian and Sri Lankan Roman Catholics are among the young people whose perspectives will feature in this chapter. A Church of Scotland minister who provided contextual information for this research project provided another reason: his church (unlike the Church of England south of the border) had handed over its schools to the control of the state in the education reforms of the 1870s and, not anticipating the divergence between the Church and other social institutions of the modern era, had lost that connection with the lives of young people and their families.

The educational situation for Roman Catholics in Scotland is quite different from that of their Church of Scotland neighbours. Roman Catholic education started in the nineteenth century to serve a poor, largely Irish immigrant community often discriminated against. The poverty of the community meant that the Roman Catholic Church could not support the system it had established, and in the Education (Scotland) Act of 1918 the schools were integrated into the public system while the Church retained its management role and approval of staffing appointments. The schools were intended to provide for the spiritual needs of the pupils and also, through educational achievement, to promote social mobility and access to mainstream society. The schools have indeed proved more effective than non-denominational schools in enabling their working-class pupils to gain good qualifications so that the occupational status of the community has risen (see Paterson 2000, 227). This success could be seen as a reason for the discontinuation of the separate education system, but those who support the continuation of Roman Catholic schools in Scotland increasingly see their value in terms of not social mobility but their distinctive ethos, whether that ethos is manifested in concern for the spiritual development of their own pupils or in the contribution that the norms, values and trust promoted through Catholic education can make to fairness and democracy in wider society (ibid., 155) or in a mission to offer an example of Christian living amid the social confusion and moral ambiguities of the modern world (Bradley 2000, 168–169). These aims can be found within the *Charter for Catholic Schools in Scotland* produced on behalf of the Bishops' Conference of Scotland.[4]

The continuing existence of Roman Catholic schools in Scotland thus stands against trends towards institutional divergence (a separation of church, state, education) and the fragmentation of memory and identity (individual, family, religion, institution) that have been proposed as characteristics of modernization (Hervieu-Léger 2000, 127). This chapter presents perspectives from pupils at one of the Roman Catholic schools. Their case could be viewed as a counterpoint to the studies of teenage 'no-religion' or the 'do-it-yourself religion' mentioned earlier. But it is more than this: as well as being members of this church school, these young people are also part of a society (and consciously so) marked by secularization – an in-between position that feeds into their thinking. Another influence on their thinking is awareness of being part of a religiously plural society and of a religiously plural community within their own school where minorities from other faith traditions also attend. The *Charter for Catholic Schools in Scotland* encourages such awareness and advocates 'the promotion of respect for different beliefs and cultures and for inter-faith dialogue'. Young people's recognition of religious diversity is the central focus of the overarching Diversity project in which this small case study is located. It has interest in relation to the validation theme introduced in the introduction, as the young people gave evidence of a concern, not only to find validation of their own faith position, but also to validate the different faith positions (the beliefs, practices and values) of those they encountered directly or through their learning.

Perspectives from St Albert's RC High School

St Albert's RC High School[5] is a highly respected and academically successful Roman Catholic comprehensive school in Edinburgh. Four groups of six pupils (aged 14–15) were interviewed for the research. These were selected to include a wide range of perspectives on religion and degrees of practice; the majority were Roman Catholic and only one professed to have no religion. The sample included pupils of different ethnic backgrounds. The groups were differentiated by religiosity using the teacher's knowledge. Group A was a group of Roman Catholics with regular and irregular practice, including one girl from Sri Lanka. Group B included pupils with Roman Catholic identity, but they were non-practising or only infrequently participated in church worship – one of these pupils described himself as having no religion. Group C consisted of Muslim and Sikh pupils. Group D was chosen for being regularly practising Roman Catholics particularly interested in religion, including three pupils who served regularly in church, one with a mixed Italian-Scottish family background, one with a Polish family background (third generation) and one who had migrated from Poland five years ago. For this chapter it is the perspectives of those identifying as Roman Catholics which will be explored with the focus on validation of faith, comprising religious identity, beliefs, practices and values.

Being religious in a secular society

The presence in the groups of pupils with in-depth experience of other societies helped to contextualize the case of St Albert's by comparison. Pupils from or with relations in Poland, for example, contrasted the traditional acceptance of religion and religious practice there with the decline of the religious habit in Edinburgh:

> Like 80 per cent of society in Poland are Christian – they follow their religion so they go to church every week and kind of here not many people do that any more.
>
> (D)[6]

For this boy, brought up in Poland, church attendance was a natural part of life: 'I just go to church every Sunday.' His classmate described not just a difference of practice but a contrast between Polish warmth and Scottish reserve:

> I've got Polish family – my grandparents were from Poland and I go there for summer holidays quite often and I find that, yeah, it's a completely different atmosphere like I feel here that people don't join in really with the responses with the singing but in Poland I think – it's just everything seems to be warmer.
>
> (D)

His own first communion, he felt, did not get the community interest and endorsement that it would have had in his home country. The girl from Sri Lanka reported similar contrasts between people in Edinburgh who 'don't go to church that often' and Sri Lanka where it is 'in the culture' to pray every day and 'everyone has to go to church like Catholics and stuff' (A). The Italian-Scot described the place in Italy where his family come from, where going to church is about worship but is also about community: it is 'very important to people' because it 'brings people together'; 'I'm not sure', he admitted, 'that it is as much here as it is in Italy' (D). Although the pupils' reminiscences may be coloured by nostalgia, they clearly had something to say about the context in which they and their fellows now conduct themselves as young Catholics. Their Scottish peers picked up the same theme of the secularization of society and presented it in generational terms: one declared that people today 'find it harder to believe'; 'I'd say this generation isn't as believing as the last' (D); another viewed it as more a loss of interest rather than loss of faith: 'it's not like [people] are losing their faith in God, it's maybe as the generations pass, they just, I don't know, just losing interest' (D); a third explained that 'because it's modern times now', their generation had different interests ('computers and stuff') to distract them (D). They also mentioned negative images (the 'bad messages') and trivialized messages ('TV shows will make fun') that make people 'kind of think that religion mustn't be very good' (B).

In such a society, the believing and practising are faced with these questions: If religious faith is not important to everyone around you, why should it be to you? If religious observance is not something in which everyone around you engages, why do you? It is at this point that the question of validation comes in: in a secular context it is not just the validation of religious beliefs but of religious believing; it is not just validation of religious actions but of religious acting.

Reflecting the prominence given to concepts of 'autonomy' and 'individualization' in contemporary studies of youth religion, this chapter takes self-validation as the first of four validation regimes used to analyze the young people's contributions to discussion. It offers some examples of young people attempting a 'go it alone' religion, but also shows how for the other pupils different forms and authoritative sources of validation were needed to stabilize their meanings. At the other end of the spectrum, institutional validation has a particular significance for these young people, exercising in their lives the combined force of church and school, closely bound in identity, management and ethos, in personnel and in liturgical provision. In the absence of wider community involvement, some form of mediation is often needed to bring the individual young person into the orbit of the religious institution, whether that entails conferring identity, offering guidance or modelling practice. For these young people, the dominant mediating influence in bringing them to religion was the family – a reason for considering the family as a third validation regime, although it is not included in Hervieu-Léger's model.

Institution and family can be viewed as 'vertical validation' regimes, passing down an inheritance or memory to a new generation in a hierarchical power relationship. Hervieu-Léger's regimes included validation between equals, what could be termed 'horizontal validation' regimes.[7] Her second, 'communal', regime is the validation between equals, a community of believers who share a common interpretation of their relationship to the world and the shared way of life that common interpretation implies; she writes of orders, congregations, movements, devotional groups (Hervieu-Leger 2001, 168). Among the schools participating in the Diversity project, those (in Northern Ireland and the Hebrides) with strong Christian Unions could well be said to contain such communally validating groups, but there was little sign of such a phenomenon at St Albert's. The members of Group D, selected as being particularly religious, had been chosen for their individual religiosity rather than any group identity. For this reason, communal validation is not a category applied to the findings from St Albert's. Another regime of 'horizontal validation' is that of mutual validation where there is an ethos of equality, a fellowship and positive disposition towards understanding each other, but without uniformity of belief and practice. Among the pupils in this case study, mutual validation relates both to peer endorsement (or otherwise) of each other's religious expression and an approach to be taken with those of different faiths; it is the point at which the desire for the validation of one's own faith transfers to validation of the faith of others.

Self-validation

Any analysis of pupils' comments for signs of self-validation has to acknowledge that the discussions have to some extent falsified the findings; anything pupils said about their private religion in this setting was necessarily expressed publicly and shared with others, perhaps seeking mutual validation from other members of the group within the structure of the research event. There were nevertheless indications that some of them valued the self-referential, 'do it yourself' approach to religion identified by Linda Woodhead and others (see earlier). For example, there is evident self-belief and self-reliance in the following statement and explicit rejection of external authorities. At the same time the altruistic direction of this pupil's sense of justice confirms that a self-validating religion or worldview is not necessarily a selfish one:[8]

> Being a moral person is like justice, like standing up not just for yourself but for other people and I think that I live by just doing what you believe in, not what others want you to do and you have to like trust and have faith in yourself as well.
>
> (A)

The emphasis on living by 'what you believe in' reflects the value placed on authenticity, on being true to oneself. The globalization and pluralization of the religious landscape afford a multiplicity of religious options for those who grant themselves the liberty to pick and choose their own religion. Such freedom was exercised by the pupil who made the following comment as she brought her subjective judgement and personal preference to bear on her choice of religion from the variety on offer:

> I always try to work out which one's better or which one's the most desirable to be with because of what's in it.
>
> (D)

However, few of the young people at St Albert's gave the impression that self was the only, or even primary, foundation for their beliefs, actions and values – other sources of validation were needed. Several indicated how their sense of self was shored up by a received identity and religion, accepted on authority beyond themselves. All but one accepted for themselves an inherited religious identity and that identity was for most more than a label. Among the respondents were the following:

- The pupil for whom going to mass every Sunday was 'special to me', who felt 'lucky' to have been brought up in a religion, 'so lucky to have Catholicism . . . because it feels important to have some belief' (D);
- The pupil for whom serving at the altar was 'very much a big part of my life' (D);
- The pupil who, in his attempts to lead a good life found 'it's religion that keeps you on that track' (D);
- The pupil who related stories from the Bible to his own life with a view to 'making it better' and to 'be more helpful towards others and be more understanding' (A).

The role of the family in shaping the young people's interpretation of their world and their actions within it was a prominent theme. In particular they mentioned the knowledge of right and wrong that had been instilled in them by their parents and their religious upbringing within the family circle. The following quotation suggests an interplay between external forms of validation (family, church) and self-realization:

> Up until a year ago or something I thought I would stop because I just went for my parents basically, but now I think that I would continue to go to church . . . there was a point when I just realized that I wasn't going for my parents any more but I wanted to go.
>
> (A)

This account records the significant moment reached when what had been enforced by others becomes an authentic act of one's own that embeds self in community. Among the pupils at St Albert's, the influence of family and organized religion on values, behaviours and beliefs was generally more marked than any expressions of self-reliance in these respects.

Institutional validation

Under the heading of institutional validation there are three interconnected aspects of the young people's lives to consider: their consciousness of being Catholic, their connection with the local church and their attendance at a Roman Catholic school. From their contributions it was evident that these young Catholics generally considered their religious identity to be inherited through their family. For most it was more than just a label, being viewed as crucial to their formation as moral and believing persons. Even those less practising pupils spoke of the Ten Commandments as the guide for living and professed orthodox Catholic belief systems – 'I believe in Jesus and that he was the Messiah and how there is God and he sent his Holy Spirit' (B) – although whether they did so on the authority of the Church or of their parents who had assimilated the teachings of the Church was a point for discussion. The dependency of morals on Catholic teaching was boldly expressed by one of the more devout pupils – 'if you had a religion that says do wrong, you'd do wrong. Catholicism says to do what's right, so you do what's right' (D) – while another gave a concrete example of how that moral obligation might be cemented through a commitment made at first communion:

> When I took first communion, we kind of made a promise that we won't smoke and drink until above 18. And sometimes people try to make me like smoke or drink, but then I can think back, I've done a promise and I'm more influenced by that so I just say 'no'.
>
> (D)

It is an example where behaviour different from society's expectations is validated by Catholicism.

Sylvia Collins-Mayo wrote of young people's need for 'ontological security', as mentioned earlier; it was evident from several comments that these pupils considered Catholicism to be part of their ontological definition. As one said about coming to a Roman Catholic school, 'It's just who I am' (A). A discussion of poverty provided instances of this ontological significance, first with the idea that for Catholics one's poverty or wealth was not computed in monetary terms: 'If you're Catholic, you don't have to be poor if you have no money; if you have friends and love someone, that kind of makes you rich as well' (D). Second, a contrast was made between their understanding of what they understood to be the fixed state of being in Hinduism and the possibilities for transformation of one's state in Catholicism:

> There's nothing in Catholicism to say you can't be [changed] – like just going back to the Hinduism you could only be a poor person – you can be the best poor person, but in Catholicism it's like even if you are a poor person, you can get better and you don't always have to be poor.
>
> (D)

Pupils found that St Albert's School, through its curriculum, religious provision and ethos, reinforced this image of the Catholic self and did so without putting them under too much pressure:

> I think the school's pretty good for maintaining like the fact that it is a Catholic school and teaching you enough about religion, but not overly

religious at the same time, so it's quite relaxed and modern in the way of religious views.

(A)

They claimed that the school was teaching them to be 'good Catholics', that teachers 'try and modernize things from the Bible and say like you should try to do this' and that 'they take lessons that you learn from the religion and put it into your work and use that as a way to try and help you' (A). The training was not just in knowledge of their own faith but in engagement with issues of justice affecting the wider world:

> It's about not just Catholic religion or religion in general, it's more about – like the fairness in teachings how to be like a good Catholic.
>
> (B)

In religious observance as well as moral teaching there was an institutional convergence between church and school. St Albert's has the structures in place for regular Catholic observance: daily prayers; mass in the school hall; observance of saints' days; an oratory; the ministry of a sister from the convent up the road, including facilitated meditation sessions; and the involvement of the Dominicans who celebrate mass for the school community. These observances are not obligatory, but the provision is there if needed:

> At school it's like, because the oratory is open at break and lunch and things so it's like people can come and pray when they want and it's not like we have to pray before and after lunch, we can just pray when we feel the need to.
>
> (B)

While mass is well attended by the school community, the opportunities for the daily office and private prayer are only taken up by a few. Some recalled their experience in Roman Catholic primary schools and the greater insistence on their participation in worship there. A couple of them would have appreciated a continuation of that regime in secondary school: 'I don't go [to daily worship] because I forget about it each morning; I think it should be more that you have to go' (A). Others felt the greater freedom of St Albert's more appropriate for their stage in life: 'In primary it was much more religious and I was more comfortable with it then; I don't know if I would be comfortable if it were like that now' (B).

In relation to church, the Catholic pupils represented a wide range of practice: those who go every Sunday and pray every day, those who go occasionally on a Sunday and on special feast days, those who just go for Christmas and Easter, those who do not go at all. That lack of attendance is not related to lack of belief is evident in statements like 'I do believe in God and the Bible and I believe in all that, but I'm not really someone that goes to church' (B) and 'I haven't been to church in a while actually . . . I still believe and all that, but I just haven't been to church' (A). Neither did lack of attendance affect their Catholic identity, as one girl stated:

> I don't really go to church – I don't go regularly and I don't go on occasions either, but I am a Catholic 'cos my grandparents were Catholics and they gave it on to me, so I don't really practise it but it's there.
>
> (A)

Those who did not attend church regularly did not as a rule attribute their lack of attendance to any negativity towards the church. There was an admission from one that as he got older he found church 'a bit boring' (B), but generally pupils saw the fault as being on their side, they were 'quite busy' (A) or 'just sleep through church time' (B) or just drifted away without having a real reason why – it 'just happened' (A). The relationship of these pupils to the church could be described as 'believing and belonging but not going'. It was also noticeable that the infrequent attendees felt they should go more often or they expressed an intention of doing so as they got older: 'I might get up a bit earlier and go – make a bit of effort' (B); 'I might practise a little bit more – I'll try to go to church like every week' (B). Even the bored pupil declared his intention to 'start going again' (B). There was security in the continuing existence of this religious home (church and faith), independent as it is from the pupils' own construction, as a centre to which they can return at a later point in their lives. These attitudes to the Church have elements in common with Davie's construct of 'vicarious religion' (Davie 2006, 2007, 140–141), whereby churches have significance and meaning to a wider public than those who currently attend regularly and are 'just there' for times when individuals want to attend or get involved; as with the prayer facilities in school, they are there when people 'feel the need'. A personal and a communal need for the ministries of the Church at times of crisis were reported by the boy who turned to and re-engaged with the church on the death of his father, and by several pupils who reported how a celebration of the mass had gathered the school community together in the hall to remember and pray for a teacher who had died recently.

Family validation

It was very evident from the discussions that the influence of family on religious identity, practice and values was very strong; that influence tended in the direction of institutional religion, both brokering and validating the role of church and church school in the religious formation of their sons and daughters. The young people revealed why their parents made the selection of St Albert's as the setting for their secondary education. The academic record of the school was mentioned as one attraction, but its Catholic identity was more prominent in parents' thinking, the criteria for the parents' choice being continuity of family identity, belief and religious practice:

> Both my mum and dad's side are like strong Catholic so they wouldn't let me go into other like non-Catholic schools.
>
> (A)

> My mum thought it would be positive to be in an atmosphere with people who . . . I think both her and I like the things that they believe in, it's what I believe in as well, so she thought it was a good atmosphere and community.
>
> (A)

> Because we're Catholic and we go to church every Sunday, so I just think [my mum] wanted to sort of highlight that.
>
> (A)

As with the school, so with the church: it was above all the family that cemented the young people's sense of belonging and involvement. The patterns of attendance during childhood years at least were largely determined by family: 'All my family is Christian so I've been brought up Christian and I just go to church every Sunday' (D); this was so whether they attended every Sunday or whether they did not go every week 'because we're quite busy, we go whenever we can' (A). Where the young people's practice had dropped off from the level of their parents, the family example had established a habit that was still part of their horizon and to which several of them said they might well return as they got older; childhood experience of churchgoing had had an impact on the young people's outlook in other ways:

> To be honest, I think it's kind of like partly how you've been brought up [that affects your attitudes to religion] 'cos I was brought up going to church and that, so I have quite a strong belief, but I don't really go any more.
>
> (B)

Pupils also reported cases of the establishment of religious habits in the home encouraged by parents and grandparents; models of religious devotion set by the adults had given the young people examples to imitate and something to aspire to.

> My mum, she's a very strong Catholic . . . she goes to church every day; she's free so she goes as often as she can and every evening or every morning she encourages us, like me and I've got two brothers, to say a prayer to thank God for what he gave us and just to say like a wee prayer.
>
> (D)

> I used to say prayers – the compline – the whole little booklet. I used to say it at night on my own because when my grandfather – when I was

with him, we used to say it at night and the prayers were really nice and he'd say the Hail Mary in Latin and I really liked that so I started saying it myself.

(D)

Alongside the transmission of faith and modelling of religious practice, parents were credited with a decisive influence over the development of the young people as moral beings. In pupils' discussions of the comparative influence of peers and parents on interpretations of right and wrong, the parents clearly won out. In almost all cases parents' judgement was deemed to be wiser, although it was not always followed. It is hard to distinguish between the impact of church and parents on the values of the younger generation as their moral teaching so often coincided: 'my parents have always raised me to believe in God and to just follow his commands' (D). Parents and church reinforced each other's role – biblical injunctions had the force of parental stricture:

> Like the Bible has an influence in my life but I don't think it would influence something that I do majorly in my life, like if I was told to steal something I wouldn't do it, because my parents told me that's wrong; you shouldn't do that and I wouldn't do it.
>
> (A)

The authority of the parent is shored up by the teaching of the church:

> I know this might sound weird but like 'obey your parents' you know – I feel so bad if I do something against my mum. Sometimes you want to do it, but you have something inside saying 'don't do it', like someone told you not to.
>
> (A)

The vertical orientation of this regime, conveying religious identity, practice, belief and values from older to younger generations is evident. The expectation of several non-practising or infrequently practising pupils that they might increase their engagement as they get older may reflect an understanding of themselves as part of that vertical chain of transmission; such a view was evident in the resolve of one non-attender to return to church in order to support the religious development of a young relation:

> But like my wee cousin, she's only like one and she got baptized and stuff and when she's older I'm going to take her to church so I might start going again.
>
> (B)

There were a few indications, however, of a gentle rattling of the chain, particularly when it encountered the contrariness of the teenage years. This was found not just in the interruption in patterns of attendance but in the questioning by some who did attend. As one regular churchgoer admitted:

> My parents brought me up as Catholic, I go to church every week but I don't quite follow it in the way they've wanted me to because I'm always asking questions.
>
> (D)

Another reported how his critical comments to his parents on the content of Sunday worship – his attempts to 'catch them out' – was shaking elements of his mother's faith:

> They'll try to get me into discussing what was said [in church] and then I'll try and catch them out. My mum says she's kind of stopped believing in half the stuff since I came.
>
> (D)

In their questioning and criticisms these young people were exploring a two-way, more equal relationship than the traditional hierarchy of parent and child. This section began with a family validation akin to institutional validation, but shifts in family relations could result in a regime closer to mutual validation.

In her study of the faith of Generation Y, Collins-Mayo et al. both note the significant role of family in conferring on a young person a sense of self, and record a shift in relationships between parents and children from a traditional vertical transmission model to a friendship model where the autonomy of the individual young person within the family is prioritized (Collins-Mayo et al. 2010, 33–34). It is a trend entailing both gain and loss, the loss being the break in continuity of cultural (and religious) memory. Pupils in Group D engaged with this issue, attributing the decline of religion in society and the disinheritance of the younger generation of their religion to a rupture in the 'chain of memory' at family level. Parents were criticized for failing to 'enforce' their religion:

> I think it's important for parents to enforce the religion and bring you to mass and because maybe as a child – maybe as a small baby, parents might not bring them – they might think oh they'll cry or – I don't know – they may just not bring them but I was brought from a very early age, like always brought, always brought to mass. That's just something – parents have got to enforce the religion or the children won't know about their religion – if the parents don't tell them, how are the children to know?
>
> (D)

The significance of the parental validating role is acknowledged in the final question. Another pupil continued the theme by setting out in a kind of mathematical progression how 'marrying out' of the religion will lead to the religious memory dying out:

> People might marry into non-religious people and that would affect the children because it's like a big choice whether to keep going with the religion or not and then if half of the people don't, then those children – then it will just eventually fade out.
>
> (D)

Mutual validation

Church, school and family proved to be powerful influences on young people's self-understanding; this section moves from this vertical axis of influence to the horizontal axis of peer group. The first question is what validation the young person's religious self receives from his/her peers in the context of a secular and religiously plural society; the answer seems to be not very much. A few reported infrequent conversations about personal faith and belief with their peers. One mentioned a particular classmate who would 'ask me some question about what I think' (D) on religious questions, the nature of the discussion being a sharing of opinions rather than debate. Another spoke of a cross-faith discussion with some Muslim friends – 'When we talk, I talk about Christians and they talk about Muslims and kind of share ideas' (D) – again the intention was to hear about each other's views and experiences, as the pupil was emphatic that they were not trying to convince each other. The only criterion for mutual validation is, according to Hervieu-Léger, 'the authenticity of the individual quest that expresses itself there by all who are participating' (Hervieu-Léger 2001, 170). The comment of another pupil, using the example of a third party,[9] gives an idea of what else is entailed beyond talking and sharing ideas:

> If you meet someone and, say, they do something like you want to go to the cinema with them and they say, 'I've got to pray with my family', you might think, 'well, I'm your friend, do you not think I'm more important than doing that because you can do that any time', but there's probably a valid reason for them doing it and there *would* be a valid reason for them doing it, so that I think you'd be able to understand that reason.
>
> (A)

This pupil used the language of 'validity' in this example of religious practice in a secular environment. The validity of the person's action needs acknowledgement; understanding is called for. The example also sets up a tension between a vertical axis of family and traditional practice and a horizontal axis of peer group. Religion – the need to pray – is not being rejected for itself, but for its incompatibility with the friendship relationship and peer group sociability. The theme of incompatibility with peer group norms was repeated by several young people; in this context religion is seen as an 'uncool sort of thing' (A), to choose

Religious and Moral Education[10] as an examination subject 'is not exactly good for your street cred' (A), and a return as teenagers to the more rigorous prayer regime of the Roman Catholic primary would be 'uncomfortable':

> It's more because you wouldn't feel like part of a group sort of because maybe your friends wouldn't say the prayers, but you would, so then they'd neglect you.
>
> (B)

Elements that gave strength to the young people's religious self in another context – memory and prescribed codes of morality – became problematic within the sphere of the peer group. The verticality of tradition was rejected for modernity: 'people might think [religion's] quite archaic like some parts of it, 'cos some parts are very old-fashioned' (A); that of authority is rejected in favour of a 'do it yourself' morality: 'most people try to be bad and cool – that's what they think it's cool to go against it' (A).

According to these young people, religion is not something they discuss much with each other outside RME lessons; the peer group is rarely a source of validation of their religious identity, behaviours and beliefs. Engagement with other religions as conducted in their RME classes, however, appears to open up more fruitful opportunities for mutual validation: it gives an opportunity to talk about one's own religion in a parallel relationship with other religions rather than in a struggle between religion and secularity, tradition and modernity. The relationship with religion in this context is different:

> It's more like looking at a religion whether it's your religion or not – it's more like everyone's looking at it rather than being part of it, so you could still be involved in it but you're still learning.
>
> (A)

What the pupils reported remained at a surface level; they were not 'part of it', but nevertheless felt validated in their engagement, learning and curiosity: 'It's interesting to see how other religions feel about their gods – like in Hinduism how they have many gods and we have one' (B). It was also a context where the young people did the validating so that there was an emphasis, as they related to others, on their attitudinal rather than religious profile, on their disposition rather than faith; key words were 'tolerance', 'understanding', 'respect' and 'listening'. These concepts help the young people negotiate their way through the potentially confusing diversity with which they are faced.

> It's important for like people to know about other religions so they're like tolerant of them so they can understand what other people believe.
>
> (D)

> I think it's important that [pupils] need to take it seriously and just listen to other people – hear their views.
>
> (D)

One group was keen to contrast the open attitudes of their own generation to other religions with the negativity of their grandparents' generation, so emphasizing a break in continuity on this issue. The young people's approval was nevertheless conditional. The key criterion used to validate other traditions was the acknowledgement of a non-specific 'something'. This was frequently used to endorse different religions:

> There's always something, whether it's God or whether it's the Holy Spirit or whether it's like Shiva or something like that – it's something to pray to – I think it's about hope, because you've got something to hope for.
>
> (D)

> I think that in every religion there's always something – like if you die, there's always an afterlife like even if you've done something you'll go somewhere – there's always an afterlife.
>
> (D)

While the object of other people's beliefs was left open, the pupils' respect for difference had its limits when it encountered non-belief. The bolder of them were prepared to argue with non-believers and to try to 'convince them that there is something' (D), to 'convert them so that they believe in something because it always helps in life' (D) or to 'always try to convince people like that – try to believe something, not necessarily Catholic or Christian but just something' (D). It was in their discussion of encounter with those who do not believe that the young people showed how crucial belief was to their own self-fulfilment:

> I would think not believing in God or not believing in anything, I think it would be sad, I think inside I would be unhappy in some way because if you didn't believe in anything . . . – you're a kind of poor person inside.
>
> (D)

> And I think it's very important to believe in something 'cos it kind of gives you more strength in your life.
>
> (D)

As the data reported in previous sections show, the 'something' that these young people themselves believe in and whom they view as strength and richness is the God known and taught through the Catholic tradition.

Conclusion

This chapter began with problems of identity, with fragmentation of memory, with disconnect of the individual from collective tradition, and, in this context of instability, with the need of young people for ontological security. The special position of Roman Catholic schools within the Scottish education system has given access to a group of young people who manifest a pattern of self-understanding and religiosity different from many subjects of Generation Y research studies, as individuals nurtured within a traditional religious framework, yet living in what (census figures suggest) is a largely secularized community. Their words throw light on both environments and the relationship between them. The young people in this group realize their ontological security through a convergence of vertical influences (in home, school and church) which define and validate their religious self. These influences are bound up with 'tradition', 'authority', 'lineage', 'heritage' and 'collective memory'. The threatened or broken condition of all of these has been the food of much discussion between sociologists of religion, and yet they retain a significance in the lives of the young people. They recognized the persistence of a religious tradition that is not only present for them now, but has a past significance in their personal biography and family history and a future significance, providing both a constant possibility of return for those whose current commitment is weak and an eschatological promise of 'something to hope for'. Even where religious practices had dropped off from the rigour of their earlier years (in family or Roman Catholic primary), it appeared in almost all cases that identity and beliefs remained strong. These young people cannot be taken to represent Scotland's young Roman Catholics as a whole (there will be instances where negative experiences in family, school and home have acted to undermine security and trust), but they consistently portrayed their relations with church, school and family as a positive foundation on which to build their sense of authentic self.

This stable yet dynamic religious foundation contrasts with the less stable and age-limited mutual validation regime of peer group. In terms of the young people's religious growth this was a relatively infertile environment, unfavourable to religion; here some of them would avoid certain activities or topics of conversation in order not to be excluded or 'neglected' by the group or not to lose their 'street cred'. Examples of avoidance of some activities and participation in others they knew to be wrong in order to 'fit in' reveal the challenges of being authentic in the face of such social pressures. For other pupils it was not a case of suppressing their religious selves; rather they felt no interest or desire to introduce this aspect of their lives into the secular teenage world. This stage in life – keeping up with your peers, sleeping in late on a Sunday morning, doing things you later feel embarrassed about, trying to score points off your parents, losing your temper with your sister – was known to be transitory, which need not affect Catholic identity, religious belief or future patterns of involvement.

Outside the sphere of family and church, the young people were living in a society that was not only secular but also religiously plural; a plurality experienced at school through contact with peers of other religions and through education about different faiths in RME. From this encounter (according to the young people's self-presentation) another identity was developing that was tolerant, respectful, interested in others, one that helps them organize the varied mass of information they receive about religion. The atmosphere of equality, recognition and reciprocal learning in which these encounters were managed set up the conditions for mutual validation. Where the pupils expressed serious-ness about their engagement with religious difference, there was evident interest in the authenticity of the other. There was a circularity in the young people's move between their own identities and views and the identities and views of those they encountered, however: the emphasis on having a belief in 'something' indicates that their validation of the other depends on that other possessing the level of ontological security that they themselves have acquired through the combined collective memories of family, school and church.

Notes

1 Gordon Brown gave his speech at Dalgety Bay Primary School, 20 September 2014 (viewed live on BBC TV).
2 While the drop-off of religious affiliation was greater in Scotland than elsewhere, it should be noted that the 2010 census in Scotland asked a different question ('What religion, religious denomination or body do you belong to?') from that used in England and Wales ('What is your religion?') or from the two questions asked in Northern Ire-land ('What religion, religious denomination or body do you belong to?' 'What religion, religious denomination or body were you brought up in?').
3 The decrease in Church of Scotland membership and communicants is sharper still (see http://www.scotsman.com/news/politics/top-stories/church-of-scotland-struggling-to-stay-alive-1-3391152, access date: 6 May 2015).
4 See http://www.sces.uk.com/catholic-schools-charter.html, access date: 6 May 2015.
5 The name of the school has been changed to preserve anonymity.
6 Letters after quotations indicate the discussion group to which the pupils belonged.
7 The vertical and horizontal distinction applied to this context is not made by Hervieu-Léger. It echoes Amin Maalouf's distinction between vertical and horizontal heritage (Maalouf 2000).
8 It accords with Ulrich Beck's 'altruistic individualism' (Beck and Beck-Gernsheim 2002, 162).
9 The pupil possibly had the prayer regime of a Muslim young person in mind.
10 In Scotland, religious education is known as religious and moral education (RME).

References

Beck, Ulrich, and Elisabeth Beck-Gernsheim. 2002. *Individualization*. London: Sage.
Bradley, Joseph M. 2000. 'Catholic Distinctiveness: A Need to Be Different?' In *Scotland's Shame? Bigotry and Sectarianism in Modern Scotland*, ed. Tom M. Devine, 159–174. Edin-burgh: Mainstream.
Collins-Mayo, Sylvia, Bob Mayo, Sally Nash with Christopher Cocksworth. 2010. *The Faith of Generation Y*. London: Church House.
Collins-Mayo, Sylvia, and Pink Dandelion. eds. 2010. *Religion and Youth*. Farnham: Ashgate.
Davie, Grace. 1994. *Religion in Britain since 1945*. Oxford: Blackwell.
———. 2006. 'Vicarious Religion: A Methodological Challenge.' In *Everyday Religion: Observ-ing Modern Religious Lives*, ed. Nancy Ammerman, 21–36. New York: Oxford University Press.
———. 2007. *Sociology of Religion*. London: Sage.
Day, Abby. 2009. 'Believing in Belonging: An Ethnography of Young People's Constructions of Belief.' *Culture and Religion* 10 (3): 263–278.

————. 2011. *Belief and Social Identity in the Modern World: Believing in Belonging.* Oxford: Oxford University Press.

Francis, Leslie F., and Mandy Robbins. 2004. 'Belonging without Believing: A Study in the Social Significance of Anglican Identity and Implicit Religion among 13–15 Year-old Males.' *Implicit Religion* 7 (1): 37–54.

Hervieu-Léger, Danièle. 2000. *Religion as a Chain of Memory.* Trans. Simon Lee. Cambridge: Polity Press.

————. 2001. 'Individualism, the Validation of Faith, and the Social Nature of Religion in Modernity.' In *The Blackwell Companion to the Sociology of Religion*, ed. Richard K. Fenn, 161–175. Oxford: Blackwell.

Ipgrave, Julia. 2012. 'Relationships between Local Patterns of Religious Practice and Young People's Attitudes to the Religiosity of their Peers.' *Journal of Beliefs and Values* 33 (3): 261–274.

Maalouf, Amin. 2000. *On Identity.* London: Harvill Press.

Paterson, Lindsay. 2000. 'Salvation through Education? The Changing Social Status of Scottish Catholics.' In *Scotland's Shame? Bigotry and Sectarianism in Modern Scotland*, ed. Tom M. Devine, 145–158. Edinburgh: Mainstream.

Taylor, Charles. 1991. *The Ethics of Authenticity.* Cambridge, MA: Harvard University Press.

Voas, David. 2010. 'Explaining Change over Time in Religious Involvement.' In *Religion and Youth*, ed. Sylvia Collins-Mayo and Pink Dandelion, 25–32. Farnham: Ashgate.

Wallis, Simeon. 2014. 'Ticking the "No Religion" Box: A Case Study amongst "Young Nones".' *Diskus* 16 (2): 70–87.

Woodhead, Linda. 2010. 'Epilogue.' In *Religion and Youth*, ed. Sylvia Collins-Mayo and Pink Dandelion, 239–241. Farnham: Ashgate.

7 The matter of context
The case of two community schools in Wales

Elisabeth Arweck

Introduction

This chapter reports data collected during visits to community schools in two locations: one the suburb of a large city in the south of Wales, the other a large village in rural mid-Wales. While the school in the former was fairly large and multicultural, the school in the latter was fairly small and monocultural. These differences allow for comparison and contrast between the schools regarding pupils' attitudes to religious diversity. This chapter explores how the geographical and social context in which young people are growing up shapes their attitudes to religious diversity and their perceptions of their own and other people's religious or non-religious positions.

This chapter comprises three sections. The first draws the profiles of the two schools (including the socio-economic contexts of the schools, their catchment areas and ethos) based on information extracted from documents, such as Ofsted reports, documents relating to the school (e.g. prospectus, policies), and information available on the schools' websites. These details are supplemented by fieldnotes where possible.[1] The second section describes the young people who took part in the focus group discussions in order to contextualize the data collected in the schools for the diversity project. The third section reports data from the group discussions, examining pupils' responses to the question of difference in relation to religion, their perceptions of their own and peers' (non)religious stances, the relevance they attributed to their social and geographical contexts, and their views of and attitudes towards religious diversity or its lack in their respective schools. The conclusion draws some of the main points together at the end.

Profiles of the schools[2]

School A

At the time of the school visit, School A[3] was a co-educational comprehensive school, located on the south-western outskirts of a large city in Wales. School A is situated in a suburb and draws the majority of its pupils from the surrounding area (which includes housing estates). The school opened in the late 1950s. The age range of pupils is 11–18. In 2008, the number of pupils on roll was 1,200 (school website, access date: 8 May 2015), with 189 in the sixth form (inspection report 2008). These numbers have risen slightly since 2008: 1,280 and 200, respectively (school website, access date: 8 May 2015). The school's catchment area included a number of socially disadvantaged areas, with 34 per cent of pupils entitled to free school meals, a figure well above the regional and national average (school website, access date: 8 May 2015). By 2014, this figure had risen to 36 per cent, still well above the average for Wales (17.7 per cent). Also, just over 50 per cent of the pupils came from the fifth most deprived areas in Wales (inspection report 2014). The school's intake represented the full range of abilities, but was significantly skewed towards the less able (ibid.). The number of pupils with special educational needs (SEN) and of those with statements amounted to around 23 per cent (229 and 42, respectively) (inspection report 2008), rising in 2014 to 29 per cent (pupils on SEN register) and 4 per cent (pupils with a statement, again to above average levels). For Wales as a whole, the percentage of pupils with a statement is 2.5 per cent (inspection report 2014).

The school was a large multicultural establishment, with many pupils of minority ethnic heritage, speaking around 34 home languages between them. Just over 11 per cent (136) received support in English as an additional language (inspection report 2008). The school's website also speaks of a multi-ethnic and multicultural school (access date: 8 May 2015). The inspection report of 2014 stated that around a third (30 per cent) of pupils had a minority ethnic or mixed-race background, a quarter did not use English as their main language at home and very few spoke Welsh as their first language.[4] The school received funding to provide this support in lessons and to work with subject departments in the development of suitable teaching materials and methods (prospectus).[5] Neither the inspection reports nor the school prospectus provided any precise figures for the composition of the pupil body. The perceptions of the pupils in the focus groups (see later) varied in this regard: the non-religious Y10 group indicated the presence of three major segments: sizeable groups of Muslims and non-religious pupils, both roughly the same size, and a smaller group of Christians. By contrast, the pupils in the religious Y10 group said that 'quite a few religions' and 'many different ethnic groups' were present, although the main religions present were Christianity and Islam. They also stated that not many in their year group 'really strongly believe in religion'. The non-religious Y9 group also referred to a wide range of backgrounds, listing Muslims, Christians, Hindus, atheists, Buddhists, Sikhs and 'probably' Jains, echoed by a pupil in the 'non-religious' Y11 group, who commented that 'it's a multicultural school, there's a lot of different religions in there.'

The inspection in early 2008 found the school requiring significant improvement; the follow-up inspection in early 2009 recorded that the school had made good progress. This meant that it could be removed from the list of schools requiring significant improvement (re-inspection report 2009). One of the recommendations (of the 2008 inspection) related to the statutory requirement for a daily act of collective worship. By the time of the re-inspection, resources and activities had been put in place to support the act of worship in tutor groups. This encouraged pupils to consider, discuss and reflect on a range of relevant topics, which were linked to the school's weekly theme and 'thought for the day' (re-inspection report 2009).[6] The subsequent inspection in early 2014 reported that the school's performance and prospects for improvement were 'good', meaning that, by Ofsted's criteria, the school had 'many strengths and no important areas requiring significant improvement'. 'Good performance' related to a number of aspects, including pupils' achievements, progress (regarding knowledge, understanding and skills), literacy and numeracy skills, behaviour and social skills, the quality of teaching, and levels of care and guidance. (inspection report 2014)

Religious education (RE) was part of the curriculum for Years 7–9 (Key Stage 3) and Years 10 and 11 (Key Stage 4), as was Welsh for all year groups (prospectus). However, none of the pupils spoke Welsh as a first language and none of the subjects was taught through the medium of the Welsh language (inspection report 2008).[7] Pupils in Key Stage 3 (Years 7–9) studied RE in order to develop their knowledge and understanding of the major world religions, with Year 7 focusing on Hinduism, Sikhism, Islam and Christianity, Year 8 looking at general aspects, such as belonging, worship, prayer and festivals, and Year 9 dealing with the notions of prejudice, suffering and inspirational people. In Key Stage 4, pupils could study RE at GCSE level, either as a short or a full course, and at AS and A2 level, with modules on religion and ethics and Buddhism (school website, access date: 8 May 2015).

The school's aims were based on creating success, realizing potential and generating lifelong learning (inspection report 2008). The school's motto was 'Learning and Respect' (prospectus), which one Y10 pupil cited, and its 'Behaviour and Discipline Policy' aimed to ensure, for example, that pupils were 'aware of the importance of honesty and respect' and 'aware of the importance of understanding and respecting the beliefs and opinions of others, including those whose religion and culture may be different from their own' (prospectus). The ethos of respect was reflected in inspectors' statements that pupils showed respect for diversity and that pupils from other cultures were well integrated (inspection report 2008). The school thus recognized the diversity of pupils and provided an extensive and flexible curriculum for them. Whether they had been brought up in the local community or had arrived more recently, the pupils from ethnic minority groups had integrated seamlessly, making this an outstanding strength of the school. (ibid.)[8] RE contributed to the school's ethos in making it clear that it was about understanding different beliefs, cultures and perspectives on the world and God and in enabling pupils to develop as individuals and citizens in a diverse, multicultural society. Further, RE sought to encourage pupils to develop respect, tolerance and sensitivity to others, especially to those whose faith and beliefs are different from their own. (school website, access date: 8 May 2015) The school thus developed pupils' moral attitudes through an emphasis on fostering respect and consideration for others. Pupils learnt about issues to do with prejudice, honesty, choice and responsibility, and showed concern for others by initiating and enthusiastically supporting events that raised substantial sums for local and national charities (inspection report 2008).

School B

At the time of the school visit, School B was a co-educational comprehensive school, located in a village in rural mid-Wales. The village lies in a former slate quarrying area. The village is quite large (about 1,700 inhabitants) and the majority (88 per cent) of its population are Welsh speaking. The village and the surrounding area are the school's catchment area. (inspection report 2009)[9] The school is thus a bilingual community secondary school, described as 'a naturally Welsh school, embedded in the community it serves'. The annual intake was between 70 and 100 pupils. (ibid.) The age range of pupils in the school is 11–18. The number on roll was 507 in late 2009, including 65 pupils in the sixth form (inspection report 2009).

There were privileged and disadvantaged groups among the pupils. According to the Welsh Index for Multiple Deprivation of 2008, the five wards in the school's catchment area are among the half most deprived wards in Wales. Ten per cent of the pupils were entitled to free school meals, which was similar to the county average, but lower than the national percentage of 16.2 per cent and lower than the figure recorded in the previous inspection in 2004. (inspection report 2009) The 'Handbook for Parents' put the percentage of pupils living in an area classed among the 20 per cent most deprived parts of Wales in 2013 as 0.4. According to the Governors' Annual Report 2013–2014, the percentage of pupils entitled to free school meals increased to 13.4 per cent.

The pupil body consisted almost entirely of pupils from a white background (see also inspection report 2009); 87 per cent spoke Welsh and 13 per cent English as their first language (ibid.). The Y8 pupils said that they were taught in a mix of Welsh and English and that it varied from lesson to lesson, but the mix was unrelated to the subject. The Welsh speakers found switching between Welsh and English sometimes difficult because they could not think of the English words. This was also evident in the delivery of the RE teacher and a trainee teacher whose lesson I observed. One pupil struggled with Welsh, despite being Welsh, as English was the language spoken at home. The English-speaking pupils in the Y8 group struggled with Welsh. Displays in the RE classroom were in Welsh or in English.[10]

The school accepted pupils from the full range of abilities. There were 82 pupils with SEN and 19 (approx. 4 per cent) had a statement (the national average was 3.2 per cent) (inspection report 2009). According to the 'Handbook', the percentage of pupils subject to school action plus or with a statement of SEN in 2013 was 11.6.

According to the inspection report of 2009, the standards of teaching at the school were good and the curriculum met the needs of the pupils very well. However, progress in the pupils' standards of achievement had not yet been reflected in the GCSE results (ibid.). However, the Governors' Annual Report 2013–2014 suggested an upward trend in this regard.

According to the inspection report of 2009, the curriculum was enriched through a wide range of extracurricular activities, which contributed well to pupils' personal and cultural development. Further, the school provided extensive opportunities for promoting pupils' moral, social and cultural development. Respect towards others was evident in the life of the school. However, the provision for pupils' spiritual development was not as effective. The 2009 inspection report did not include details about RE, although it commented on other subject areas. The school's 'Handbook for Parents' (available on its current website, access date: 27 July 2015) includes a brief note about the provision of RE, stating that the equivalent of one lesson of RE (a statutory obligation) is part of Humanities in Years 7–9 and through a modular method in Key Stages 4 and 5 within the personal and social education programme. The 'Handbook' also states that a key stage service and four class services are held every week and that relevant resources, Christian in nature, are available at the school.

The Governors' Annual Report for 2013–2014 includes the school's mission statement, which aims to provide the best possible education for pupils and to help them develop and practise all their talents and become responsible members of a bilingual and European society. The school's Welsh motto stresses the importance of nurturing character and personality and one of the curricular aims is about pupils learning about achievements in various spheres, including the humanities and religion. The pastoral aims include the nurture of a civilized society in the context of self-respect as well as respect, tolerance and concern for others. The 'Handbook' includes the school's general code of conduct which highlights the values of respect (e.g. for fellow pupils, people and the school), honesty and responsibility.

The focus groups in the schools

School A

There were six focus groups in School A: two groups each of Y9, Y10 and Y11 pupils. The pupils were divided into religious and non-religious groups, with a religious and non-religious set in each year. The focus groups consisted of five to six pupils each, with an even split between the genders in the Y9 and Y10 groups and a mainly female presence in the Y11 groups.[11] The pupils in the non-religious Y11 group were not all from the same class. It was noticeable that the discussion in this group was dominated by one or two voices, with the others not very forthcoming, despite repeated encouragement.[12] The religious Y11 group consisted of three Christians (Protestant, Catholic, Irish Protestant; two female, one male), two Muslims (female), and a pupil from a Pakistani and Indian background. In this group everybody contributed (sometimes after some encouragement), although the male pupil dominated at times. In the Y10 groups, there were two pupils who had a mixed-faith background. One (male) described himself as 'half-caste', indicating that he had been brought up in the Muslim faith, but decided that this was not for him when he was put into care at the age of 12. The other pupil (female) had a Christian mother and a Hindu father.

The focus groups had been put together by the RE teacher who had taken careful note of our criteria and had asked for volunteers. The time allocated to each focus group was an hour.

School B

In School B, there were three focus groups, involving pupils from Y8, Y11 and Y13. The groups were a mixture of religious and non-religious pupils. Most of them spoke Welsh as their first language, which reflects the catchment area of the school. The groups varied in size. The Y8 group was neatly divided into three male and three female pupils. All of them said they did not have a religion, with one (female) stating that she was a former Jehovah's Witness. The Y11 group comprised about 10 pupils who were a mixture in terms of having a religion, not having a religion or not being sure whether they had a religion.[13] By contrast, the Y13 group included two male and two female pupils, who all said they did not have a religion, which they indicated was the case for most pupils in the school. For this group, not having a religion was accidental rather than choice: had they been born into a religious family, they would be religious.

In this school, too, the RE teacher had organized the focus groups, but there was no indication of the criteria according to which pupils and year groups had been selected. The time allocated to each group was 45 minutes.

How context influences pupils' attitudes and perspectives

As indicated, this chapter seeks to how the geographical and social contexts in which the young people in the two schools were growing up influenced their attitudes and outlooks. The following elicits from the data the extent to which the particular school and community context shaped young people's perceptions of their own and other people's religion or lack of religion.

School A

School's A embeddedness in the fairly diverse community of a large city was reflected in the composition of the school's pupil body and the pupils' general perception that different religious and ethnic groups as well as non-religious stances were represented. Given the school's ethos, which was, as described earlier, inclusive and stressed the importance of pupils' respect for and understanding of the religious beliefs and cultures of others, the pupils in this school had experience of diversity (in the wider sense) and had opportunities to develop skills to deal with it, such as practising respect and consideration for others. Hence the school's outstanding strength, according to the inspection report of 2008, that pupils showed respect for diversity, that pupils from other cultures were well integrated and that pupils learnt about prejudice and responsibility.

Difference and contexts

Although there was great variety in the way the pupils in the focus groups understood and approached their religious beliefs and practice or the lack of any such beliefs or practice and in the way they perceived religion (whether in positive, negative or neutral terms), they generally welcomed the encounter with people from different cultures and with different religious perspectives – it would be boring, one pupil said, if everyone were the same – and open to others. For example, some pupils in the non-religious Y10 group said they were open towards people who had a faith.[14]

> I think it's always good to meet new people and explore different cultures, like if yours just was nothing, then it would be like boring.
>
> (Y10/1, male)[15]

> It's good to meet new people of other religions and then you're experiencing their religions.
>
> (Y10/1, female)

> It's interesting. There's quite a few religions. – It's great learning it in lesson, but when you've got it going on around you, you learn it better from that.
>
> (Y10/2, male)

Some of those who said they were religious felt themselves part of a family which had a distinct religious (and also ethnic) identity (e.g. Irish Protestant, Pakistani Muslim, Indian Christian) and part of a particular religious community which had distinct beliefs and practices. Although the pupils could point to differences between religious and non-religious peers (e.g. regarding restrictions and rules of religious teachings and discipline), they generally upheld the notion of individual freedom (the right to choose to be religious or not) and (non-religious) Y11 pupils pointed out that religion did not enter in the way pupils at the school thought about each other. They suggested that religion was not that prominent in school – religious pupils practised at home rather than expressing their religion in school. This made 'everyone the same'. Therefore, although there were differences, these did come out that much in school.

> Do you mean: how different is it between people? Quite a bit, but because it's a multi-cultural school, there's a lot of different religions in here, but I don't think anyone thinks differently that much of other people because of their religion – if that makes sense.
>
> (Y11/1, female)

> This school is really multi-cultural, so we can mix with them, Christian people, Indian people, and it's not a big problem, but . . .
>
> (Y11/2, female)

Everyone's the same in school really.

(Y11/1, female)

There's no like any segregated groups type of things [in this school], like you get in prison, all the white people and all the blacks and all the Chinese, it's not like that. Most people are quite inter-mixed.

(Y11/2, male)

On the one hand, religion (religious practice) was more of a private (and domestic) matter rather than something that people advertised publicly. On the other hand, some people (mainly 'those that really strongly believe in religion', as one Y11 pupil stated) wanted to express their religion and wanted others to join in, yet the current level of prejudice made it advisable sometimes not show one's religion openly.

I don't think people are that *fond* on *expressing* their religion to them. There are some people who [. . .] go into the middle of town and they have the Bible in one hand and a loudspeaker outside and try and get people to join them, but I think the majority of people just keep it to themselves. Like maybe in the house there might be a cross or something or a picture of Jesus or Allah or something like that.

(Y11/2, male)

The somewhat discreet presence of religion may also be related to the (non-religious) Y10 pupils stating that religion was not a topic they thought much about, even if they readily discussed it in the focus group. However, the situation was different outside school. Although the non-religious Y11 group found it difficult to articulate this, their comments suggested that, while the multi-cultural context of the school was not a place which underlined difference as pupils mixed with one another, other areas were different. This seemed partly to depend on the concentration of ethnic/religious groups in particular parts of the town.

It depends what estate you are . . . It's not just the way it is. In [name of a part of the town] there are a lot of Muslims and there are quite a lot of people there, but where I live up in [name of another part of the town] there aren't as many. There are a few people there, but it's mainly like Christians up there or like agnostic people.

(Y11/2, male)

The context beyond the city was also important in highlighting differences between religions, locations like Northern Ireland, with its particular dynamic between Protestants and Catholics, or the Middle East, where political tensions between Palestine and Israel also meant tensions between Jews and Muslims – a point which relates back to the link between religion and ethnicity.

When I used to live in Belfast there was always a *big* thing between the Protestants and the Catholics.

(Y11/2, male)

Actually, sometimes it does make a difference because Christian people don't want to mix with Muslims and so on and it can be sometimes quite difficult. (Y11/2, female) – Like [the] Palestine-and-Israel-type thing because the Jews and the Muslims, they don't really like to be mixed with each other, really.

(Y11/2, male)

Returning to the context of the school, here, different sub-contexts can be identified in which encounters took place and took particular forms. One such sub-context was RE where, for example, the mix of religious and non-religious pupils could lead to lively debates and sometimes clashes. Y10 pupils (religious) indicated that such debates could lead to disagreements, some fierce, between pupils representing different stances. In this context, religious pupils who felt themselves to be a minority were afraid to declare their religion or join the debates, while those who felt confident about their religion had their say. For two pupils in this Y10 group, speaking out was motivated by the need to stand up for what they believed; for two others, speaking out was less about their own position than about the negative attitude towards them personally as religious individuals. For them, the issue was mutual respect: they wished to convey the message, 'I respect you and your opinions. Please respect me and my opinions.' (I shall return to the value of respect later in the text.)

It does create *a lot of* debates like when we're in class and stuff, because a majority of children in our year I would say are *not* religious.

(Y10/2, female)

I think both sides of the argument can be quite narrow-minded concerning aspects of other religions or with someone being an atheist or whatever. . . . it's not nice to be . . . not to be labelled one religion, but to be labelled 'she *has* to do this because she's *this* religion'.

(Y10/2, female)

Yeah, even people who are [religious], I'd say, that they don't feel confident to say anything about it because there's such a majority who *aren't*, but the minority who *are* can get quite heated in class with debates about differences in ideas and stuff like that.

(Y10/2, female)

With *me* it's actually people who are maybe more negative towards me *because* of my religion and not because of what I say, but how I *act* and how I act towards religion and towards other people. For me it's not as if I have to say 'Christianity is the big thing and everyone else is wrong'. For me it's 'I can believe this, but you can believe another thing, but don't disrespect. Don't disrespect the way I think and how I feel about how I am.'

(Y10/2, female)

While pupils in this school were generally happy to discuss religious matters in lessons, as this was part of the curriculum (the structured activities in the school), some felt less comfortable to do so in other sub-contexts within the school, such as the playground. In such situations, a range of factors came into play: pupils' sense of competence and privacy, the particular expectations and assumptions about them, risk of embarrassment, whether religion came up in conversations at all, others' interest in their religion, others' sensitivity regarding religious matters.

No [I wouldn't feel comfortable], because I don't believe in it and if you start something you don't want to discuss, you wouldn't know what to say.

(Y10/1, male)

You might even be embarrassed to talk about it sometimes, if they were the sort of people who just laughed at it or something or maybe ignored it completely.

(Y9/2, male)

I've got many friends that have been very embarrassed about talking about it in front of other people, but I'm quite an open person so I don't mind talking about it in front of anybody.

(Y9/2, female)

But some people would want to know what you believe. (Y9/2, female) – Because they'd gain more knowledge of different religions, so then they'd have a more open mind to talk to different religious people and they know more about them before they've even met them.

(Y9/2, male)

Thus, overall, how much young people displayed and discussed about their own (non)religious stances depended on the 'kind of community you are in', as a Y11 pupil commented, which again points to context in terms of place and people. The kind of community young people are in prompts them which aspects of themselves to foreground or which parts of their identities to show; they know what is to be 'front behaviour' in a given setting (Goffman 1959) or they display 'multiple cultural competence' (Jackson and Nesbitt 1993), 'integrated plural identities' (Østberg 2000) or 'intercultural competence' (e.g. Deardorff 2009).

Such competence is also related to the value of respect, which was part of the school's ethos, enshrined in its motto, 'Learning and Respect'. 'Respect' was one of the most cited values – 'Obviously, respect other people's religion and what they believe' (Y9/2, male) – which some religious pupils derived from the teachings of their religion. As the quote suggests, respect was both individual and collective: respecting the former automatically implies respecting the latter. This was important to realize, the non-religious Y9 group pointed out, because showing lack of respect towards individuals prompted solidarity from the collective:

> Some people, like with the Muslims and all the other groups, they kind of like stay together, whereas in our year they're all separate, so if you annoy one they all start going over you. Because if you don't respect one religion like the whole religion . . . if you don't respect one person with one religion, it's kind of like seen as like you don't respect the whole religion.
>
> (Y9/1, male)

The school could be an influence in instilling values such as respect: 'What you've been taught as a younger child from your parents and from teachers' (Y9/2, male). Respect also meant recognizing peers' reluctance to discuss any matters relating to religion and thus not forcing the issue. Further, respect implied equality, in the sense of considering all religions to be of equal value, as they shared common traits, and treating everyone (whether religious or not) the same. Some pupils went as far as saying that the various religions were different ways of thinking about or approaching 'the same thing'. However, as pointed out earlier, respect had to be mutual, entailing respect for others and being respected by others.

Attitudes to diversity and context

As indicated earlier, pupils were generally positive about the presence of different backgrounds in the school, also because it presented opportunities to learn about these. However, they were also aware of negative aspects, such as arguments and racist behaviour between pupils with different (non)religious stances, which underlined differences. However, the positive outweighed the negative.

> Some people have [a] discussion and pull other people in, to like back them up and then other people and it carries on, so it creates like one big argument.
>
> (Y9/1, female)

> Because some people come out with the wrong words, like racial comments, and that creates fights, but otherwise we get friends from different religions, so we get to learn more about each other.
>
> (Y9/1, male)

> Sometimes, there's disagreements, but most of the time we get along – well, we always get along really.
>
> (Y9/1, male)

When asked whether they wanted to see a wider range of backgrounds in the school than there was already, the views in the focus groups were mixed, reflecting the groups' perceptions of the composition of the pupil body.

The following section follows pupils' views through the respective year groups, rather than differentiating the views of religious and non-religious pupils, in order to create some symmetry with the data from School B, where the focus groups were mixed in terms of religious and non-religious pupils.

The non-religious Y9 group thought the school probably had as much of a range as it could have – in terms of both ethnic and religious backgrounds. It was not a question of not being able to cope with a greater mix – an increase 'wouldn't make a difference because we've got that much [already]' (Y9/1, male). Although people from different backgrounds (religious or not) initially found it difficult to get on with another, once trust had built, things became easier (as already indicated) – again, the reference to learning and developing skills in dealing with diversity.

This group made an interesting observation about the way young people mixed in the school, relating this both to age and to the areas where young people grow up: older year groups segregated into 'black' and 'white', but their own year group mixed. The older pupils tended to stick with those they had grown up with or with those who lived in the same part of town as they did – in that sense, their neighbourhood was replicated in the school – or they were too shy to mix. This pupil group referred back to individuals' freedom to choose, in this case, the freedom to choose with whom to associate; their own choice was to mix, because 'colour doesn't make a difference' (Y9/1, male). This group did not distinguish between skin colour and religion – neither seemed to matter, but it had been a learning process for them; they had been scared to begin with, but making *one* friend from a different religious/ethnic background built trust and respect for the other's religion and religious practice. Again, this points to dealing with diversity as an acquired skill.

> It's because we live in different parts of [name of town] and they each know each other more so they just don't bother.
>
> (Y9/1, female)

> We'd normally like be scared because this is like your first year, you don't want to mix in with anyone bad and then because you don't really know about much and then when you get *one* friend, you get attached, then you start bonding and then . . . – Yes, if you like them, then we just let them do what they've got to do with their religion.
>
> (Y9/1, male)

The religious Y9 group seemed non-committal about whether they wanted more of a mix in their school or less or leave it at the level it was. Religion was a neutral factor in their friendships. They, too, affirmed individuals' freedom to choose, in their case, whether to wear religious symbols (at school or at work).

The headscarf ban in countries like France prompted one pupil to comment that it did not make sense to speak of 'Christian' countries with only Christian inhabitants. This group saw value in different kinds of people being together (e.g. in a neighbourhood or a school like theirs). There should not be less of a range, 'because we are all the same people', although this did not mean that everybody would get on with one another. Dealing with disagreement or conflict was not to get involved. Where that was not possible, 'You do what you think is right, even if it may not be right.' The way forward was to find common ground rather than dwell on differences. Disagreements, when they arose in the school, were not 'huge': they sorted themselves out and rarely ran along religious lines.

The non-religious Y10 group articulated a somewhat paradoxical view: on the one hand, a limit of diversity had been reached in the school; on the other hand, they welcomed a wider of range of backgrounds, even if the different religions and ethnicities would not automatically get on with one another. This view was related to their perception of a strong Muslim presence and 'a lot of people' who did not have a religion; thus religions other than Islam and Christianity were hardly represented. Different beliefs would make for difficulties (and complexity), especially where the differences were not huge (e.g. in the case of Catholics and Protestants).

> You say 'Christian and Muslim'; I think it's more non-religious and then Muslim rather than Christians. – Because none of my friends really like in school are Christian. (Y10/1, male) Thinking about it, barely anyone was actually Christian in school. Like if you go round and ask people . . .
>
> (Y10/1, male)

For this group, too, individuals' respective backgrounds did not decide friendships or relationships – someone's religion was a given. They pointed out that young people did 'just get on with' dealing with diversity.

> In a way I don't think it [religion] would get brought up. Say like [name], one of our friends, everyone knows he's a Muslim, but then none of [them] ever talk about it, but then we don't ignore it, we know he's a Muslim and we accept that, it never comes up.
>
> (Y10/1, male)

Again, mutual respect was the key to (non-)religious people getting on with another. Differences might create barriers, but they need not. One pupil pointed out that their generation did not dwell on differences or insist on erasing them – they let them stand. Another commented on young people's willingness to understand other points of view and identify shared ground.

> I think this generation's a lot more mature than the last [. . .]. The adults are more biased to their own thing, they're more headstrong. Say if they're not

religious, everyone has to be non-religious. Say, if they're Muslim, everyone has to be Muslim, whereas we're all like, our generation, is just like you can be what you wanna be.

(Y10/1, male)

The religious Y10 group thought that an even wider range of backgrounds in the school would provide further opportunities to learn, although one pupil wondered whether the existing range could in fact be extended. This group valued the existing variety: it was a positive feature; it opened their minds and allowed them to learn. It was thus educative and well-nigh indispensable to their education.

Yeah there's so many different religions and cultures and there's 52 languages spoken here and it's just . . . and there are different religions and it just really opens your eyes and I've learnt *so* much more about different cultures and things.

(Y10/2, female)

I couldn't imagine leaving school without knowing about different religions and different cultures and things.

(Y10/2, female)

They, too, thought that pupils in the school generally got on well with one another, with little or no racism. There was general acceptance that they were in school to learn. In fact, it was part of their learning to get on with people who were different from themselves (a comment echoed by other young people cited earlier).

Sometimes there are some very narrow-minded people who have *ideas* that maybe aren't their own . . . and they speak them and that gets them into trouble and they get other people in trouble. There's always going to be that, but generally on the whole there's not a lot of racism or discrimination that goes on because we just accept each other, because we're all here for one purpose, to learn.

(Y10/2, female)

You're always going to meet people who are different and the earlier you start really the easier it gets.

(Y10/2, female)

Whether everybody got on with one another depended on both sides: again (mutual) respect was the crucial element, coupled with an attitude that avoids arguments or dwells too much on differences. This group saw a potential for problems between religious and non-religious people because of the risk of argument. More or better knowledge about religions and being diplomatic, open-minded and respectful facilitated understanding. This group perceived non-religious people to be narrow-minded: they lacked knowledge about religion(s), were set in their views and had rejected religion when something had gone wrong in their lives. The (negative) influence of the media and the way the next generation of young people were brought up would shape the future situation at the school.

For the non-religious Y11 group, the broad range of ethnic and religious backgrounds in the school was important, but it did not matter how broad the range was. Having the range was important so that they could be educated about different approaches and get to know different people. This was what shaped one's opinions and views.

> Yeah, I think it's important. – I don't think it [how wide the range is] *matters* really. I think it's good that there are different things because you learn more out of lessons as well. Because people in other schools, a lot of them are not really as multicultural as this, so they'll have a lot of different views to us, because they don't know people themselves.
>
> (Y11/1, female)

In this group's perception, the pupils in the school generally got on with one another and religion was not a divisive issue, which would – 'hopefully' – continue. That some groups, like Muslim boys, tended to stick together 'needed sorting out' (they should mix more), but they had no suggestions how this might be done. Religion could be a 'not so positive factor' in relating to religious people, but it was better to have open discussions and clarify one's assumptions, even if this involved 'a little argument'. This group thought it was difficult for people from different religions to get on and understand each other and they had mixed views about religious and non-religious people doing so. Although dialogue would promote understanding, it would not happen automatically. They pointed out that school helped to create understanding by providing a platform for discussions – 'School does it a lot because we talk equally normally about Muslims and Christians' – in RE and assembly (daily act of worship). How to create the right atmosphere which facilitated such discussions outside lessons was another question they could not answer.

> It's good having discussions. – [. . .] – It *is* good to talk to them about it because you understand more rather than have your own opinion on them and . . . like think of them in a different way.
>
> (Y11/1, female)

> Yeah [in the discussions we have in RE], but that's only one lesson a week, so I don't know how you do it more. We talk about it in assembly as well. I'm not sure out of school how you do it.
>
> (Y11/1, female)

The religious Y11 group also considered the school's multicultural and multireligious character as a positive. Given their perception of a mainly Christian and Muslim presence, they thought that the range of religions in the school could be broader.

> It [the school] isn't really *that* multi cultural; well, with nationalities it is, but it is just mainly Christians and Muslims. I don't think there are any Hindus, there are a few of other religions, but it's mainly those two religions. – [. . .] – Oh yeah, we could have more depth in other religions.
>
> (Y11/2, male)

If the range were broader, everyone could get on with everybody else, because, as pointed out earlier, religion was secondary to individuals' personality and ethnic/national backgrounds. The understanding between pupils and the way pupils from different backgrounds got on with one another were at the right level, even if 'there's always room for improvement,' but 'it's a lot better than it is in many other schools, probably'. Things were likely to change if different populations moved into the school's catchment area, thus changing the social context in which the school is embedded. Again, this highlights the role of context(s).

School B

School's B location in the monocultural rural setting of a mainly Welsh-speaking area was reflected in the composition of the school's pupil body (almost entirely of white background) and the pupils' embeddedness in the local culture, with most pupils using Welsh as their first language. Although the school's ethos was, as described earlier, inclusive and stressed the importance of pupils' respect towards others, the pupils in this school had fewer opportunities to experience diversity (in the wider sense) and thus fewer opportunities to develop skills to deal with diversity. However, the inspection report of 2009 noted that extensive extracurricular activities promoted pupils' personal and cultural as well as moral and social development, although it also noted that the provision for pupils' spiritual development was not as effective (as also indicated in the school's profile). Our visit to the school did not offer any opportunity to gather information about these aspects of the school, but the largely non-religious pupil body may be connected to pupils' spiritual development.

Difference and contexts

The focus groups mirrored the particular constellation of religious and non-religious people in this geographical context. The majority of the pupils said they did not have a religion, which, they indicated, was the case for most pupils in the school. Some had grown up with a religion, mostly in a Christian denomination, but had stopped practising entirely or only retained loose links with occasional attendance (for social/family reasons). They thus had no close connection with a religious community or place of worship. A small minority said they had a religion or were not sure whether they had. A Y11 pupil from a mixed-faith background said that neither his Hindu father or his Christian mother 'force me to go to church'. The pupils indicated that the parental generation had little if any connection with religion, while the grandparental generation still practised. Overall, theirs was not a churchgoing village community, although the majority who were religious were Christians.

This context also shaped the way pupils related to religion. In this regard, there were differences between the age groups. The Y13 pupils thought about religion in both positive and negative terms: religion was part of life and formed a bond in society, but could ignite wars and spark discrimination.

> I think that religion can keep societies together. [. . .] the fact that they share certain beliefs in common.
>
> (Y13, male)

> . . . the negative bit, there's been wars and stuff over religion and religion is supposed to be like a peaceful thing and people conflicting over it for no apparent reason, because they don't *believe* in other people's religion.
>
> (Y11, female)

In this group, not having a religion meant not having a religion *yet*. The implication was that they were open to and curious about religion and they expected to make a (personal) choice at a later point in their lives. Those who belonged to a religious community were different in terms of the way non-religious pupils perceived religious peers. The pupils referred to a Roman Catholic fellow pupil who 'got a bit bullied outside class' and to the way 'cliques' formed in school. Some Y11 pupils saw difference in terms of morality (the moral dimensions of religion[s] influenced people's thought and action) and approach (some religions are inclusive, others exclusive), but other pupils pointed out that morals were not the reserve of religious people – everyone adhered to some moral code.

Interestingly, the younger age groups (Y8 and Y11) generally did not discuss religion outside RE lessons, although they were happy to do when it arose. By contrast, the Y13 pupils said they had lively discussions about religion with one another, both inside and outside the classroom, often triggered by topics raised in RE and philosophy, such as life after death, suffering or the concept of God. Curiosity and the wish to understand better made these discussions spill into social times. The pupils debated differences in approach, for example, a factual/ scientific versus a scripture-based approach. Having gone beyond learning the basic facts about different religions (e.g. Judaism and Christianity), they had studied RE and philosophy at GCSE and AS level. Thus RE had opened their minds to religion, which had caused a shift from atheist to agnostic positions and kindled belief in God. Some also sparred with their atheist parents about religious matters.

Another topic of discussion showed a difference between the age groups. The younger age groups (Y8 and Y11) found it very difficult to relate to the question about the values which guided their behaviour. Some prompting elicited 'treat others with respect and love,' 'treat others as you want to be treated yourself' and 'do not lie.' However, the older Y13 pupils readily cited respect, equality, honesty, and being non-judgemental and open-minded and again pointed out that such values did not necessarily derive from religion.

> It's like respect and equality and stuff.
>
> (Y13, female)

> Try not to be judgemental before you get to know someone, I think that's important.
>
> (Y13, female)

The pupils in all the groups thought that such qualities were either inborn or instilled by parents and friends, but not by school – school was about skills needed for future employment (thus not a formative influence in that regard) because it exposed them to different people and because it depended on how they related to teachers.

> Especially when you go to secondary school, you mix a lot with people that have different values to you and different beliefs and how they should act around other people.
>
> (Y11, female)

> I think it depends on the teacher. If you respect the teacher and they respect you, then you will listen.
>
> (Y13, female)

When asked to comment on commonalities between different religions, all three groups pointed out that all religions shared some aspects and differed in others, although some had more in common than others, for example, Christianity and Islam had more in common than Islam and Buddhism. A Y11 pupil suggested that Buddhism was close to a non-religious stance.

The non-religious pupils in all three groups were somewhat divided on the question whether their stance influenced the way they treated religious people (some had friends who were religious), but they indicated that everybody was the same (whether religious or not) and that they were guided by respect and tolerance in dealing with religious people, to the point of watching what they said in case they might offend. One pupil commented that her family expected her to treat an ordained aunt with 'more respect'.

> Everybody is the same, even if they're religious or not.
>
> (Y8, male)

I would just treat everybody the same.

(Y8, female)

I have a friend from town, she's a Mormon. I act differently around her. [. . .] I just don't act me sometimes. [. . .] Cause they don't get to do a lot of stuff.

(Y8, female)

If I did have a friend like [a] Muslim or that culture, I don't know, I would be afraid to say something wrong. I would double-check what I'm saying. Sometimes you will offend and then they won't talk to me ever again.

(Y8, male)

Yes, my aunty was ordained when I was younger and it's always like you have to have more respect and that's what she's saying out and stuff. It's weird.

(Y11, female)

Respect was linked to individuals' right to choose commitment to a religion. This made religion a personal or private matter and a matter of mutual respect in that religious people should not proselytize and '*we* should also respect *them*.'

It's all well and great saying '*they* should respect *us*', but *we* should also respect *them*. A lot of people turn round and say 'you've got to go from assembly because it's a Christian assembly', when really they wouldn't have a problem sitting in on it.

(Y11, female)

Not having a religion, Y13 pupils commented, meant being less biased, being more open towards all religions and not trading in truth claims.

It's completely up to the individual what religion they choose to follow.

(Y13, female)

If it's their religion and it's an important part of *them*, but to *me* because he follows his religion, I don't mind that, that doesn't make them any different to who they are; [. . .] I'm fine with that,

(Y11, male)

I don't really have a religion and these people, they choose what they believe in and it doesn't really affect how I think about anything at all, it's just they've got their things and I've got my things.

(Y11, male)

As long as they don't try to drag you into their religion.

(Y11, male)

Yes, because maybe if you have one religion you could be biased to see other different religions, but as we don't have one specific religion, we can see everybody as quite equal.

(Y13, male)

Yeah, if someone was [. . . Jewish], maybe they would say 'your belief is totally wrong. Nothing's correct' [. . .]; but as someone with no religion, [. . . I] can say 'no, you can't say, he's wrong because maybe you're wrong', so I think it's best if I have no religion.

(Y13, male)

Similar to the pupils in School A, family friends or school had raised their awareness of religious people. In their case, too, the initial perception of religious people as strange (unfamiliar) gave way to greater understanding as they learnt about the beliefs and practices of different religions. As in School A, this bears out the contact hypothesis.

Yeah, my uncle's friend who lives in [name of town], he's a very strong Muslim and I remember [. . . when he went] to his house and he had to take his shoes off at the door and make sure he was totally clean before he entered the house and stuff.

(Y13, female)

Maybe it could be more critical at that time [when you were young], because maybe you'd never heard the religion, you know the stuff they're doing, like Jews with kosher meals and all that. Maybe at the time we work out what they're doing, but I've [. . . got] more into it in GCSEs and understanding why, and your opinion has changed that way.

(Y13, male)

If you get it in Year 7 and 8 and 9, really, you don't really understand, but I suppose it's a bit pointless then, because to us, we don't know anything about any religion, we've never really come across any religion, except for our own, but then as you move up to GCSE, if you pick it in GCSE, then you learn the reasons behind and you respect the religion a lot more as you learn more about it.

(Y13, female)

Only the older pupils (Y13) indicated that having religious friends had an effect on their own positions: they wondered at times why religion was not part of their lives. They could see that religion connected people to a community and provided a refuge in difficult times. However, being part of a community depended on where you lived, as there were areas with only a handful of, for example, Muslims or Jews. In this regard, these pupils were looking forward to a school trip to Auschwitz (Poland), which they thought would give them the opportunity to see an area with a sizeable Jewish community and to move from textbook knowledge to firsthand experience. Thus living in a multicultural country had the advantage of learning about religion and its importance in people's lives. The discussion of these points also revealed these pupils' awareness of the diversity *within* religions – the different strands within, for example, Christianity and Judaism.

> Yeah, definitely because if you think about somebody who has faith, it just makes me question why can't I have that. They have something . . . (Y13, male) . . . to hold on to. (Y13, female) Concrete. (Y13, female)

> I suppose it's nice to have that, because you've got a whole community with you, haven't you?
>
> (Y13, female)

> I think the location you're in is very important with that as well, because if you just have a community like [. . . this one], then you just have maybe a few Muslims, a few Jews; maybe it wouldn't click as much, but, say, you go somewhere which is a Jewish community with loads more than here, it would work better like that.
>
> (Y13, male)

> Where we're going [in Poland], it's the Jewish community, it's gonna be a totally new experience for us, which is good because we've learned about it in GCSE and last year, so we're not new to it.
>
> (Y13, male)

> And they think the fact that Britain is a very multicultural nation, it's quite a positive thing because it makes us more aware of that religion and the fact that it plays an important part in people's lives.
>
> (Y13, male)

Attitudes to diversity and contexts

Regarding pupils' attitudes to diversity and views about greater variety in school, different aspects emerged from the three focus group discussions.

The attitudes of the Y8 group to 'the other' seemed to be guided by caution. One pupil commented that he would watch what he might say to a religious friend, because he was afraid of offending him/her (see earlier comment). Another 'used to think that Jews were really wrong' and would not be friends with a Jew. A third said it was alright to be friends with people from other backgrounds, but going on an aeroplane with them was a different matter. Other comments suggested caution with regard to forming friendships with those from a background different from theirs. This group's perception was that there was quite a mix of religious/ethnic back-grounds in the school, but they conceded after some probing that, numeri-cally speaking, pupils from non-white backgrounds were tiny minorities. Their comments also suggested that the minority pupils tended to stick with each other.

The opinions in this group were divided about the question whether they would welcome a greater variety: only one pupil would welcome it, two would not and two were non-committal. The first pupil saw the opportunity to be open to and to respect other people. The first pair of pupils saw potential for conflict, basing this view on their observations. There was also the fear that Welsh language and culture would be threatened. The second pair of pupils wanted things to stay as they were.

> I think if we had more mix, we'd have more chance to be open to other people, you'd be able to respect other people's backgrounds.
>
> (Y8, female)

> I don't think it would be right because there's sometimes fights, some people fight because of skin colour [. . .] and more of it will cause chaos.
>
> (Y8, male)

> I think we should stay how we are.
>
> (Y8, female)

> But if there are more people from different continents, it kills out lan-guages, like with Chinese people going to England and it's killing the English language and in Wales the English language is killing the Welsh language.
>
> (Y8, female)

A greater mix in the school would cause problems: religious pupils would have negative views about non-religious pupils; religious practice would interfere with the school timetable; 'spite' would drive some religious minorities away. It is interesting to note that *religious* pupils would be the source of the perceived problems, not non-religious pupils.

> Because like the people with religion probably try and put the people without religion down.
>
> (Y8, female)

> I think the school will have a big problem, too, because some people medi-tate morning, afternoon and . . . [that] will be at school time and they have to go to another place.
>
> (Y8, male)

Jews – if they come to our school and pray, somebody will spite them and then they will go to a school out of the country, it will hurt them.

(Y8, male)

Some preconceived ideas, if not prejudice, about religious people were reflected in some comments:

People get the wrong idea because I used to think that Jews were really wrong. I used to think that Jews were really bad and it was their fault that the world war happened. [. . .] I don't know [why I thought that]; it's like when I was in . . . [primary] school, I used to think really strongly that it was [the] Jews' fault that loads of people died and it wasn't until later on that I found out that it was actually them that were being [ab]used.

(Y8, female)

I don't want to be racist at all, but I don't trust black people, like when I'm in the aeroplane and getting frustrated because there's all the story and the stupid stuff about they're going to bomb innocent countries.

(Y8, male)

The Y11 group seemed more open to other faiths, but also aware of the effect of the media: people were likely to judge others by their appearance and jump to conclusions. This group's opinions were divided about the benefit of a greater mix of backgrounds in the school: a pupil who had grown up in London wanted greater variety and another suggested that a mix would make it easier to get to know people.

A bigger mix. I moved from somewhere that's just outside London to up here and it's so weird, because here you see no one except for people from the area, no one's basically moved in except for a few people and there's no mix; therefore people basically have the same opinion as their parents on a lot of things, which really isn't good, because people should have their own opinions because of what they see around them.

(Y11, female)

I really want a different mix because it teaches you more about different religions and stuff so it's more helpful for you to get used to them.

(Y11, female)

This group's views also differed as to how well pupils from different backgrounds would get on with one another. One pupil recognized that pupils in this school had not grown up with a range of different religions and therefore considered them as somewhat strange, but felt confident that (mutual) respect and willingness to learn about them would lead to greater acceptance. Again, what they learnt in school was important: if RE included religions other than Christianity, this would promote acceptance and understanding. Another was sceptical, saying that local people did not easily accept people from outside the area. A third challenged this as being too much of a generalization.

> I personally think [that] because we haven't been brought up with different religions and all that, some of them will think it's a bit weird and they will start wondering, but I think quite a few of the kids in school *do* respect other religions and I think they will just carry on and I think they will be fascinated to learn about these other people, because we only really learn about Christianity in school, but if we learnt more about different religions, we'd accept them more in the community.
>
> (Y11, male)

> A lot of people in this school have problems enough accepting English people, so what would happen, if people came in from loads of other countries. I would dread to think – and especially from those different religions – because *a lot of* people, not everyone, but *a lot of* people here are really closed minded and aren't willing to accept other people for who they are.
>
> (Y11, female)

This group saw potential difficulties for people from different faith backgrounds who feel strongly about their faith to get on with one another and with people who have no faith. However, such difficulties might be smoothed out over time, as people got to know each other better and learnt not be afraid of one another. The element of the unknown and unfamiliar would have to be overcome, a point which, again, refers to the relevance of the contact hypothesis.

> I imagine it would be temporary because eventually people would get to know each other and [. . .] get to know how each other operate and learn to accept each other.
>
> (Y11, female)

> . . . because people tend to be scared of what they don't know.
>
> (Y11, female)

This group explicitly commented on the specific situation in this geographical location: the rural Welsh village setting shaped people's attitudes and outlook and made people from outside conspicuous.

> I think it's difficult for English people to come to such a closed Welsh community because everything is so Welsh here. If you go to somewhere like [name of a near-by town] or a bigger city [. . .] they wouldn't stand out as much.
>
> (Y11, female)

One pupil articulated her perception of the place of Christianity in a multi-cultural UK, suggesting that it had receded in the presence of other religious traditions and that the UK was no longer a Christian country – quite a different take of the view reported earlier (School B) which stated that the notion of a 'Christian country' was no longer tenable.

> I think there's no religion in this country because we just have so many people just came from everywhere, it's just mixed and it would be a bit hypocritical from everybody if you were to write a Christian article, even though it's supposed to be a Christian country, that people like from other nationalities would complain. We have a mosque in [name of a near-by city] and you wouldn't see a chapel in a Muslim country, it would be burnt down.
>
> (Y11, female)

The same pupil's comment that homosexuality should not be allowed, if this were a Christian country, because the Bible prohibited it, was challenged by other pupils who said that being homosexual and being Christian was not mutually exclusive.

The older pupils (Y13) said they would welcome greater diversity in the school, although not everybody in the school would be ready for it, especially the younger pupils. They pointed out that RE had prepared the ground for them, which was not the case for the lower classes. Greater diversity would thus make for conflict in the school, although pupils would adapt over time. However, an element of potential conflict would remain, with pupils forming camps and polarization between religious positions.

> I wouldn't have no problem [*sic*] at all with it; I'd be like 'OK, just more people in the school', but there are some kids, I could think of a few, that would probably make their lives hell if they came here.
>
> (Y13, female)

> The younger kids would have a problem coping with that. We have some kids . . . they would go on the defensive. I could think of a few kids that would go on the defensive and there would be a lot of bullying about it, especially in year 11, 10 and 9.
>
> (Y13, female)

This group had not given any thought to the question of how people from different religions might get on with one another and how religious people might get on with each other and with non-religious people, but again they saw potential for conflict.

Conclusion

This chapter sought to compare and contrast young people's attitudes to religious diversity in two different locations in Wales: one a suburban context in the south of Wales, the other a rural context in mid-Wales. Both schools were community schools, but different in a number of respects: size and composition (School A fairly large and multicultural; School B fairly small and monocultural);

prominence of Welsh culture (in School B a majority of Welsh speakers and Welsh used in lessons, thus having a distinct Welsh identity; in School A the main medium being English and pupils having a wide range of home languages); the proportions of religious and non-religious pupils (a non-religious minority among other minorities in School A; a non-religious majority in School B); location (suburban vs. rural); catchment area (multicultural vs. monocultural). However, both schools shared an ethos which emphasized respect.

The views of the young people in the two schools show variety, both within each school and across the two schools. This chapter results from an analysis of the group discussions which aimed to reveal the extent to which pupils' attitudes to (non)religion and diversity were shaped by the geographical and social contexts in which they are growing up. It is clear that the context, composition and ethos in School A provided an range of opportunities – both organized by the school and just occurring as part of daily school life – for pupils to learn about and develop skills for dealing with diversity. Overall, pupils' attitudes towards religious peers were positive and marked by tolerance. By contrast, the context and composition of School B afforded pupils fewer opportunities to learn about and develop skills for dealing with diversity. In this school, it is interesting to note the difference in pupils' attitudes related to age: while the younger age groups (Y8 and Y11) were somewhat cautious and dealt in preconceived ideas about religious people, the older pupils (Y13) were more open and curious about religion and religious people – looking forward to, for example, a trip to Auschwitz to broaden their horizons. In this regard, the role of RE revealed itself to be of great importance: lacking the presence of multicultural peers, RE is the portal through which the world of religions is opened up.

Another aspect of the schools emerges as playing an important role: school ethos. In both schools, the value of respect – which, as many pupils pointed out, had to be mutual – proves an essential ingredient in young people's attitudes to diversity. It is a kind of dependable approach and the ultimate default position which fits all situations. Respect transcends context and difference and allows people of any background, whether religious or not, to get on with another. Thus, where respect is an integral part of the school ethos, this value is instilled in young people and guides their approach to other people.

Finally it is interesting to note the difference in perspectives between the two schools with regard to the relationship between religious and non-religious pupils. Given the multicultural composition of School A, non-religious pupils represented a minority among other minorities, but the other minorities all represented religious positions. Thus the perspective within which the focus groups in School A articulated their opinions was the perspective of the religious, in other words, religious peers were their reference points which oriented their comments. However, given the monocultural character of School B, where non-religious pupils were in the majority, the non-religious stance was the standpoint from which pupils viewed and expressed their opinions. Hence also the comment that 'we [the non-religious] have to respect them [the religious].' This difference between the schools suggests that the multicultural and multireligious diversity was the given situation in School A, while the non-religious majority was the given 'fact' in School B. Future research may prove worthwhile in probing the dynamics of such constellations further and the areas where the views of religious and non-religious young people overlap.

Notes

1 In order to avoid any clues for identification, details about inspection reports and school documents are not included in the bibliography.

2 The profile of School A is more detailed than that of School B because more documentation was available.

3 The names of the schools and any details that may identify them are not included here in order to preserve anonymity.

4 In 2014, the percentage of pupils receiving specialist support to improve their English was 25 per cent, but it is not clear whether this applies exclusively to pupils who use English as an additional language (inspection report 2014).

5 A 'pupil deprivation grant' currently supports the school's provision for disadvantaged pupils. The grant targets literacy and numeracy skills, further curriculum opportunities for pupils, attendance and enhancement of teaching and learning. (document on school website, access date: 8 May 2015)

6 Other recommendations (of the 2008 inspection) related to raising standards in all subjects, raising standards of teaching and learning, reducing high levels of absenteeism and motivating pupils to learn effectively, improving pupils' behaviour and key skills (re-inspection report 2009). According to a news report, progress in pupils' achievement was evident by 2013, when the GCSE pass rate reached 81 per cent. The school's current website (access date: 8 May 2015) states examination results of over 77 per cent of pupils achieving at least five GCSEs at A★–C.

7 According to a news report in early 2015, the school is to be relaunched and renamed, with a Welsh-medium school to be created on its site.

8 In 2014, the inspectors judged the school's learning environment to be 'good', stating that the school had a clear and well-established inclusive ethos and community that successfully celebrated the diverse nature of its pupil body and the local area (inspection report 2014).

9 The details in this section mainly rely on the full inspection report of October 2009 and the author's fieldnotes, as at the time of the visit the website of the school was under construction and no prospectus was available. The school has a website now, which includes most of the information in both Welsh and English. The school has not been inspected since 2009.

10 The Governors' Annual Report for 2013–2014 (school website, access date: 27 July 2015), which is mainly in Welsh, states that Welsh is the natural language of communication in school and that the school aims to encourage pupils' bilingual development, expecting pupils to study Welsh up to the end of Year 11.

11 The non-religious Y11 group consisted entirely of female pupils and the religious Y11 group consisted of five female pupils and one male pupil.

12 This group seemed less articulate, which could have been due to (1) their inability to express what they thought, (2) the pupils not having thought about the issues the questions raised or (3) the pupils not being particularly interested in the questions. It may have been a combination of these aspects. As this group seemed to need quite a bit of prompting and explaining, there may be a case for aspects (1) and (2) to apply more than aspect (3).

13 A female teaching assistant was present during this focus group, but there was no explanation why this was the case.

14 The differences in the way young people in this project understood and approached their (non)religious identities are described in more detail in Arweck (2013).

15 The details in parentheses provide details about the pupils, given their year group and gender. 'Y10/1' indicates, for example, that this is a pupil from group 1 of the Y10 focus groups.

References

Arweck, Elisabeth. ' "I've been Christened, but I don't Really Believe in It": How Young People Articulate their (Non)Religious Identities and Perceptions of (Non)Belief.' In *Social Identities between the Scared and the Secular*, ed. Abby Day, Christopher R. Cotter, and Giselle Vincett, 103–125. Farnham: Ashgate, 2013.

Deardorff, Darla K., ed. 2009. *The SAGE Handbook of Intercultural Competence.* Thousand Oaks, CA: Sage.

Goffman, Erving. 1959. *The Presentation of Self in Everyday Life.* New York: Doubleday.

Jackson, Robert, and Eleanor Nesbitt. 1993. *Hindu Children in Britain.* Stoke-on-Trent: Trentham Books.

Østberg, Sissel. 2000. 'Islamic Nurture and Identity Management: The Lifeworld of Pakistani Children in Norway.' *British Journal of Religious Education* 22 (2): 91–103.

8 Religious diversity as a personal and social value

Impressions from a multicultural school in London

Elisabeth Arweck

Introduction

This chapter reports data from focus group discussions with young people attending a large community school in inner London. Over three-quarters of pupils in this school were from minority ethnic backgrounds, thus making for a multicultural and multi-ethnic pupil body. The visit to the school showed that the school celebrated the presence of a wide range of cultural groups and that its ethos underpinned the promotion of a cohesive community. The chapter explores whether the school's ethos was reflected in the young people's views and attitudes regarding the multicultural composition of their school and whether they valued growing up in this kind of social context. The chapter thus revolves around the question whether the young people in this school considered religious diversity as being of personal and social value.

This chapter comprises eight sections. The first two sections draw the profile and ethos of the school in terms of the characteristics that can be derived from documents, such as Ofsted reports, documents relating to the school (e.g. prospectus, policies) and information available on the school's website. This information is supplemented by fieldnotes where possible.[1] The section about the school's profile also sets the socio-economic context of the school and its catchment area and provides general information about the school. In the third section, the groups of young people who took part in the focus group discussions are described in order to contextualize the data collected in the school for the diversity project. The following four sections report data from the group discussions, examining pupils' responses to the question of difference in relation to religion, their conversations about religion with their peers and family, how they related to values and their general attitudes to (religious) diversity. The questions about these topics sought to draw out young people's views of and attitudes to the multicultural composition of their school and how they situated themselves within that context. The conclusion draws some of the main points together at the end.

Profile of the school

At the time of the school visit, Meynard Green[2] was a co-educational comprehensive community school located in North London catering to pupils aged 11–19. Since September 2012, the school operates as an academy[3] under the leadership of the same headteacher who was in post when our school visit took place in July 2010. With about 1,200 pupils on roll, Meynard Green is a larger than average school.[4] It is regularly oversubscribed. The school achieved Business and Enterprise Specialist status in 2003 and became a Creative Partnership core school in 2006. (Ofsted 2008)

Meynard Green is characterized by a comprehensively multi-ethnic pupil body, which was one of the reasons why it was chosen for our project. According to the Ofsted inspection report of 2008, over three-quarters of the pupils were from minority ethnic groups, with the largest groups of Asian or Asian British heritage and black or black British Caribbean heritage. Around 20 per cent were from a range of white backgrounds. The Ofsted reports of 2004 and 2008 also noted a high proportion of pupils whose first language was believed not to be English, although for few pupils English was not a familiar language. This suggests that a high number of pupils in the school had knowledge of another language besides English, which they would use in their homes and communities.

Ofsted further reported (2008) that the school community successfully celebrated its multi-ethnicity and that pupils said they got on well together. This, the report noted, was a consequence of effective personal development and well-being and good spiritual, moral, social and cultural development.[5] This was also reflected in the inclusive relationships and the atmosphere of trust and mutual respect that prevailed in the school. The pupils valued the school's racial and cultural diversity. (Ofsted 2008)

The school was further characterized by a fairly high pupil mobility, with a substantial number entering and leaving during the school year and many late entrants having gaps in their formal schooling. Some of these were refugees or asylum seekers. (Ofsted 2008) High pupil mobility is a challenge for a school, in terms of integrating newcomers and providing for their learning needs regarding both language proficiency and academic achievement. Another area Ofsted examines is attainment between primary and secondary school. It noted in 2004 that the levels pupils had reached in primary schools before attending this school were below the national average in most year groups, but were closer to the national average in the younger year groups. This indicates the school's ability to raise academic achievement.

Another, somewhat unusual, characteristic reported by Ofsted (2004, 2008) was that boys outnumbered girls in each year group. However, pupils were taught in mixed gender groups, with only one boys-only group in each year (school prospectus 2010).

Ofsted also looks at the proportion of pupils with special educational needs (SEN), including those with so-called statements, noting a steady increase over the years: it was broadly in line with the national average in 2004 (Ofsted 2004), had increased by 2008 (Ofsted 2008), with the proportion higher than in most schools, and remained above average in 2012 (Ofsted 2012). Finally, regarding the socio-economic profile of the catchment area of the school, Ofsted assesses this by looking at the proportion of pupils entitled to free school meals. In Meynard Green, this rate has been consistently above the national average (2004, 2012) or even well above the national average (2008). Both aspects – SEN and socio-economic profile – present particular challenges for schools and the way they rise to these attests to the quality of their provision.

Our school visits also sought to identify the status of religious education (RE) in the schools – how it was taught, who taught it, how it fitted into the timetable, what syllabus was followed, how it fitted with related curriculum elements (e.g. citizenship, collective worship) and so forth. In Meynard Green, RE was located within the humanities faculty and taught in lesson blocks within history and geography. This meant that there were no discrete RE lessons. For example, in Years 10 and 11, pupils took a course with three units, consisting of Christianity and Islam, Patterns and Places, and the United States since 1960. An assignment linked the three units. Citizenship was a separate subject within the humanities faculty. The head of RE was a non-specialist, having a degree in history. According to the school's prospectus, the relevant SACRE (Standing Advisory Council for Religious Education)[6] had granted a so-called determination, which lifts the requirement for Christian worship at the school.[7] Thus acts of broadly based collective worship took place either in the tutor group or as part of a larger school assembly using the Thought for the Week as a theme. However, RE was taught according to the agreed syllabus of the relevant local authority.

The school's ethos

Given the school's diverse pupil body and Ofsted's comments on the harmonious relationships in the school community, we looked at the school's documents to find out whether there were any explicit statements about its approach to religious and cultural diversity and its strategy for achieving a friendly and co-operative atmosphere. The school's code of conduct (prospectus) set out clearly what was expected in terms of pupils' behaviour in the school's spaces (classroom, corridors, playgrounds) and towards people (teachers, fellow pupils). The stated aims of the school (prospectus) included the promotion of a friendly, welcoming community in which each individual is valued and their talents and achievements celebrated, the promotion of respect for individual and cultural diversity, and the provision of opportunities for the development of the whole person (spiritual, moral, intellectual and physical). The school's aims thus encompass the value of the individual and his/her talents and the value of an environment where diversity is an asset and respect for diversity is the adhesive which binds all parts together into a community.

The school's aims were reinforced in its stated vision and mission: the school intended to prepare pupils for a world of continuous change, it endeavoured to eradicate disadvantage and promoted social equality, it believed in every young person's potential to achieve, no matter his/her background (e.g. school website, access date: 8 May 2015).

The school's aims, vision and mission thus refer to diversity (understood in the broader sense, including religious diversity) and the need to cultivate respect for individual and cultural diversity. They also refer to values, such as equality, in terms of equal opportunities and equal treatment and of being valued as a person. The latter also tie in with the emphasis on the nurture of the whole person, with reference to schools being required to promote the spiritual, moral, intellectual and physical development of pupils.

Evidence that Meynard Green is successful in achieving its aims and vision is Ofsted rating it as a 'good school'.[8] This rating applies to the school's overall effectiveness, the quality of teaching in the school, pupils' behaviour and safety, and the leadership and management of the school. With regard to religious and cultural diversity, the respect the school aims at is noted in Ofsted's (2012) comment that 'a respect for diverse faiths, ethnic backgrounds and cultures permeates the extremely harmonious atmosphere.' This is also borne out by pupils feeling safe and bullying being rare. In that regard, the school adhered to a zero tolerance policy, to which the pupils taking part in our focus group discussions also pointed (discussed later). Thus, the school's leadership and management have established an inclusive school where all students are well supported. (Ofsted 2012)

In terms of pupils' personal development, the way in which the curriculum supports aspects of this is outstanding, Ofsted noted, with many lessons and displays helping to develop pupils' appreciation of spiritual, moral, social and cultural issues. Various curriculum elements were covered in different subjects but linked up with one another – for example, pilgrimages in religious education; apartheid in personal, social and health education; fair trade in geography; civil rights in the United States in history. (Ofsted 2012)

There were thus a number of aspects in the curriculum and the way the school operated as a community which underpinned the promotion of respect for diversity (in the wider sense). These included the following: first, a strong ethos of inclusion in terms of socio-economic background, ability (special educational needs, gifted and talented young people, new entrants), cultures, religions, ethnicities, visitors to the school and so forth. Second, positive and respectful relationships between teachers and pupils created a strong sense of collaborative working and ensured continuity for pupils, also given low staff turnover, which is especially important for tutor groups. This aspect of the school was immediately palpable during our visit, in terms of us observing teachers and pupils relating to each other and staff and pupils relating to us as visitors. Third, pupils were encouraged to develop a can-do attitude, to be innovative and creative, but also to be able to handle uncertainty and to respond to change. Fourth, the school offered a wide range of extracurricular activities, maintained close links with parents and the local community and made links beyond the immediate neighbourhood – for example, through international activities. Finally, the school offered a range of award schemes, such as the Duke of Edinburgh Award[9]. All these aspects provided a structure which acted like scaffolding for the skills and values with which the school aimed to equip its pupils.

The focus groups in the school

Four groups took part in our project: a group of Year 8 pupils (aged 12–13), a group of Year 9 (aged 13–14) pupils, and two Year 10 pupils (aged 14–15).[10] The groups were mixed in the following terms:

- pupils identifying as religious or non-religious (perhaps not surprisingly, given the school's composition, more pupils identified with a religion);
- religions (e.g. Christian, Muslim) and ethnicities (also, occasionally, combined, e.g. Egyptian-Turkish);
- understandings of Christian (including Jehovah's Witness), Muslim (Nation of Islam was perceived as separate) and 'no religion' (see Arweck 2013);
- gender (usually fairly evenly split between male and female).

Each group comprised 6–7 pupils.[11] The discussions with each group lasted for a school period (50 minutes). All the pupils were keen to take part in the discussions and were thus interested to engage with the questions and readily expressed their views. Also, they seemed comfortable with one another with regard to voicing their opinions. In the Y8 group, more explanations and prompting were needed to elicit responses. The older pupils (Y10) had more nuanced perspectives of issues relating to religion and religious diversity.

The question of difference

In order to draw out young people's views of and attitudes to the multicultural composition of their schools, one of the questions asked was whether being (non)religious made them different in relation to others. In the Y8 group, the general opinion on this question was that this was not the case – neither stance set them apart in any way. They indicated openness and curiosity towards (other) religious people. They would note the differences in relation to where they stood themselves, but would not be judgemental:

> I don't think it makes any difference. Just because I don't have a religion doesn't mean I'm not gonna be friends with everyone that does have a religion and care what their religion is. Not that I don't care, but it doesn't make a difference to how I see them.
>
> (Y8, female)

> I don't judge people by their religion. It's what they believe.
>
> (Y8, female)

> [The way I relate to people who have a different religion to mine is] still with interest; it's just that I don't believe what they believe. I like to find out

what they believe, but personally I don't believe in what they do. I don't have anything against them or anything.

> (Y8, male)

Context did not seem to play a role in this regard – their respective attitudes would prevail pretty much anywhere – nor did context have an impact:

> It's pretty much everywhere. Just because you're at school doesn't mean you have to be nice to everyone, but you choose to be, it's not just because the teacher's there or you're gonna be in trouble, because everywhere else you're like that, really.

> (Y8, female)

However, context played a role in what religion one might adopt or grow into, as one pupil pointed out. If one's family was Christian, one would be most likely to be Christian oneself:

> I think that sometimes it's got something to do with family. If you have people in your family who are Christians, you would probably be Christian. My family are all Christian, it's just my mum and my dad and me and my sister and my grandma on my mum's side.

> (Y8, gender?[12])

Another commented that one's religion may appear to be strict to outsiders, but did not appear to be strict from the point of view of those who adhered to it:

> If you have a really strict religion and some other people think, 'oh, maybe they're too strict' and stuff, it's just the way you are. It doesn't really feel too strict, because you've been brought up like that.

> (Y8, female)

Here, context is related to where one is positioned – inside a religion or outside it – and this shapes individuals' perception of what is 'normal' and what is not, if 'too strict' is assumed to be 'not normal'.

Although the pupils in this group conceded that certain religious practices made some difference, this did not weigh heavily, as they could work round such things (e.g. activities that were not allowed for some or dietary requirements) and make allowances. For example, it would not raise barriers to sharing meals:

> If you can't do something and someone else could do the thing that you're not allowed, you say, 'oh they can do that and when they come back from doing that, we can just go on with our normal life.'

> (Y8, female?)

> [If someone follows a particular diet, it does] not [make] so much [difference], because if you know that person and you know what you can't eat and what they can't eat, then you can kind of work around it quite easily.

> (Y8, male)

The same question elicited two sets of views in the Y9 group, with some saying that it made no difference, while others pointing out aspects which made
believers different from non-believers:

> Day-to-day life is normal, like you go to school and you get a job and things
> like that, but like [name of fellow pupil] said, it's different if you follow a
> religion.
>
> (Y9, female)

> You go home and at home it's your home, you'd have your parents, your
> siblings, but the things you do might be different, like what you eat or what
> clothes you wear and stuff like that, that's a difference, but in general what
> you do and how you do it is different.
>
> (Y9, female)

For believers, life revolved around religion, in terms of what they thought about
and practised (rituals, festivals, observance of dress codes), and this directed their
purpose in life:

> People who do believe have like a purpose in life, because they think and
> they spend their time celebrating festivals and following religion, but those
> who disbelieve [*sic*] don't, so that makes a difference.
>
> (Y9, female)

Further, religious people were perceived by others in a particular way:

> I don't think it [religion] makes it different, but people *see* you in another
> way, another kind of way.
>
> (Y9, male)

And there were positive aspects of having religion in one's life, by setting people
on the right path and preventing them from doing 'bad stuff', thus giving clear
direction, purpose and guidance:

> Having a religion can set you on the right path of life, like to be successful,
> because you're not really supposed to do bad stuff when you follow a reli-
> gion, you're supposed to do good stuff. You're not supposed to sin.
>
> (Y9, female)

There was also the prescriptive side of religion – what is (not) permissible – or
requirements such as tithing or giving *zakat*:

> Yeah, like some religions there's different things that you're allowed to do
> and what you're not allowed to do. Some religions, you can't drink and
> stuff like that.
>
> (Y9, male)

> You see sometimes in some religions . . . you have to like give up money; like my religion, you have to give 10% of your salary, so . . . for some people it's hard.
>
> (Y9, male)

This set religious people apart in some way from everyday 'normal' life – 'They have values,' as one pupil said (Y9, female), which have consequences. Rules and requirements could also separate religious people from their friends, because they had to give priority to other things and this excluded certain activities:

> And also it's easy because you know what to do, because you've got either the Bible or the Qur'an; it says what you're allowed to do or not to do, but also like if you see your friends doing something that you can't do, it might be difficult that way, because you want to do it, but you can't.
>
> (Y9, female)

Not having a religion freed one from prescriptions and obligations, but this freedom afforded no guidance or resort in difficult situations:

> Yeah, basically if you haven't got a religion, then it's almost as if you've got freedom. – [. . .] – Yeah, but then, there's always things that you might not know what to do in certain things, but when you've got a religion, it's like a pack and you know what to do in certain situations basically.
>
> (Y9, female)

There was thus a trade-off for religious people, on the one hand having (to observe or follow) rules and requirements, and on the other hand having guidance.

Context (school or outside school) did not seem to play a significant role, because even if one could identify people's religion, everyone was treated the same, everybody was equally different, given the school's multicultural composition:

> Yeah [there isn't a huge difference in school], because you normally, you can see what religion you are, but it doesn't matter because everyone is treated similarly.
>
> (Y9, female)

> Because we're so mixed in the school and outside, it's normal for us to encounter other people from different religions, different backgrounds.
>
> (Y10/2, male)

> [Outside school – at home and where we live] it's still the same. It don't [*sic*] really matter what religion you are, I reckon.
>
> (Y9, male)

However, the pupils in the Y10 groups pointed out that difference did come to the fore in different areas in the school and in different geographical locations. For example, in school, the playground may be different from the canteen. While difference made no difference in the former, it may do in the latter, given different dietary requirements:

> In the playground, there isn't really a big difference between like what religion you are, if you're Muslim or Christian or atheist or whatever, because if there's like a group of people playing football that you really like, the religion doesn't come into it, but sometimes in the canteen, people who are Muslim don't eat ham and so on. It's different parts of the school and it's the context again; it depends on what you're doing in the school.
>
> (Y10/2, male)

As to geography, diversity was perceived to be a feature of life in London, where it was 'everywhere', contrary to the countryside, where 'everyone's Christian' and is expected to conform to Christian practice ('everyone goes to church'):

> London is like a diverse place, you will find different people everywhere you go.
>
> (Y10/1, female)

> When you go to the countryside, it's really different. It sounds out of context, but everyone's all Christian; everyone all believes the same thing; everyone goes to church; if you don't go to church, everyone goes 'oh why weren't you at church?' and when you come here [to the city], it's just a lot more free and there's still lots of churches, but there's also mosques and synagogues.
>
> (Y10/2, female)

The second quote suggests that, both in terms of individual practice and architecture, the countryside's uniform Christian character is restricting, while the city's diverse religious character is liberating.

Further, the ubiquity and natural presence of diversity engendered openness and curiosity towards 'the other', to the point of some Christian pupils joining their Muslim peers during Ramadan in order to experience the effects of fasting:

> When we play, there's loads of us and I mostly play with a group that's mostly Muslim, but there's a few Christian boys there as well and because this is a [. . .] class where we're just all boys, we just play football all the time, but sometimes when we like go and talk a bit, [. . .] the Christian boys, because they've spent so much time with the Muslims, they know loads about Islam and they even like try fasting during Ramadan and they do different things just to try it out and it's really nice, because I think people

appreciate it more and they understand each other more when they try things like that and they discuss it openly.

(Y10/2, male)

Thus different religious views and practices did not create lines of division, but brought out positive values in young people, such as tolerance, flexibility and accommodation.

The older year groups (Y10) also displayed awareness of the internal diversity of religions and related religion to culture which they understood in terms of country of origin:

People have morals based on religion and other things and I think it just changes [according to what] your cultural beliefs are and your ritual routines. – [How would you distinguish cultural beliefs from religions ones?] – Normally like you'd say someone's from Pakistan, you wouldn't say they're a Muslim from Pakistan or something like that. Culture is more like country.

(Y10/2, female)

In that sense, religion was just one aspect of difference or being different and thus only one among possible distinctive features:

We're all different and we all have different beliefs, so it doesn't really matter if people are different.

(Y10/1, female)

[It does] not really [make a difference in the school] because it's multi-cultural, so you're always going to find different religions, different races in each class, so you don't really feel different, you're all the same, really, you're in a group of different people.

(Y10/1, male)

Doesn't everything make you different, not just religion?

(Y10/2, female)

Conversations about religion

There was great variation among the focus groups as to whether they discussed religious matters with friends. Some pupils said they avoided such conversations, giving various reasons. One reason was to stay away from competitive comparison between religions, as the need to respect other stances made such comparison invidious:

If there's a group of different cultures, I don't think people really like to talk to each other about religion, because sometimes it may become a bit competitive of which religion is *better*, which you can't really tell because everyone has the right to believe in what they believe in.

(Y9, male)

Another reason was not to have to launch into long explanations about one's own particular beliefs and practices, especially when they did not fall into known denominational categories, as this Jehovah's Witness indicated:

Some people will ask what religion I am and then I will say 'Jehovah's Witness' and they say 'what's that?' and then you have to go into detail about it. – [And you're happy to do that?] – Sometimes. It's kind of a long explanation.

(Y8, female)

A third reason was to avoid causing offence, which was often due to lack of knowledge. Not being sure about details regarding a particular religion made it safer not to broach that topic at all:

You would normally joke with probably your family or your friends, you wouldn't go to someone and say that, that you don't really know because they might take it . . .

(Y10/2, female)

However, there were those who were happy to discuss religion, although again the circumstances for doing so varied. For some, the conversations needed to be triggered by someone or something – a relative or something happening in school. Others felt they needed to be really close friends to talk about religion, suggesting that a certain level of trust was needed:

Me and my friend, we talk a lot about religion and I think it's real interesting to talk about, because you're not always talking about silly stuff and football and stuff like that; you're talking about something that *every*one has a *different* opinion on. – Yeah. My best friend's Christian, so he will tell me something about Christianity and I'll tell him stuff about Islam and there would never be a point where we would become angry at each other, it would just be like we'll just talk about something until we get bored and then we'll start again.

(Y10/2, male)

The degree to which young people were comfortable with each other can be measured by whether they felt they could make jokes about each other's religions:

We're so comfortable nowadays we can make not like really bad jokes, but just like make jokes about people's religions and no-one cares. – [So you're not afraid to offend in any way?] – Yeah, because we all know that we're OK with these different religions, because we're all hanging out with people from these different religions and so we can make jokes about it and it doesn't really matter because . . .

(Y10/2, male)

Yeah, because I think, if you understand a religion and you start making jokes about it, people would be like 'errrr', you should stop, but if you know about it and that person's your friend, I think it's alright to some extent.

(Y10/2, male)

Where such conversations took place, there was the chance to explore each other's religions and even share some practices, as the earlier quotation about Ramadan demonstrated. Dialogue of this kind could set a chain in motion: it fostered appreciation of other religions and insights; insights in turn promoted understanding and understanding broke down stereotypes and stereotyping, as the following quotes show.

I think people appreciate it more and they understand each other more when they try things like that and they discuss it openly.

(Y10/2, male)

Yeah, it gives you an insight on it [*sic*], so you can understand it.

(Y10/2, male)

I think when you talk about religion, it kind of gets away from the stereotyping that other people could push on you really.

(Y10/2, male)

The question of values

The young people articulated various values, such as respect, tolerance and openness, *indirectly* when contributing to the discussions, as indicated in some of the quotes cited earlier. When asked specifically about values that motivated or guided their attitudes towards others, they responded in various ways. Some found it hard to relate to the notion of values, even when the question was rephrased or an example offered. Questions about what guided their behaviour led to answers which suggested principles which had been instilled in them, but they were now not conscious of them. These pupils were clear about right and wrong, being able to give examples (e.g. treating people with respect, not harming someone) and aware that their actions had consequences:

Well, you know the consequences, if you're gonna do something bad.

(Y8, female)

You do [know], but you just know it's wrong or you know it's right.

(Y8, male)

You get punishments if you do something wrong.

(Y8, gender?)

I think, although we all know what's right and wrong, we *do* tend to break them at times, for different occasions and circumstances.

(Y10/1, male)

Pupils in this category often referred to the sources which guided them – themselves, parents, friends, school – so they tended to think in terms of knowing instinctively what was right, taking this knowledge as a given ('you just know') and learning from other people's experiences. This included the occasional reference to scripture as a source of guidance:

It's probably like 'is it good?', like what you're doing. If your friends say, 'do you want to go out somewhere?' and you have to ask for permission to do something and you don't ask for permission, you just go, you kind of grow up in a way where you have to think about it. – [So you would refer back to your parents for guidance?] – Yeah.

(Y8, male?)

You've had the influence that something like breaking into someone's house is wrong.

(Y8, male)

You might have the experience that maybe one of your friends has already had that decision and they might have got it right or wrong.

(Y8, female?)

If you're a Christian and you were gonna do something that you knew in other religions was quite bad and had like serious consequences, then you could look in the Bible and it would tell you.

(Y8, female)

The phrasing of the previous quotes shows that some pupils found it difficult to pin down or articulate what guided or informed their actions, although they knew that their upbringing had played an important role. Some of the older pupils (Y10) were able to express this difficulty:

I understand the question [about values]; I just don't know how I'd answer it.

(Y10/2, female)

I understand it, but when you think about the question, you sort of get it.

(Y10/2, male)

It's hard to answer.

(Y10/2, male)

Other pupils clearly connected values with religion, in terms of guidelines or general rules (what is or is not allowed):

If you have a religion, you kind of follow the guidelines and you follow it.

(Y8, female)

Depending on your religion probably. It'll be like smoking or something like that in your religion, it'll be considered wrong and someone maybe considers it right . . . [so that kind of gives guidance].

(Y8, male)

Some identified particular values which religion underpinned. A Year 9 pupil (female), for example, immediately related values to her religion (Islam) which commanded that she honour others, from which she derived the value of respect. This was echoed by another pupil in the same group who added the principle of treating others as one would like to be treated oneself:

Yeah, because I'm a Muslim; you'd said that you're meant to honour people, that's a value, so you'd think you must be respectful and you think about it.

(Y9, female)

There's certain things in my religion as well that you shouldn't and should do, like respect your elders, treat them like you'd like to be treated and things like that.

(Y9, female)

A third pupil also related values to religion, pointing to the way religious teach-ings prioritized some things and put others second, suggesting different levels of importance or a hierarchy of values:

It [the word 'values'] means what you think is important and, according to your religion, what you think should become first and what other things should come after.

(Y9, female)

A third set of pupils did not relate values to religion, pointing out that one did not need to be religious to have values – they could be understood as general ethical principles, as this pupil expressed:

[It's] relatively easy [to answer this question]. So like I value loyalty and telling the truth and morals are *really* important; even though I consider [myself] not having a religion, I still believe in certain things that other religious people might believe in as well . . . so, yeah, morals are really important.

(Y10/1, female)

This statement reflects similar comments from other pupils who pointed out that just because they did not follow or identify with a religion did not mean that they were immoral or unprincipled people.

As the earlier comment about treating others as one would want to be treated oneself implies, the relational aspect of values, such as respect and loyalty, was emphasized by a number of pupils: these were qualities that one hoped to find in other people (e.g. friends). Conversely, such values also applied in the sense of disregarding other people's bad behaviour and taking a forgiving attitude:

Like . . . ignore people when they're doing something bad to you. Always respect your parents and others as well . . . yeah, respect as well.

(Y9, male)

Pupils who could relate to the concept of values cited a range, including respect, honesty, truth, loyalty, kindness and being a moral person. Respect was cited the most, often accompanied by the remark that it relied on mutuality:

You can't always follow them, but I try to stay calm, be kind to people and respect. I think respect is the main value, really, because if you respect people, they respect you and you can live happily.

(Y10/2, male)

The mutual aspect of respect also made for harmonious coexistence with others, as this pupil stated:

Yeah, like for example if . . . you can't always follow them, but I try to stay calm, be kind to people and respect. I think respect is the main value, really, because if you respect people, they respect you and you can live happily.

(Y10/2, male)

However, it was also important to practise one's values even when the people one dealt with did not share them, making adherence to one's values a value in itself, as this pupil conveyed:

Basically, the whole point of life is to interact with others and if you can't use your own values, if you're in a group with loads of people who like don't share the same values as you and you have to interact, you have to just carry on, so sometimes you keep all of them, that's a good point.

(Y10/2, male)

In this regard, context came into play, as it was easier to adhere to one's values in the company of like-minded people, such as one's family:

> I think it's hard to keep your values outside in society, because you're just mixed with other people from different cultures and some of the values that you might have, they might not have, [. . .] so it's harder, but when you're at home it's a lot easier because you're with people . . . [with like minds].
>
> (Y10/2, male)

The discussion in one of the Y10 groups revealed that some values depended on context. This group discussed non-violence after one pupil had cited it in connection with being a vegetarian:

> I'm a vegetarian. [. . .] that's kind of similar to religion in a way, if you think about it. I wouldn't consider using violence.
>
> (Y10/2, female)

Others took issue with this stance: while violence was not necessary or acceptable as an act of aggression or gratuitous brutality, they argued, it could be a last resort in some situations as an act of just defence and thus override any religious injunction against it:

> I don't believe in non-violence. I don't believe it [violence] is necessary, but people will have the view that violence is only necessary at the very last point. – [As a last resort?] – Yeah, I mean some people would say that, like Ghandi, because he said 'no violence' and what we are learning in history is that he said that if all the Jews died in the holocaust, they would have the moral win, but violence is necessary in very extreme circumstances.
>
> (Y10/2, female)

> It's uncomfortable hearing it, but if you think about it, it's kind of true, because I sort of don't feel comfortable hearing like [someone] saying 'violence is right', but in a way it is and when you think about it, it's kind of . . . yeah, it is the last resort, because if people don't listen otherwise, that's the only thing you can do.
>
> (Y10/2, male)

This points to a more nuanced understanding of values and the ability to bring different considerations to bear in situations presenting ethical dilemmas.

Attitudes towards diversity

The discussion about values had already elicited the view that one had to treat people as one wanted to be treated oneself, although it was not clear what motivated this principle. One of our questions asked whether pupils' own views of or attitude to religion influenced the way they treated others. The pupils' responses were generally of two kinds: although some took it at face value, the majority interpreted it in terms of *other people's religion* being the influential factor, not their own. However, regardless of how the question was interpreted, there was general agreement in the groups that everybody should be treated the same – as a person, not as a representative of a particular religion or stance, and regardless of one's own position:

> For me, everyone's the same. It's just who you believe in. So if I met someone on the street and they are a Muslim or a Hindu, I don't really care because they're still a person.
>
> (Y9, female)

> I agree with [fellow pupil], like you shouldn't treat people differently because of what they believe and who they are.
>
> (Y9, female)

> I see them as who they are, not what religion they come from, what colour they are.
>
> (Y9, male)

Being brought up in a particular religion would, however, shape one's attitudes towards others:

> Yes, because especially if you're brought up from young, from your parents, they teach you the basics and what you should believe in, so that I'm Christian, but if I was born into another family who doesn't believe in anything I'd believe in different stuff, so it depends what you . . . [inaudible].
>
> (Y9, female)

Also, particular religions might have teachings about how to encounter others and thus make adherents more open:

> I think maybe if you are a really happy person and your religion said that you should always be open, so you might try and meet them a bit more.
>
> (Y8, female)

This view was countered by another pupil who commented that such an attitude would still not discriminate between people of different faiths:

> But then you would do that to everyone, so you wouldn't see the difference between meeting people of other religions.
>
> (Y8, female)

However, being religious created immediate affinity between people of the same faith:

> I guess if you meet someone like in a church and you know they're Christian you'll probably . . . it's like common ground, so you get to know them better than someone in school, but in general it doesn't really matter.
>
> (Y9, female)

Being religious also created an understanding of the way other religious people's lives were determined by their beliefs and practice:

> I don't think it does. I think I just understand other people's religions and I would not judge that religion because I'm not part of that religion.

I wouldn't say 'that religion's wrong and this religion's right', because if you are with any religion and you follow that religion, you're gonna be a good person. That's basically it.

(Y10/2, male)

As the previous quote indicates, there was also a strong emphasis on not being judgmental about anybody's (non)religious stance, at least not openly, as the following quote illustrates:

I follow my religion and I understand that people believe different things, but to myself I think that some people are wrong in what they think, but I'll never say it, because that's their free choice and I've got no right to tell them what to believe, but what I think is my right as well and I can think whatever I want really. – [You're going back to respect, aren't you?] – Yeah.

(Y10/2, male)

The value of diversity

For the pupils in Meynard Green, diversity was a fact of life: for most of them their upbringing in the school's catchment area had exposed them to people from different religions and ethnicities at a very early stage – they saw it as part of everyday life, just as they perceived London to be a multicultural environment overall, as mentioned earlier. People from different backgrounds were part of where they lived and part of their growing up, beginning in nursery. They were 'used to it' and they might live in a street where different religious festivals would be celebrated, such as Divali, Christmas and Eid. Religion was not a defining factor when dealing with people, a point which had been made earlier.

It's because of where you've been brought up as well, with like your next-door neighbours can be different races, different religions. – You just grew up around it.

(Y9, male)

Where I live, there's a lot of different people and there's all these different cultures, different religions, so I didn't really become aware because I'd already seen these people.

(Y9, female)

In like nursery you have kids with headscarves on and you just kind of . . . it's just your lifestyle and you're just used to it.

(Y8, female)

I think it's always sort of been there.

(Y10/1, female)

It's not a conscious thing. You just know it.

(Y10/2, male)

Living in London your whole life, really the multi cultural aspect. It isn't really an incredible thing to you because it's been with you all your life, so it's just something that you've come to expect. You don't exactly take it for granted, but you appreciate the fact that you have this multicultural community, but then, since you've had it your whole life, it's not really an incredible thing to you, it's something you just expect to see. [It's matter of fact.]

(Y10/1, male)

Thus, attending a school which was diverse in terms of cultures and religions was seen in a positive light, as this prepared one for life and made one knowledgeable about the wide range of religions that exist beyond the world religions:

It kind of prepares you for like society when you grow up. Like say, if you went to a school where everybody is the same colour skin as you, everybody practises the same religion, the same culture as you and then like if you go out in the world of work and you're in an office with all these different kinds of people, you don't know how to go about with it because you're so used to being around people who are just like you.

(Y9, female)

I think it's really good because it gives you sort of like experience that you couldn't get before you go out into the world of work and everything, you just see that there's so much diversity.

(Y10/1, female)

Yeah, and now we know pretty much every major religion.

(Y10/1, male)

And small religions sometimes, like not the religions that stand out like Christianity.

(Y10/1, female)

It also meant that pupils from non-mainstream religions felt less conspicuous, because they were part of a wide range, as a Jehovah's Witness pupil indicated:

I really like it here, because like in my primary school everybody has Christians so when I changed into a Jehovah's Witness, they were like, 'oh Jehovah's Witness' and some teachers didn't really like it.

(Y8, male)

Some young people commented that the plurality of backgrounds around them made them more open and curious about other people and broadened their horizons, making them global citizens. The more they learnt, the more comprehensive their picture of the world became and the variety made for lively discussions in class, which supported the learning.

> It just makes us more open to it, because there are so many religions.
>
> (Y8, female?)

> I like to question religions. Because I don't know much about other religions, so I like to question why people believe in gods and why they believe.
>
> (Y10/1, male)

> We always get into big discussions in my class in humanities, which is really good and *every*one contributes, it's not just some.
>
> (Y8, female)

However, living with diversity required mutual respect, as indicated earlier, so that people from diverse backgrounds could get on with one another:

> As long as you provide the right respect for other people's religions. (Y10/1, female) – Like you respect someone because you want them to respect you back.
>
> (Y10/1, female)

> If you don't have a problem with the other religions, they don't have a problem with your religion, you'll get on fine.
>
> (Y9, male)

Respect would also facilitate relationships with and among those who felt strongly about their religious stance and considered their religion to be 'the truth'. Lack of respect would communicate the message that the other's religion was wrong. Respect further meant not trying to change other people, thus tolerating how they lived and what they believed, while carrying on with what one believed to be right oneself. This suggests some equality regarding religions. However, respect did not preclude value judgements about the other religion(s), but it would seek out the common ground with the other religion (e.g. belief in God, righteous living, moral standards).

> Surely you can actually believe that what you believe is the truth – and I'm sure people with religions do – but you can't say to everyone else, 'this is the truth, you're wrong' because by saying to everyone else, 'this is the truth', even if you don't explicitly say, 'yours is wrong', it is basically the same thing as saying 'yours is wrong'.
>
> (Y10/1, female)

You should just keep it inside. If you think it's right and you're right, then fine, live your life the right way and don't try and change other people because that's just wrong. (Y10/1, female) – If you were really religious, wouldn't you think other religions were wrong? (Y10/1, male) – No, I respect other religions. (Y10/1, female) – I know you respect them. I'm just saying that you'd say Judaism is the wrong way to interpret gods or life and Muslims the right way, would you say 'that religion is wrong'? (Y10/1, male) – in a way, yeah, but . . . I believe there is a God a long time and they've believed it for time, so I'm not going to say, 'oh you're *wrong*' or anything like that, but they still believe in God, that's the main thing, that they believe in God and they live their life right and they don't go out killing people or robbing, stuff like that. They just live their life right and do right things and not like change the world for [the] wrong reasons. (Y10/1, female)

Those who held extreme views or had a closed mindset, for example, people with racist views or people who claim their own religion to be the only 'true religion' and any other religion was wrong, were difficult if not impossible to get on with:

> It depends. If you're a racist or if you really don't like that person for their religion, it depends, but normally people just get on.
>
> (Y9, male)[13]

> I think there have been one or two incidences in the school where a person says 'your religion is all wrong and mine is the correct religion' and I don't think this is the right school for them to be making those kind of comments and some people might actually take much more offence to it as well.
>
> (Y10/1, male)

> It depends; if that person's always in your face, saying 'your religion is wrong, your religion is wrong', but if that person just says that 'I think my personal religion is right', it wouldn't really bother me that much, because everyone is entitled to their own opinion.
>
> (Y9, female)

Extremism could also include religious dress, as a Muslim pupil in Y10 pointed out when he stated that there was no explicit requirement in the Qur'an for women to cover themselves entirely and, when he was young, totally veiled Muslim women had scared him. This is a point which (non-Muslim) pupils in other groups also made. For this pupil, one should be true to one's religion to a certain extent, but wearing the full burka went beyond that.[14]

Being exposed to different perspectives could be challenging, for example, when religious young people felt confronted with existential questions from fellow pupils who did not identify with a religion, which they were not able to answer from their own faith perspective:

> There's someone in my class [. . .], they don't have a religion [. . .]. She'll start questioning, like 'how come there's illnesses, how come there's things

like . . .?' – things you can't answer basically, so I don't know, it kind of puts you in an awkward situation because you can't answer certain things especially like . . . because I haven't got much knowledge about my religion because I'm still young, but it's just awkward basically, so I try to avoid it.

(Y9, female)

As the previous quote indicates, harmonious relations require a certain discipline – such as the practice of respect – and in some cases this could mean avoiding argument or keeping one's distance. In one group it was pointed out that religion was just *one* of the topics people formed opinions on and discussed and thus was not the *only* source of potential contention. This implies that the discipline of respect applies to any interaction between people.

I think it happens in any situation with any kind of other opinions, you know, like even over *small* little things like favourite foods and stuff. If you said, 'my favourite food is this and yours is wrong because that's not a good one', then . . . It's just not the religion, it's for everything.

(Y10/1, female)

In one of the Y10 groups, pupils pointed to the general secular nature of society and the potential clash between religious practices. This meant that, in order to fit in, some young religious people tended to tone down their religious identity when away from home.[15] Deference to peer pressure weakened their religious identity, while friends who shared their religious tradition reinforced it. Thus difference created spaces which marginalized individuals' religious identity (social acceptance being in tension with religious identity), while likeness or sameness created spaces where this identity had a place and was validated. However, where difference involved respect and acceptance, religious identity neither weakened nor did it have to be downplayed.

I think society now is way more secular than what it used to be, so there's a lot of people that don't really believe in religion that much and, say, if you're hanging around someone that doesn't have a religion or has a different religion and they do stuff that's OK with their religion, but it's not with yours, then you're . . . kind of stuck, because you don't know. I think when young people are out with their friends, they tend to become *less* religious and they kind of think, 'I'll put it aside and then when I go back home then I'll start, I'll go back up again.' But I think this kind of peer pressure that you would have, that you have to fit in, that you have to do something that would make you fit in, because if you don't, then you'll just be like a social outcast and no-one would want to be with you.

(Y10/2, male)

Also it's important, like I said before, how your friends know about your religion and that they respect it, because when you go out with your friends that know about what you believe and what you do and what you can't do and they know it and they respect it, then . . . you can keep your religion and it doesn't weaken because they respect it and they don't see it as different. They see it as different, but they don't see it as weird, so it's like they accept you but . . . I don't know how to really put it, but if your friends basically know what your religion is and what you do and you don't do, then your religion doesn't really weaken, so you have to make sure that your friends know about what you do and you inform them and they tell you and they try it out and everything.

(Y10/2, male)

It was also clear that pupils' attitudes were shaped by the school's approach to diversity and ethos, which is about being respectful towards different religions, not just by their upbringing. This ethos is school policy which instils respectful behaviour in pupils, as described earlier and documented in the Ofsted reports. The pupils knew that intolerance was not tolerated in school:

Yes, they do tend to make it a big thing if you say something out of line in this school because it's *so* diverse and it's so wrong to say something like that to some people.

(Y10/1, female)

Conclusion

This chapter has sought to show how young people attending a large multi-cultural community school in London perceive religious and cultural diversity and to what extent the ethos of the school is reflected in their attitudes. As described, the school's approach to the diverse composition of the pupil body was to treat it as an asset and its ethos of inclusivity led its promotion of a cohesive community within and beyond the school. While the school placed emphasis on the development of the individual learner – both in terms of academic achievement and acquisition of personal skills – it did so with reference to pupils' social contexts, including school and the wider community. All these different aspects provided external and internal scaffolding for pupils' education and development.

The case of this school thus shows that school ethos and related policies can have a big impact on young people's attitudes to diversity. For most of the pupils in this school, there was a continuum of home, school and wider community – most of them had grown up and lived in the catchment area of the school. They had encountered difference and diversity in various guises (religious, ethnic, cultural) and combinations from an early age and had come to see them as part of everyday life. Thus, in this respect, the contexts in which they were embedded were similar and reinforced each other – hence the pupils' perception of London as a multicultural city and their view that they would meet and deal with people of all kinds of backgrounds once they moved from education into employment. In that sense, (religious) diversity was a value and had value, as being exposed to it and learning to deal with it had personal and practical benefits: it broadened pupils' horizons, made them knowledgeable about the range of religions and prepared them for adult life.

As described earlier, the school's commitment to and practice of inclusion operated in a range of areas – not just religion, culture and ethnicity – thus addressing diversity in the wider sense of the term. The school's aims, vision and mission encompassed aspects related both to the individual (his/her value, talents, potential, etc.) and to the social context in which the individual is embedded (home, school, wider community), placing emphasis on diversity as a positive asset and on respect as a kind of the passe-partout attitude which provides the common platform for a diverse community to stand and build on.

Meynard Green also points to the importance and facilitating power of good relationships between pupils and teachers, the role of RE in forming young people's attitudes and the importance of interaction between pupils which are grounded in mutual respect and trust – not just in the classroom, but also in extracurricular activities and in the playground. In this regard, common interests and shared activities foster intercultural and interreligious understanding by allowing young people to do things together without any particular focus on religious or cultural background. Their schooling is thus an kind of apprenticeship for life in terms of people skills, including the challenges they may face, which will, as they pointed out, stand them in good stead in later life.

Notes

1 In order to avoid any clues for identification, details about Ofsted reports and school documents are not included in the bibliography.
2 In order to preserve the anonymity of the school, a pseudonym is used.
3 Academies are part of the growing variety of school types, created with the launch of the Academies Programme in 2000 under Tony Blair's Labour Government as a way of reorganizing failing schools. These are independent community (state) schools which are outside the authority of the Local Authority, often supported by corporate sponsorship. The Academy Act of 2010, passed by the Conservative-Liberal Coalition Government, introduced changes to the academy concept, allowing successful state-maintained schools to become academies (see e.g. Walford 2014).
4 At the time of the Ofsted inspection in 2004, the number on roll was 1,180. By 2008, this had increased to 1,214 (Ofsted 2008).
5 Schools have a statutory obligation to attend to the spiritual, moral, social and cultural (SMSC) development of pupils, which they usually do by taking a cross-curricular approach (see also later).
6 Since 1988, local authorities need to establish SACREs which advise and monitor the locally agreed syllabus for RE. Although RE is a statutory element of the basic curriculum, it is not a National Curriculum subject; it is the responsibility of the Children's Services Authority (CSA) through its SACRE. The National Association of SACREs (NASACRE) supports the work of SACREs on a national level.
7 The Education Act of 1988 made a daily act of collective worship a legal requirement for schools in England and Wales, stipulating that it 'shall be wholly or mainly of a broadly Christian character'.

8 Ofsted's ratings are: 1 – outstanding; 2 – good; 3 – satisfactory; 4 – inadequate.
9 This (inter)national award was established in 1956 by the Duke of Edinburgh and is aimed at young people aged 14–24. It consists of a tailored programme of activities at three levels designed to develop skills for life and work.
10 As the pupils in Year 11 (aged 15–16) were sitting GCSE (General Certificate of Secondary Education) examinations, the school felt it was not appropriate for them to take part in the project.
11 The groups were composed as follows: in Y8, three male, three female, with four religious (Christian, Muslim, Jehovah's Witness) and two (female) no religion; in Y9, three male, three female, with five religious (Christian, Muslim, Nation of Islam) and one (female) no religion; in Y10 (group 1), three male, four female, with four religious and three no religion; in Y10 (group 2), three male, three female, with five religious, one (female) no religion and one mixed (Egyptian-Turkish).
12 Background noise outside the room where this focus group took place makes it hard to distinguish male from female voices in the recording, hence the question mark about gender in some of the quote attributions.
13 The focus group took place some time after Nick Griffin of the BNP (British National Party) had been on the panel of BBC1's 'Question Time' programme (October 2009). There were several references to the BNP and its political stance, probably partly due to the controversy around the fact that Nick Griffin had been invited on to the panel. Pupils were clear that the presence of a person like Nick Griffin in the school would lead to tension and conflict, but there was also the view that some would befriend him to show how misguided his views were.
14 The way young people related to religious dress and clothing is explored in a separate publication (see Francis, Village and McKenna forthcoming; Arweck 2016).
15 Similarly, a pupil in another London school indicated that she adhered to (and insisted on) Jewish dietary rules at home, but not elsewhere: 'I keep a kosher house in my house, but if I'm going out I'm not kosher outside, but if like some of my friends will come in [to the house] with food, I'll be like "I'm not sure if you can have that in my house".' (Y11, female)

References

Arweck, Elisabeth. 2013. ' "I've been Christened, but I don't Really Believe in It": How Young People Articulate their (Non)Religious Identities and Perceptions of (Non)Belief', In *Social Identities between the Scared and the Secular*, ed. Abby Day, Christopher R. Cotter, and Giselle Vincett, 103–125. Farnham: Ashgate.

———. 2016. 'Religion Materialized in the Everyday: Young People's Attitudes towards Material Expressions of Religion', In *Religion and Material Culture*, ed. Tim Hutchings and Joanne McKenzie. Farnham: Ashgate. (forthcoming)

Francis, Leslie J., Andrew Village, Ursula McKenna and Gemma Penny. 'Freedom of Religion and Freedom of Religious Clothing and Symbols in School: Exploring the Impact of Church Schools in a Religiously Diverse Society.' In *Religion and Human Rights* Vol. 5, ed. Hans-Georg Ziebertz and Carl Sterkens. Leiden: Brill. (forthcoming)

Walford, Geoffrey. 2014. 'Academies, Free Schools, and Social Justice (Introduction).' *Research Papers in Education* 29 (3): 263–267.

Part Three

Quantitative perspectives

9 Does RE work and contribute to the common good in England?

Leslie J. Francis, Gemma Penny and Ursula McKenna

Introduction

The distinctive place of religious education within the state-maintained sector of schools in England is a direct consequence of the long, complex and pivotal role of the Christian churches in establishing and shaping that sector (see Francis 1987). Formative voluntary societies like the National Society established in 1811, the British and Foreign School Society established in 1814 and the Catholic Poor School Committee established in 1847 had established a mechanism for creating schools throughout England; from 1833 they were supported by government grants in aid of private subscriptions (Cruickshank 1963; Murphy 1971; Chadwick 1997). It was inevitable that religious education was seen as part of the raison d'être of a public system of schools. When the state first introduced a mechanism for creating schools independently of voluntary societies under the 1870 Education Act, the resulting Board Schools could have opted not to include religious education (Rich 1970). As the Cross Commission in 1888 revealed, however, very few Board Schools followed that approach. Religious education seemed to be there as part of the English school system and seemed to be destined to stay there.

The 1944 Education Act, in a major attempt to re-engineer the partnership between church and state in the provision of a national network of public schools, legislated for the provision of 'religious instruction' within all schools that were not church foundations (Dent 1947). In return, some denominations felt confident to relinquish some of their control over church schools, resulting in the creation of two forms of church school: voluntary controlled schools, which were in the control of the local education authority; and voluntary aided schools that remained in control of the churches. Two further features of the provisions for religion made within the 1944 Education Act deserve reporting. In voluntary controlled schools and schools without a church foundation, religious education was to be taught according to 'a locally agreed syllabus'. This kind of syllabus was agreed within each local education authority by a committee consisting of the local education authority, local teachers, local representatives of the Church of England and local representatives of other denominations present in the area. Parents were given the statutory right to withdraw their children from attendance at religious education classes. The 1988 Education Reform Act left the basic architecture of the provision for religious education engineered by the 1944 Education Act unchanged (Cox and Cairns 1989).

While the legislative framework within which religious education in England has remained largely unchanged since 1944, the actual provision within schools has changed beyond recognition (for a current review see Gates and Jackson 2014). The developments have embraced changed aims and objectives for the subject, the emergence of national guidelines intended to influence the locally agreed syllabi and the introduction of syllabi for examination-based programmes alongside other subjects for GCSE.

Assessment of student responses to religious education in England has been a long-established enterprise engaging both quantitative and qualitative perspectives. The oldest established tradition has been concerned with locating students' attitudes towards religious education alongside their attitudes towards other areas of the curriculum, going back to an early study by Lewis (1913). A series of studies conducted in this area throughout the 1960s, 1970s and 1980s generated a relatively unambiguous picture locating religious education at the lowest position, at the least favourable end of the attitudinal continuum (Garrity 1960; Williams and Finch 1968; Ormerod 1975; Keys and Ormerod 1976; Harvey 1984; Francis 1987). For example, Roma Williams and Stewart Finch (1968), whose study embraced 14 school subjects, reported that religious education was assigned the thirteenth rank position by boys and the eleventh rank position by girls with regard to usefulness, and the thirteenth rank position by both boys and girls with regard to interest. T. J. Harvey (1984) reported that religious education was assigned among 18 school subjects, sixteenth place by boys and seventeenth place by girls.

During the 1960s, a series of studies, working from a range of different perspectives, attempted to look more deeply into aspects of students' approaches to religious education, including studies by Harold Loukes (1961, 1965); Violet Madge (1965, 1971); Ronald Goldman (1964, 1965); Kenneth Hyde (1965); Edwin Cox (1967); Reginald Rees (1967); and Colin Alves (1968). During the 1970s and 1980s, attention was drawn to researching religious language comprehension (Turner 1978) and religious attitudes (Francis 1978, 1986). During the 1990s, contributions were made to understanding the spiritual and religious backgrounds, concerns, interests and development of young people in England by the Children and Worldviews Project (Erricker et al. 1997), by the Children's Spirituality Project (Hay and Nye 1998) and by the work of the Warwick Religions and Education Research Unit (Jackson 1997). The primary relevance of these studies for the religious education agenda resided in the seriousness with which they took the voices of young people themselves, and some of them had enormous impact on reshaping the philosophy and curriculum in the classroom (see, for example, Goldman 1965; Jackson 1997). Many questions, however, remained unanswered concerning the contribution of religious education to the lives of young people themselves growing up in England or to the broader life of English society.

Within the context of the AHRC/ESRC Religion and Society Programme, a challenge was placed for the religious education community by the provocative title of the project initiated at Glasgow University by Jim Conroy: 'Does Religious Education Work?' (see Conroy, Lundie and Baumfield 2012; Conroy et al. 2013). The present chapter takes up this challenge.

In his own response to this question, Conroy's investigation employed a range of methods: multi-model ethnographic approach (see Walford 2008) within 24 schools (some with a religious character and some without a religious foundation); professional seminars using the Delphi method (Baumfield et al. 2011); textbooks and policy analyses; participant research; and an online questionnaire made available to students in participating schools. Conroy's interpretation of the meaning of his research question is interesting and crucial. He is concerned with the self-understanding of the subject, with the way in which it is delivered in the classroom and with the way in which students perceive its delivery. On this interpretation, Conroy's data led him to the conclusion that religious education is not working effectively and not delivering efficiently. There is at the heart of the matter a problem of meaning with and within religious education.

Of particular relevance to the present chapter are the data that Conroy collected from the students themselves, both through the ethnographic and interview component of the project and through the online survey. A focus group in a London community school led to the following observation:

> The sense of boredom and scepticism . . . points to one of RE's central challenges: coherence as to purpose and meaning. Pupils appear to have absorbed the view that the purposes of RE are vague and possibly meaningless and that RE primarily serves as a forum for expressing personal opinions.
>
> (Conroy, Lundie and Baumfield 2012, 316)

The online survey corroborated the view from the qualitative perspective that RE as a subject is concerned with sharing opinions rather than reaching significant conclusions. According to these data, the students rated RE as less important than other subjects and as not of real practical value:

> That most pupils did not ascribe any utilitarian worth to RE is a double-edged sword, as they enjoyed not feeling any pressure, but did not see any need to 'press for meaning'.
>
> (Conroy et al. 2012, 320)

The statistics on which these conclusions are based are reported in Conroy et al. (2013, 199–215), where hints are also given about the response rate to the online survey (ibid., 191–192). A total of 535 responses were received as a consequence of targeting 'class groups across the schools' ($N = 24$), although no information is given regarding the number of class groups or the size of the groups. Just over half considered that religious education classes are interesting (55 per cent).

Just under half considered that religious education is an important subject in their school (48 per cent), but the proportion fell to just over a quarter who considered that religious education would be useful when they are applying for jobs or university (27 per cent). In terms of the content of religious education classes, 69 per cent agreed that in RE they discuss issues a lot more than in other classes; 53 per cent agreed that in RE they listen to the teacher talking a lot more than in other classes; 37 per cent agreed that in RE they just talk about issues all the time; 30 per cent agreed that in RE they write a lot more than in other classes; and 20 per cent agreed that in RE they watch videos all the time.

In the introduction to the study, Conroy et al. (2013, 2) rightly observe that the structure of the research question 'Does religious education work?' entails asking 'what would count as working?' The present chapter proposes to approach that question in a somewhat different but complementary way. The primary interest of the present chapter is whether religious education works in the sense of having an impact on the students. One way of expressing that interpretation of the research question is to ask whether groups of students who experience a particular kind of religious education display significantly different outcomes from students who do not share that experience. Such an interpretation does not necessarily depend on specifying what the outcomes of religious education may be, since in this sense 'to work' does not necessarily mean to deliver specified outcomes. Rather it may mean to effect an outcome, and that outcome may be either positive or negative. Nonetheless, a research design capable of answering this question would be complex and expensive. At best it would entail a longitudinal study involving measures before and after the delivery of the programme of religious education and a control group, not so exposed to the programme, against which the outcomes could be measured.

Other, less expensive approaches to the research question rely on cross-sectional studies comparing differences between two groups of students at one point in time and, in this case, noting significant differences between the two groups exposed to religious education and not exposed to it. The limitation with this approach is that the findings are correlational but not necessarily causational. Indeed, there may be contaminating factors at play, like the different motivations of students who participate in the religious education programme and those who do not. One way of dealing with the problems is to rephrase the research question within the context of ethos theory.

Ethos theory recognizes the complex system of interactions that exist within different groups of students attending different schools or engaging in different programmes. Ethos theory maintains that what distinguishes one group from another is the totality of values and attitudes within the group. On this account, it is the values and attitudes of the group that comprise the ethos within which individual students exist and which plays a part in shaping and nurturing the individual's worldview. Working with this understanding of ethos theory, Leslie Francis and Gemma Penny (2013a) explored the distinctive characteristics of students attending Anglican secondary schools across England by comparing the collective worldview of 3,124 students (13 to 15 years of age) attending 15 Anglican secondary schools alongside the collective worldview of 4,929 students attending 25 comparable schools with no religious foundation. The worldview of these two groups of students was profiled over 10 value domains defined as Christian beliefs, church and society, non-traditional beliefs, personal aims in life, personal wellbeing, attitudes towards school, attitudes towards sexual morality, attitudes towards substance use, attitudes towards right and wrong, and attitudes towards the environment. Two main conclusions were drawn from the data: that the collective worldview of students attending Anglican secondary school was not greatly different from the collective worldview of students attending comparable schools with no religious character, and that the collective worldview of students attending Anglican schools generates an ethos consistent with a predominantly secular culture.

Research question

Working within the same theoretical framework as Francis and Penny (2013a), the present chapter is now in a position to reframe its approach to the primary question 'Does religious education work?' by exploring the collective worldview of a group of students who are engaged with studying religious education as an *examination* subject in England today. The provision of religious education in school up to this level is likely to have engaged their attention seriously enough to commend religious education as an examination subject. The worldview of this group of students is compared with the worldview of students who are not taking religious education as an examination subject.

In this project, the notion of worldview has been shaped to concentrate on three specific domains, with each domain defining a specific research question. The first domain is concerned with religious worldview and comprises four areas: religious beliefs, religious affect, religious environment and religious discussion. The first research question tests whether the groups of students (those taking RE as an examination subject and those not taking RE as an examination subject) differ in their levels of religiosity. In other words, has the RE group self-selected because they are religiously inclined?

The second domain is concerned with the experience of religious education in school and comprises three areas: the part played by religious education (alongside other influences) in shaping views about religion, the contribution of religious education to shaping views about the six main religious groups in England, and the contribution of religious education to shaping appreciation of life in a religiously plural society. Given the statutory requirement that all students attend religious education classes (apart from those specifically withdrawn from those classes by their parents), students should have some experience of religious education in school. The second research question tests whether the two groups of students (those taking RE classes as an examination subject and those not taking RE as an examination subject) differ in their evaluation of religious education.

The third domain is concerned with living with religious diversity and comprises four areas: attitudes towards religions, attitudes towards religious plurality, attitudes towards cultural diversity, and attitudes towards religious distinctiveness. The third research question tests whether the two groups of students (those taking RE classes as an examination subject and those not taking RE as an examination subject) differ in their attitudes towards religious diversity.

In view of the significant effect of sex differences on attitudes towards religious education and attitudes towards religion (Francis and Penny 2013b), this comparison is conducted among a single sex group. In view of the specific tendency for male students to be less favourably disposed than female students towards religious education, the comparison is conducted among male students. In view of the different expectations placed on religious education within schools with a religious character and schools without a religious foundation, this comparison is conducted among male students attending schools without a religious foundation.

Method

Procedure

As part of a large multi-method project on religious diversity designed to examine the experiences and attitudes of young people living in multicultural and multi-faith contexts throughout the UK, classes of Year 9 and Year 10 students in England (13–15 years of age) were invited to complete a questionnaire survey during 2011 and 2012. The participants were guaranteed confidentiality and anonymity and given the choice not to participate. The level of interest shown in the project meant that very few students decided not to take part in the survey. The sampling frame set out to compare data from at least 2,000 students (1,000 males and 1,000 females) from England, Northern Ireland, Scotland, Wales and London (as a special case), with half of the students attending schools with a religious character within the state-maintained sector (Anglican, Catholic and joint Anglican and Catholic) and half of the students attending schools without a religious foundation within the state-maintained sector.

Instrument

The *Religious Diversity and Young People* survey was designed for self-completion, using mainly multiple-choice questions and Likert scaling on 5 points: agree strongly, agree, not certain, disagree and disagree strongly. In the present analysis, 11 groups of items were identified from the instrument to map the following three themes: the students' religious worldview, experiences of religious education in schools and living with religious diversity.

Participants

In England, completed questionnaires were submitted by 528 male students in schools without a religious foundation.

Analysis

The data were analyzed by means of SPSS, employing chi square 2 × 2 contingency tables, combining the 'agree strongly' and 'agree' responses into one category and the 'disagree strongly', 'disagree' and 'not certain' responses into the second category. When discussing these data in the following narrative, the text will refer to RE students and non-RE students.

Results

Theme one: religious worldview

The first thesis tested by the present chapter is that the two groups of students (those taking RE classes as an examination subject and those not taking RE classes as an examination subject) display no significant differences in their religious worldview. This was tested against four sets of items concerning religious beliefs, religious affect, religious environment and religious discussion.

Religious beliefs

The section on religious beliefs explored four areas: belief in God, belief in life after death, belief in heaven and belief in hell. The data make it clear that there was no significant difference in the levels of religious belief between the two groups of students (Table 9.1). Thus, 31 per cent of RE students and 27 per cent of non-RE students believed in God; 37 per cent of RE students and 35 per cent of non-RE students believed in life after death; 31 per cent of RE students and 35 per cent of non-RE students believed in heaven; and 26 per cent of RE students and 30 per cent of non-RE students believed in hell. There is no evidence to suggest that students in the RE examination classes were motivated to study the subject because of higher levels of religious belief.

Religious affect

The section on religious affect explored affective responses to God, prayer and church. The data make it clear that there was no significant difference in the

Table 9.1 Religious beliefs

	RE %	Non-RE %	χ^2	$p<$
I believe in God.	31	27	1.40	NS
I believe in life after death.	37	35	0.15	NS
I believe in heaven.	31	35	0.84	NS
I believe in hell.	26	30	1.02	NS

religious affect expressed by the two groups of students (Table 9.2). In terms of attitudes towards God, 17 per cent of both groups said that they knew that God is very close to them; 22 per cent of RE students and 19 per cent of non-RE students said that they knew God helps them; and 49 per cent of RE students and 43per cent of non-RE students found it hard to believe in God. In terms of attitude towards prayer, 17 per cent of RE students and 13 per cent of non-RE students felt prayer helps them a lot. In terms of attitude towards church, 36 per cent of RE students and 35 per cent of non-RE students thought going to a place of worship is a waste of their time. There is no evidence to suggest that students in the RE examination classes were motivated to study the subject because of more positive affect towards the place of religion in their personal lives.

Religious environment

The section on religious environment explored two aspects of the connection between personal religious belief and life: the connection between personal faith and individual living and the connection between personal faith and the religious support of friends and family. The data make it clear that there was no significant difference in the religious environment of the two groups of students (Table 9.3). In terms of their own lives, between 16 per cent and 19 per cent of

Table 9.2 Religious affect

	RE %	Non-RE %	χ^2	$p<$
I know that God is very close to me.	17	17	0.05	NS
I know that God helps me.	22	19	0.56	NS
I find it hard to believe in God.	49	43	2.26	NS
Prayer helps me a lot.	17	13	1.32	NS
I think going to a place of worship is a waste of my time.	36	35	0.09	NS

Table 9.3 Religious environment

	RE %	Non-RE %	χ^2	$p<$
My life has been shaped by my religious faith.	19	16	1.24	NS
When making important decisions in my life, my religion plays a major role.	15	12	0.95	NS
Most of my friends think religion is important.	7	8	0.76	NS
My parents think religion is important.	25	21	1.53	NS

the two groups claimed that their life has been shaped by their religious faith. Between 12 per cent and 15 per cent of the two groups claimed that, when making important decisions in their life, their religion plays a major role. In terms of family and friends, between 7 per cent and 8 per cent of the two groups claimed that most of their friends think religion is important. Between 21 per cent and 25 per cent of the two groups claimed that their parents think religion is important. There is no evidence to suggest that students in the RE examination classes were motivated to study the subject because of greater saliency in their religious environment.

Religious discussion

The section on religious discussion explored the extent to which students talk about religion with their grandparents, their father, their mother and their friends. The data demonstrate that, although RE students were no more likely than non-RE students to talk about religion with their grandparents, they were more likely to do so with father, mother and friends (Table 9.4). Thus, 15 per cent of RE students and 10 per cent of non-RE students often talked about religion with grandparents; 21 per cent of RE students and 13 per cent of non-RE students often talked about religion with father; 24 per cent of RE students and 13 per cent of non-RE students often talked about religion with mother; and 27 per cent of RE students and 14 per cent of non-RE students often talked about religion with friends. These findings may be interpreted in two ways. One account suggests that more frequent conversations with parents and friends led to interest in RE as an examination subject. The other account suggests that taking RE as an examination subject led to more conversations with friends and parents. The fact that the two groups of students did not differ in terms of levels of religious belief, religious affect or religious environment suggests that the second account may be the more plausible and that RE classes may lead to more conversations about religion.

Theme two: experiencing religious education

The second thesis tested by the present chapter is that the two groups of students (those taking RE classes as an examination subject and those not taking RE classes as an examination subject) display no significant differences in their

Table 9.4 Religious discussion

	RE %	Non-RE %	χ^2	p<
I often talk about religion with my grandparents.	15	10	3.38	NS
I often talk about religion with my father.	21	13	6.35	.01
I often talk about religion with my mother.	24	13	10.76	.001
I often talk about religion with my friends.	27	14	13.39	.001

experience of religious education in schools. This was tested against three sets of items concerning the part played by religious education in shaping students' views about religion (alongside other influences); the contribution of religious education to shaping views about the six main religious groups in England; and the contribution of religious education to shaping appreciation of life in a religiously diverse society.

Main influences

The section on main influences explored and compared the perceived influences exerted by four sources on views about religion: school, television, the Internet and friends. The data demonstrate that even among those not studying RE as an examination subject, school was perceived as having been more influential than television, the Internet or friends (Table 9.5). While 47 per cent of non-RE students said that their views about religion had been shaped by studying religion at school, the proportions fell to 25 per cent influenced by television, to 19 per cent influenced by the Internet and to 18 per cent influenced by friends. Compared with non-RE students, more RE students attributed the influence of school in shaping their views about religion (64 per cent compared with 47 per cent) and also the influence of television (40 per cent compared with 25 per cent). There is no significant difference between the two groups in terms of influence attributed to Internet (19 per cent and 26 per cent) or to friends (18 per cent and 21 per cent). Here is some evidence to suggest that as an examination subject RE does work both in shaping students' views about religion and in focusing their attention on the presence of religion on television.

Studying religions at school

The section concerning the impact of school on shaping views about religious traditions was influenced by the way in which the religious question for the 2011 census in England was designed, listing the main traditions as Christian, Buddhist, Hindu, Muslim, Jewish and Sikh. The data demonstrate that even among those not

Table 9.5 Main influences

	RE %	*Non-RE %*	χ^2	*p<*
Studying religion at school has shaped my views about religion.	64	47	16.48	.001
Television has influenced my views about religion.	40	25	13.23	.001
The Internet has influenced my views about religion.	26	19	3.53	NS
My friends have influenced my views about religion.	21	18	0.79	NS

studying RE as an examination subject, studying religion at school has had some impact (Table 9.6). Among the non-RE group, studying religion at school has shaped views about Buddhists (33 per cent), Christians (38 per cent), Hindus (29 per cent), Jews (35 per cent), Muslims (34 per cent) and Sikhs (28 per cent). In all cases the percentages were significantly higher among the RE group, where agreement that studying religion at school has shaped views about Buddhists rose from 33 per cent to 46 per cent, about Christians from 38 per cent to 55 per cent, about Hindus from 29 per cent to 45 per cent, about Jews from 35 per cent to 46 per cent, about Muslims from 34 per cent to 53 per cent and about Sikhs from 28 per cent to 44 per cent. Here is some evidence that as an examination subject RE does work in shaping views about all the six major faith traditions evident in England.

Understanding religious and cultural difference

The section concerning the influence of studying religion at school in promoting understanding of religious and cultural difference focused on the three areas of religious difference, denominational difference and racial difference. The data demonstrate that even among those not studying RE as an examination subject, studying religion at school was rated as helpful in understanding people from other religions by 66 per cent, helpful in understanding people from other racial backgrounds by 61 per cent, and helpful in understanding people from other denominations by 45 per cent (Table 9.7). In all cases the percentages

Table 9.6 Studying religions at school

	RE %	Non-RE %	χ^2	p<
Studying religion at school has shaped my views about . . .				
Buddhists	46	33	9.71	.01
Christians	55	38	16.08	.001
Hindus	45	29	14.82	.001
Jews	46	35	7.46	.01
Muslims	53	34	18.38	.001
Sikhs	44	28	14.62	.001

Table 9.7 Understanding religious and cultural difference

	RE %	Non-RE %	χ^2	p<
Studying religion at school helps me understand people from other religions.	81	66	15.62	.001
Studying religion at school helps me understand people from other denominations.	60	45	11.13	.001
Studying religion at school helps me understand people from other racial backgrounds.	74	61	10.45	.001

were significantly higher among the RE group, where the proportions rose from 66 per cent to 81 per cent in respect of understanding people from other religions, from 61 per cent to 74 per cent in respect of understanding people from other racial backgrounds, and from 45 per cent to 60 per cent in respect of understanding people from other denominations. Here is some evidence that as an examination subject RE does work in promoting understanding of religious and cultural differences.

Theme three: living with religious diversity

The third thesis tested by the present chapter is that the two groups of students (those taking RE classes as an examination subject and those not taking RE classes as an examination subject) display no significant differences in their attitudes towards living with religious diversity. This was tested against four sets of items concerning attitudes towards religions, attitudes towards religious plurality, attitudes towards cultural diversity and attitudes towards religious distinctiveness.

Attitudes towards religions

The section on attitudes towards religions explored two themes: respect for the place of religion in society and the negative consequences of religion within society. The data demonstrate that RE students showed a significantly higher level of respect for religion, compared with non-RE students, but nonetheless retained a similar critical stance on the negative consequences of religion within society (Table 9.8). On the one hand, 71 per cent of RE students agreed that we must respect all religions, compared with 58 per cent of non-RE students, and 66 per cent of RE students agreed that all religious groups in Britain should have equal rights, compared with 56 per cent of non-RE students. On the other hand, RE students were significantly more likely to consider that religious people are often intolerant of others (42 per cent compared with 33 per cent) and not significantly less inclined to consider that religion brings more conflict than peace (45 per cent compared with 51 per cent). Here is some

Table 9.8 Attitudes towards religions

	RE %	Non-RE %	χ^2	$p<$
We must respect all religions.	71	58	9.39	.01
All religious groups in Britain should have equal rights.	66	56	5.65	.05
Religious people are often intolerant of others.	42	33	4.54	.05
Religion brings more conflict than peace.	45	51	2.06	NS

Table 9.9 Attitudes towards religious plurality

	RE %	Non-RE %	χ^2	p<
I would be happy to go out with someone from a different denomination.	62	45	16.08	.001
I would be happy to go out with someone from a different faith.	62	44	18.28	.001
I would be happy about a close relative marrying someone from a different denomination.	62	47	11.99	.001
I would be happy about a close relative marrying someone from a different faith.	67	51	14.67	.001

evidence that as an examination subject RE does work to promote respect for religious diversity.

Attitudes towards religious plurality

The section on attitudes towards religious plurality drew on the social proximity thesis to test the acceptability of close personal relationships across denominational and faith boundaries. The data demonstrate that there was a significantly more positive attitude towards religious plurality among RE students compared with non RE students (Table 9.9). The RE students were more likely to be happy to go out with someone from a different denomination (62 per cent compared with 45 per cent) or with someone from a different faith (62 per cent compared with 44 per cent). The RE students were more likely to be happy about a close relative marrying someone from a different denomination (62 per cent compared with 47 per cent) or someone from a different faith (67 per cent compared with 51 per cent). Here is some evidence that as an examination subject RE does work to provide acceptance of religious diversity.

Attitude towards cultural diversity

The section on attitudes towards cultural diversity explores awareness of and attitudes towards diversity within the local school and within the local neighbourhood. The data demonstrate that there was a (small) significantly higher level of acceptance of cultural diversity among RE students (Table 9.10). RE students were more likely than non-RE students to feel that having people from different religious backgrounds makes their school or college an interesting place (52 per cent compared with 43 per cent) or makes where they live an interesting place (43 per cent compared with 35 per cent). RE students were more likely than non-RE students to feel that people who come from

Table 9.10 Attitude towards cultural diversity

	RE %	Non-RE %	χ^2	p<
Having people from different religious backgrounds makes my school/college an interesting place.	52	43	5.02	.05
People who come from different countries make my school/college an interesting place.	54	43	6.08	.05
People from different religious backgrounds make where I live an interesting place.	43	35	3.92	.05
People who come from different countries make where I live an interesting place.	47	41	1.95	NS

Table 9.11 Attitudes towards religious distinctiveness

	RE %	Non-RE %	χ^2	p<
Christians should be allowed to wear crosses in school.	70	58	8.33	.01
Muslims should be allowed to wear the burka in school.	47	39	4.11	.05
Sikhs should be allowed to wear the turban in school.	61	51	4.89	.05
Jews should be allowed to wear the Star of David in school.	65	52	8.76	.01
Hindus should be allowed to wear the bindi in school.	58	49	4.01	.05

different countries make their school or college an interesting place (54 per cent compared with 43 per cent). RE students were not, however, significantly more likely than non-RE students to feel that people who come from different countries make where they live an interesting place (47 per cent compared with 41 per cent). Nonetheless, here is some evidence that as an examination subject RE does work to promote acceptance of cultural diversity.

Attitudes towards religious distinctiveness

The section on attitudes towards religious distinctiveness explored the acceptance of distinctive religious clothing within school across a range of faith traditions. The data demonstrate that there was a higher level of acceptance across all faith traditions by the RE students compared with the non-RE students (Table 9.11). The RE students were more likely to agree that in school Christians should be allowed to wear crosses (70 per cent compared with 58 per cent), Muslims should be allowed to wear the burka (47 per cent compared with 39 per cent), Sikhs should be allowed to wear the turban (61 per cent compared with 51 per cent), Jews should be allowed to wear the Star of David (65 per cent compared with 52 per cent), and Hindus should be allowed to wear the bindi (58 per cent compared with 49 per cent). Here is further evidence that as an examination subject RE does work to promote acceptance of religious distinctiveness.

Conclusion

This chapter, stimulated by the provocative and challenging title of Conroy's project ('Does Religious Education Work?'; Conroy et al. 2013) set out to explore from an empirical perspective one specific issue, namely whether the pursuit of RE as an examination subject worked in the sense of having an identifiable impact on the worldviews of students enrolled in the programme, thereby contributing to the common good. The issue was explored, within the context of ethos theory, by comparing a group of 279 male students in England who were engaged with RE as an examination subject with a group of 249 comparable male students who were not engaged with RE as an examination subject. To this end three specific theses were tested.

The first thesis was that the two groups of students (those taking RE classes as an examination subject and those not taking RE classes as an examination subject) display no significant differences in their religious worldviews. This thesis was supported by the data. This is a crucial finding in the sense that it suggests that the two groups of students were not differently motivated by personal religion. Consequently, if differences were to emerge between the two groups in terms of the understanding of religious diversity or attitudes towards religious diversity, such differences could not simply be attributed to greater levels of personal religiosity. In other words, there must be other influences at work.

The second thesis was that the two groups of students (those taking RE classes as an examination subject and those not taking RE classes as an examination subject) display no significant differences in their experiences of religious education in schools. This thesis was *not* supported by the data. Students in the RE classes attributed more influence to school in shaping their views about religion both in general and across each of the six main faith traditions represented in England. Students in the RE classes attributed more influence to school in helping them understand people from other religious backgrounds and from other racial backgrounds. Here is some evidence that as an examination subject RE works to promote religious understanding, to build on inclusive society and to promote community cohesion, thereby contributing to the common good.

The third thesis was that the two groups of students (those taking RE classes as an examination subject and those not taking RE classes as an examination subject) display no significant differences in their attitudes towards living with religious diversity. This thesis was *not* supported by the data. Students in the RE classes showed greater respect for religious diversity, greater acceptance of religious diversity and greater acceptance of religious distinctiveness. Here is some further evidence that as an examination subject RE works to build a society in which religious and cultural diversity is understood, embraced and welcomed, thereby contributing to the common good.

The question 'Does religious education work?' clearly receives different answers depending on the context in which the question is asked and the methodology that is employed to address the question. The empirical evidence for the present study suggests that there are indeed ways in which RE currently works in England and ways in which life in the current climate of religious diversity in England might be more fragile and more volatile if RE were to be given less serious attention and less secure resourcing.

References

Alves, C. 1968. *Religion and the Secondary School*. London: SCM.

Baumfield, V. J., J. C. Conroy, R. Davies, and D. Lundie. 2011. 'The Delphi Method: Gathering Expert Perspectives in Religious Education.' *British Journal of Religious Education* 34 (1): 5–19.

Chadwick, P. 1997. *Shifting Alliances: Church and State in English Education*. London: Cassell.

Conroy, J. C., D. Lundie, and V. Baumfield. 2012. 'Failures of Meaning in Religious Education.' *Journal of Beliefs and Values* 33 (3): 309–323.

Conroy, J. C., D. Lundie, R. A. Davis, V. Baumfield, L. P. Barnes, T. Gallagher, K. Lowden, N. Bourque, and K. Wenell. 2013. *Does Religious Education Work? A Multidimensional Investigation*. London: Bloomsbury.

Cox, E. 1967. *Sixth-form Religion*. London: SCM.

Cox, E., and J. M. Cairns. 1989. *Reforming Religious Education: The Religious Clauses of the 1988 Education Reform Act*. London: Kogan Page.

Cruickshank, M. 1963. *Church and State in English Education*. London: Macmillan.

Dent, H. J. 1947. *The Education Act 1944: Provisions, Possibilities and some Problems* (3rd ed.). London: University of London Press.

Erricker, C., J. Erricker, C. Ota, D. Sullivan, and M. Fletcher. 1997. *The Education of the Whole Child*. London: Cassell.

Francis, L. J. 1978. 'Measurement Reapplied: Research into the Child's Attitude towards Religion.' *British Journal of Religious Education* 1 (2): 45–51.

———. 1986. 'Denominational Schools and Pupil Attitude towards Christianity.' *British Educational Research Journal* 12 (2): 145–152.

———. 1987. 'The Decline in Attitude towards Religion among 8–15 Year Olds.' *Educational Studies* 13 (2): 125–134.

Francis, L. J., and G. Penny. 2013a. 'The Ethos of Anglican Secondary Schools Reflected through Pupil Values: An Empirical Enquiry among 13- to 15-Year-Olds.' In *Anglican Church School Education: Moving beyond the First Two Hundred Years*, ed. H. Worsley, 131–148. London: Continuum.

———. 2013b. 'Gender Differences in Religion.' In *Religion, Personality and Social Behaviour*, ed. V. Saroglon, 191–209. New York: Psychology Press.

Garrity, F. D. 1960. 'A Study of the Attitude of some Secondary Modern School Pupils towards Religious Education.' Unpublished M.Ed. dissertation. Manchester: University of Manchester.

Gates, B., and R. Jackson. 2014. 'Religion and Education in England.' In *Religious Education at Schools in Europe. Part 2: Western Europe*, ed. M. Rothgangel, R. Jackson, and M. Jäggle, 65–98. Vienna: Vienna University Press.

Goldman, R. J. 1964. *Religious Thinking from Childhood to Adolescence*. London: Routledge and Kegan Paul.

———. 1965. *Readiness for Religion*. London: Routledge and Kegan Paul.

Harvey, T. J. 1984. 'Gender Differences in Subject Preference and Perception of Subject Importance among Third Year Secondary School Pupils in Single-sex and Mixed Comprehensive Schools.' *Educational Studies* 10 (3): 243–253.

Hay, D., and R. Nye. 1998. *The Spirit of the Child*. London: Fount.

Hyde, K. E. 1965. *Religious Learning in Adolescence*. University of Birmingham Institute of Education, Monograph No. 7. London: Oliver and Boyd.

Jackson, R. 1997. *Religious Education: An Interpretive Approach*. London: Hodder and Stoughton.

Keys, W., and M. B. Ormerod. 1976. 'Some Factors Affecting Pupils' Subject Preferences.' *Durham Research Review* 36 (7): 1109–1115.

Lewis, E. O. 1913. 'Popular and Unpopular School Subjects.' *Journal of Experimental Pedagogy* 2: 89–98.

Loukes, H. 1961. *Teenage Religion*. London: SCM.

———. 1965. *New Ground in Christian Education*. London: SCM.

Madge, V. 1965. *Children in Search of Meaning*. London: SCM.

———. 1971. *Introducing Young Children to Jesus*. London: SCM.

Murphy, J. 1971. *Church, State and Schools in Britain 1800–1970*. London: Routledge and Kegan Paul.

Ormerod, M. B. 1975. 'Subject Preference and Choice in Co-educational and Single Sex Secondary Schools.' *British Journal of Educational Psychology* 45 (3): 257–267.

Rees, R. J. 1967. *Background and Belief*. London: SCM.

Rich, E. E. 1970. *The Education Act 1870*. London: Longmans.

Turner, E. B. 1978. 'Towards a Standardised Test of Religious Language Comprehension.' *British Journal of Religious Education* 1 (1): 14–21.

Walford, G. 2008. 'The Nature of Educational Ethnography.' In *How to Do Educational Ethnography*, ed. G. Walford, 1–15. London: Tufnell Press.

Williams, R. M., and S. Finch. 1968. *Young School Leavers*. London: HMSO.

10 Testing the 'worlds apart' thesis

Catholic and Protestant schools in Northern Ireland

Leslie J. Francis, Gemma Penny and Philip Barnes

Introduction

Writing in the *American Psychologist* in the late 1990s, Ed Cairns and John Darby (1998) described Northern Ireland as having been and as remaining a deeply divided country, politically, socially and religiously. It is the established and celebrated religious division between Catholics and Protestants that is regarded by many as the most basic and fundamental (Barnes 2005a, 2005b). This religious division is reflected in a variety of ways: in geographical location, in employment and in housing, as much as in churches and even in recreation and sport (Dunn 1995; Hargie and Dickson 2003). One of the most obvious and striking illustrations of the religious divisions within society is that of education, where the majority of schools have been in the past and remain at present religiously segregated: less than 5 per cent of the school population attend 'integrated' schools. The educational system in Northern Ireland generally distinguishes between Catholic schools and state schools, which by their nature and constitution are non-denominational, non-confessional and are, in principle, open to those of any or no religious persuasion (Greer 1988). Nevertheless, in practice, most Catholics attend Catholic schools and most Protestants attend state schools. For this reason, it is generally not thought inappropriate to speak, at least colloquially, of the division between Catholic schools and Protestant schools, and this is the practice adopted by the present chapter. The religiously segregated nature of schooling is particularly noteworthy because, unlike the divisions that result from individual and community choices, it is a division supported and funded by the state. Indeed, unlike Catholic voluntary aided schools in England and Wales, in Northern Ireland Catholic schools are *fully* funded by the state.

Although the segregated nature of education in Northern Ireland currently commands the interest of researchers, this was not always the case. In one sense, such a clearly segregated system makes the task of the empirical scientist straightforward. The two research populations are easily identified and distinguished. In another sense, however, the clarity of segregation and the highly politicized context within which the dual school system is located makes the task of the empirical scientist not only difficult but also controversial. Direct comparisons between Catholic and Protestant could be used to reinforce sectarian stereotypes or to encourage judgements of superiority and accusations of injustice. It is perhaps not surprising, therefore, that few serious attempts at comparative research and analysis have been made in this field.

A qualitative approach to the question concerning differences between Catholic and Protestant schools in Northern Ireland was initiated by Murray (1982, 1983, 1985). Murray carried out his study of two neighbouring schools, one Catholic and one Protestant, using participant observation. At a curricular level, the schools were found to be almost indistinguishable apart from the content of and approach towards religious instruction. However, at a more general cultural level, Murray found that the two separate systems of schooling reflected the two dominant cultures of the province. The two schools were, Murray suggested, 'worlds apart'.

One quantitative approach to the question was initiated by E. B. Turner (1970). In 1968, Turner carried out a study exploring attitudes towards religion among boys attending secondary schools in Belfast. This study found that the attitudes towards religion of boys at Catholic schools were significantly more positive than the attitudes of boys at Protestant schools. This was again found to be the case in 1979 when Turner repeated his study (Turner, Turner and Reid 1980), and in 1987 when L. D. Rose (1987), under Turner's guidance, carried out a further replication of the research among a sample of girls.

An alternative initiative to pioneer quantitative research exploring the religious and social worldview of students attending Catholic and Protestant schools in Northern Ireland was undertaken by John E. Greer of the University of Ulster, Coleraine, during the 1970s. In 1979, after conducting a number of smaller research projects, Greer employed the Francis Scale of Attitude toward Christianity (Francis 1978) to embark on a major investigation of the religious attitudes of a sample of students aged between 8 and 16 years attending 28 schools across Belfast (Greer 1981, 1982). This study found that, overall, students had fairly positive attitudes towards religion, but that attitudes declined steadily for the whole sample from the sixth year of primary school to the fourth year of secondary school. From the seventh year of primary school to the fourth year of secondary school, students attending Catholic schools were significantly more favourable towards religion than students attending Protestant schools. Other findings revealed that students attending Catholic schools were much more inclined to believe in God and to attend church regularly than students attending Protestant schools. These results supported the earlier conclusion reached by Turner (1970; Turner, Turner and Reid 1980) that students attending Catholic schools in Northern Ireland were significantly more religious than comparable students attending Protestant schools.

Intrigued by his original findings and recognizing the potential of comparative research, Greer decided to build on his 1979 study in two different ways. First, he initiated a series of studies to replicate his earlier research in order to produce an ongoing profile of students' attitudes towards religion in Northern Ireland (Francis and Greer 1990, 1999). Second, he broadened his research focus beyond a concern for attitude towards religion to include a range of indicators of religious beliefs, practices and moral judgements. It is research of this type with which the present chapter is concerned. In 1984 Greer administered a broad-ranging questionnaire throughout 10 Protestant and 10 Catholic schools to one form four, one form five and one form six class in each school. A total of 1,177 students participated: 606 in Protestant schools (292 boys and 314 girls) and 571 in Catholic schools (254 boys and 317 girls). The findings indicated significant and consistent differences in the religious profiles of the two denominational groups, but not complete contrast (see Greer and Francis 1990).

In 1998 efforts were made to replicate and to extend Greer's original 1984 study in order to examine whether differences between the two religious communities, detected specifically in respect of attitude towards Christianity, were persisting over time and were reflected more generally over a wider range of indices. On this occasion, a random sample of seven Protestant and nine Catholic schools in Northern Ireland were invited to administer a survey among their lower and upper sixth-form students. Thoroughly completed questionnaires were submitted by 2,369 students: 1,099 attending Protestant schools and 1,270 attending Catholic schools. The eight-page questionnaire was based on an instrument designed originally by Greer (1972) for use among students attending Protestant schools. The questions reflected the following areas: religious practice, including public church attendance, personal prayer and personal Bible reading; religious beliefs, including beliefs about God, Jesus, the Bible and life after death; moral values, including gambling, drunkenness, smoking, lying, stealing, sexual intercourse before marriage, capital punishment, suicide, war, use of nuclear weapons, colour prejudice and religious discrimination; and the social role of the Church, including influence over politics, morality and social problems. The data from this study led to four main conclusions (Francis et al. 2006).

First, in terms of religious practice, church attendance and Bible reading assumed different importance in the two communities. On the one hand, church attendance played a more important part in the Catholic community than in the Protestant community. Through church attendance Catholics were more open to being shaped by the culture of public liturgy and sacramental worship. On the other hand, the Bible played a more important part in the Protestant community than in the Catholic community. Through attention to Bible-reading Protestants were more open to being shaped by the authority and imagery of scripture.

Second, Protestants and Catholics seemed to nurture somewhat different beliefs about the nature of God, as reflected, for example, in their understandings of life after death. Catholics were more inclined to cherish a loving image of God concerned with rewarding believers after death, while Protestants were more inclined to cherish a judging image of God concerned with punishing unbelievers after death.

Third, Protestants and Catholics seemed to inhabit somewhat different moral universes, which in turn may reflect somewhat different understandings of the moral values espoused by their God. The God of the Protestant community seemed to be more against gambling, drunkenness, smoking, lying, stealing and sexual intercourse before marriage. The God of the Catholic community seemed to be more against capital punishment, war, the use of nuclear weapons, colour prejudice and religious discrimination. In broad terms it would seem that the Protestant moral universe is chiefly focused on personal ethics, whereas the Catholic moral universe is more focused on social ethics.

Fourth, Protestants and Catholics held somewhat different views on the Church's continuing influence on aspects of social life. Overall, the Catholic community was less sympathetic towards the Church's influence over morals and politics and more sympathetic towards the Church's involvement in social issues and the resolution of social problems.

Working within the research tradition established by Greer, more recently Mandy Robbins and Leslie Francis (2008) extended the Teenage Religion and Values Survey developed by Francis (2001) to Northern Ireland. Using this instrument, Robbins and Francis (2008) compared the responses of 712 male students attending Catholic schools with the responses of 873 male students attending Protestant schools across the following eight areas: religious beliefs, paranormal beliefs, church-related attitudes, attitudes towards sex and family life, law-related attitudes, school-related attitudes, locality-related attitudes, and personal anxiety and depression. Their data demonstrated significant differences between the two communities across all eight areas, thus sustaining the worlds apart thesis.

In terms of religious beliefs, Catholic students were significantly more likely than Protestant students to hold traditional beliefs: to believe in God (86 per cent compared with 72 per cent), to believe Jesus really rose from the dead (77 per cent compared with 65 per cent) and to believe in life after death (65 per cent compared with 58 per cent).

In terms of paranormal beliefs, Catholic students were significantly more likely than Protestant students to hold such beliefs: to believe in their horoscope (24 per cent compared with 15 per cent), to believe that fortune-tellers can tell the future (14 per cent compared with 11 per cent) and to believe that it is possible to contact the spirits of the dead (24 per cent compared with 19 per cent).

In terms of church-related attitudes, Catholic students were significantly more likely than Protestant students to be positive towards the church: to want their children to be baptized/christened in church (88 per cent compared with 69 per cent), to maintain that religious education should be taught in schools (78 per cent compared with 61 per cent) and to feel that Christian ministers/ priests do a good job (64 per cent compared with 56 per cent). It should be noted, however, that these statistics reflect attitudes that existed before revelations about sex scandals in the church were widely known, publicized and discussed.

In terms of attitudes concerning sex and family life, Catholic students were significantly more likely than Protestant students to hold a traditional perspective: to maintain that contraception is wrong (18 per cent compared with 14 per cent), to maintain that abortion is wrong (71 per cent compared with 52 per cent) and to maintain that divorce is wrong (45 per cent compared with 33 per cent).

In terms of law-related attitudes, Catholic students were significantly more likely than Protestant students to disregard the law: to maintain there is nothing wrong in travelling without a ticket (28 per cent compared with 21 per cent), to maintain that there is nothing wrong in buying cigarettes under the legal age (26 per cent compared with 20 per cent) and to maintain that there is nothing wrong in buying alcoholic drinks under the legal age (37 per cent compared with 32 per cent).

In terms of school-related attitudes, Catholic students were significantly less likely than Protestant students to endorse positive views: to report that they feel happy in school (57 per cent compared with 70 per cent). Young Catholics were also more likely to report negative views: to feel worried about being bullied at school (38 per cent compared with 29 per cent).

In terms of locality-related attitudes, Catholic students were significantly more likely than Protestant students to report negative attitudes: to feel that drug-taking is a growing problem in their area (33 per cent compared with 19 per cent), to feel that drunks are a growing problem in their area (37 per cent compared with 31 per cent) and to feel that unemployment is a growing problem in their area (25 per cent compared with 19 per cent).

In terms of anxiety and depression, Catholic students were significantly more likely than Protestant students to report negative feelings: to be worried about getting AIDS (62 per cent compared with 54 per cent), to feel often depressed (50 per cent compared with 43 per cent) and to have considered taking their own life (26 per cent compared with 20 per cent).

In a second article drawing on data from the Teenage Religion and Values Survey in Northern Ireland, Robbins (2012) compared the responses of 682 female students attending Catholic schools with the responses of 832 female students attending Protestant schools across all 15 areas covered by the survey, including: personal wellbeing, worries, counselling, school, work, religious beliefs, church and society, the supernatural, politics, social concerns, sexual morality, substance abuse, right and wrong, leisure, and my area. On the basis of this detailed analysis, Robbins concluded that there were significant similarities in aspects of the worldviews of young women shaped within Catholic schools and of young women shaped within Protestant schools as well as wide-ranging differences. Engaging with Murray's thesis advanced in the 1980s that the students educated in these two types of school are worlds apart (Murray 1982, 1983, 1985), Robbins concluded: 'While in some ways young women remain "worlds apart"; in other ways they inhabit the common universe of adolescent experiences' (2012, 171).

Research question

Against this background, the aim of the present chapter is to draw on the Young People's Attitudes to Religious Diversity project to examine the extent to which young people living in Northern Ireland today remain worlds apart or the extent to which they inhabit the common universe of adolescent experience, drawing on the vocabulary proposed by Robbins (2012). The present study advances knowledge beyond Robbins's study in three ways. Although only recently published, Robbins's data were collected in the early 2000s; the present data were collected during 2011 and 2012. Robbins's data drew on the general values map proposed by Francis (2001); the present study focuses on some issues more directly relevant to the theme of religious diversity. Robbins profiled the views of female students; the present study profiles the views of male students.

Method

Procedure

As part of a large multi-method project on religious diversity designed to examine the experiences and attitudes of young people living in the multicultural and multi-faith context of the UK, classes of Year 10 and Year 11 students in Northern Ireland (13 to 15 years of age) were invited to complete a questionnaire survey during 2011 and 2012. The participants were guaranteed confidentiality and anonymity and were given the choice not to take part in the survey. The level of interest shown in the project meant that very few students decided not to participate. The sampling frame set out to capture data from around 2,000 students in Northern Ireland, with half attending Catholic schools within the state-maintained sector and half attending Protestant schools within the state-maintained sector.

Instrument

The *Religious Diversity and Young People* survey was designed for self-completion, using mainly multiple-choice questions and Likert scaling on 5 points: agree strongly, agree, not certain, disagree and disagree strongly. In the present analysis, 10 groups of items were identified from the instrument to map the following areas: attitudes towards religion, attitudes towards Protestants, attitudes towards Catholics, shaping views about Protestants, shaping views about Catholics, accepting religious plurality, living with religious plurality, living with cultural diversity, studying religion in school and accepting religious clothing worn in school.

Participants

In Northern Ireland, completed questionnaires were submitted by 888 male students, 452 attending Catholic schools and 436 attending Protestant schools.

Analysis

The data were analyzed by means of SPSS, employing chi square in 2 × 2 contingency tables, combining the 'agree strongly' and 'agree' responses into one category and the 'disagree strongly', 'disagree' and 'not certain' responses into the second category. Throughout the following analysis and commentary, the short-hand is applied consistently of referring to students attending Catholic schools as Catholic students and of referring to students attending Protestant schools as Protestant students.

Results

Attitudes towards religion

The analysis begins by examining students' overall attitude towards religion by exploring two themes: their impression of the place of religion and religious people in political and social life and their support for religious diversity. On these issues the data demonstrate more consensus than difference between the two religious groups (Table 10.1). Similar proportions of Catholic students and Protestant students take the view that religion brings more conflict than peace (60 per cent and 54 per cent) and that religious people are often intolerant of others (47 per cent and 46 per cent). Similar proportions of Catholic students and Protestant students agree that we must respect all religions (73 per cent and 69 per cent). However, Protestant students are significantly less likely than Catholic students to maintain that all religious groups should have equal rights (64 per cent compared with 72 per cent).

Attitudes towards Protestants

Attitudes towards Protestants were assessed by four items, three expressing positive attitudes and one expressing a negative attitude. Overall, the data demonstrate that Catholic students are less likely than Protestant students to endorse the positive items but are not more likely to endorse the negative item (Table 10.2). In terms of the positive items, while 86 per cent of Protestant students have friends who are Protestants, the proportion falls to 73 per cent among Catholic students. While 45 per cent of Protestant students are interested in finding out about Protestants, the proportion falls to 35 per cent among Catholic students. While 56 per cent of Protestant students feel that a lot of good is done in the world by Protestants, the proportion falls to 46 per

Table 10.1 Attitudes towards religion

	Cath %	Prot %	χ^2	p<
Religion brings more conflict than peace.	60	54	2.62	NS
Religious people are often intolerant of others.	47	46	0.01	NS
We must respect all religions.	73	69	2.33	NS
All religious groups in Britain should have equal rights.	72	64	6.40	.01

Table 10.2 Attitudes towards Protestants

	Cath %	Prot %	χ^2	p<
I have friends who are Protestants.	73	86	23.14	.001
I am interested in finding out about Protestants.	35	45	9.25	.01
A lot of good is done in the world by Protestants.	46	56	7.99	.01
A lot of harm is done in the world by Protestants.	42	39	0.99	NS

Table 10.3 Attitudes towards Catholics

	Cath %	Prot %	χ^2	p<
I have friends who are Catholics.	89	76	25.56	.001
I am interested in finding out about Catholics.	48	38	7.77	.01
A lot of good is done in the world by Catholics.	62	44	30.04	.001
A lot of harm is done in the world by Catholics.	31	46	20.19	.001

cent among Catholic students. In terms of the negative item, 39 per cent of Protestant students feel that a lot of harm is done in the world by Protestants, as do 42 per cent of Catholic students.

Attitudes towards Catholics

Attitudes towards Catholics were assessed by the same four items employed to assess attitudes towards Protestants. The figures in the two tables (Table 10.2 and Table 10.3) mirror each other in terms of the positive items, but not in terms of the negative item. The data demonstrate that Protestant students are less likely than Catholic students to endorse the positive items, but are more likely to endorse the negative item. In terms of the positive items, while 76 per cent of Protestant students have friends who are Catholics, the proportion rises to 89 per cent among Catholic students. While 38 per cent of Protestant students are interested in finding out about Catholics, the proportion rises to 48 per cent among Catholic students. While 44 per cent of Protestant students feel that a lot of good is done in the world by Catholics, the proportion rises to 62 per cent among Catholic students. At the same time, Protestant students are more likely to endorse the negative item: 46 per cent of Protestant students feel that a lot of harm is done in the world by Catholics, compared with 31 per cent of Catholic students.

Table 10.4 Shaping views about Protestants

	Cath %	Prot %	χ^2	$p<$
My views about Protestants have been influenced by . . .				
friends	50	45	3.15	NS
my father	43	41	0.31	NS
my mother	39	44	2.17	NS
television	43	33	10.07	.01
Internet	30	21	8.90	.01
studying religion at school	68	45	49.58	.001

Shaping views about Protestants

The next issue explored by the study concerns students' perception of the factors that have shaped their views about Protestants. Protestant students' perception of what has shaped their views about their own religious group give equal weight to the influences of school, friends, father and mother (each of which are rated between 41 per cent and 45 per cent). Less weight is given to television (33 per cent) and to the Internet (21 per cent). The data also demonstrate (Table 10.4) that there are no significant differences in the proportions of Catholic students and Protestant students who rate the influence of friends (50 per cent and 45 per cent), father (43 per cent and 41 per cent) and mother (39 per cent and 44 per cent). On the other hand, Catholic students are more likely than Protestant students to feel that their views on Protestants have been influenced by television (43 per cent compared with 33 per cent), by the Internet (30 per cent compared with 21 per cent) and by studying religion at school (68 per cent compared with 45 per cent).

Shaping views about Catholics

Students' perceptions of the factors that shaped their views about Catholics were assessed by the same six themes employed to assess the factors that shaped views about Protestants. The data demonstrate that Catholic students rate each of these six factors more highly than Protestant students (Table 10.5). Thus, 57 per cent of Catholic students feel that their views about Catholics have been influenced by their mother, compared with 37 per cent of Protestant students. The comparisons for the influence of father is 54 per cent and 36 per cent, for the influence of friends 49 per cent and 36 per cent, for the influence of television 45 per cent and 33 per cent, for the influence of the Internet 32 per cent and 19 per cent and for the influence of studying religion at school 71 per cent and 46 per cent. It is this final comparison that emphasizes the role of Catholic schools in shaping their students' views about Catholics themselves.

Table 10.5 Shaping views about Catholics

	Cath %	Prot %	χ^2	p<
My views about Catholics have been influenced by . . .				
friends	49	36	17.25	.001
my father	54	36	27.51	.001
my mother	57	37	36.22	.001
television	45	33	13.65	.001
Internet	32	19	21.17	.001
studying religion at school	71	46	58.89	.001

Table 10.6 Accepting religious plurality

	Cath %	Prot %	χ^2	p<
I would be happy to go out with someone from a different denomination.	68	62	3.50	NS
I would be happy about a close relative marrying someone from a different denomination.	62	54	6.58	.01
Where I live there is a lot of discrimination again Catholics.	46	50	1.74	NS
Where I live there is a lot of discrimination against Protestants.	55	30	57.94	.001

Accepting religious plurality

Attitudes towards religious plurality were assessed by exploring two themes: perception of the levels of religious discrimination in the students' locality and students' willingness to embrace close relationships with individuals from a different denomination. The data demonstrate that on these issues there are both similarities within and differences between the attitudes of Catholic students and Protestant students (Table 10.6). In terms of perceived levels of discrimination, Catholic students and Protestant students perceive similar levels of discrimination against Catholics, but dissimilar levels of discrimination against Protestants. Thus 46 per cent of Catholic students and 50 per cent of Protestant students feel that, where they live, there is a lot of discrimination against Catholics. However, while 55 per cent of Catholic students feel that there is a lot of discrimination against Protestants, the proportion falls to 30 per cent among Protestant students. In terms of willingness to embrace close relationships with individuals from a different denomination, there are no significant differences between

Catholic students and Protestant students regarding the acceptance of personal relationships, although there are significant differences regarding acceptance of familial relationships. Thus 68 per cent of Catholic students and 62 per cent of Protestant students would be happy to go out with someone from a different denomination. However, while 62 per cent of Catholic students would be happy about a close relative marrying someone from a different denomination, the proportion falls to 54 per cent among Protestant students.

Living with religious plurality

The experience of living with plurality was assessed by three items, exploring cultural differences, ethnic differences and religious differences. The data showed no significant differences in the responses of Catholic students and Protestant students to these items (Table 10.7). Thus 44 per cent of Catholic students and 40 per cent of Protestant students considered that, where they live, people who come from different countries get on well together. There was a slightly less positive view on religious differences, but again there were no significant differences between Catholic students and Protestant students. Thus 34 per cent of Catholic students and 37 per cent of Protestant students considered that, where they live, people from religious backgrounds get on well together. Similarly, 32 per cent of Catholic students and 37 per cent of Protestant students considered that, where they live, people respect religious differences.

Living with cultural diversity

In order to focus in closer detail on students' perceptions of the contribution made by diversity to their own environment, two further questions were raised about the students' school and two further questions were raised about the students' locality. The data demonstrated that there were no significant differences in the perceptions of Catholic students and Protestant students regarding their locality, but there were significant differences between the two groups regarding their schools (Table 10.8). In terms of locality, 43 per cent of Catholic

Table 10.7 Living with religious plurality

	Cath %	Prot %	χ^2	$p<$
Where I live, people who come from different countries get on well together.	44	40	1.08	NS
Where I live, people from different religious backgrounds get on well together.	34	37	0.67	NS
Where I live, people respect religious differences.	32	37	1.90	NS

Table 10.8 Living with cultural diversity

	Cath %	Prot %	χ^2	$p<$
People who come from different countries make where I live an interesting place.	43	42	0.18	NS
People from different religious backgrounds make where I live an interesting place.	37	40	0.95	NS
People who come from different countries make my school/college an interesting place.	43	48	1.35	NS
Having people from different religious backgrounds makes my school/college an interesting place.	47	56	7.64	.01

students and 42 per cent of Protestant students feel that people who come from different countries make where they live an interesting place; 37 per cent of Catholic students and 40 per cent of Protestant students feel that people from different religious backgrounds make where they live an interesting place. In terms of school, 43 per cent of Catholic students and 48 per cent of Protestant students feel that people who come from different countries make their school or college an interesting place. However, while 56 per cent of Protestant students feel that people from different religious backgrounds make their school or college an interesting place, the proportion falls to 47 per cent among Catholic students.

Studying religion in school

Religious education in schools in Northern Ireland is concerned with religious diversity in a much broader sense than that concerned with Protestants and Catholics. The next stage of the study was concerned with assessing the extent to which students' perceived the influence of studying religion in school as shaping their views about the six main religious traditions represented in the UK: Buddhism, Christianity, Hinduism, Islam, Judaism and Sikhism. The data demonstrated that there are some significant differences between the experiences of Catholic students and Protestant students (Table 10.9). In terms of three of the religions, students in the two types of schools seem to experience the same level of influence, namely Buddhism, Hinduism and Sikhism. In terms of all three Abrahamic religions, however, students in Catholic schools seem to experience a higher level of influence. Thus, 33 per cent of Catholic students and 35 per cent of Protestant students feel that studying religion at school has shaped their views about Buddhists, 30 per cent of Catholic students and 31 per cent of Protestant students feel that studying religion at school has shaped their views about Hindus, and

Table 10.9 Studying religion in school

	Cath %	Prot %	χ^2	$p<$
Studying religion at school has shaped my views about . . .				
Buddhists	33	35	0.28	NS
Christians	67	51	25.89	.001
Hindus	30	31	0.25	NS
Jews	61	40	39.76	.001
Muslims	51	37	15.87	.001
Sikhs	20	16	2.83	NS

20 per cent of Catholic students and 16 per cent of Protestant students feel that studying religion at school has shaped their views about Sikhs. The situation regarding the Abrahamic religions, however, is different. While 67 per cent of Catholic students feel that studying religion at school has shaped their views about Christians, the proportion falls to 51 per cent among Protestant students. While 61 per cent of Catholic students feel that studying religion at school has shaped their views about Jews, the proportion falls to 40 per cent among Protestant students. While 51 per cent of Catholic students feel that studying religion at school has shaped their views about Muslims, the proportion falls to 37 per cent among Protestant students. This difference may reflect the fact that the textbooks required by the Catholic Church to be used in schools includes (compulsory) material on Islam and Judaism. By contrast, state Protestant schools do not use religiously approved textbooks and the diversity of curriculum content that results can mean that Islam and Judaism receive limited or very little coverage (it may be that some state schools do not study religions other than Christianity).

Accepting religious clothing

One way of assessing attitudes towards the six religious traditions is to explore students' views regarding the acceptability of distinctive religious clothing in school. These attitudes were explored in respect of the Christian cross, the Hindu bindi, the Jewish kippah/yarmulke, the Muslim burka and the Sikh turban. The data demonstrated that Catholic students are significantly more open than Protestant students to all six religious groups being allowed to wear religious clothing in school (Table 10.10). Thus 68 per cent of Catholic students and 57 per cent of Protestant students agreed that Christians should be allowed to wear crosses in school. The same pattern persisted in respect of the Hindu bindi (59 per cent and 46 per cent), the Jewish kippah/yarmulke (59 per cent and 49 per cent), the Muslim burka (58 per cent and 44 per cent) and the Sikh turban (62 per cent and 49 per cent).

Table 10.10 Accepting religious clothing

	Cath %	Prot %	χ^2	p<
Christians should be allowed to wear crosses in school.	68	57	11.55	.001
Hindus should be allowed to wear the bindi in school.	59	46	14.98	.001
Jews should be allowed to wear the kippah/ yarmulke in school.	59	49	9.33	.01
Muslims should be allowed to wear the burka in school.	58	44	18.36	.001
Sikhs should be allowed to wear the turban in school.	62	49	14.88	.001

Conclusion

In order to test the 'worlds apart' thesis, the present study set out to build on a small but significant stream of quantitative research concerned with profiling and comparing the worldviews of students attending Catholic and Protestant secondary schools in Northern Ireland. This research tradition was pioneered by John Greer in the 1970s (Greer 1981, 1982; Francis and Greer 1990, 1999; Greer and Francis 1990) and continued more recently by studies reported by Francis et al. (2006), Robbins and Francis (2008) and Robbins (2012). Building on this research tradition, the present study extended previous work by focusing specifically on areas concerned with religious diversity and by testing Robbins's (2012) thesis that there is much in common between the worldviews of two groups of Catholic and Protestant students and that there are some significant differences. In her study Robbins (2012) concluded that in some areas the students were worlds apart, yet in other areas 'they inhabit the common universe of adolescent experience.'

The present study identified 10 areas relevant to exploring religious diversity and appropriate for profiling and comparing the views of students attending Catholic schools and students attending Protestant schools. These areas were defined as follows: attitudes towards religion, attitudes towards Protestants, attitudes towards Catholics, shaping views about Protestants, shaping views about Catholics, accepting religious plurality, living with religious plurality, living with cultural diversity, studying religion in school and accepting religious clothing worn in school. Overall, the evidence drawn from across these 10 areas supports Robbins's contention that, in spite of there being some commonality between the experiences and worldviews of students educated in Catholic secondary schools and students educated in Protestant secondary schools, there remain some significant differences between the two groups. The most important differences that can still support the 'worlds apart' thesis arise in four areas.

First, Catholic students and Protestant students see themselves in a significantly different way from the way in which they are perceived by the other group of students. Protestants have a more positive image of themselves compared to the image of Protestants held by Catholics. Catholics have a more positive image of themselves compared to the image of Catholics held by Protestants.

Second, school plays a more important part in shaping the views of Catholic students concerning both Catholics and Protestants than is the case for Protestant students. Both television and the Internet also play a more important part in shaping views of Catholics and Protestants for Catholic students than for Protestant students.

Third, Catholic students feel that their schools have a greater influence, compared with Protestant students, on shaping their views not only on Christianity, but also on the other Abrahamic religions, Islam and Judaism. This difference does not extend further, however, to influence views on Buddhism, Hinduism and Sikhism.

Fourth, Catholic students are significantly more positive than Protestant students in accepting outward signs of religious clothing in school. The greater acceptance of Catholic students to the Christian cross is extended to greater acceptance of the Hindu bindi, the Jewish kippah/yarmulke, the Muslim burka and the Sikh turban.

The present study has provided a profile of attitudes towards religion and attitudes towards religious diversity among students attending Protestant schools and Catholic schools in Northern Ireland during 2011 and 2012. In order to provide a sharp focus to the analysis, the data have been confined to one sex (males) and to a narrow age range (Year 10 and Year 11 classes). The current analyses are now worth extending to female students and the data collection is worth extending across a wider age range. Given both the continuing importance of religious diversity in Northern Ireland and the current climate of religious and social change, there is also every value in replicating this study in the not-too-distant future in order to monitor the changing responses of young people to religious diversity.

References

Barnes, L. P. 2005a. 'Religion, Education and Conflict in Northern Ireland.' *Journal of Beliefs and Values* 26 (2): 123–138.
———. 2005b. 'Was the Northern Irish Conflict Religious?' *Journal of Contemporary Religion* 20 (1): 53–67.
Cairns, E., and J. Darby. 1998. 'The Conflict in Northern Ireland: Causes, Consequences and Controls.' *American Psychologist* 53 (7): 754–760.
Dunn, S. 1995. *Facets of the Conflict in Northern Ireland.* London: Macmillan.
Francis, L. J. 1978. 'Attitude and Longitude: A study in Measurement.' *Character Potential* 8: 119–130.
———. 2001. *The Values Debate: A Voice from the Pupils.* London: Woburn Press.
Francis, L. J., and J. E. Greer. 1990. 'Measuring Attitudes towards Christianity among Pupils in Protestant Secondary Schools in Northern Ireland.' *Personality and Individual Differences* 11 (8): 853–856.
———. 1999. 'Attitude toward Christianity among Secondary Pupils in Northern Ireland: Persistence of Denominational Differences?' *British Journal of Religious Education* 21 (3): 175–180.

Francis, L. J., M. Robbins, L.P Barnes, and C. A. Lewis. 2006. 'Religiously Affiliated Schools in Northern Ireland: The Persistence of Denominational Differences in Pupils' Religious and Moral Values.' *Journal of Empirical Theology* 19 (2): 182–202.

Greer, J. E. 1972. 'Sixth-form Religion in Northern Ireland.' *Social Studies* 1: 325–340.

———. 1981. 'Religious Attitudes and Thinking in Belfast Pupils.' *Educational Research* 23 (3): 177–189.

———. 1982. 'Growing up in Belfast: A Study of Religious Development.' *Collected Original Resources in Education* 6 (1): fiche 1, A14.

———. 1988. 'The Churches and Educational Provision in Northern Ireland.' In *Christian Education in a Pluralist Society*, ed. V. A. McClelland, 135–159. London: Routledge.

Greer, J. E., and L. J. Francis. 1990. 'The Religious Profile of Pupils in Northern Ireland: A Comparative Study of Pupils Attending Catholic and Protestant Secondary Schools.' *Journal of Empirical Theology* 3 (2): 35–50.

Hargie, O., and D. Dickson. 2003. *Researching the Troubles: Social Science Perspectives on the Northern Ireland Conflict*. Edinburgh: Mainstream.

Murray, D. 1982. *A Comparative Study of the Culture and Character of Protestant and Catholic Primary Schools in Northern Ireland*. Unpublished DPhil dissertation. Ulster: New University of Ulster.

———. 1983. 'Schools and Conflict.' In *Northern Ireland: The Background to the Conflict*, ed. J. Darby, 136–150. Belfast: Appletree Press.

———. 1985. *Worlds Apart: Segregated Schools in Northern Ireland*. Belfast: Appletree Press.

Robbins, M. 2012. 'Denominational Identity and Cultural Heritage: A Study among Adolescents Attending Protestant and Catholic Secondary Schools in Northern Ireland.' In *Religious Identity and National Heritage: Empirical Theological Perspectives*, ed. F.-V. Anthony and H.-G. Ziebertz, 171–193. Leiden: Brill.

Robbins, M., and L. J. Francis. 2008. 'Still Worlds Apart: The Worldviews of Adolescent Males Attending Protestant and Catholic Secondary Schools in Northern Ireland.' *Research in Education* 80 (1): 26–36.

Rose, L. D. 1987. *A Comparative Analysis of the Religious Attitudes of Adolescents in a State Controlled and Church Controlled School in Northern Ireland and France*. Unpublished BEd dissertation. Belfast: The Queen's University of Belfast.

Turner, E. B. 1970. *Religious Understanding and Religious Attitudes in Male Urban Adolescents*. Unpublished PhD dissertation. Belfast: Queen's University of Belfast.

Turner, E. B., I. F. Turner, and A. Reid. 1980. 'Religious Attitudes in Two Types of Urban Secondary Schools: A Decade of Change?' *Irish Journal of Education* 14: 43–52.

11 Growing up Catholic in Scotland

Not one Catholic community but three

Leslie J. Francis, Gemma Penny and Peter Neil

Introduction

Growing up Catholic in England and Wales and in Scotland has meant being part of a religious community outside of the Established Church. As a consequence of Reformation history in England and Wales, the Established Church was the Church of England (Reformed and Episcopal) and in Scotland the Church of Scotland (Reformed and Presbyterian). Many social and educational consequences of this history survived through the twentieth century (Hornsby-Smith 1978, 1987, 1991, 1999).

The introduction of a religious question into the national censuses for England and Wales and for Scotland for the first time in 2001 allowed data on the religious profile of the population to be reported in the same way as a range of other areas of social significance (see Aspinall 2000; Weller 2004; Sherif 2011). Unlike England and Wales, however, the census question on religion in Scotland allowed the Christian response to be subdivided into denominational categories. The precise question asked in the census in Scotland was: 'What religion, religious denomination or body do you belong to?' As in England and Wales, the question was voluntary. The data from the 2001 census demonstrated that overall 16 per cent of the population in Scotland self-identified as Catholic. There were very significant regional variations, with the highest concentration in Inverclyde (38 per cent), North Lanarkshire (27 per cent), West Dunbartonshire (36 per cent), Glasgow City (34 per cent), Renfrewshire (25 per cent), East Dunbartonshire (24 per cent), South Lanarkshire (24 per cent) and East Renfrewshire (22 per cent).

The 2011 census for Scotland showed little overall change in the proportion of the population who self-identified as Catholic (16 per cent) and the regional variations also remained fairly constant. Regions with greater numbers of Catholics included North Lanarkshire (35 per cent), West Dunbartonshire (33 per cent), Glasgow City (27 per cent), East Dunbartonshire (22 per cent) and South Lanarkshire (22 per cent). Regions with smaller Catholic communities included the Orkney Islands (3 per cent), Shetland Islands (4 per cent), Aberdeenshire (5 per cent) and the Scottish borders (6 per cent).

One of the main justifications for including the religious question within the 2001 census for England and Wales and for Scotland was the argument that religious identity is a matter of public significance (Francis 2003) in the sense that self-assigned religious affiliation, like ethnicity, may serve as a significant predictor of social and personal differences. This is a thesis that can be tested, to some extent, by the exploration of the connection between religious identity and a range of social and personal attitudes. The British Social Attitudes Survey provides one mechanism for exploring this issue with specific reference to those who self-identify as Catholics.

The most thorough and sustained exploration of the British Social Attitudes Survey to explore the connection between religious identity and social and personal attitudes is still provided by Robin Gill (1999). Subsequent analyses have continued to illustrate a range of ways in which a distinctive profile emerges among Catholics both in comparison with non-affiliates and in comparison with members of other denominations. For example, Anne Barlow, Simon Duncan, Grace James and Alison Park (2001) found a significant association between religious affiliation and cohabitation. While 14 per cent of non-affiliates were cohabiting, the proportions fell to 8 per cent among Catholics, 7 per cent among Anglicans, 5 per cent among other Christians and 2 per cent among those affiliated with non-Christian traditions. While 66 per cent of other Christians, 65 per cent of Anglicans and 55 per cent of Catholics took the view that people who want children ought to get married, the proportion fell to 38 per cent among non-affiliates. Leslie Francis (2003) found a significant association between religious affiliation and participation within altruistic voluntary groups. While 21 per cent of non-affiliates claimed such participation, the proportions rose to 25 per cent among Catholics and 34 per cent among Anglicans.

More recently Alison Park and Rebecca Rhead (2013) drew on British Social Attitudes Survey data to chart the changing profile of the connection between religious affiliation and attitudes towards sex, marriage and parenthood. According to this analysis, the proportions of Catholics who said that premarital sex is always or mostly wrong fell from 32 per cent in 1983 to 26 per cent in 1993, 16 per cent in 2003 and 11 per cent in 2012. For non-affiliates, the proportions fell from 11 per cent in 1983 to 5 per cent in 1993, 5 per cent in 2003 and 2 per cent in 2012.

Teenage religions and values survey

Although the British Social Attitudes Survey holds good potential for illuminating the social significance of religious affiliation, the major drawback with this source concerns the number of participants interviewed each year (for example 3,248 in 2012). For this reason denominational groups within the sample remain quite small. The Teenage Religion and Values Survey was designed in the 1990s to address this weakness by developing a database of sufficient size to bring religious minorities into clear visibility (34,000 cases). The project concentrated on 13- to 15-year-old students for two reasons: one pragmatic and one strategic. Pragmatically, it was possible to generate a representative sample of this age group through schools at relatively low cost. Strategically, it was argued that the toughest test for the continuing social significance of religion would be among young people where the effects of secularization may be most pronounced.

The Teenage Religion and Values Survey was introduced by Francis (2001a) in *The Values Debate*. Subsequently the data are analyzed in four papers specifically exploring the connection between religious affiliation and personal and social attitudes (Francis 2001b, 2001c, 2008a, 2008b). Taken together these four papers provided insight into what it meant to be growing up Catholic in England and Wales in the 1990s. Concentrating specifically on female students, Francis (2008a, 2008b) found significant differences between Catholics and non-affiliated young people across the six areas of personal wellbeing, personal worries, personal support, social awareness, views on sex and views on substances.

In terms of personal wellbeing, Catholic students were more likely than non-affiliated students to report that they felt their life had a sense of purpose (63 per cent compared with 50 per cent) and less likely to report that they had sometimes considered taking their own life (29 per cent compared with 32 per cent). In spite of higher levels of overall personal wellbeing, Catholic students were more likely to experience some social insecurities. They were more likely to worry about being bullied at school (33 per cent compared with 29 per cent) and more likely to worry about their attractiveness to the opposite sex (43 per cent compared with 39 per cent). Catholic students were more likely to experience personal support at home. They were more likely to find it helpful to talk about problems with their mother (58 per cent compared with 55 per cent) and with their father (26 per cent compared with 23 per cent).

In terms of social awareness, Catholic students were more likely than non-affiliated students to show concern for the environment and for world development. Thus 67 per cent of Catholic students were concerned about the risk of pollution to the environment, compared with 63 per cent of non-affiliated students. Similarly, 77 per cent of Catholic students were concerned about the poverty of the third world, compared with 60 per cent of non-affiliated students.

Overall Catholic students held somewhat more conservative views than non-affiliated students on sex. Thus 14 per cent of Catholics considered sexual intercourse outside marriage as wrong, compared with 9 per cent of non-affiliated students; 19 per cent of Catholics considered divorce as wrong, compared with 13 per cent of non-affiliated students; and 53 per cent of Catholics considered abortion as wrong compared with 38 per cent of non-affiliated students. On the other hand, Catholic students did not differ greatly from non-affiliated students in their views on tobacco and alcohol. Thus, 15 per cent of non-affiliated students considered it is wrong to become drunk and so did 17 per cent of

Catholics; 35 per cent of non-affiliated students considered it is wrong to smoke cigarettes and so did 35 per cent of Catholics.

Catholic identities

Although self-assigned religious affiliation as Catholic by itself provides significant predictive power in respect of a range of individual differences of personal and social importance, religious affiliation by itself is properly seen to be an inadequate (or even suspect) indicator of religiosity (Voas and Bruce 2004). According to some commentators, self-assigned religious affiliation may be construed fully as an indicator of cultural identity (see Fane 1999), while for other commentators this cultural identity continues to encase attitudes and values rooted in the religious tradition (see Bibby 1985, 1987). It is for such reasons that the social scientific study of religion often takes religious practice (worship attendance) into account alongside religious affiliation in order to generate a more nuanced account of religious identity.

Following earlier evidence marshalled by Francis (1986) in England, Josephine Egan and Francis (1986) in Wales, Francis and Egan (1987) in Australia, Francis and Egan (1990) in the United States and Francis and Gibson (2001) in Scotland, Francis (2002) suggested that Catholic schools were currently hosting not one coherent community of students, but four overlapping communities that inhabited discernibly different worldviews. Alongside non-Catholic students Francis proposed distinguishing between three groups of Catholic students, namely groups characterized as practising Catholics (who attend church most Sundays), sliding Catholics (who attend church some Sundays but less than weekly) and lapsed Catholics (who never attend church on Sunday). Francis (2002) tested the thesis that these three groups of Catholic students differed in significant ways one from another by exploring two sets of values, namely religious values and moral values. In both domains the highest value scores were recorded by practising Catholic students and the lowest value scores were recorded by lapsed Catholic students, with the sliding Catholic students occupying the middle position.

Research question

Against this background, the aim of the present chapter is to draw on the Young People's Attitudes to Religious Diversity project to test three theses. First, that lapsed Catholic students differ in significant ways in their attitudes and values from non-affiliated students. Second, that sliding Catholic students differ in significant ways in their attitudes and values from lapsed Catholic students. Third, that practising Catholic students differ in significant ways in their attitudes and values from sliding Catholic students. Building on the study reported by Francis (2002), the present study focuses on female students.

Method

Procedure

As part of a large multi-method project on religious diversity designed to examine the experiences and attitudes of young people living in the multicultural and multi-faith context of the UK, classes of students in the second and third years of secondary education in Scotland (13 to 15 years of age) were invited to complete a question-naire survey during 2011 and 2012. The participants were guaranteed confidential-ity and anonymity and were given the choice not to take part in the survey. The level of interest shown in the project meant that very few students decided not to participate. The sampling frame set out to capture data from at least 2,000 students in Scotland, with half attending Catholic schools within the state-maintained sector and half attending non-denominational schools within the state-maintained sector.

Instrument

The *Religious Diversity and Young People* survey was designed for self-completion, using mainly multiple-choice questions and Likert scaling on 5 points: agree strongly, agree, not certain, disagree and disagree strongly. In the present analysis, 12 groups of items were identified from the instrument to map the following areas: religious identity, religious conversation, religion and life, Christian beliefs, religious affect, non-conventional beliefs, religion and education, religion and society, accepting religious plurality, living with religious plurality, living with cultural diversity and accepting religious differences.

Participants

In Scotland, completed questionnaires were submitted by 1,439 female students. From this group, 510 identified themselves as having no religious affiliation and 475 as Catholics, among whom 95 never attended church (lapsed Catholics), 219 attended church sometimes but less frequently than weekly (sliding Catho-lics) and 161 attended church weekly (practising Catholics).

Analysis

The data were analyzed by means of SPSS, employing chi square 4×2 contingency tables, combining the 'agree strongly' and 'agree' responses into one category and the 'disagree strongly', 'disagree' and 'not certain' responses into the second category.

Results

Religious identity

The analysis begins by exploring students' perceptions of the importance they attribute to their own religious identity and how this relates to their perception of their parents' religiosity. The data demonstrate clear differences among the

Table 11.1 Religious identity

	None %	Laps %	Slid %	Prac %	χ^2	$p<$
My religious identity is important to me.	2	16	36	54	268.11	.001
My mother's religious identity is important to her.	5	26	35	72	314.83	.001
My father's religious identity is important to him.	5	15	27	49	176.93	.001
My parents think religion is important.	3	23	36	84	431.60	.001
My grandparents think religion is important.	18	42	58	72	203.15	.001

four groups of students (Table 11.1). While just 2 per cent of non-affiliates feel that their religious identity is important to them, the proportions rise to 16 per cent among lapsed Catholics, 36 per cent among sliding Catholics and 54 per cent among practising Catholics. While just 5 per cent of non-affiliates feel that their mother's religious identity is important to her, the proportions rise to 26 per cent among lapsed Catholics, 35 per cent among sliding Catholics and 72 per cent among practising Catholics. While just 5 per cent of non-affiliates feel that their father's religious identity is important to him, the proportions rise to 15 per cent among lapsed Catholics, 27 per cent among sliding Catholics and 49 per cent among practising Catholics. A similar pattern emerges when the students were invited to assess the importance attributed to religion by their parents and their grandparents. While just 3 per cent of the non-affiliates consider that their parents think religion is important, the proportion rises to 23 per cent among lapsed Catholics, 36 per cent among sliding Catholics and 84 per cent among practising Catholics. While 18 per cent of non-affiliates consider that their grandparents think religion is important, the proportions rise to 42 per cent among lapsed Catholics, 58 per cent among sliding Catholics and 72 per cent among practising Catholics. These findings confirm that lapsed Catholics, sliding Catholics and practising Catholics inhabit very different religious cultures.

Religious conversation

The second set of items explored the extent to which levels of conversation about religion varied among the four groups of students. The data demonstrate that the differences identified in the previous section (in terms of religious identity) are clearly reflected in the present section on religious discussion (Table 11.2). While just 6 per cent of non-affiliates often talk about religion with their friends, the proportions rise to 13 per cent among lapsed Catholics, 9 per cent among sliding Catholics and 27 per cent among practising Catholics. While just 6 per cent of non-affiliates often talk about religion with their

Table 11.2 Religious conversation

	None %	Laps %	Slid %	Prac %	χ^2	$p<$
I often talk about religion with my friends.	6	13	9	27	63.61	.001
I often talk about religion with my father.	6	10	18	36	94.35	.001
I often talk about religion with my grandparents.	7	16	24	44	120.60	.001
I often talk about religion with my mother.	7	10	26	53	187.69	.001

father, the proportions rise to 10 per cent among lapsed Catholics, 18 per cent among sliding Catholics and 36 per cent among practising Catholics. While just 7 per cent of non-affiliates often talk about religion with their grandparents, the proportions rise to 16 per cent among lapsed Catholics, 24 per cent among sliding Catholics and 44 per cent among practising Catholics. While just 7 per cent of non-affiliates often talk about religion with their mother, the proportions rise to 10 per cent among lapsed Catholics, 26 per cent among sliding Catholics and 53 per cent among practising Catholics. These findings confirm that lapsed Catholics, sliding Catholics and practising Catholics experience quite different levels of conversation about religious matters.

Religion and life

The third set of items explored the extent to which the connection between religion and life varied among the four groups of students. The data demonstrate that there are clear differences among the four groups in this regard (Table 11.3). While just 4 per cent of non-affiliates consider that their life has been shaped by their religious faith, the proportions rise to 10 per cent among lapsed Catholics, 27 per cent among sliding Catholics and 52 per cent among practising Catholics. While just 4 per cent of non-affiliates consider that their religion plays a major role when making important decisions in their life, the proportions rise to 13 per cent among lapsed Catholics, 18 per cent among sliding Catholics and 48 per cent among practising Catholics. This perception of the connection between religion and life is validated by the responses of the four groups concerning overall levels of wellbeing. Nearly two-fifths of non-affiliates (37 per cent) feel that their life has a sense of purpose, but the proportions rise to 46 per cent among lapsed Catholics, 53 per cent among sliding Catholics and 71 per cent among practising Catholics. Three-fifths of non-affiliates (59 per cent) find life really worth living, but the proportions rise to 64 per cent among lapsed Catholics, 70 per cent among sliding Catholics and 79 per cent among practising Catholics. These findings confirm that lapsed Catholics, sliding Catholics and practising Catholics experience different levels of psychological wellbeing.

Table 11.3 Religion and life

	None %	Laps %	Slid %	Prac %	χ^2	$p<$
My life has been shaped by my religious faith.	4	10	27	52	214.82	.001
When making important decisions in my life, my religion plays a major role.	4	13	18	48	181.21	.001
I feel my life has a sense of purpose.	37	46	53	71	61.19	.001
I find life really worth living.	59	64	70	79	24.46	.001

Table 11.4 Christian beliefs

	None %	Laps %	Slid %	Prac %	χ^2	$p<$
I believe in God.	8	50	59	83	385.08	.001
I believe in life after death.	35	56	58	64	61.20	.001
I believe in heaven.	33	62	66	88	176.34	.001
I believe in hell.	27	48	48	60	71.43	.001

Christian beliefs

The fourth set of items explored the connection between Catholic identity and Christian beliefs among the four groups of students. The data demonstrate a clear linkage between levels of Catholic involvement and levels of Christian belief (Table 11.4), but there is also a very clear difference between lapsed Catholic and the non-affiliated students. Thus, 50 per cent of lapsed Catholics believe in God compared with 8 per cent of non-affiliates; 56 per cent of lapsed Catholics believe in life after death, compared with 35 per cent of non-affiliates; 62 per cent of lapsed Catholics believe in heaven, compared with 33 per cent of non-affiliates; and 48 per cent of lapsed Catholics believe in hell, compared with 27 per cent of non-affiliates. The linkage between Catholic involvement and Christian belief is equally clear. While 50 per cent of lapsed Catholics believe in God, the proportions rise to 59 per cent among sliding Catholics and 83 per cent among practising Catholics. While 56 per cent of lapsed Catholics believe in life after death, the proportions rise to 58 per cent among sliding Catholics and 64 per cent among practising Catholics. While 62 per cent of lapsed Catholics believe in heaven, the proportions rise to 66 per cent among sliding Catholics and 88 per cent among practising Catholics. While 48 per cent of lapsed Catholics and 48 per cent of sliding Catholics believe in hell, the proportion rises to 60 per cent among practising Catholics. These findings confirm that the three groups of Catholics hold significantly different levels of Christian belief.

Religious affect

The fifth set of items turns attention from Christian belief to religious affect, to the attitudinal dimension of religion. These items explore whether the different levels of Christian belief endorsed by the four groups of students are reflected in different attitudes towards religious faith. These items focus on God, prayer and worship. The data demonstrate that lapsed Catholics hold a more positive attitude than non-affiliates towards God, prayer and worship (Table 11.5). Thus 26 per cent of lapsed Catholics say that God means a lot to them, compared with 2 per cent of non-affiliates; 20 per cent of lapsed Catholics say that God helps them to lead a better life, compared with 3 per cent of non-affiliates; 21 per cent of lapsed Catholics say that prayer helps them a lot, compared with 4 per cent of non-affiliates; and 31 per cent of lapsed Catholics dismiss going to church as a waste of time, compared with 41 per cent of non-affiliates. The data also demonstrate the linkage between Catholic involvement and religious affect. The proportions who agree that God means a lot to them rises from 26 per cent among lapsed Catholics to 39 per cent among sliding Catholics and 69 per cent among practising Catholics. The proportions who agree that God helps them to lead a better life rises from 20 per cent among lapsed Catholics to 37 per cent among sliding Catholics and 57 per cent among practising Catholics. The proportions who agree that prayer helps them a lot rises from 21 per cent among lapsed Catholics to 30 per cent among sliding Catholics and 52 per cent among practising Catholics. The proportions who agree that going to a place of worship is a waste of their time falls from 31 per cent among lapsed Catholics to 23 per cent among sliding Catholics and 8 per cent among practising Catholics.

Non-conventional beliefs

The sixth set of items widened the discussion from conventional Christian beliefs to explore the connection between Catholic identity and non-conventional beliefs, concerned with horoscopes, contacting the spirits of the dead, fortune-telling and tarot cards. The data demonstrate that in this area there were no significant differences in terms of the levels of endorsement

Table 11.5 Religious affect

	None %	Laps %	Slid %	Prac %	χ^2	$p<$
God means a lot to me.	2	26	39	69	346.73	.001
God helps me to lead a better life.	3	20	37	57	264.82	.001
Prayer helps me a lot.	4	21	30	52	199.79	.001
I think going to a place of worship is a waste of my time.	41	31	23	8	72.90	.001

offered by the four groups (Table 11.6). Indeed the levels of acceptance of non-conventional beliefs were almost identical among non-affiliates and among practising Catholics. Thus 38 per cent of non-affiliates believe in their horoscope and so do 37 per cent of practising Catholics; 35 per cent of non-affiliates believe it is possible to contact the spirits of the dead and so do 38 per cent of practising Catholics; 23 per cent of non-affiliates believe fortune-tellers can tell the future and so do 24 per cent of practising Catholics; 18 per cent of non-affiliates believe tarot cards can tell the future and so do 14 per cent of practising Catholics.

Religion and education

The seventh set of items explored the connection between Catholic identity and views on the connection between religion and education. The data demonstrate that support for religious education in school is clearly linked with Catholic identity (Table 11.7). While 32 per cent of non-affiliates agree that religious education should be taught in school, the proportions rise to 53 per cent among lapsed Catholics, 61 per cent among sliding Catholics and 76 per cent among practising Catholics. Moreover, Catholic students who are more

Table 11.6 Non-conventional beliefs

	None %	Laps %	Slid %	Prac %	χ^2	$p<$
I believe in my horoscope.	38	46	43	37	3.90	NS
It is possible to contact the spirits of the dead.	35	47	42	38	7.38	NS
Fortune-tellers can tell the future.	23	32	23	24	3.51	NS
Tarot cards can tell the future.	18	25	17	14	5.11	NS

Table 11.7 Religion and education

	None %	Laps %	Slid %	Prac %	χ^2	$p<$
Religious education should be taught in school.	32	53	61	76	117.38	.001
Learning about different religions in school is interesting.	25	23	48	62	97.52	.001
I am in favour of Christian schools.	21	48	51	69	150.59	.001
I am in favour of Muslim schools.	18	24	27	33	18.26	.001

actively involved in the life of the church are also those who are more supportive of religious education embracing other religious traditions. While 25 per cent of non-affiliates and 23 per cent of lapsed Catholics feel that learning about different religions in schools is interesting, the proportions rise to 48 per cent among sliding Catholics and 62 per cent among practising Catholics. The data also demonstrate that support for Christian schools is clearly linked with Catholic identity. While 21 per cent of non-affiliates are in favour of Christian schools, the proportions rise to 48 per cent among lapsed Catholics, 51 per cent among sliding Catholics and 69 per cent among practising Catholics. Moreover, the Catholic students who are more actively involved in the life of the church are also those who are more supportive not only of Christian schools, but also of Muslim schools. While 18 per cent of non-affiliates are in favour of Muslim schools, the proportions rise to 24 per cent among lapsed Catholics, 27 per cent among sliding Catholics and 33 per cent among practising Catholics.

Religion and society

The eighth set of items explored the connection between Catholic identity and views on the connection between religion and society. The data demonstrate that lapsed Catholics hold a more inclusive attitude than non-affiliates towards religious diversity within society (Table 11.8). While 55 per cent of non-affiliates say that all religious groups in Britain should have equal rights, the proportion rises to 72 per cent among lapsed Catholics. While 61 per cent of non-affiliates say that we must respect all religions, the proportion rises to 70 per cent among lapsed Catholics. However, practising Catholics are then shown to hold a more inclusive attitude than lapsed Catholics. Thus 77 per cent of practising Catholics say that all religious groups in Britain should have equal rights, compared with 72 per cent of lapsed Catholics, and 88 per cent of practising Catholics say that we must respect all religions, compared with 70 per cent of lapsed Catholics. The data also demonstrate that the connection between Catholic identity and inclusivity is reflected in more general support for equality. Thus 67 per cent of practising Catholics say that promoting equality in society is important to them, compared with 52 per cent of sliding Catholics, 51 per cent of lapsed Catholics

Table 11.8 Religion and society

	None %	Laps %	Slid %	Prac %	χ^2	p<
All religious groups in Britain should have equal rights.	55	72	69	77	32.48	.001
We must respect all religions.	61	70	74	88	45.82	.001
Promoting equality in society is important to me.	33	51	52	67	68.66	.001
Religious people are often intolerant of others.	19	23	23	21	1.47	NS

and 33 per cent of non-affiliates. Although practising Catholics are more inclusive in their attitude towards diversity, they are as alert as non-affiliates to the dangers of religious intolerance. Similar proportions of all four groups agree that religious people are often intolerant of others: 19 per cent of non-affiliates, 23 per cent of lapsed Catholics, 23 per cent of sliding Catholics and 21 per cent of practising Catholics.

Accepting religious plurality

The ninth set of items took the analysis of religious inclusivity one step further by exploring the connection between Catholic identity and acceptance of religious plurality. The data demonstrate that lapsed Catholics positively embrace close personal relationships with others from different denominational or different faith backgrounds (Table 11.9). Thus, 62 per cent of lapsed Catholics would be happy to go out with someone from a different denomination and 60 per cent would be happy to go out with someone from a different faith; 59 per cent of lapsed Catholics would be happy about a close relative marrying someone from a different denomination and 66 per cent would be happy about a close relative marrying someone from a different faith. The data also show that practising Catholics are more positive than lapsed Catholics about embracing such close personal relationships. Going out with someone from a different denomination is acceptable to 62 per cent of lapsed Catholics, 63 per cent of sliding Catholics and 76 per cent of practising Catholics. Going out with someone from a different faith is acceptable to 60 per cent of lapsed Catholics, 71 per cent of sliding Catholics and 77 per cent of practising Catholics. A close relative marrying someone from a different denomination is acceptable to 59 per cent of lapsed Catholics, 62 per cent of sliding Catholics and 70 per cent of practising Catholics. A close relative marrying someone from a different faith is acceptable to 66 per cent of lapsed Catholics, 71 per cent of sliding Catholics and 78 per cent of practising Catholics.

Table 11.9 Accepting religious plurality

	None %	Laps %	Slid %	Prac %	χ^2	$p<$
I would be happy to go out with someone from a different denomination.	47	62	63	76	48.11	.001
I would be happy to go out with someone from a different faith.	50	60	71	77	53.84	.001
I would be happy about a close relative marrying someone from a different denomination.	45	59	62	70	39.25	.001
I would be happy about a close relative marrying someone from a different faith.	55	66	71	78	37.44	.001

Living with religious plurality

The tenth set of items tested whether the greater acceptance of religious plurality by practising Catholics was reflected in the way in which they perceived
their local neighbourhood. The data demonstrate that there is little difference
between the perceptions of non-affiliates and lapsed Catholics in this area
(Table 11.10). Thus, 35 per cent of non-affiliates and 32 per cent of lapsed
Catholics feel that where they live, people from different religious backgrounds
get on well together; 41 per cent of non-affiliates and 35 per cent of lapsed
Catholics feel that where they live, people from different countries get on well
together; and 34 per cent of non-affiliates and 34 per cent of lapsed Catholics
feel that where they live, people respect religious differences. There are, however, significant differences between the perspectives of practising Catholics and
lapsed Catholics. While 32 per cent of lapsed Catholics feel that where they live,
people from different religious backgrounds get on well together, the proportions rise to 54 per cent among sliding Catholics and 61 per cent among practising Catholics. While 35 per cent of lapsed Catholics feel that where they live,
people who come from different countries get on well together, the proportions
rise to 49 per cent among sliding Catholics and 62 per cent among practising
Catholics. While 34 per cent of lapsed Catholics feel that where they live, people
respect religious differences, the proportions rise to 44 per cent among sliding
Catholics and 56 per cent among practising Catholics.

Living with cultural diversity

The eleventh set of items developed the previous theme of living with religious plurality one step further to consider more broadly the notion of living
with cultural diversity, both within the local school and within the local area.
The data demonstrate that of the four groups it is the practising Catholics
who hold the most positive attitude towards living with cultural diversity
(Table 11.11). Practising Catholics are twice as likely as non-affiliates to feel
that having people from different religious backgrounds makes their school
or college an interesting place (71 per cent compared with 36 per cent), with

Table 11.10 Living with religious plurality

	None %	Laps %	Slid %	Prac %	χ^2	$p<$
Where I live, people from different religious backgrounds get on well together.	35	32	54	61	50.94	.001
Where I live, people who come from different countries get on well together.	41	35	49	62	27.29	.001
Where I live, people respect religious differences.	34	34	44	56	28.10	.001

Table 11.11 Living with cultural diversity

	None %	Laps %	Slid %	Prac %	χ^2	$p<$
Having people from different religious backgrounds makes my school/college an interesting place.	36	45	58	71	73.60	.001
People who come from different countries make my school/college an interesting place.	30	42	39	66	64.82	.001
People from different religious backgrounds make where I live an interesting place.	25	28	32	51	40.47	.001
People who come from different countries make where I live an interesting place.	26	26	34	58	58.42	.001

the middle ground being occupied by lapsed Catholics (45 per cent) and sliding Catholics (58 per cent). Practising Catholics are more than twice as likely as non-affiliates to feel that people who come from different countries make their school or college an interesting place (66 per cent compared with 30 per cent), with the middle ground being occupied by lapsed Catholics (42 per cent) and sliding Catholics (39 per cent). Practising Catholics are twice as likely as non-affiliates to feel that people from different religious backgrounds make where they live an interesting place (51 per cent compared with 25 per cent), with the middle ground being occupied by lapsed Catholics (28 per cent) and sliding Catholics (32 per cent). Practising Catholics are twice as likely as non-affiliates to feel that people who come from different countries make where they live an interesting place (58 per cent compared with 26 per cent), with the middle ground being occupied by lapsed Catholics (26 per cent) and sliding Catholics (34 per cent).

Accepting religious differences

The twelfth set of items explored the extent to which the four groups held different views on the acceptability of distinctive religious dress worn in school. The data demonstrate that lapsed Catholics and non-affiliates hold similar views in relation to Christians and Muslims (Table 11.12): 52 per cent of non-affiliates and 55 per cent of lapsed Catholics accept that Christians should be allowed to wear crosses in school; 52 per cent of non-affiliates and 54 per cent of lapsed Catholics accept that Muslims should be allowed to wear the headscarf in school. At the same time, lapsed Catholics are slightly more accepting than non-affiliates in relation to Sikhs, Jews and Hindus: 49 per cent of non-affiliates and 55 per cent of lapsed Catholics support the Sikh turban in school; 47 per cent of non-affiliates and 54 per cent of lapsed Catholics support the

Table 11.12 Accepting religious differences

	None %	Laps %	Slid %	Prac %	χ^2	$p<$
Christians should be allowed to wear crosses in school.	52	55	68	75	37.17	.001
Muslims should be allowed to wear the headscarf in school.	52	54	57	73	21.36	.001
Sikhs should be allowed to wear the turban in school.	49	55	55	73	28.59	.001
Jews should be allowed to wear the kippah/yarmulke in school.	47	54	55	68	24.12	.001
Hindus should be allowed to wear the bindi in school.	47	53	53	69	23.59	.001

Jewish kippah/yarmulke in school; 47 per cent of non-affiliates and 53 per cent of lapsed Catholics support the Hindu bindi in school. The data also demonstrate that practising Catholics are more accepting than lapsed Catholics or sliding Catholics of religious clothing in school: 75 per cent of practising Catholics support the Christian cross in school, compared with 68 per cent of sliding Catholics and 55 per cent of lapsed Catholics; 73 per cent of practising Catholics support the Muslim headscarf in school, compared with 57 per cent of sliding Catholics and 54 per cent of lapsed Catholics; 73 per cent of practising Catholics accept the Sikh turban in school, compared with 55 per cent of sliding Catholics and 55 per cent of lapsed Catholics; 68 per cent of practising Catholics accept the Jewish kippah/yarmulke in school, compared with 55 per cent of sliding Catholics and 54 per cent of lapsed Catholics; 69 per cent of practising Catholics accept the Hindu bindi in school, compared with 53 per cent of sliding Catholics and 53 per cent of lapsed Catholics.

Conclusion

This chapter set out to test the thesis proposed in an earlier study by Francis (2002) that the Catholic community in Scotland needs to be conceptualized not as one homogenous community (united around one common set of values and beliefs), but as three overlapping communities, all of which are differentiated from the religiously unaffiliated, but in varying degrees. This thesis was operationalized by taking seriously self-assigned religious affiliation as identifying the Catholic community and then by distinguishing within the community according to three levels of religious practice. Drawing on vocabulary employed in previous studies, those who never attend church were characterized as lapsed Catholics, those who attend church weekly as practising Catholics and those who attend church less than weekly as sliding Catholics. This thesis was tested among 985 female students (attending schools with a religious character or schools without a religious character in Scotland) against 12 groups of items mapping the following themes: religious identity, religious conversation, religion and life, Christian beliefs, Religious affect, non-conventional beliefs, religion and education, religion and society, accepting religious plurality, living with religious plurality, living with cultural diversity and accepting religious differences. Four main conclusions emerge from these analyses.

The first conclusion concerns the distinctive profile of practising female Catholic students in Scotland. These are a group of young people who come from backgrounds where parents and grandparents take their religion seriously and where mothers in particular encourage conversations about religion. They allow their religion to shape their lives and enjoy a real sense of purpose in life. Practising Catholics keep their faith in God and believe in both heaven and hell. They take their faith in God seriously and that means a lot to them. Practising Catholics support the connections between religion and education and welcome an approach to religious education that gives space to teaching about different religions. They adopt an inclusive approach to respecting all religions and to promoting equality in society. Practising Catholics accept religious plurality and welcome the development of close personal relationships developing across religious boundaries. They acknowledge the benefits of living with cultural diversity. Practising Catholics accept and support the rights of all religious groups to wear distinctive religious clothing in school.

The second conclusion concerns the significant differences between the worldview espoused by practising Catholics and the worldview espoused by lapsed Catholics. Lapsed Catholics come from backgrounds where parents and grandparents are less likely to take their religion seriously and where they are much less likely to engage in conversations about religion. Lapsed Catholics are much less likely to see the connection between religion and daily living. They are much less likely to feel a sense of purpose in their lives. Lapsed Catholics are less likely than practising Catholics to believe in God, to believe in heaven or to believe in hell, and yet overall their levels of belief still remain quite high. The difference is much stronger in the area of religious affect. While lapsed Catholics may still believe in God, that belief does not mean a great deal to them. Lapsed Catholics are less supportive of the place of religious education in school and much less interested in learning about different religions. Lapsed Catholics are less concerned with matters of social equality and religious diversity. For lapsed Catholics religion is generally less salient for their worldview. They are less conscious of the contribution made by faith groups to their local community and they are less tolerant of the rights of fellow students to wear distinctive religious clothing in school.

The third conclusion is the category of sliding Catholic occupying real territory between the worldview of lapsed Catholics and the worldview of practising Catholics across the majority of the 12 areas analyzed. For example, the home background of sliding Catholics is more supportive of religion than is the case among lapsed Catholics, but less supportive of religion than is the case among practising Catholics.

The fourth conclusion is that there remain important differences between the worldview of lapsed Catholics and the worldview of religiously unaffiliated students. In other words, self-assigned religious affiliation unsupported by current practice of worship attendance is not an empty or meaningless category. Compared with the non-affiliates, lapsed Catholics have a stronger religious presence in their home background among parents and grandparents. Lapsed Catholics have more conversations about religion with parents and grandparents. Lapsed Catholics are more likely to see a connection between religion and life and they are more likely to feel their life has a sense of purpose. Lapsed Catholics are much more likely than non-affiliates to believe in God and to believe in life after death. Lapsed Catholics hold a more positive attitude towards the Christian faith. They hold a more positive attitude towards religious education and towards Christian schools. Compared with non-affiliates, lapsed Catholics adopt a more inclusive approach to respecting all religions and to promoting equality in society. Lapsed Catholics show more support for religious plurality and for welcoming close personal relationships developing across religious boundaries.

Overall, therefore, the thesis is supported that the Catholic community in Scotland needs to be conceptualized not as one homogenous community (united around one common set of values and beliefs), but as three overlapping communities, all of which are differentiated from the religiously unaffiliated, but in varying degrees. The implication of this conclusion is to recognize the inadequacy of trying to profile the religious landscape of a nation by relying solely on the assessment of religious affiliation. A much richer account is provided when religious affiliation is nuanced against religious practice.

References

Aspinall, P. 2000. 'Should a Question on "Religion" Be Asked in the 2001 British Census? A Public Policy Case in Favour.' *Social Policy and Administration* 34 (5): 584–600.

Barlow, A., S. Duncan, G. James, and A. Park. 2001. 'Just a Piece of Paper? Marriage and Cohabitation.' In *British Social Attitudes: The Eighteenth Report*, ed. A. Park, J. Curtice, K. Thomson, L. Jarvis, and C. Bromley, 29–57. London: Sage.

Bibby, R. W. 1985. 'Religious Encasement in Canada: An Argument for Protestant and Catholic Entrenchment.' *Social Compass* 16 (3): 287–303.

———. 1987. *Fragmented Gods: The Poverty and Potential of Religion in Canada.* Toronto: Irwin.

Egan, J., and L. J. Francis. 1986. 'School Ethos in Wales: The Impact of Non-practising Catholic and Non-Catholic Pupils on Catholic Secondary Schools.' *Lumen Vitae* 41 (2): 159–173.

Fane, R. S. 1999. 'Is Self-assigned Religious Affiliation Socially Significant?' In *Sociology, Theology and the Curriculum*, ed. L. J. Francis, 113–124. London: Cassell.

Francis, L. J. 1986. 'Roman Catholic Secondary Schools: Falling Rolls and Pupil Attitudes.' *Educational Studies* 12 (2): 119–127.

———. 2001a. *The Values Debate: A Voice from the Pupils.* London: Woburn Press.

———. 2001b. 'Religion and Values: A Quantitative Perspective.' In *The Fourth R for the Third Millennium: Education in Religion and Values for the Global Future*, ed. L. J. Francis, J. Astley and M. Robbins, 47–78. Dublin: Lindisfarne Books.

————. 2001c. 'The Social Significance of Religious Affiliation among Adolescents in England and Wales.' In *Religious Individualisation and Christian Religious Semantics*, ed. H.-G. Ziebertz, 115–138. Münster: LIT Verlag.

————. 2002. 'Catholic Schools and Catholic Values: A Study of Moral and Religious Values among 13–15 year old Pupils Attending Non-denominational and Catholic Schools in England and Wales.' *International Journal of Education and Religion* 3 (1): 69–84.

————. 2003. 'Religion and Social Capital: The Flaw in the 2001 Census in England and Wales.' In *Public Faith: The State of Religious Belief and Practice in Britain*, ed. P. Avis, 45–64. London: SPCK.

————. 2008a. 'Self-assigned Religious Affiliation: A Study among Adolescents in England and Wales.' In *Religion, Spirituality and the Social Sciences: Challenging Marginalisation*, ed. B. Spalek and A. Imtoual, 149–161. Bristol: Policy Press.

————. 2008b. 'Family, Denomination and the Adolescent Worldview: An Empirical Enquiry among 13- to 15-year-old Girls in England and Wales.' *Marriage and Family Review* 43 (1–2): 185–204.

Francis, L. J., and J. Egan. 1987. 'Catholic Schools and the Communication of Faith: An Empirical Inquiry.' *Catholic School Studies* 60 (2): 27–34.

————. 1990. 'The Catholic School as "Faith Community": An Empirical Enquiry.' *Religious Education* 85 (4): 588–603.

Francis, L. J., and H. M. Gibson. 2001. 'Growing up Catholic in a Scottish City: The Relationship between Denominational Identity, Denominational Schools, and Attitude toward Christianity among Eleven to Fifteen Year Olds.' *Catholic Education: A Journal of Inquiry and Practice* 5 (1): 39–54.

Gill, R. 1999. *Churchgoing and Christian Ethics*. Cambridge: Cambridge University Press.

Hornsby-Smith, M. P. 1978. *Catholic Education: The Unobtrusive Partner*. London: Sheed and Ward.

————. 1987. *Roman Catholics in England: Studies in Social Structure since the Second World War*. Cambridge: Cambridge University Press.

————. 1991. *Roman Catholic Beliefs in England: Customary Catholicism and Transformations of Religious Authority*. Cambridge: Cambridge University Press.

————. 1999. *Catholics in England 1950–2000: Historical and Sociological Perspectives*. London: Bloomsbury.

Park, A., and R. Rhead. 2013. 'Changing Attitudes towards Sex, Marriage, and Parenthood.' In *British Social Attitudes: The Thirtieth Report*, ed. A. Park, C. Bryson, E. Clery, J. Curtice, and M. Phillips, 1–32. London: NatCen Social Research.

Sherif, J. 2011. 'A Census Chronicle: Reflections on the Campaign for a Religious Question in the 2001 Census for England and Wales.' *Journal of Beliefs and Values* 32 (1): 1–18.

Voas, D., and S. Bruce. 2004. 'The 2001 Census and Christian identification in Britain.' *Journal of Contemporary Religion* 19 (1): 23–28.

Weller, P. 2004. 'Identity, Politics, and the Future(s) of Religion in the UK: The Case of the Religious Question in the 2001 Decennial Census.' *Journal of Contemporary Religion* 19 (1): 3–21.

12 Schools with a religious character and community cohesion in Wales

Leslie J. Francis, Gemma Penny and Tania ap Siôn

Introduction

Religious diversity and community cohesion in Wales

Wales has long been a nation that embraces religious diversity. The classic count of public church attendance conducted alongside the national census in 1851 drew public attention to the comparative strengths of the different Christian denominations. At that time the Established Church of England did not rate highly at the top of the list (see Jones and Williams 1976). In the 1850s, religious diversity was measured in terms of denominational identity and experienced in terms of denominational rivalries and competition. Matters of geography, social class and linguistic background (Welsh as first language) all contributed to the rich tapestry of denominational difference.

Inclusion of the religious question in the national census for England and Wales for the first time in 2001 (see Aspinall 2000; Francis 2003; Weller 2004; Sherif 2011) provided an objective opportunity to profile religious diversity in Wales from a different conceptual framework. The Census White Paper (1999) which proposed the religious question to parliament rejected the opportunity to raise a statistical enquiry into denominational affiliation and offered instead a conceptual framework designed to establish the strengths of what were reportedly the six largest religious groups in England and Wales: Christian, Buddhist, Hindu, Muslim, Jewish and Sikh, preceded by 'none' and followed by 'other (please write in)'. Unusually in the context of the national census, the religious affiliation question was voluntary in a way that allowed the output statistics to include the additional category of 'not stated'. In the early 2000s religious diversity in Wales was measured in terms of religious group affiliation and experienced as part of a wider issue of pluralism. Still, however, matters of geography, social class and linguistic background (now languages other than Welsh as first language) contributed to the rich tapestry of religious group differences.

Across England and Wales, the religious question in the 2001 census found that 72 per cent of the population could be defined as Christian, 3 per cent as Muslim, 1 per cent as Hindu and under 1 per cent as either Buddhist, Jewish or Sikh; 15 per cent had no religious affiliation and 8 per cent chose not to answer the optional question on religion. There were however some clear differences in the levels of religious diversity recorded in England and Wales. For example, in both England and Wales, around 72 per cent of the population could be classified as Christian. In England around 6 per cent were classified as affiliated with one of the other five listed religions, but in Wales this proportion fell to 2 per cent. In Wales the largest religious group after Christians at 72 per cent were Muslims at 1 per cent, accounting for 22,000 individuals. The Muslim population was concentrated in major cities, including Wrexham in North East Wales and Swansea and Cardiff in South Wales, with the highest density in Cardiff at 4 per cent.

After considerable debate regarding ways of modifying the 2001 census question on religious affiliation during the process of shaping the 2011 census, the decision was made to rerun the same question a decade later. The advantage of this is that it becomes possible to assess how responses to the same question change over time. The headline reading from the 2011 census was that in Wales the proportion of endorsement of the Christian category reduced from 72 per cent to 58 per cent, with consequent increase in the proportion claiming no religious affiliation from 19 per cent to 32 per cent.

The significance of religious diversity in relation to Welsh economic, cultural and social life was recognized by the Welsh Government explicitly through the convening of the Faith Forum which is chaired by the first minister, with the purpose of facilitating dialogue between the Welsh Government and the major faith communities in Wales at a national level. In addition to representatives of Christian denominations, there are also Muslim, Jewish, Sikh, Buddhist, Hindu and Baha'i representatives on the Faith Forum.

The Welsh Government's community cohesion strategy, however, is focused on developing and resourcing responses at the local community level, as reflected in the publication *Getting on Together: A Community Cohesion Strategy for Wales* (Welsh Assembly Government 2009). The strategy is focused around five key areas, which are identified as learning, housing, communication, promoting equality and social inclusion, and preventing violent extremism and strengthening community cohesion.

This strategy emphasizes the value of local partnerships, the important role of organizations that are working at community level and readily acknowledges that the engagement of people living in communities is vital. A community which works well together in these ways (the five key areas) is also a community which is likely to be resilient when external challenges arise or internal tensions develop (Welsh Assembly Government 2009, 3).

The place of education and schools in relation to community cohesion was specifically recognized by the Welsh Government through the publication of *Faith in Education* (Welsh Government 2011) and *Respect and Resilience – Developing Community Cohesion: A Common Understanding for Schools and Their Communities* (Welsh Assembly Government 2011).

Faith in Education was produced in collaboration with representatives of providers of publically funded schools with a religious character in Wales. The document made a significant policy statement through asserting the Welsh

Government's commitment to schools with a religious character as part of its celebration of the diversity of cultures present in Wales and described its aim as outlining 'the nature of schools with a religious character in Wales at the present time, to delineate the ethos and character of these schools, to challenge preconceptions, and to emphasise and celebrate diversity' (Welsh Government 2011, 2). Although in terms of descriptive scope *Faith in Education* was restricted to provision as it relates to the Church in Wales and the Roman Catholic Church, it claimed wider use and relevance extending to other Christian denominations and other faiths.

Respect and Resilience was published as a guidance document that aimed to support the development of community cohesion and prevent violent extremism in all secondary schools, pupil referral units, special schools and other educational settings in Wales. The document defined community cohesion, described what the UK Government and the Welsh Assembly Government was doing to prevent violent extremism, identified effective approaches to community cohesion for schools and their communities and provided more specific advice and guidance for schools in the areas of leadership, working with others, the curriculum and teaching, intervention and support, and managing risks and responding to events. As this document content illustrates, community cohesion in Wales at this time also needs to be understood in relation to the conceptually separate but related issue of the prevention of violent extremism, which is articulated from a political perspective in the Welsh Government's 'Prevent' strategy.

State-maintained schools in Wales

The state-maintained system of education in England and Wales has its roots in an historical context firmly shaped by the Christian churches. The original initiative to build schools came not from the state, but from voluntary philanthropy stimulated by religious principles. In 1808 a group of Free Churchmen founded the Royal Lancasterian Society from which the British and Foreign Schools Society emerged in 1814. In 1811 a group of Anglicans founded the National Society 'for the education of the children of the poor in the principles of the established church'. In 1847 the Roman Catholic Church established the Catholic Poor School Committee. The Education Act of 1870 was not designed to supplant these church schools, but to fill the gaps where church-related initiatives proved to be too slow or less than adequate. The fuller history of these initiatives has been well rehearsed by Marjorie Cruickshank (1963), James Murphy (1971) and Priscilla Chadwick (1997).

The debate about the divisive nature of church schools in England and Wales took a new turn in the early 1980s in the light of the changing composition of British society and the transforming effects of immigration. At this point the debate was shaped by discourse about cultural and ethnic diversity and behind this was a less well-articulated concern about religious diversity. In the early 1980s this debate was informed by the Runnymede Trust and by the government's Committee of Enquiry.

From the Runnymede Trust, Ann Dummett and Julia McNeal (1981), in their study *Race and Church Schools*, argued that church schools were having a mixed effect. In some areas, where there was a black Christian community, church schools had the effect of creating multiracial institutions. In other areas, where the black community was not Christian, church schools had the effect of preventing multiracial institutions.

The Committee of Enquiry into the education of children from ethnic minority groups brought the church school question into central focus in their report *Education for All* (Swann Report 1985). After reviewing the arguments for and against separate voluntary schools for other ethnic and religious groups, the majority voice of the committee stressed 'misgivings about the implications and consequences of "separate" provision of any kind'. Having come to this view, the majority voice of the Committee faced the consequence that

> our conclusions about the desirability of denominational voluntary aided schools for Muslims or other groups, by extension seriously call into question the long established dual system of educational provision in this country and particularly the role of the Churches in the provision of education . . . We believe therefore that the time has come for the DES [Department of Education and Skills], in consultation with religious and educational bodies, to consider the relevant provisions of the 1944 Act to see whether or not alterations are required in a society that is now radically different.
>
> (Swann Report 1985, 514)

Six members of the Committee of Enquiry dissented from this conclusion and formulated a completely different minority recommendation, not only supporting the provisions of the 1944 Education Act concerning voluntary schools, but also clearly wishing to see other ethnic and religious groups enabled to benefit from these provisions. The minority voices stressed the opposite view: 'We believe that it is unjust at the present time not to recommend that positive assistance should be given to ethnic minority communities who wish to establish voluntary aided schools in accordance with the 1944 Education Act' (Swann Report 1985, 515). The clear division of opinion within the Committee of Enquiry provided a good indication of the political sensitivities raised by the discussion in the mid-1980s.

In his article 'Should the State Fund Faith Based Schools?', Robert Jackson (2003) revisited the arguments for and against schools with a religious character. According to Jackson, the debate about state funding for schools with a religious character in England and Wales intensified at the beginning of the twenty-first century in the light of the events of 11 September 2001 in the United States. In his review, Jackson identified four main arguments in favour of state funding for schools with a religious character, namely that they provide a positive response to racism; promote justice and fairness for children, parents and religious communities; offer education of a high quality; and promote social cohesion and integration of minority communities into the democratic life of the state. Jackson balances these four arguments in favour of state funding for schools with a religious character by five main arguments against state funding for such schools, namely that they limit the personal autonomy of students; impose on students a restricted view of a religion promoted by sponsoring bodies; use state finance to fund proselytization or mission; disadvantage other schools through entry procedures that select the most able students; and erode social cohesion by separating students of different religious and non-religious backgrounds.

It is the fifth of these arguments that is directly relevant to the concern of the present study regarding the role of schools with a religious character in the preparation of students for life in a religiously diverse society. In this connection Jackson concludes:

> The most convincing argument against faith based schools lies in their potential to create barriers between groups, thereby eroding social harmony. Although there is some force in . . . [the] argument that the politics of faith based education has drawn minorities into democratic practices and institutions, any benefit could be out weighed by the fact that faith based education necessitates the separation of children by religion. There is also a danger, in some cases, that separation by religion could also mean separation by 'ethnicity'.
>
> (Jackson 2003, 97)

Nearly three decades after their report *Race and Church Schools* (Dummett and McNeal 1981), the Runnymede Trust re-entered the debate on the role of schools with a religious character by publishing a second report, *Right to Divide? Faith Schools and Community Cohesion* (Berkeley 2008). Here was a research project asking the question 'whether a school system with faith schools could also promote equality and cohesion' (ibid., 2). The project consulted with over a thousand people, including 'parents, students, professionals, and policy-makers from a range of faith backgrounds as well as those who do not subscribe to any religion' (ibid., 1). The aim of the consultation was 'to assess whether faith schools are well placed to deliver their obligations' (ibid., 4) in the following areas: encouraging students to share a sense of belonging; helping students develop a positive appreciation of diversity; removing barriers to inequality; and building strong partnerships between people from different backgrounds.

The six key recommendations put forward by the Runnymede Trust were, in one sense, very supportive of schools with a religious character. Such schools are supported as affirming government policies committed to increasing choice and diversity in the education sector. In another sense, however, the types of schools with a religious character being supported by the Runnymede Trust are very different from many of those currently supported within the state-maintained system in England and Wales. The first call from the Runnymede Trust is for schools with a religious character to cease to include faith criteria within their admissions policies. The argument is pitched as follows:

Faith schools should be for the benefit of all in society rather than for just a few. If faith schools are convinced of their relevance for society, then that should apply equally for all children. With state funding comes an obligation to be relevant and open to all citizens . . . All parents should be given access to what faith schools claim is a distinctive ethos.

(Berkeley 2008, 4)

The recommendation is based on the following evidence:

Our research has found that commitment to the promotion of cohesion is not universal, and for many faith schools not a priority . . . Too often, there remains a resistance to learning about other faiths when faith schools are seen as the spaces in which singular faith identities and traditions are transmitted.

(Berkeley 2008, 4–5)

Research aim

Against this background, the aim of the present study is to address the problem from an empirical perspective by posing the general question as to whether students educated in schools with a religious character in Wales hold attitudes that are more or less conducive to life in a religiously diverse society. This research aim situates the present study within the broader literature concerned with exploring the effects of schools with a religious character on students' attitudes, values and behaviours (see, for example, recent studies reported by Francis 2002; Lankshear 2005; Francis and Penny 2013; Francis et al. 2014; Village and Francis 2015). The study by Leslie Francis and Gemma Penny (2013) offers a useful conceptual framework on which to ground the present analysis. This study profiled the collective worldview of 3,124 students (13–15 years of age) attending 15 Anglican schools alongside the collective worldview of 4,929 students attending 25 schools with no religious foundation across 10 value domains: Christian beliefs, church and society, non-traditional beliefs, personal aims in life, personal wellbeing, attitudes towards school, attitudes towards sexual morality, attitudes towards substance use, attitudes towards right and wrong, and attitudes towards the environment.

Method

Procedure

As part of a large multi-method project on religious diversity designed to examine the experiences and attitudes of young people living in multicultural and multi-faith contexts throughout the UK, classes of Year 9 and Year 10 students in Wales (13–15 years of age) were invited to complete a questionnaire survey. The participants were guaranteed confidentiality and anonymity and were given the choice not to participate. The level of interest shown in the project meant that very few students decided not to take part in the survey. The sampling frame set out to compare data from at least 2,000 students (1,000 males and 1,000 females) from England, Northern Ireland, Scotland, Wales and London (as a special case), with half of the students attending schools with a religious character within the state-maintained sector (Anglican, Catholic and joint Anglican and Catholic) and half of the students attending schools without a religious foundation within the state-maintained sector.

Instrument

The *Religious Diversity and Young People* survey was designed for self-completion, using mainly multiple-choice questions and Likert scaling on 5 points: agree strongly, agree, not certain, disagree and disagree strongly. In the present analysis, 14 groups of items were identified from the instrument to map the following three themes: the religious worldview of the students, attitudes towards religion and religious diversity, and shaping attitudes towards religion and religious diversity.

Participants

In Wales, completed questionnaires were submitted by 1,087 students in schools with a religious character (519 males, 561 females and 7 of undisclosed sex) and by 1,241 students in schools without a religious foundation (603 males, 632 females and 6 of undisclosed sex). Among the students attending schools with a religious character, 768 were from four Catholic schools, 140 from one Church in Wales school and 179 from one joint Catholic and Church in Wales school.

Analysis

The data were analyzed by means of SPSS, employing chi square 2 × 2 contingency tables. When discussing these data in the following narrative, the text will be simplified by referring to schools with a religious character as religious schools and to schools without a religious foundation as secular schools.

Results

Theme one: the religious worldview of students

The first thesis tested by the present analysis is that the two groups of students (attending religious schools and attending secular schools) display no significant differences in their religious worldviews. This thesis was tested against five sets of items, concerning religious identity, religious discussion, religious self-assessment, religious beliefs and religion in schools.

Religious identity

The section on religious identity explored two key issues: the importance that students attributed to religion in their own lives and the importance that they perceived those in their immediate environment attribute to religion. The data demonstrate that religious identity is significantly more salient for students in religious schools across both of these areas (Table 12.1). Thus 32 per cent of students in religious schools consider that their religious identity is important to them, compared with 15 per cent of students in secular schools. Students in religious schools are also more likely to consider that their friends, their parents and their grandparents think religion is important. While 16 per cent of students in religious schools say most of their friends consider religion important, the proportion falls to 7 per cent among students in secular schools. While 35 per cent of students in religious schools say their parents think religion is important, the proportion falls to 17 per cent of students in secular schools. While 44 per cent of students in religious schools say their grandparents think religion is important, the proportion falls to 27 per cent of students in secular schools. Religious schools in Wales are places where students are more likely to see religion as a matter of importance.

Religious discussion

The section on religious discussion explored the opportunities students experienced to discuss religion with their friends and family. The data demonstrate that students attending religious schools have more opportunities to talk about religion at home with their family (Table 12.2). While 26 per cent of students in religious schools often talk about religion with their mother, the proportion falls to 15 per cent in secular schools. While 22 per cent of students in religious schools often talk about religion with their grandparents, the proportion falls to 14 per cent in

Table 12.1 Religious identity

	Rel %	Sec %	χ^2	p<
My religious identity is important to me.	32	15	93.5	.001
Most of my friends think religion is important.	16	7	42.6	.001
My parents think religion is important.	35	17	100.3	.001
My grandparents think religion is important.	44	27	75.0	.001

Table 12.2 Religious discussion

	Rel %	Sec %	χ^2	p<
I often talk about religion with my friends.	17	14	3.6	NS
I often talk about religion with my father.	18	13	12.2	.001
I often talk about religion with my grandparents.	22	14	23.6	.001
I often talk about religion with my mother.	26	15	45.4	.001

secular schools. While 18 per cent of students in religious schools often talk about religion with their father, the proportion falls to 13 per cent in secular schools. On the other hand, students in religious schools are no more likely than students in secular schools to talk about religion with their friends (17 per cent and 14 per cent, respectively). Religious schools in Wales are places where students are more likely to be supported by religious conversation in the home.

Religious self-assessment

The section on religious self-assessment explored how students rated themselves as religious or spiritual beings and how they rated religion as playing a part in shaping their lives. The data demonstrate that religion plays a stronger part in the lives of students in religious schools (Table 12.3). While 37 per cent of students in religious schools describe themselves as religious, the proportion falls to 16 per cent in secular schools. While 24 per cent of students in religious schools describe themselves as spiritual, the proportion falls to 18 per cent in secular schools. Twice as many students in religious schools consider that their life has been shaped by their religious faith (27 per cent, compared with 13 per cent in secular schools). Twice as many students in religious schools consider that when making important decisions in their life, religion plays a major role (21 per cent, compared with 11 per cent in secular schools). Religious schools in Wales are places where religion is more likely to influence students' outlook on life.

Religious beliefs

The section on religious beliefs explored two key religious issues: belief in God and belief in life after death. The data demonstrate that religious belief is significantly stronger among students in religious schools (Table 12.4). Half of

Table 12.3 Religious self-assessment

	Rel %	Sec %	χ^2	p<
I am a religious person.	37	16	123.0	.001
I am a spiritual person.	24	18	10.1	.001
My life has been shaped by my religious faith.	27	13	76.5	.001
When making important decisions in my life, my religion plays a major role.	21	11	52.9	.001

Table 12.4 Religious beliefs

	Rel %	Sec %	χ^2	p<
I believe in God.	52	27	154.7	.001
There is only one God.	41	18	150.4	.001
I believe in life after death.	53	42	32.7	.001
I believe in heaven.	57	39	69.8	.001
I believe in hell.	47	32	57.3	.001

the students in religious schools (52 per cent) believe in God, compared with a quarter of the students in secular schools (27 per cent). Students in religious schools are also more likely to assert that there is only one God (41 per cent, compared with 18 per cent). In the religious schools, roughly the same proportion of students believe in life after death as believe in God (53 per cent and 52 per cent, respectively). In the secular schools, more students believe in life after death than believe in God (42 per cent compared with 27 per cent); nonetheless belief in life after death is higher in religious schools. A similar pattern appertains to belief in heaven and hell. Thus 57 per cent of students in religious schools believe in heaven, compared with 39 per cent in secular schools; 47 per cent of students in religious schools believe in hell, compared with 32 per cent in secular schools. Religious schools in Wales are places where there is a higher level of religious belief.

Religion in schools

The section on religion in schools explored understanding and appreciation of the place of religious education within school life. The data demonstrate that religion is more highly valued by students in religious schools than by students in secular schools (Table 12.5). While only 6 per cent of students in secular schools agree that school should hold a religious assembly every day, the proportion rises significantly to 11 per cent in religious schools. While 52 per cent of students in secular schools agree that religious education should be taught in schools, the proportion rises significantly to 62 per cent in religious schools. While 43 per cent of students in secular schools agree that learning about religion in school is interesting, the proportion rises to 53 per cent in religious schools. Students in religious schools are also more likely than students in secular schools to agree that citizenship should be taught in school (38 per cent, compared with 31 per cent). Religious schools in Wales are places where there is a higher level of commitment among the students to support the place of religion within the life of the school.

Theme two: attitudes towards religions and religious diversity

The second thesis tested by the present analysis is that the two groups of students (attending religious schools and attending secular schools) display no significant differences in their attitudes towards religions and religious diversity. This

Table 12.5 Religion in schools

	Rel %	Sec %	χ^2	$p<$
Religious education should be taught in school.	62	52	23.0	.001
Citizenship should be taught in school.	38	31	10.1	.001
Schools should hold a religious assembly every day.	11	6	15.3	.001
Learning about different religions in school is interesting.	53	43	22.0	.001

thesis was tested against five sets of items concerning attitudes towards religions, accepting religious plurality, living with religious plurality, living with cultural diversity and accepting religious clothing.

Attitudes towards religions

The section on attitudes towards religions explored two key issues: the extent to which students perceived religion to be socially disruptive and the extent to which students supported religious inclusivity in contemporary culture. The data demonstrate partial support for the thesis that students in religious schools are less likely to endorse negative views concerning religion and more likely to endorse positive views concerning religion (Table 12.6). Only one of the two negative items that portrays religion as socially disruptive receives lower endorsement from students in religious schools. While 51 per cent of students in secular schools agree that religion brings more conflict than peace, the proportion falls to 44 per cent among students in religious schools. On the other hand, there is no significant difference in the proportions of the two groups of students who agree that religious people are more intolerant than others (31 per cent in secular schools and 28 per cent in religious schools). Only one of the two positive items that support religious inclusivity receives higher endorsement from students in religious schools. While 66 per cent of students in secular schools agree that we must respect all religions, the proportion rises to 72 per cent in religious schools. On the other hand, there is no significant difference in the proportions of the two groups of students who agree that all religious groups in Britain should have equal rights (62 per cent in secular schools and 66 per cent in religious schools). Religious schools in Wales are places where there is a slightly more positive attitude towards religions.

Accepting religious plurality

The section on accepting religious plurality explored the students' acceptance of two levels of social proximity (personal relationships and relationships within the wider family) and two levels of religious difference (denomination and faith groups). The data demonstrate that there are no significant differences between students in religious schools and students in secular schools in acceptance of

Table 12.6 Attitudes towards religions

	Rel %	Sec %	χ^2	p<
Religion brings more conflict than peace.	44	51	9.4	.01
Religious people are often intolerant of others.	28	31	3.0	NS
We must respect all religions.	72	66	10.5	.001
All religious groups in Britain should have equal rights.	66	62	3.2	NS

religious proximity conceptualized through social proximity (Table 12.7). In terms of personal relationships, 53 per cent of students in secular schools would be happy to go out with someone from a different denomination and so would 56 per cent of students in religious schools. Similarly, 53 per cent of students in secular schools would be happy to go out with someone from a different faith and so would 56 per cent of students in religious schools. In terms of relationships within the wider family, 49 per cent of students in secular schools would be happy about a close relative marrying someone from a different denomination and so would 53 per cent of students in religious schools. Similarly, 59 per cent of students in secular schools would be happy about a relative marrying someone from a different faith and so would 60 per cent of students in religious schools. Religious schools in Wales are not places that seem either to encourage or to discourage greater acceptance of social proximity with people from other religious backgrounds, in comparison with secular schools.

Living with religious plurality

The section on living with religious plurality explored the students' perceptions of the levels of acceptance of cultural and religious diversity within their locality. The data demonstrate that there are no significant differences in the perceptions of students in religious schools and of students in secular schools on this issue (Table 12.8). Half of the students in both types of school feel that, where they

Table 12.7 Accepting religious plurality

	Rel %	*Sec %*	χ^2	*p<*
I would be happy to go out with someone from a different denomination.	56	53	2.2	NS
I would be happy to go out with someone from a different faith.	56	53	1.7	NS
I would be happy about a close relative marrying someone from a different denomination.	53	49	3.7	NS
I would be happy about a close relative marrying someone from a different faith.	60	59	0.3	NS

Table 12.8 Living with religious plurality

	Rel %	*Sec %*	χ^2	*p<*
Where I live, people who come from different countries get on well together.	51	50	0.7	NS
Where I live, people from different religious backgrounds get on well together.	48	45	1.7	NS
Where I live, people respect religious differences.	42	42	0.0	NS

live, people who come from different countries get on well together (50 per cent in secular schools and 51 per cent in religious schools). Just under half of the students in both types of school feel that, where they live, people from different religious backgrounds get on well together (45 per cent in secular schools and 48 per cent in religious schools). Just over two-fifths of the students in both types of school feel that, where they live, people respect religious difference (42 per cent in secular schools and 42 per cent in religious schools). Religious schools in Wales are not places that seem to colour their students' perception of the responses to cultural and religious diversity in their locality, either positively or negatively, in comparison with secular schools.

Living with cultural diversity

The section on living with cultural diversity explored the students' attitudes towards cultural diversity, in terms of living alongside people who come from different countries and people who belong to different religious backgrounds. Both of these issues were explored in terms of two levels of proximity (the educational context and the local community). The data demonstrate that students in religious schools are more likely to perceive cultural diversity as having a positive impact on their school (Table 12.9). While 45 per cent of students in secular schools feel that having people from different religious backgrounds makes their school or college an interesting place, the proportion rises to 54 per cent in religious schools. While 38 per cent of students in secular schools feel that people who come from different countries make their school or college an interesting place, the proportion rises to 45 per cent in religious schools. On the other hand, students in religious schools are no more likely to perceive cultural diversity as having a positive impact on their locality. Similar proportions of students in both types of schools feel that people from different religious backgrounds make where they live an interesting place (35 per cent in religious schools and 35 per cent in secular schools). Similar proportions of students in both types of school feel that people who come from different countries make where they live an interesting place (41 per cent

Table 12.9 Living with cultural diversity

	Rel %	Sec %	χ^2	p<
Having people from different religious backgrounds makes my school/college an interesting place.	54	45	16.6	.001
People who come from different countries make my school/college an interesting place.	45	38	11.0	.001
People from different religious backgrounds make where I live an interesting place.	35	35	0.1	NS
People who come from different countries make where I live an interesting place.	41	38	2.3	NS

in religious schools and 38 per cent in secular schools). Religious schools in Wales are places in which students may feel more positive about cultural diversity within the school environment, but this does not extend to their views on the wider community.

Accepting religious clothing

The section on accepting religious clothing examined the extent to which students found visible expressions of religious identity and religious differences acceptable within their schools. The data demonstrate that there is slightly greater acceptance of outward signs of Christian identity in religious schools, but that this does not extend to greater acceptance of outward signs associated with other faith traditions (Table 12.10). On the one hand, while 55 per cent of students in secular schools agree that Christians should be allowed to wear crosses in school, the proportion rises to 61 per cent in religious schools. On the other hand, there are no significant differences in the proportions of students who feel that: Muslims should be allowed to wear a headscarf in school (52 per cent in secular schools and 54 per cent in religious schools) or the burka in school (47 per cent in secular schools and 50 per cent in religious schools); Sikhs should be allowed to wear the turban in school (52 per cent in secular schools and 54 per cent in religious schools); Jews should be allowed to wear the kippah/yarmulke in school (50 per cent in secular schools and 52 per cent in religious schools); Hindus should be allowed to wear the bindi in school (51 per cent in secular schools and 53 per cent in religious schools). Religious schools in Wales are not places in which fellow students wishing to wear the Muslim headscarf or burka, the Sikh turban, the Jewish kippah/yarmulke or the Hindu bindi would be either more welcome or less welcome than would be the case in secular schools.

Table 12.10 Accepting religious clothing

	Rel %	*Sec %*	χ^2	*p<*
Christians should be allowed to wear crosses in school.	61	55	8.5	.01
Muslims should be allowed to wear the headscarf in school.	54	52	0.6	NS
Muslims should be allowed to wear the burka in school.	50	47	2.8	NS
Sikhs should be allowed to wear the turban in school.	54	52	1.7	NS
Jews should be allowed to wear the kippah/yarmulke in school.	52	50	0.4	NS
Hindus should be allowed to wear the bindi in school.	53	51	0.3	NS

Theme three: shaping attitudes towards religions and religious diversity

The third thesis tested by the present analysis is that the two groups of students (attending religious schools and attending secular schools) display no significant differences in their perceptions of the factors that have shaped their attitudes towards religions and religious diversity. This was tested against two sets of items concerning the importance of different sources of influence and concerning the specific influence of school on shaping views about different religious traditions.

Sources of influence

The section on the sources of influence explored the relative weight given to the influence of parents, friends, media and school in influencing views about religion. The data demonstrate that students in religious schools are significantly more conscious of the factors that have influenced their views about religion, in comparison with students in secular schools, and are more likely to attribute influence to parents, friends and school (Table 12.11). While 28 per cent of students in secular schools feel that their mother has influenced their views on religion, the proportion rises to 45 per cent in religious schools. While 23 per cent of students in secular schools feel that their father has influenced their views on religion, the proportion rises to 34 per cent in religious schools. While 18 per cent of students in secular schools feel that their friends have influenced their views on religion, the proportion rises to 26 per cent in religious schools. While 56 per cent of students in secular schools feel that studying religion in school has shaped their view about religion, the proportion rises to 65 per cent in religious schools. On the other hand, there is no significant difference between the two groups of students in terms of the proportions who attribute influence to television (33 per cent in secular schools and 36 per cent in religious schools) and to the Internet (21 per cent in secular schools and 25 per cent in religious schools).

Table 12.11 Sources of influence

	Rel %	*Sec %*	χ^2	*p<*
My mother has influenced my views about religion.	45	28	82.2	.001
My father has influenced my views about religion.	34	23	34.1	.001
My friends have influenced my views about religion.	26	18	21.2	.001
Studying religion at school has shaped my views about religion.	65	56	19.2	.001
Television has influenced my views about religion.	36	33	1.7	NS
The Internet has influenced my views about religion.	25	21	3.9	.05

Table 12.12 Studying religion in school

	Rel %	*Sec %*	χ^2	*p<*
Studying religion at school has shaped my views about . . .				
Buddhists	28	36	18.8	.001
Christians	59	49	22.4	.001
Hindus	33	40	11.6	.001
Jews	40	39	0.1	NS
Muslims	37	36	0.0	NS
Sikhs	22	31	20.1	.001

Religious schools in Wales are places in which students are more conscious of the factors that have shaped their views on religion.

Studying religion at school

The section on studying religion at school explored the extent to which students felt that studying religion at school had shaped their views about the adherents of the six main religious traditions identified within the 2001 census for England and Wales: Buddhists, Christians, Hindus, Jews, Muslims and Sikhs. The data demonstrate three main patterns in the findings (Table 12.12). First, students in religious schools are more likely to say that studying religion at school has shaped their views about Christianity (59 per cent compared with 49 per cent). Second, students in religious schools are less likely to say that studying religion at school has shaped their views about Buddhists (28 per cent compared with 36 per cent), Hindus (33 per cent compared with 40 per cent) or Sikhs (22 per cent compared with 31 per cent). Third, students in religious schools are neither more nor less likely to say that studying religion at school has shaped their views about Jews (40 per cent compared with 39 per cent) or Muslims (37 per cent compared with 36 per cent). Religious schools in Wales are places in which students may spend more time learning about Christianity and less time learning about Buddhists, Hindus and Sikhs, compared with students in secular schools, although they are likely to give comparable time to learning about Jews and Muslims.

Conclusion

This chapter set out to test the thesis proposed by the report *Right to Divide?* that schools with a religious character in Wales fail to prepare students for life in a religiously and ethnically diverse society and so fail to promote community cohesion. This thesis was examined against data provided by 1,087 students attending schools with a religious character alongside 1,214 students attending schools without a religious foundation. The analysis examines three themes: the religious worldview of students, students' attitudes towards religions and religious diversity, and students' perceptions of the influences shaping their attitudes towards religion and religious diversity. The following main conclusions emerge from these analyses.

The first conclusion concerns significant differences in the emphasis placed on a religious worldview within the two types of schools. Schools with a religious character in Wales are places where students are more likely to see religion as a matter of importance, where students are more likely to be supported by religious conversation in the home, where religion is more likely to influence students' outlook on life, where there is a higher level of religious belief, and where there is a higher level of commitment among the students to support the place of religion in the life of the school. These differences may well reflect the admissions policies of the schools with a religious character. Drawing together students who share a religious worldview may generate an environment in which peer support helps to normalize and sustain a religious worldview.

The second conclusion concerns the general lack of significant differences in attitudes towards religion and religious diversity within the two types of schools. Schools with a religious character in Wales are places where students hold only a slightly more positive attitude towards religion, where students are neither more nor less likely to accept social proximity with people from other religious backgrounds (in comparison with schools without a religious foundation), where students are neither more nor less likely to perceive religious discrimination in their neighbourhood, where students are neither more nor less likely to feel positive about cultural diversity in their local neighbourhood (although they are slightly more positive about cultural diversity in their school), and where students are neither more nor less open to expressions of religious clothing being worn in school.

The third conclusion concerns the factors that shape attitudes towards religion and religious diversity. Schools with a religious character in Wales are places where students are more conscious of the factors that have shaped their views on religion. They also have a different account from students in schools without a religious character regarding the way in which their schools prioritize religious learning. Schools with a religious character in Wales are places in which students may spend more time learning about Christianity and less time learning about Buddhists, Hindus and Sikhs, although they are likely to give comparable time to learning about Jews and Muslims.

Taken together, these three conclusions suggest that schools with a religious character in Wales are producing students neither more adequately nor less adequately prepared for life in a religiously and ethnically diverse society, in comparison with schools without a religious foundation. While schools with a religious character cannot, on the basis of these data, be accused of failing to promote community cohesion as well as schools without a religious foundation, nor can they be applauded for making a positive contribution to community cohesion. These data do however offer a serious critique of the evidential basis for the criticism of schools with a religious character advanced by the Runnymede Trust in their report *Right to Divide? Faith Schools and Community Cohesion* (Berkeley 2008). Although this report refers to taking evidence from students themselves, there is no evidence offered in the report regarding the strategies for sampling young people, for framing the collection of data or for analyzing the findings.

References

Aspinall, P. 2000. 'The Challenges of Measuring the Ethno-cultural Diversity of Britain in the New Millennium.' *Policy and Politics* 28 (1): 109–118.

Berkeley, R. 2008. *Right to Divide? Faith Schools and Community cohesion.* London: Runnymede Trust.

Census White Paper. 1999. *The 2001 Census of Population.* London: HMSO.

Chadwick, P. 1997. *Shifting Alliances: Church and State in English Education.* London: Cassell.

Cruickshank, M. 1963. *Church and State in English Education.* London: Macmillan.

Dummett, A., and J. McNeal. 1981. *Race and Church Schools.* London: Runnymede Trust.

Francis, L. J. 2002. 'Catholic Schools and Catholic Values: A Study of Moral and Religious Values among 13–15 year old Students Attending Non-denominational and Catholic Schools in England and Wales.' *International Journal of Education and Religion* 3 (1): 69–84.

———. 2003. 'Religion and Social Capital: The Flaw in the 2001 Census in England and Wales.' In *Public Faith: The State of Religious Belief and Practice in Britain,* ed. P. Avis, 45–64. London: SPCK.

Francis, L. J., D. W. Lankshear, M. Robbins, A. Village, and T. ap Siôn. 2014. 'Defining and Measuring the Contribution of Anglican Secondary Schools to Students' Religious, Personal and Social Values.' *Journal of Empirical Theology* 27 (1): 57–84.

Francis, L. J., and G. Penny. 2013. 'The Ethos of Anglican Secondary Schools Reflected through Pupil Values: An Empirical Enquiry among 13- to 15-year-olds.' In *Anglican Church School Education,* ed. H. Worsley, 131–150. London: Continuum.

Jackson, R. 2003. 'Should the State Fund Faith Based Schools? A Review of the Arguments.' *British Journal of Religious Education* 25 (2): 89–102.

Jones, I. G., and D. Williams, eds. 1976. *The Religious Census of 1851: A Calendar of the Returns Relating to Wales (Volume 1, South Wales).* Cardiff: University of Wales Press.

Lankshear, D. W. 2005. 'The Influence of Anglican Secondary Schools on Personal, Moral and Religious Values.' In *Religion, Education and Adolescence: International Empirical Perspectives,* ed. L. J. Francis, M. Robbins, and J. Astley, 55–69. Cardiff: University of Wales Press.

Murphy, J. 1971. *Church, State and Schools in Britain 1800–1970.* London: Routledge and Kegan Paul.

Sherif, J. 2011. 'A Census Chronicle: Reflections on the Campaign for a Religious Question in the 2001 Census for England and Wales.' *Journal of Beliefs and Values* 32 (1): 1–18.

Swann Report. 1985. *Education for All.* London: HMSO.

Village, A., and L. J. Francis. 2015, in press. 'Measuring the Contribution of Roman Catholic Secondary Schools to Students' Religious, Personal and Social Values.' *Catholic Education* (September).

Weller, P. 2004. 'Identity, Politics, and the Future(s) of Religion in the UK: The Case of the Religious Question in the 2001 Decennial Census.' *Journal of Contemporary Religion* 19 (1): 3–21.

Welsh Assembly Government. 2009. *Getting on Together: A Community Cohesion Strategy for Wales.* Cardiff: WAG.

———. 2011. *Respect and Resilience – Developing Community Cohesion: A Common Understanding for Schools and their Communities.* Cardiff: WAG.

Welsh Government. 2011. *Faith in Education.* Cardiff: WAG.

13 The personal and social significance of diverse religious affiliation in multi-faith London

Leslie J. Francis and Gemma Penny

Introduction

The religious landscape of England and Wales has undergone rapid and radical change since the early 1950s. On the one hand, church attendance has declined and churches and chapels have been demolished or have turned to secular uses (country cottages and inner-city warehouses). Some commentators have spoken confidently of *The Making of Post-Christian Britain* (Gilbert 1980), and of *The Death of Christian Britain* (Brown 2001). On the other hand, other major world faiths have taken root, especially in some of the major cities. Mosques, temples, gurdwaras and synagogues witness these traditions nestling alongside long-established churches and chapels. Some commentators have spoken confidently of the growth of religious diversity throughout the UK (see Parsons 1993, 1994; Wolffe 1993; Weller 2008) and especially within London.

Religion itself is far from being a simple or unidimensional construct. The public face of religious diversity is generally discussed in terms of religious affiliation (Christian, Muslim, Sikh, no religion and so on) rather than in terms of religious beliefs or religious practice. Religious affiliation is both the most readily available and least understood indicator of religiosity within the social scientific literature. It is readily available because religious affiliation is regarded as an aspect of personal and social identity (like sex, age and ethnicity) and properly included within public enquiries like the national census. In this sense, religious affiliation is regarded as belonging to the public and social domain, in marked contrast to religious beliefs and religious practices which are generally regarded as belonging to the private and personal domain, properly protected from public scrutiny. Religious affiliation is poorly understood because both conceptually and empirically it seems to function quite differently from the ways in which other indicators of religiosity (like beliefs and practices) function. As a consequence, religious affiliation acts as a relatively poor predictor of other religious indicators.

The debate about the usefulness of religious affiliation as an indicator in social research was brought to particular prominence in England and Wales in the six-year period prior to the 2001 national census, when the introduction of a religious affiliation question within the census was seriously debated for the first time (Francis 2003; Weller 2004; Sherif 2011). Similar debates have occurred in other countries such as New Zealand (Statistics New Zealand 1998).

Initially, the Office for National Statistics (ONS) was highly perplexed by the proposal (initiated through the Inner Cities Religious Council and Churches Together in England) to introduce a religious question. The two challenges for the senior managers of the ONS were to grasp the complexity of religion and to see the public utility of information about religion. The initial rebuff to the Inner Cities Council was signed by John Dixie on behalf of the ONS:'this is not a priority for Census users' (Sherif 2011, 2). Pressed further, however, the ONS agreed to convene a consultative group, the Religious Affiliation Sub-Group of the Census Content Working Group (chaired by Leslie J. Francis) to scope the issue further. This group consistently advanced two points of clarification.

The first point of clarification focused on the variety of meaning that 'a religious question' may suggest. The argument was made as follows:

> Debates within this area distinguish clearly between three distinct dimensions of religion, which are generally characterised as: belief; practice, affiliation. Questions about religious belief belong to the domain of personal matters. The census should not be concerned with matters of religious belief. Questions about religious practice (like attendance at places of worship) demonstrate the interface between the personal and the public dimension of religion. It is not proposed that the census should be concerned with religious practice. Questions about affiliation touch most closely the public and social dimensions of religion. It is proposed that the census should include a question on religious affiliation.
>
> (Sherif 2011, 4)

The second point of clarification focused on the public utility of information about religion. The argument was made as follows:

> First, scientific research in areas (for example) of psychology, sociology, gerontology and health care is pointing increasingly to the importance of religious indicators for predicting a range of practical outcomes. For example, international empirical research indicates the different patterns of social support required by the religious elderly, the speedier recovery rate from certain illnesses among some religious subjects, the different patterns of substance abuse among religious teenagers, and so on . . . In other words, knowing about the distribution of religion within society could promote the more effective and efficient targeting of resources, and indicate the presence of fresh partners in provision.
>
> (Indicative Business Case for the Religion Question
> in the 2001 Census, paragraph 2.5)

The controversial issue in connecting those two points (the focus on religious affiliation and the focus on the public utility of information about religion) _date about whether religious affiliation serves as a reliable, _cient indicator of religion being capable of predicting useful vari- _on matters of public significance. This is an empirical matter open to serious scientific investigation. Examples of how such investigation has been conducted in England and Wales can be found in analyses undertaken on data provided by the British Social Attitudes Survey and by the Teenage Religion and Values Survey.

Religious affiliation in London

London was included as a 'special case' within the Young People's Attitudes to Religious Diversity project, alongside England, Northern Ireland, Scotland and Wales, on the assumption that the religious profile of the population of London was highly distinctive. The data generated by the religious question within the 2011 census (http://www.ons.gov.uk) validated the assumption. In England as a whole, 7.2 per cent of the population left the voluntary question on religion unanswered, 24.7 per cent reported no religion, 59.4 per cent Christian, 5.0 per cent Muslim, 1.5 per cent Hindu, 0.5 per cent Jewish, 0.8 per cent Sikh, 0.5 per cent Buddhist and 0.4 per cent as 'other religion'. A very different picture emerged in London, with 8.5 per cent of the population leaving the voluntary question on religion unanswered, 20.7 per cent reporting no religion, 48.4 per cent Christian, 12.4 per cent Muslim, 5.0 per cent Hindu, 1.8 per cent Jewish, 1.5 per cent Sikh, 1.0 per cent Buddhist and 0.6 per cent as 'other religion'.

Comparisons made between the findings from the two censuses in 2001 and 2011 demonstrated some interesting differences between London and England as a whole. Similar to the rest of England, the proportion of those who self-assigned as Christian declined in London, but London experienced the lowest decrease (below 10 per cent). London also had the smallest increase in those claiming no religion and the highest increase of Muslims (4 per cent).

In 2011, of all areas in England, London had the highest proportion of Muslims, Hindus, Jewish, Buddhists and people of 'other religions'. Five of the top 10 local authorities with the largest proportion of Muslims were in London: Tower Hamlets, Newham, Redbridge, Waltham Forest and Brent. Tower Hamlets had the highest proportion of Muslims at 35 per cent. Four of the top five local authorities with the largest proportion of Hindus were in London: Harrow, Brent, Redbridge and Hounslow. Harrow had the highest proportion of Hindus at 25 per cent. Three of the top five local authorities with the highest proportion of Jews were in London: Barnet, Hackney and Camden. Barnet had the highest proportion of Jews at 15 per cent. Four of the top five local authorities with the highest proportion of Buddhists were in London: Greenwich, Kensington and Chelsea, Westminster, and Hounslow. Greenwich had the highest proportion of Buddhists at 2 per cent.

Personal and social correlates of religious affiliation

The British Social Attitudes Survey, which has been conducted almost every year since 1983 (excluding 1988 and 1992), provides a broad and reliable source of data across a range of personal and social attitudes. In principle these data should provide an interesting opportunity to test the thesis that religious affiliation functions as a significant predictor of attitudes and values that are of personal and social importance. Indeed, significant contributions to this debate have been made by chapters published in annual reviews employing these data, including Nina Stratford and Ian Christie (2000); Anne Barlow et al. (2001); Stratford, Theresa Marteau and Martin Bobrow (2001); Arthur Gould and Stratford (2002); Park and Paula Surridge (2003); Patrick Sturgis et al. (2004); Anthony Heath, Jean Martin and Gabriella Elgenius (2007); Elizabeth Clery, Sheila McLean and Miranda Phillips (2007); Barlow et al. (2008); David Voas and Rodney Ling (2010); Sonia Exley (2012); Lois Lee (2012); Park and Rebecca Rhead (2013); and Heath, Mike Savage and Nicki Senior (2013). Findings from the British Social Attitudes Survey on the religious and social significance of self-assigned religious affiliation have also been published in a number of independent papers, including Bernadette Hayes (1995); Hayes and Manussos Marangudakis (2001); Francis (2003); and Barlow et al. (2005). The majority of these studies, drawing on the British Social Attitudes Survey data, focused on differences between Christian denominations while treating all other religious traditions as one group.

As Francis, Emyr Williams and Andrew Village (2011) discovered when they set out to explore the connection between marital status and religious affiliation, generally the major faith traditions apart from Christianity are insufficiently represented within the annual participation of the British Social Attitudes Survey to provide meaningful analyses. Francis, Williams and Village (2011) circumvented this problem by collapsing sets of annual surveys to create larger datasets. The 11 surveys conducted between 1983 and 1995 (recognizing no surveys were conducted in 1988 and 1992) generated a total of 10,014 cases, among whom there were 199 Muslims, 158 Hindus, 136 Jews, 56 Sikhs and 30 Buddhists. The 10 surveys conducted between 1996 and 2005 generated a total of 13,914 cases, among whom there were 507 Muslims, 200 Hindus, 170 Jews, 96 Sikhs and 56 Buddhists. In their analyses Francis, Williams, and Village (2011) confirmed that marital status varied among the different religious traditions.

A more sustained attempt to explore the religious and social significance of self-assigned religious affiliation across the faith traditions has been demonstrated by recent analyses of the data generated by the Teenage Religion and Values Survey, conducted in the 1990s among 13- to 15-year-old students across England and Wales (see Francis 2001a). For example, Francis (2001b, 2001c) compared the responses of young people who self-identified as Christians (13,676), Muslims (349), Sikhs (125), Hindus (125) and Jews (71), alongside those who owned no religious affiliation (13,360).

In the first of these two papers, Francis (2001b) profiled the association between faith-group affiliation and aspects of religious belief, personal values, family values and social values. In terms of religious belief, the data demonstrated a closer association between affiliation and belief among non-Christian faith groups than among Christians. Thus belief in God was reported by 92 per cent of Muslims, 79 per cent of Hindus, 74 per cent of Sikhs and 65 per cent of Jews, compared with 55 per cent of Christians. At the same time, belief in God was not restricted to those who owned religious affiliation: 24 per cent of non-affiliates also believed in God.

In terms of personal values, a clear association was found between faith-group affiliation and purpose in life, although levels of purpose in life varied from one faith group to another. While 50 per cent of young people who belonged to no faith group reported that their life had a sense of purpose, the proportions rose to 51 per cent among Sikhs, 61 per cent among Christians, 62 per cent among Hindus, 64 per cent among Jews and 68 per cent among Muslims.

In terms of family values, a clear association was found between faith-group affiliation and support received in the home from the mother. The differences, however, were not always in favour of the faith groups. While 47 per cent of young people who belonged to no faith group found it helpful to talk about their problems with their mother, the proportions fell to 45 per cent among Sikhs and to 40 per cent among Hindus, but rose to 52 per cent among Muslims, 53 per cent among Christians and 71 per cent among Jews.

In terms of social values, a clear association was found between faith group affiliation and attitudes towards the police. While 51 per cent of young people who belonged to no faith group considered that the police do a good job, the proportions fell to 49 per cent among Muslims, 40 per cent among Hindus and 35 per cent among Sikhs, but rose to 55 per cent among Jews and 59 per cent among Christians.

In the second paper pursuing this theme, Francis (2001c) provided analyses on the association between faith-group affiliation and attitudes towards school, sex, alcohol, environment and leisure. In terms of attitude towards school, there was a clear association between faith-group affiliation and bullying. While 25 per cent of young people who belonged to no faith group were worried about being bullied at school, the proportions rose to 30 per cent among Christians, 31 per cent among Muslims, 32 per cent among Jews, 34 per cent among Sikhs and 39 per cent among Hindus.

In terms of attitude towards sex, a clear link remained between faith-group affiliation and more traditional views. While 10 per cent of young people who belonged to no faith group took the view that it is wrong to have sexual intercourse outside marriage, the proportions rose to 15 per cent among Christians, 23 per cent among Jews, 23 per cent among Sikhs, 27 per cent among Hindus and 48 per cent among Muslims.

In terms of attitude towards alcohol, a clear link between faith-group affiliation and more traditional views also persisted. While 17 per cent of young people who belonged to no faith group took the view that it is wrong to become drunk, the proportions rose to 21 per cent among Christians, 21 per cent among Jews, 33 per cent among Sikhs, 33 per cent among Hindus and 68 per cent among Muslims.

In terms of attitude towards environmental issues, some interesting differences emerged between faith groups. While 63 per cent of young people who belonged to no faith group expressed concern about the risk of pollution to the environment, the proportions fell slightly to 61 per cent among both Muslims and Sikhs, but rose to 68 per cent among Hindus, 72 per cent among Christians and 76 per cent among Jews.

In terms of attitude towards leisure, some clear differences emerged in terms of issues concerning parental supervision. While 19 per cent of young people who belonged to no faith group and 20 per cent of Christians said that their parents prefer them to stay at home as much as possible, the proportions dropped to 11 per cent among Jews, but rose to 39 per cent among Hindus, 51 per cent among Muslims and 57 per cent among Sikhs.

A more recent exploration of the religious and social significance of self-assigned religious affiliation in England and Wales was reported by Francis and Mandy Robbins (2014), drawing on a sample of 567 16- to 18-year-old students, comprising 244 Christians, 111 Muslims and 212 non-affiliated students. This study explored two main areas. First, the analysis identified eight themes concerning religious beliefs: the Bible, the Qur'an, Jesus, Muhammad, Jesus and justice, Muhammad and justice, experiencing God and the theology of religions. Second, the analysis identified six themes concerning the connection between religion and matters of public concern: religion and personal life, religion and public life, religion and the state, social rights, the rights of women and children, and sex and morality. The data highlighted some areas of commonality and some areas of strong divergence between the three groups, demonstrating how the religious and social significance of self-assigned religious affiliation holds salience in some areas rather than others.

Research question

Against this background, the aim of the present chapter is to draw on the Young People's Attitudes to Religious Diversity project to test two main theses among students attending secondary schools in London. The first thesis is that self-assigned religious affiliation serves as a predictor of significant differences in the personal worldview and experience of young people. The second thesis is that self-assigned religious affiliation serves as a predictor of significant differences in the social worldview of young people.

These two broad and general theses are sharpened in the light of the data made available by the 'Diversity project', both in terms of the themes covered by the survey and in terms of the range of respondents to the survey. In terms of themes covered by the survey, eight areas are available to explore personal worldview and experiences: religious identity, religious importance, religious self-assessment, religious conversation, religious influences, religious beliefs, personal wellbeing and social wellbeing. Five areas are available to explore social worldview: attitudes towards religions, attitudes towards religious plurality, living with religious plurality, living with cultural diversity and living with religious differences. In terms of the range of respondents within the London schools accessed by the survey, alongside religiously unaffiliated students, there were sufficient numbers of students within three religious traditions to enable profiles to be generated: Christian students, Hindu students and Muslim students.

Method

Procedure

As part of a large multi-method project on religious diversity designed to examine the experiences and attitudes of young people living in the multicultural and multi-faith context of the UK, classes of Year 9 and Year 10 students in London (13–15 years of age) were invited to complete a questionnaire survey during 2011 and 2012. The participants were guaranteed confidentiality and anonymity and were given the choice not to take part in the survey. The level of interest shown in the project meant that very few students decided not to participate. The sampling frame set out to capture data from at least 2,000 students in London, with half attending schools with a religious character within the state-maintained sector and half attending schools without a religious foundation within the state-maintained sector.

Instrument

The *Religious Diversity and Young People* survey was designed for self-completion, using mainly multiple-choice questions and Likert scaling on 5 points: agree strongly, agree, not certain, disagree and disagree strongly. In the present analysis, 13 groups of items were identified from the instrument to map the following areas: religious identity, religious importance, religious self-assessment, religious conversation, religious influences, religious beliefs, personal wellbeing, social wellbeing, attitudes towards religions, attitudes towards religious plurality, living with religious plurality, living with cultural diversity and living with religious differences.

Participants

In London, completed questionnaires were submitted by 2,296 students. The following analyses are based on 1,250 who self-identified as Christians, 231 who self-identified as Hindus, 227 who self-identified as Muslims and 505 who self-identified as having no religious affiliation. The remaining 83 students comprised small numbers of Buddhists (15), Sikhs (15) and Jews (8), alongside other groups and some missing cases, and were excluded from the present analysis.

Analysis

The data were analyzed by means of SPSS, employing chi square 4 × 2 contingency tables, combining the 'agree strongly' and 'agree' responses into one category and the 'disagree strongly', 'disagree' and 'not certain' responses into the second category.

Results

Theme one: personal worldview and experience

The first thesis tested by this chapter is that self-assigned religious affiliation serves as a predictor of significant difference in the personal worldview and experience of young people. This thesis is tested against eight areas defined as religious identity, religious importance, religious self-assessment, religious conversation, religious influence, religious beliefs, personal wellbeing and social wellbeing.

Religious identity

The section on religious identity explored students' perceptions of the importance that they attribute to their own religious identity and their perceptions of the importance attributed to religious identity by their parents. The data demonstrate that the saliency of religion varies from group to group with the highest levels among Muslims (Table 13.1). Thus 88 per cent of Muslim students said their religious identity is important to them, followed by 67 per cent of Hindus, 47 per cent of Christians and 10 per cent of non-affiliates. In terms of parental religious identity, 82 per cent Muslim students said their father's religious identity is important to him, followed by 69 per cent of Hindus, 35 per cent of Christians and 12 per cent of non-affiliates. Similarly 94 per cent of Muslim students said that their mother's religious identity is important to her, followed by 84 per cent of Hindus, 62 per cent of Christians and 20 per cent of non-affiliates. Self-assigned religious affiliation predicts different levels of saliency for religion in the lives of young people and in the lives of their parents.

Table 13.1 Religious identity

	None %	Hindu %	Musl %	Chri %	χ^2	$p<$
My religious identity is important to me.	10	67	88	47	462.69	.001
My father's religious identity is important to him.	12	69	82	35	441.40	.001
My mother's religious identity is important to her.	20	84	94	62	488.18	.001

Religious importance

The section on religious importance explored students' perceptions of the importance attributed to religion by their grandparents, parents and friends. The data demonstrate that the highest level of religious social support is perceived by Muslims (Table 13.2). Thus 93 per cent of Muslims considered that their parents think religion is important, followed by 79 per cent of Hindus, 59 per cent of Christians and 14 per cent of non-affiliates. Similarly 88 per cent of Muslims considered that their grandparents think religion is important, followed by 85 per cent of Hindus, 53 per cent of Christians and 29 per cent of non-affiliates. The same pattern also followed in terms of peers where 64 per cent of Muslims considered that their friends think religion is important, followed by 43 per cent of Hindus, 32 per cent of Christians and 22 per cent of non-affiliates. Self-assigned religious affiliation predicts different levels of social support for maintaining a religious worldview.

Religious self-assessment

The section on religious self-assessment explored the ways in which students perceive themselves religious or spiritual individuals and the part religion plays in shaping their lives. The data demonstrate that awareness of the connection between religion and individual lives varies from group to group, with the greatest awareness evident among Muslim students (Table 13.3). Thus 72 per cent of

Table 13.2 Religious importance

	None %	Hindu %	Musl %	Chri %	χ^2	$p<$
Most of my friends think religion is important.	22	43	64	32	134.32	.001
My parents think religion is important.	14	79	93	59	535.21	.001
My grandparents think religion is important.	29	85	88	53	328.08	.001

Table 13.3 Religious self-assessment

	None %	Hindu %	Musl %	Chri %	χ^2	$p<$
I am a religious person.	2	49	72	56	512.56	.001
I am a spiritual person.	12	29	33	30	68.81	.001
My life has been shaped by my religious faith.	8	55	68	41	320.50	.001
When making important decisions in my life, my religion plays a major role.	6	48	72	38	348.36	.001

Muslim students rated themselves as a religious person, followed by 56 per cent of Christians, 49 per cent of Hindus and 2 per cent of non-affiliates. Similarly 33 per cent of Muslim students rated themselves as a spiritual person, followed by 30 per cent of Christians, 29 per cent of Hindus and 12 per cent of non-affiliates. Two-thirds of Muslim students (68 per cent) said that their life has been shaped by their religious faith, followed by 55 per cent of Hindus, 41 per cent of Christians and 8 per cent of non-affiliates. Nearly three-quarters of Muslim students (72 per cent) said that their religion plays a major role when they are making important decisions in their life, followed by 48 per cent of Hindus, 38 per cent of Christians and 6 per cent of non-affiliates. Self-assigned religious affiliation predicts different levels of awareness of the importance of religion in shaping life.

Religious conversation

The section on religious conversation explored the extent to which students talk about religion with those closest to them. The data demonstrate that conversation about religion varies from group to group, with the greatest frequency evident among Muslims (Table 13.4). Two-thirds of Muslim students (66 per cent) often talk about religion with their mother, followed by 50 per cent of Hindus, 40 per cent of Christians and 18 per cent of non-affiliates. Over half of Muslim students (54 per cent) often talk about religion with their father, followed by 39 per cent of Hindus, 26 per cent of Christians and 18 per cent of non-affiliates. Over two-fifths of Muslim students (43 per cent) often talk about religion with their grandparents, followed by 39 per cent of Hindus, 21 per cent of Christians and 11 per cent of non-affiliates. Nearly half of Muslim students (48 per cent) often talk about religion with their friends, followed by 30 per cent of Hindus, 30 per cent of Christians and 25 per cent of non-affiliates. Self-assigned religious affiliation predicts different levels of engagement in religious conversation.

Religious influence

The section on religious influence explored the way in which students evaluated the influence of parents, friends and school on shaping their views about religion. The data demonstrate that school had an important part to play in

Table 13.4 Religious conversation

	None %	Hindu %	Musl %	Chri %	χ^2	$p<$
I often talk about religion with my mother.	18	50	66	40	179.13	.001
I often talk about religion with my father.	18	39	54	26	114.32	.001
I often talk about religion with my grandparents.	11	39	43	21	131.16	.001
I often talk about religion with my friends.	25	30	48	30	39.72	.001

Table 13.5 Religious influence

	None %	Hindu %	Musl %	Chri %	χ^2	$p<$
My mother has influenced my views about religion.	29	72	67	66	229.57	.001
My father has influenced my views about religion.	31	67	63	50	111.69	.001
My friends have influenced my views about religion.	19	30	37	35	43.51	.001
Studying religion at school has shaped my views about religion.	60	79	61	71	38.54	.001

Table 13.6 Religious beliefs

	None %	Hindu %	Musl %	Chri %	χ^2	$p<$
I believe in God.	13	75	93	75	717.63	.001
I believe in life after death.	30	65	79	59	195.05	.001
I believe in heaven.	23	55	96	76	543.93	.001
I believe in hell.	17	45	92	56	394.80	.001

shaping views about religion among all four groups: 79 per cent of Hindus, 71 per cent of Christians, 61 per cent of Muslims and 60 per cent of non-affiliates (Table 13.5). Mother had a stronger part to play among Hindus (72 per cent), Muslims (67 per cent) and Christians (66 per cent), compared with non-affiliates (29 per cent). Father, too, had a stronger part to play among Hindus (67 per cent), Muslims (63 per cent) and Christians (50 per cent), compared with non-affiliates (31 per cent). Compared with parents, friends had a less important part to play in shaping views about religion among Muslims (37 per cent), Christians (35 per cent) and Hindus (30 per cent), although this was still higher than among non-affiliates (19 per cent). Self-assigned religious affiliation predicts different forms of influence in the development of religious views.

Religious beliefs

The section on religious beliefs explored the two areas concerning belief in God and belief in life after death. The data demonstrate that in both of these areas the highest level of belief was recorded among Muslims (Table 13.6). Thus nearly all Muslim students (93 per cent) believed in God, followed by 75 per cent of Hindus, 75 per cent of Christians and 13 per cent of non-affiliates. Four out of five Muslim students (79 per cent) believed in life after death, followed by 65 per cent of Hindus, 59 per cent of Christians and 30 per cent of non-affiliates.

Table 13.7 Personal wellbeing

	None %	Hindu %	Musl %	Chri %	χ^2	$p<$
I feel my life has a sense of purpose.	45	65	79	67	100.62	.001
I find life really worth living.	63	73	71	76	29.17	.001
I often feel depressed.	34	26	24	27	11.92	.008
I have sometimes considered taking my own life.	24	20	17	14	27.79	.001

Nearly all Muslim students (96 per cent) believed in heaven, followed by 76 per cent of Christians, 55 per cent of Hindus and 23 per cent of non-affiliates. Nearly all Muslim students (92 per cent) believed in hell, followed by 56 per cent of Christians, 45 per cent of Hindus and 17 per cent of non-affiliates. Self-assigned religious affiliation predicts very different levels of religious belief.

Personal wellbeing

The section on personal wellbeing explored two areas of wellbeing, concerning positive affect and negative affect. The data demonstrate that both positive affect and negative affect vary from group to group (Table 13.7). Negative affect was highest and positive affect was lowest among non-affiliates, with some variation among the religious groups. While 45 per cent of non-affiliates felt that their life has a sense of purpose, the proportions rose to 65 per cent among Hindus, 67 per cent among Christians and 79 per cent among Muslims. While 63 per cent of non-affiliates found life really worth living, the proportions rose to 76 per cent among Christians, 73 per cent among Hindus and 71 per cent among Muslims. In terms of negative affect, 24 per cent of Muslims, 26 per cent of Hindus and 27 per cent of Christians often felt depressed, with the proportion rising to 34 per cent among non-affiliates; 14 per cent of Christians, 17 per cent of Muslims and 20 per cent of Hindus had sometimes considered taking their own life, with the proportion rising to 24 per cent among non-affiliates. Self-assigned religious affiliation predicts different levels of personal wellbeing.

Social wellbeing

The section on social wellbeing explored vulnerability and bullying. The data demonstrate that levels of victimization and bullying vary from group to group (Table 13.8). Both Muslims and Hindus reported a higher level of bullying in comparison with Christians and non-affiliates. Thus 17 per cent of Hindus and 23 per cent of Muslims felt that they were bullied because of their religion, compared with 7 per cent of Christians and 3 per cent of non-affiliates. In a similar

Table 13.8 Social wellbeing

	None %	Hindu %	Musl %	Chri %	χ^2	$p<$
I am bullied because of my religion.	3	17	23	7	102.33	.001
I am bullied because of my race or colour.	8	21	20	12	35.76	.001
I am bullied because of my language.	3	13	8	5	32.77	.001
I am bullied because my family comes from another country.	7	10	13	7	14.41	.01

vein 21 per cent of Hindus and 20 per cent of Muslims felt that they were also bullied because of their race or colour, compared with 12 per cent of Christians and 8 per cent of non-affiliates. Likewise, 13 per cent of Hindus and 8 per cent of Muslims were bullied because of their language, compared with 5 per cent of Christians and 3 per cent of non-affiliates; 10 per cent of Hindus and 13 per cent of Muslims were bullied because their family came from another country, compared with 7 per cent of Christians and 7 per cent of non-affiliates. Self-assigned religious affiliation predicts different levels of social wellbeing.

Theme two: social worldview

The second thesis tested in this chapter is that self-assigned religious affiliation serves as a predictor of significant differences in the social worldview of young people. This thesis is tested against five areas defined as attitudes towards religions, attitudes towards religious plurality, living with religious plurality, living with cultural diversity and living with religious differences.

Attitudes towards religions

The section on attitudes towards religions explored two related areas: respect for religious inclusivity and evaluation of the social face of religion. The data demonstrate that Muslim students and Hindu students showed the highest commitment to religious inclusivity (Table 13.9). Thus 94 per cent of Muslims and 93 per cent of Hindus agreed that we must respect all religions, compared with 80 per cent of Christians and 72 per cent of non-affiliates; 87 per cent of Muslims and 87 per cent of Hindus agreed that all religious groups in Britain should have equal rights, compared with 68 per cent of Christians and 69 per cent of non-affiliates. At the same time, non-affiliated students showed the highest level of criticism of the social face of religion. Thus 59 per cent of non-affiliates considered that religion brings more conflict than peace, compared with 45 per cent of Christians, 44 per cent of Hindus and 37 per cent of Muslims. Similarly

Table 13.9 Attitudes towards religions

	None %	Hindu %	Musl %	Chri %	χ^2	$p<$
We must respect all religions.	72	93	94	80	72.20	.001
All religious groups in Britain should have equal rights.	69	87	87	68	66.56	.001
Religion brings more conflict than peace.	59	44	37	45	42.97	.001
Religious people are often intolerant of others.	37	31	24	30	13.59	.001

Table 13.10 Attitudes towards religious plurality

	None %	Hindu %	Musl %	Chri %	χ^2	$p<$
I would be happy to go out with someone from a different denomination.	70	60	54	67	22.39	.001
I would be happy to go out with someone from a different faith.	67	62	52	65	24.63	.001
I would be happy about a close relative marrying someone from a different denomination.	68	57	39	65	65.31	.001
I would be happy about a close relative marrying someone from a different faith.	72	61	44	60	56.29	.001

37 per cent of non-affiliates considered that religious people are often intolerant of others, compared with 31 per cent of Hindus, 30 per cent of Christians and 24 per cent of Muslims. Self-assigned religious affiliation predicts different attitudes towards religions.

Attitudes towards religious plurality

The section on attitude towards religious plurality explored the social proximity thesis in two ways: personal relationships and relationships involving close relatives. The data demonstrate that the Hindu and Muslim students are less open to crossing religious boundaries in this way (Table 13.10). In terms of personal relationships, 60 per cent of Hindus and 54 per cent of Muslims said they would be happy to go out with someone from a different denomination, compared with 67 per cent of Christians and 70 per cent of non-affiliates; 62 per cent of Hindus and 52 per cent of Muslims said they would be happy to go out with someone from a different faith, compared with 65 per cent of Christians and 67 per cent of non-affiliates. In terms of relationships involving close relatives, 57 per cent of Hindus and 39 per cent of Muslims said they would be happy

Table 13.11 Living with religious plurality

	None %	Hindu %	Musl %	Chri %	χ^2	p<
Where I live, people who come from different countries get on well together.	61	71	71	68	12.35	.01
Where I live, people from different religious backgrounds get on well together.	59	75	70	64	19.98	.001
Where I live, people respect religious differences.	53	70	63	57	19.88	.001

about a close relative marrying someone from a different denomination; 61 per cent of Hindus and 44 per cent of Muslims said they would be happy about a close relative marrying someone from a different faith. Self-assigned religious affiliation predicts different attitudes towards religious plurality.

Living with religious plurality

The section on living with religious plurality explores perceptions of community cohesion and mutual acceptance. The data demonstrate that Hindu and Muslim students are more positive about these matters (Table 13.11). Thus 71 per cent of Hindus and 71 per cent of Muslims felt that, where they live, people who come from different countries get on well together, compared with 68 per cent of Christians and 61 per cent of non-affiliates. Similarly 75 per cent of Hindus and 70 per cent of Muslims felt that, where they live, people from different religious backgrounds get on well together, compared with 64 per cent of Christians and 59 per cent of non-affiliates. Likewise, 70 per cent of Hindus and 63 per cent of Muslims felt that, where they live, people respect religious differences, compared with 57 per cent of Christians and 53 per cent of non-affiliates. Self-assigned religious affiliation predicts differences in attitudes towards living with religious plurality.

Living with cultural diversity

The section on living with cultural diversity explored the impact of cultural diversity and religion on perceptions of the local school or college and the local neighbourhood. The data demonstrate that Hindu and Muslim students hold a more positive attitude towards cultural diversity (Table 13.12). In terms of local school or college, 81 per cent of Hindus and 82 per cent of Muslims said that having people from different religious backgrounds makes their school or college a more interesting place, compared with 60 per cent of Christians and 60 per cent of non-affiliates; 76 per cent of Hindus and 70 per cent of Muslims said having people who come from different countries makes their school or college a more interesting place, compared with 61 per cent of Christians

Table 13.12 Living with cultural diversity

	None %	Hindu %	Musl %	Chri %	χ^2	p<
Having people from different religious backgrounds makes my school/college an interesting place.	60	81	82	60	72.49	.001
People who come from different countries make my school/college an interesting place.	56	76	70	61	33.70	.001
People from different religious backgrounds make where I live an interesting place.	45	71	65	47	68.24	.001
People who come from different countries make where I live an interesting place.	51	67	66	55	25.22	.001

and 56 per cent of non-affiliates. In terms of local neighbourhood, 71 per cent of Hindus and 65 per cent of Muslims said people from different religious backgrounds make where they live a more interesting place, compared with 47 per cent of Christians and 45 per cent of non-affiliates; 67 per cent of Hindus and 66 per cent of Muslims said people who come from different countries make where they live an interesting place, compared with 55 per cent of Christians and 51 per cent of non-affiliates. Self-assigned religious affiliation predicts differences in attitudes towards living with cultural diversity.

Living with religious differences

The section on living with religious differences explored openness to students wearing distinctive religious clothing or symbols in school. The data demonstrate that overall Hindu and Muslim students are the most open to different religious traditions being visible in school in this way, while Christian students (apart from their own tradition) display a similar profile to that of non-affiliated students (Table 13.13). Thus 88 per cent of Muslims and 79 per cent of Hindus agreed that Muslims should be allowed to wear the headscarf in school, compared with 67 per cent of Christians and 66 per cent of non-affiliates; 77 per cent of Hindus and 76 per cent of Muslims agreed that Hindus should be allowed to wear the bindi in school, compared with 63 per cent of Christians and 66 per cent of non-affiliates. Similarly 84 per cent of Muslims and 82 per cent of Hindus agreed that Sikhs should be allowed to wear the turban in school, compared with 65 per cent of Christians and 65 per cent of non-affiliates; 74 per cent of Hindus and 67 per cent of Muslims agreed that Jews should be allowed to wear the kippah/yarmulke in school, compared with 58 per cent of Christians and 60 per cent of non-affiliates Finally, 80 per cent of Hindus, 81 per cent of Muslims and 81 per cent of Christians agreed that Christians should be

Table 13.13 Living with religious differences

	None %	Hindu %	Musl %	Chri %	χ^2	$p<$
Christians should be allowed to wear crosses in school.	71	80	81	81	22.64	.001
Hindus should be allowed to wear the bindi in school.	66	77	76	63	27.62	.001
Jews should be allowed to wear the kippah/yarmulke in school.	60	74	67	58	23.45	.001
Muslims should be allowed to wear the headscarf in school.	66	79	88	67	53.28	.001
Sikhs should be allowed to wear the turban in school.	65	82	84	65	53.63	.001

allowed to wear crosses in school, compared with 71 per cent of non-affiliates. Self-assigned religious affiliation predicts differences in attitudes towards living with visible signs of religious differences.

Conclusion

This chapter set out to test two main theses regarding the connection between self-assigned religious affiliation and the worldview of young people going to school in London. The first thesis was that self-assigned religious affiliation serves as a predictor of significant differences in the personal worldview and experiences of young people. The second thesis was that self-assigned religious affiliation serves as a predictor of significant differences in the social worldview of young people. The data collected by the Young People's Attitudes to Religious Diversity project from students attending schools (with a religious character and without a religious foundation) in London allowed these theses to be tested among 1,250 Christians, 231 Hindus and 227 Muslims, alongside 505 students attending the same schools but claiming no self-assigned religious affiliation.

The first thesis was supported by the data. Comparing Christians, Hindus and Muslims alongside non-affiliated students, self-assigned religious affiliation was confirmed as a key indicator of the seriousness with which different groups take their religion. This point was demonstrated most clearly in the differences displayed among the Muslim students in comparison with students from the other faith groups. For example, the majority of young Muslims feel that their religious identity is important to them and that religion plays a major role when they make important decisions in their life. Religion is something that has been shaped by their parents and is talked about at home. The majority of young Muslims believe in God. Here is a group of young people for whom religion is a real and motivating influence in life. To understand this group of young people it would be a mistake to imagine that the disjunction between their religious worldview and the secular worldview of contemporary society is not of fundamental significance. Muslim young people enjoy a higher level of personal wellbeing (feeling a sense of purpose in their lives), but at the same time they experience a lower sense of social wellbeing (living with the anxiety of being bullied because of their religion).

The second thesis was also supported by the data. Comparing Christians, Hindus and Muslims alongside non-affiliated students, self-assigned religious affiliation was confirmed as a key indicator of the responses of different groups to living amid religious diversity. Nervousness of or antipathy towards living in religiously diverse communities was associated most not with any one religious group, but with the religiously unaffiliated. The religiously unaffiliated were more likely to see religious people as intolerant and religion as bringing more conflict than peace. The religiously unaffiliated were less likely to agree that all religious groups should have equal rights and less likely to support the rights of students to wear distinctive religious clothing or symbols in schools. While Hindus, Muslims and Christians were all keener than the religiously unaffiliated to promote religious social tolerance, some religious groups remained keen to keep social boundaries in place in their own lives. For example, Muslim students were less likely than other groups to be happy about close relatives marrying someone from a different religious background.

The two theses tested by the present chapter were shaped against the background of debate regarding the utility of information generated by the religious question in the 2001 and 2011 censuses in England and Wales. The findings from the present chapter contribute further support for the view that, among secondary school students, knowledge about self-assigned religious affiliation offers significant predictive power about matters of personal and social significance, adding to the evidence provided in earlier studies conducted among secondary school students and by Francis (2001b; 2001c) and by Francis and Robbins (2014). This growing body of evidence generated among young people could stimulate new analyses conducted on the British Social Attitudes Survey archive on more of those issues where it may be possible to combine data across different years in order to produce enough cases to support analyses by self-assigned religious affiliation as achieved, for example, by Francis, Williams and Village (2011) in respect of changing patterns of marriage, cohabitation and divorce among different faith groups between 1983 and 2005.

References

Barlow, A., C. Burgoyne, E. Clery, and J. Smithson. 2008. 'Cohabitation and the Law: Myths, Money and the Media.' In *British Social Attitudes: The Twenty-fourth Report*, ed. A. Park, J. Curtice, K. Thomson, M. Phillips, M. Johnson, and E. Clery, 29–53. London: Sage.

Barlow, A., S. Duncan, G. James, and A. Park. 2001. 'Just a Piece of Paper? Marriage and Cohabitation.' In *British Social Attitudes Survey: The Eighteenth Report*, ed. A. Park, J. Curtice, K. Thomson, L. Jarvis and C. Bromley, 29–57. London: Sage.

———. 2005. *Cohabitation, Marriage and the Law: Social Change and Legal Reform in the Twenty-first Century*. Oxford: Hart.

Brown, C. G. 2001. *The Death of Christian Britain*. London: Routledge.

Clery, E., S. McLean, and M. Phillips. 2007. 'Quickening Death: The Euthanasia Debate.' In *British Social Attitudes: The Twenty-third Report*, ed. A. Park, J. Curtice, K. Thomson, M. Phillips, and M. Johnson, 35–54. London: Sage.

Exley, S. 2012. 'School Choice: Parental Freedom to Choose and Educational Equality.' In *British Social Attitudes: The Twenty-eighth Report*, ed. A. Park, E. Clery, J. Curtice, M. Phillips, and D. Utting, 53–57. London: Sage.

Francis, L. J. 2001a. *The Values Debate: A Voice from the Pupils.* London: Woburn Press.

———. 2001b. 'Religion and Values: A Quantitative Perspective.' In *The Fourth R for the Third Millennium: Education in Religion and Values for the Global Future*, ed. L. J. Francis, J. Astley, and M. Robbins, 47–78. Dublin: Lindisfarne Books.

———. 2001c. 'The Social Significance of Religious Affiliation among Adolescents in England and Wales.' In *Religious Individualisation and Christian Religious Semantics*, ed. H.-G. Ziebertz, 115–138. Münster: LIT Verlag.

———. 2003. 'Religion and Social Capital: The Flaw in the 2001 Census in England and Wales.' In *Public Faith: The State of Religious Belief and Practice in Britain*, ed. P. Avis, 45–64. London: SPCK.

Francis, L. J. and M. Robbins. 2014. 'The Religious and Social Significance of Self-assigned Religious Affiliation in England and Wales: Comparing Christian, Muslim and Religiously Unaffiliated Adolescent Males.' *Research in Education* 92 (1): 32–48.

Francis, L. J., E. Williams, and A. Village. 2011. 'Multifaith Britain and Family Life: Changing Patterns of Marriage, Cohabitation and Divorce among Different Faith Groups between 1983–2005.' *Journal of Contemporary Religion* 26 (1): 33–41.

Gilbert, A. D. 1980. *The Making of Post-Christian Britain.* London: Longman.

Gould, A., and N. Stratford. 2002. 'Illegal Drugs: High and Lows.' In *British Social Attitudes Survey: The Nineteenth Report*, ed. A. Park, J. Curtice, K. Thomson, L. Jarvis, and C. Bromley, 119–140. London: Sage.

Hayes, B. C. 1995. 'Religious Identification and Moral Attitudes: The British Case.' *British Journal of Sociology* 46 (3): 457–474.

Hayes, B. C., and M. Marangudakis. 2001. 'Religion and Attitudes toward Nature in Britain.' *British Journal of Sociology* 52 (1): 139–155.

Heath, A., J. Martin, and G. Elgenius. 2007. 'Who Do We Think We Are? The Decline of Traditional Social Identities.' In *British Social Attitudes: The Twenty-third Report*, ed. A. Park, J. Curtice, K. Thomson, M. Phillips, and M. Johnson, 1–34. London: Sage.

Heath, A., M. Savage, and N. Senior. 2013. 'Social Class: The Role of Class in Shaping Social Attitudes.' In *British Social Attitudes: The Thirtieth Report*, ed. A. Park, C. Bryson, E. Clery, J. Curtice, and M. Phillips, 173–199. London: NatCen Social Research.

Indicative Business Case for the Religion Question in the 2001 Census Prepared by the Religious Affiliation Sub-group, May 1997.

Lee, L. 2012. 'Religion: Losing Faith?' In *British Social Attitudes: The Twenty-eighth Report*, ed. A. Park, E. Clery, J. Curtice, M. Phillips, and D. Utting, 173–184. London: Sage.

Park, A., and R. Rhead. 2013. 'Personal Relationships: Changing Attitudes towards Sex, Marriage and Parenthood.' In *British Social Attitudes: The Thirtieth Report*, ed. A. Park, C Bryson, E. Clery, J. Curtice, and M. Phillips, 1–32. London: NatCen Social Research.

Park, A., and P. Surridge. 2003. 'Charting Change in British Values.' In *British Social Attitudes: The Twentieth Report*, ed. A. Park, J. Curtice, K. Thomson, L. Jarvis, and C. Bromley, 131–159. London: Sage.

Parsons, G., ed. 1993. *The Growth of Religious Diversity: Britain from 1945. Volume 1: Traditions.* London: Routledge.

———. 1994. *The Growth of Religious Diversity: Britain from 1945. Volume 2: Issues.* London: Routledge.

Sherif, J. 2011. 'A Census Chronicle: Reflections on the Campaign for a Religious Question in the 2001 Census for England and Wales.' *Journal of Beliefs and Values* 32 (1): 1–18.

Statistics New Zealand. 1998. *2001 Census of Population and Dwellings: Preliminary Views on Content.* Wellington: Publishing and Media Services Division of Statistics New Zealand.

Stratford, N., and I. Christie. 2000. 'Town and Country Life.' In *British Social Attitudes Survey: The Seventeenth Report,* ed. R. Jowell, J. Curtice, A. Park, K. Thomson, L. Jarvis, C. Bromley, and N. Stratford, 175–208. London: Sage.

Stratford, N., T. Marteau, and M. Bobrow. 2001. 'Genetic Research: Friend or Foe?' In *British Social Attitudes: The Eighteenth Report,* ed. A. Park, J. Curtice, K. Thomson, L. Jarvis, and C. Bromley, 103–130. Aldershot: Ashgate.

Sturgis, P., H. Cooper, C. Fife-Schaw, and R. Shepherd. 2004. 'Genomic Science: Emerging Public Opinion.' In *British Social Attitudes: The Twenty-first Report,* ed. A. Park, J. Curtice, K. Thomson, C. Bromley, and M. Phillips, 117–145. London: Sage.

Voas, D., and R. Ling. 2010. 'Religion in Britain and the United States.' In *British Social Attitudes: The Twenty-sixth Report,* ed. A. Park, J. Curtice, K. Thomson, M. Phillips, E. Clery, and S. Butt, 65–86. London: Sage.

Weller, P. 2004. 'Identity, Politics, and the Future(s) of Religion in the UK: The Case of the Religious Question in the 2001 Decennial Census.' *Journal of Contemporary Religion* 19 (1): 3–21.

———. 2008. *Religious Diversity in the UK.* London: Continuum.

Wolffe, J., ed. 1993. *The Growth of Religious Diversity: Britain from 1945. A Reader.* London: Hodder and Stoughton.

Part Four

International engagement

14 Young people and religious diversity

A Canadian perspective

Lori G. Beaman, Peter Beyer
and Christine L. Cusack

Introduction

As we look at previous chapters in this volume and consider the scope and depth of studies conducted across the UK and Europe about youth, education and young people's attitudes towards religious diversity, one point is eminently clear: Canada lags far behind in analogous empirical research. With few exceptions,[1] our review of literature demonstrates that comprehensive education *about* religious diversity is either largely absent in public school[2] curricula or loosely embedded in other academic subjects such as history, social studies or citizenship education. Outside of Québec – the Canadian province which received significant scholarly attention for its implementation of a secular, compulsory programme, comparable in content to religious education (RE) – the paucity of research, and in particular the lack of ethnographic studies about teacher and student experiences with religious diversity, is disquieting.[3] We must also clarify that the idea of 'religious education' or 'religion education' can be conceptually ambiguous in the Canadian context since it has no stable meaning across provinces, referring to confessional, denomination-specific instruction in some or to world religions curricula in others.[4] Finding a common lexicon is correspondingly problematic. In contrast to other countries like the UK, where the use of the abbreviation RE immediately connotes a broadly understood model of instruction that pays heed to religious diversity, there is no Canada-wide consensus about what to even call such a programme of study. Complicating this problem of nomenclature and lack of empirical data, the issue of religion and education is, on the one hand, a non-issue for many Canadians (as we explain later). On the other hand, it is the focus of increasing levels of public scrutiny from a variety of religious and secular stakeholders pressing for change (at least concerning the questions of public support for confessional or faith-based schools or religious education in these schools). Such changes include requests for exemptions to compulsory religion courses in confessional schools and agitation for policy amendments to end public funding that exclusively serves Catholic education (primarily in the province of Ontario) (see Duffy 2012; Hammer 2014; Prince and Bishop 2014). These issues have proven to be particularly litigious over the last several decades, with Canada even coming under international censure by the United Nations Human Rights Committee for religious discrimination in the decision of *Waldman v. Canada*[5] (UNHRC 1999; UNHRC-CCPR 2006, 5). While the complex fiscal and constitutional controversies that animate debate over confessional public education are beyond the scope of this chapter, they nevertheless serve to contextualize the discussion of religion and education in Canada.[6] Collective concern (both from academia and from the vox populi) about government responses to religious diversity writ large, and religion and education in particular, however, are core research foci of the Religion and Diversity Project. Thus, the first section of this chapter offers a brief history of religion and education in Canada, a description of the Religion and Diversity Project and a snapshot of the current status of our research with observations about the most significant gaps in knowledge. The second section offers commentary on the strengths of the WRERU project's methodological approaches and how key findings about context, aversion to conflict and the theoretical footings of education *about* religion may inform our research strategies. The third section presents findings from qualitative research conducted in relation to the Religion and Diversity Project. This research focuses on how and to what extent young adults educated in Canadian school systems actually end up understanding religion and religious diversity in the context of their own religious identities, even when they have been exposed to little or no religious education in those schools. We conclude with questions about the potential benefits and possible dangers of normative approaches to teaching about religion and worldviews, how findings from the WRERU project may inform the design of our own project in Canada and the imperative of context-specific, interdisciplinary research.

Religion and education in Canada

It is an understatement to say that the topic of religion and education in Canada is a complicated affair. Religion, either as a confessional or academic subject, varies widely from province to province, resists facile categorization and requires highly contextualized examples for proper analysis. Understanding the current situation necessitates a look back to nineteenth-century constitutional agreements that shaped (and continue to influence) how religion is framed in the classroom. Any discussion of religion and education in Canada logically begins with the British North America Act, also referred to as the Constitution Act of 1867, in which the individual confederated provinces were accorded the right to 'exclusively make laws in relation to Education' and which included guarantees of public support for 'separate' Catholic and Protestant schools where these had already existed at the time of Confederation (Canada 1867, 93). Originally conceived to address concerns about religious, cultural and linguistic minorities, these arrangements created parallel systems of education in several provinces, reflecting the religious makeup of Canada's populace during that era (Dickinson and Findlay 2014). Contrary to many other Western democracies, Canada has no national ministry of education and the heterogeneous treatment of religion and religious diversity in its educational system is a reflection of how education policy evolved independently in each province. As Jennifer Wallner affirms, 'Canada is one of the most decentralized countries in the world, with provincial governments enjoying greater autonomy than their substate counterparts in other federations' (2014, 25). As to religion, this clarification sheds light on at least one reason why the educational landscape is so multifarious. Today only Québec and Newfoundland have 'secured constitutional amendments to secularize education . . . and in this way converged with the five provinces whose education systems were already secularized' (ibid., 76). Alberta, Ontario and Saskatchewan remain the three provinces with non-secularized systems, still operating under the original constitutional arrangements (Canada 1867, 93). Ontario has the distinction of being the lone Canadian province to provide 'public funding to only one religious group, to the complete exclusion of all other religions' (Bayefsky and Waldman 2007, 13).[7] However, Alberta, British Columbia, Manitoba, Québec and Saskatchewan offer some public support to 'independent' schools that may be classified as either secular or religious (Bayefsky and Waldman 2007; Dickinson and Findlay 2014, 112).[8]

The Religion and Diversity Project

The Religion and Diversity Project[9] is a seven-year (2010–2017), multimillion dollar research endeavour based at the University of Ottawa, funded by the Social Sciences and Humanities Research Council (SSHRC).[10] The project's primary goal is to explore 'the contours of religious diversity in Canada' and to deepen our understanding of how to 'respond to the opportunities and challenges presented by religious diversity in ways that promote a just and peaceful society' (Religion and Diversity Project n.d., 9). Positing 'public funding of religious schools' as a trouble spot in the broad debates concerning religious diversity and education, the project's proposal also specifies tensions around curricular content and questions of education *about* religion *versus* the denominational approaches of state-supported confessional education as areas in need of more exploration (ibid., 12). We have set aside funding issues (nevertheless acknowledging that they are inextricably linked) for the purposes of this chapter and focus on questions of how, *or even if*, public education is responding to the ongoing evolution of Canada's religious (and non-religious[11]) diversity, giving heed to 'the continued arrival and settlement of high numbers of predominantly non-Christian immigrants' (ibid., 9). This research endeavour, which intends to explore education *about* religion and worldviews in the Canadian context, must remain attentive not only to the dynamics of immigration-driven religious diversity and the rising numbers of religious 'nones' but also to the interests of the indigenous populations.[12]

Our research project on religion and education in Canada is in its initial phase. In addition to an ongoing literature review, we are compiling research on case law connected to religion and education in Canada, looking specifically at how law deals with religion in public schools. We are also mining provincial ministry of education and school board websites to gain greater insight into policies for education about religion and how religious diversity is managed on the ground. Content analysis of religion textbooks and teachers' materials will also figure prominently in our research, with particular attention paid to how religious minorities and Indigenous traditions are represented in the curricula. We are mapping relevant bachelor of education courses in at least four selected universities, looking at how (and if) pre-service teachers are being trained to teach religion and worldviews as an academic subject. In subsequent phases, we will look at both teachers' and students' experience with religious diversity, using ethnographic methods that have thus far largely been neglected in Canadian research on religion in the classroom.

Religion and education in Canada: current research status

Outside Québec and Ontario, only a modicum of scholarly attention is focused on education *about* religion. Why this dearth of research? How can it be that we are so different from our European and British counterparts in this area? The fact is we do not really talk about religion in Canada, at least not in the way it is debated in some other liberal Western democracies. Nor do we teach *about* religion in similar fashion to the long-established RE programmes in the UK, broadly speaking – hence minimal published research about the absence, presence or delivery of RE-type curricula. Working with a kind of chicken-and-egg hypothesis, we believe there is so little discussion and research about education and religion because there is so little attention paid to education about religion in public schools in Canada. What education about religion there is remains in elective courses, which are not available in all schools.

Judging from numerous legal decisions of the last decade(s) and the ongoing public outcry over the proposed Charter of Québec Values, however, it can be argued that we *do* have a vigorous public debate (and discernable collective anxiety) about some religious minorities.[13] Nevertheless, Canada has no national forum equivalent to the *Westminster Faith Debates*, for example, nor a programme such as BBC1's *The Big Questions*, that serve to nourish a spirited conversation around religion and ethics in the UK.[14] This is of course merely a partial explanation for the paucity of research and we postulate that because religion qua culture is embedded in the Canadian discourse of multiculturalism, it frequently gets subsumed into broader issues. Moreover, it is apparent that relatively few education policymakers outside the confessional system think teaching about religion is important. Interestingly, a poll conducted by the Humanist Association in British Columbia showed that 77 per cent of the respondents 'would like world religions taught in public schools', and yet such courses are quite rare and are only offered randomly in some schools (Todd 2013). One of the goals of the Religion and Diversity Project is the promotion of a robust and nuanced conversation about religious diversity. Nevertheless, those who are working on the religion and education project approach the ideas of policy creation or the standardization of teaching *about* religion and worldviews in the rest of Canada with some reserve. We put forth the plausible conjecture that even with its muted acknowledgement of religion Canadian multiculturalism has actually promoted the overarching goal of embracing diversity – that of living well together.

Keeping in mind the absence of a national discussion about religion and the concomitant scarcity of information on religious diversity curricula, we began an extensive review of Canadian literature in 2014. So far, we have compiled a bibliographic reference list with over 400 citations, which remains a work in progress. Not surprisingly, the literature shows that research on religion and education in Canada has focused largely on issues related to Québec and Ontario – the Ethics and Religious Culture (ERC) programme and Catholic schools, respectively. It is apparent that there is no systematic study of teacher training, course content, curricula, student experiences or of school policies on or about religion. This is what we do know: outside the ERC and the debate over separate school boards in Ontario, the distribution of citations within our search terms shows a significant amount of research on legal issues pertaining to religion and education in Canada. The history of Canadian schools, Charter of Rights and Freedoms issues, school funding, questions of accommodation and multiculturalism have also been explored to some degree. There are local, specific studies about the experiences of Muslim students, teachers and administrators in Muslim educational institutions, Jewish schools in Montreal and Toronto, as well as studies related to LGBTQ concerns (Bauer 1984; Azmi 2001; Collet 2007; Goldstein, Collins and Halder 2007; Goldbloom 2008; Guo 2011; Clark and MacDougall 2012; Train 2013). Our initial effort to map RE-type courses across the country reveals the most flagrant lacunae in the literature. Evidently the ERC programme in Québec stands out as the most obvious Canadian parallel to RE. Implemented in 2008, the course is obligatory in all primary and secondary institutions in the province (including, controversially, private confessional schools). The ERC programme stands out as the object of considerable attention from the media, policymakers and scholars, both in Canada and internationally, yet the education system in Newfoundland and Labrador also went through a secularization process culminating when 'the province adopted the non-denominational system at the start of the 1998–99 school year' (Higgins 2011). Since then, both primary and secondary schools in Newfoundland and Labrador offer instruction about aboriginal spirituality, Abrahamic traditions and Eastern religions (Newfoundland and Labrador 2014–2015). This evolution from confessional to secular, however, was not without controversy, with a coalition of pro-denominational education stakeholders mounting and ultimately losing their legal battles against the reorganization of the education system (Higgins 2011). In the province of Ontario, Van Arragon notes that education *about* religion can unfold in several ways: as a non-compulsory world religions elective available for secondary students (if the school opts to make it available); as an integrated component of other curricula, depending on the willingness of individual school boards; or 'through the recognition of things unique to various religions such as festivals and rituals in special classroom and school events' (2015, 338). While our preliminary research has not yet thoroughly explored RE-type curricula in other provinces, if we take Ontario as a model for the rest of Canada, we can say that if education *about* religion does occur, it happens spottily at best, with minimal standardization. Of course as our research project gains traction and we integrate more interdisciplinary scholarship, the question of how best to address gaps in knowledge will become clearer.

Learning from the WRERU findings

As we move through our own programme of research on education about religion and in thinking about religious diversity and how to live well together, we are naturally looking to other research projects to inform our own design. Given the gaps in basic knowledge about education and religion in Canada, adapting research design poses some special challenges. Moreover, such research is necessarily context specific. The unique historical contours of Northern Ireland, for example, shape both research questions and findings. This does not mean that they are irrelevant. Indeed it is probably fair to say that our shared interest in education, religion and youth means that we are all committed to the project of living well together in diverse societies, however that diversity plays out on the ground. What is increasingly clear to us is that we cannot simply replicate the research design of other projects without carefully considering the underlying assumptions contained in them and the social context within which we are conducting our research.

Before turning to findings, it is first worth reflecting on the methodological strengths of the WRERU project. There are three that stand out: first, the project uses both quantitative and qualitative methods to examine young people's attitudes to diversity. This necessary bidirectional methodological approach recognizes the importance of both big picture and ethnographic data: the qualitative results informed the quantitative measures, resulting in a robust data set. Although social scientists often talk about combining methods, few research projects actually follow through. WRERU effectively carried out a combined methods project to explore, for example, the question of whether religious education works to contribute to the common good. Francis et al. approach this through a quantitative lens, and a number of the other chapters in this volume offer responses from a qualitative approach.

The second methodological strength is equally challenging to achieve: disciplinary diversity of the team means that questions about diversity, youth and education are examined from a number of disciplinary angles, including sociology, psychology, theology and religious studies. Each discipline brings its own toolkit and resulting insights. Together, the overall response to the research questions becomes more nuanced. Empirical theology was drawn upon, for example, to consider the influence of God images in combination with psychology to examine values. These in turn combined with more sociologically focused studies on affiliation and religious practice. Rather than a territorial approach to disciplines, the researchers worked together to press their disciplines into service, creating results that examine young people's attitudes to diversity from multiple vantage points.

The third innovation relates to the first two: the WRERU team worked with the REDCo research team to both refine their own research questions as well as to contribute to a wider investigation of young people's understandings of and responses to diversity. In a globalized world, understanding one's local context in global perspective is critical. Social science has not fully caught up with this new reality. Yet in order to develop a sophisticated understanding of the social world and social problems and, more importantly, in order adequately to think about the sort of world we want to live in (see Gergen 2014), combined efforts and resources are necessary. The project is a model of how to grapple with both local and global realities as well as more pervasive patterns and differences.

In the space we have, we cannot possibly discuss all of the results reported in the previous chapters. Therefore, we briefly train our attention on those results that inform our own research, inspire our future directions and − we think − warrant particular attention by all researchers who focus on religion and education.

Context matters

This may seem like a self-evident finding and it may also seemingly contradict our earlier observation about the importance of cross-jurisdiction research. Yet the WRERU researchers demonstrate through their findings that context matters at a number of levels, including how youth experience their own religion, how religion is framed and how religious diversity is viewed. On the first aspect, Julia Ipgrave found, for example, that students with connections to Poland experienced Catholicism differently there than in Scotland − in other words, their practice as Catholics was affected by the context. This in turn affected their senses of inclusion. Elisabeth Arweck's comparative study of two schools in Wales considers context at local, national and global levels and demonstrates the impact of multicultural versus monocultural contexts. Another aspect of context that WRERU researchers were consistently attentive to were socio-economic differences/contexts. In this sense religion becomes an important, but not the only, marker of difference.

For Canadian youth, the state project of multiculturalism has been embedded in educational programmes for some time now. Thus diversity is understood through this lens. This national narrative has a particular flavour in Canada and yet we have not fully explored how it translates into what students believe about religious diversity or how they should respond to it. Yet some of our research, as reported later, has at least made a start in this respect. In general, however, religion has been largely excluded from the multicultural agenda for many years, relegated to the margins of policy, scholarly attention and analysis. Moreover, the same differences in context related to the urban/rural divide and between urban contexts are pertinent to the Canadian context and, we suspect, for most of us researching in this area.

The deep desire to avoid conflict

Perhaps the most significant contribution any of our research on young people and diversity can make is to contribute to creating and imagining a different kind of future – one in which diversity and difference are normalized and in which equality and justice are achieved in substance. An important part of such a project is the commitment to peaceful solutions. Kenneth J. Gergen (2014) argues that it is time that social sciences and humanities researchers move into the domain of futures research, committing themselves to actively shaping the future rather than engaging in research which 'mirrors' social reality.

Ipgrave's chapter on Woodside Integrated College considers the impact of an integrated school on achieving a peaceful future in historically conflict-ridden Northern Ireland. Her research demonstrates the positive outcomes of such integrated education in that students were positive about religious diversity, although less positive about religion as it related to their own community. The students had internalized the importance of equality and fairness in diversity and also an ethic of commonality. The recognition of similarity is key to developing the practice of equality beyond its theoretical imagining (Beaman 2014a). As the students said, 'There's no point in fighting.' Although Ipgrave acknowledges the limitations of the students' approaches (they see themselves as unique and somewhat separate from the rest of the community), it is worth thinking further about how this educational experiment designed to deflate religious conflict has been effective and how it might be replicated. Contact theory (Allport 1954) has developed much more sophisticated nuance, but research shows that contact with 'the other' can work to reduce conflict (see Hodson and Hewstone 2013) and in fact facilitates acceptance and understanding in societies where diverse groups of people come together.

How can this inform other research? From our previous research in the Immigrant Youth/Immigrant Young Adults studies (discussed in more detail in the next section) we know that Canadian youth too have little appetite for politics and conflict based on religion. In our future research we will build on the WRERU findings as well as our own to examine students' experiences of deflecting conflict and to explore how they think it is possible to live well together in a diverse society.

Living in a diverse society: the contribution of education about religion

Related to the deep desire to avoid conflict exhibited in the findings mentioned earlier is the question of how education about religion might contribute to society overall. We think the answer to this is somewhat site and situation specific, and we are perhaps a bit more wary of a global endorsement of education about religion than the WRERU team is. The benefits of education about religion depend on how religion is conceptualized and on students' experiences with the religious 'other'. Our reservations about endorsing RE curricula that adhere too closely to the 'world religions' model are based on concerns about exclusion:

narrow understandings of religion can serve to exclude certain groups who do not meet the definitional parameters. We can think, for example, of the controversial and negative conceptualization of 'Sheilaism' in Robert Bellah's work. Sheila, who might be described in contemporary research terms as a 'none' or 'spiritual but not religious' becomes a stand-in for all that is wrong with society (see Bellah et al. 1985; McGuire 2008). Several chapters in this volume address the issue of diverse religious practices and the 'good' society: Ipgrave's work on Northern Ireland implicitly addresses it, and Leslie Francis et al. explicitly ask 'Does RE work and contribute to the common good in England?' In their comparison of two groups of students, one of which was taking RE classes and the other not, Francis et al. found that the RE students had more positive attitudes towards living in a religiously diverse society. The results are situated in ethos theory, which sees the values and attitudes of a group as constituting the framework within which students exist. What remains unanswered is how that ethos and the values and attitudes that constitute it translate into everyday interaction. This is of course much more difficult to measure, although the qualitative studies discussed by the WRERU team in this volume shed some light on how respect and beliefs about equality translate into action.

Even if we have reservations about education about religion as a state- and peace-building project, WRERU contributes to the knowledge we need to assess the desirability of developing and advocating an RE programme. As mentioned in the introduction, RE is not on the educational or political radar in Canada in the same way that it is in the UK. The WRERU research helps us to consider how to move forward in our research and to build on the results of the Immigrant Young Adults project.

Religious and cultural identities in Canada: preliminary findings

Although there is the dearth of research in the Canadian context on religion and education, this does not mean that the research that has been done yields a correspondingly minimal understanding of how the 'products' of that education have come to understand religion, their own religious identities (or lack thereof) and the nature of religious diversity, including how that can and should be lived, how it informs the fabric of society in Canada. A series of research projects conducted since 2004, in conjunction with and in preparation for the Religion and Diversity Project, allows us to offer at least preliminary and partial answers to some key questions. How have younger Canadians who have recently emerged from our school systems come to understand religion and, in that context, religious diversity? How do they see themselves within that diversity, especially as concerns their own religious identities and how these fit into the larger framework of diversity? How do they understand this religious diversity with reference to Canadian multiculturalism – that official policy and aspect of 'national identity' that has for some time been an explicit part of school curricula?

Two research projects have sought answers to these questions; a third is under-way and beginning to report results. The first, conducted between 2004 and 2006, focused on 1.5- and 2nd-generation young adults who were at that time mostly attending Canadian universities, places to which a very large propor-tion of this broad subpopulation has significant exposure. A subsequent project, conducted between 2008 and 2010, extended the first to include a wider range of such young adults from immigrant families, including aspects of religious identity, geography and language. The third project is widening the search to include people from all backgrounds in Canada within the younger adult age range of 18–45. Although the last project is only beginning to yield preliminary adults, we can already see that the results of the earlier completed projects are being confirmed by the results from the wider population sample (Ramji 2008; Lefebvre and Triki Yamani 2011–2012; Holtmann and Nason-Clark 2012; Bea-man and Beyer 2013; Beyer and Ramji 2013; Beyer 2014).

In summarizing some of the results of this research with respect to the just stated questions, we should stress that the research was not explicitly about religion and education; the projects do not address the dearth of such research in Canada. Nonetheless the results can tell us something about what younger adults think and do about religious diversity, even if not in any direct sense how and to what extent Canadian schools are imparting understanding and appre-ciation of the religious diversity that increasingly characterizes this country, like other Western countries.

Not surprising, but nonetheless of significance, is the finding that the vast majority of young Canadians appear to end up understanding religious diver-sity as the diversity of religions, as the diversity of adherents to these religions and mostly in terms of the so-called world religions. This is the case whether they consider themselves to be among these adherents or not. However, there is also a very widespread understanding that matters are not quite so straight-forward, above all that religion and the religions bear an ambiguous relation to two other qualities, often clearly understood as spirituality and culture. Many, especially those who have strong and exclusive religious identities in terms of one of the religions, consider there to be little and even no difference among these three concepts, especially religion and spirituality. Most, however, recognize a difference and understand it as follows: religion is a collective phe-nomenon with relatively clear rules, sets of practices, and beliefs and divides itself relatively neatly into 'the religions'. Spirituality, by contrast, is something deeply personal and often quite fluid, without precise, let alone obligatory col-lective contours, even if it also involves some sort of 'greater force'. Culture is like religion in being collective; it overlaps with religion without usually being identical (cf. Beyer 2015).

This is the overall framework of understanding. When one inquires for greater detail, it becomes clear that the majority of these Canadians actually have relatively little knowledge about the 'stuff' of the religions that they know are 'out there', including not infrequently, by their own explicit confession, the religion with which they identify. The significant minority that is more 'religiously literate' has acquired this knowledge from two sources: friends or relatives who are adherents of other religions than their own or from school courses about religion (notable in the present context), either at the secondary or post-secondary level. It is perhaps even surprising that a not insignificant number have learnt about 'their own' religion primarily from or in addition to such courses, although this group is generally limited to people of Hindu and Buddhist families. Christians, Muslims, Jews and Sikhs (the other world religions most represented in the Canadian population) overwhelmingly learn about their religions from family members (usually parents), from their religious institutions and from their own extra-curricular efforts.

Although there appears to be a minority of younger Canadians who are 'anti-religion', the great majority considers religion to be a positive force in society. They value the religious diversity that Canada contains and consider it important to maintain and encourage it, along with the freedom of expression that this orientation implies. Most, but certainly not all, aver that the religions are equal in terms of value and even in terms of what they offer. No religion is better than another, just like no culture is better than another; all have something to offer. A fair proportion consider it important or an added value, in this con-text, to be able to learn about and from (other) religions, even though almost all consider that these 'good' religions can be and are sometimes 'misused' by some of their adherents. The great majority also rejects politicized religion in almost any form. Intolerance towards religion, and even certain religions, seems to be rare or, at the very least, not something that one should admit to. None of these orientations is unanimous, but those that think in opposite directions are the decided minority (or for various reasons did not end up as participants in our projects; we are not dealing with representative samples in any of the projects).

Religious diversity, understood primarily in terms of discrete religions, is thus viewed positively. Few – but certainly not none – would wish Canada to be or return to being a Christian country, in name or in fact, although most recognize the role that Christianity has played in making Canada what it is today and the degree to which Christianity still, in various ways, occupies a privileged position in the country. It is clearly still easier to be Christian in Canada than to be of another religious identity, whether restricted to one of the religions or not. By contrast, for many, Islam is the one religion that is the subject of the most preju-dicial treatment, although relatively few Muslims think this way. For Muslims the problem of Islam in Canada is a product of stereotypical media presentations with resulting ignorance and misunderstanding among the majority popula-tion. Few non-Muslims, however, will confess to Islamophobia. Paradoxically it appears that the negative media images do not result in a negative view of Islam and Muslims among this younger subpopulation.

We should stress that the positive attitude to religion and religious diversity is shared by all groups, whether they are religiously involved or not. It is an attitude that, again with the inevitable minority exceptions, is shared by people who are themselves ardently religious, who have little stake in the matter or who expressly disavow any religious identity. Religious diversity, in different words, appears to be seen as part of the Canadian multicultural reality, which the vast majority of people in this younger age group wish to celebrate, even when they criticize its degree of concrete implementation, which many of them do (Beyer 2014).

In terms of their own place within this prevailing view of religious diversity, the clear majority of the participants themselves identify as belonging to one of the religions and only one. Most people understand their place within religious diversity as adherents of one of the religions. The most common alternative is to identify with no religion; few identify explicitly with more than one of the religions or construct their religious identities by piecing together elements from more than one religion. They nonetheless often include in their accepted set of religious beliefs and practices things that do not normally belong to the religion with which they identify and they are frequently selective about what from the standard orthodoxies of their own religions they do accept. Further, a good minority do indeed consider themselves more spiritual than religious, but most of these also identify with a particular religion, although often only marginally. Another significant minority is what one can call culturally religious, meaning that they identify with a particular religion but participate in that religion only for cultural reasons, as expression of their cultural identity or for reasons of family tradition and solidarity. Overall, the ways of understanding and performing religious identities are done within the framework of the world religions, but the specific composition of those identities very often deviates from what these respondents do or might learn in world religion classes or from religious education in their (generally confessional or faith-based) schools.

Conclusion

The results of WRERU, the data from the Immigrant Youth Project and the project we are building under the Religion and Diversity framework have raised significant questions for us: What exactly is the 'problem' we are trying to solve? Is there a significant difference between levels of conflict, prejudice and misunderstanding between Canada and other Western democracies? Are there risks of reifying or essentializing religion in ways that actually promote conflicts or 'othering' in education about religion? What are the benefits of education about religion? Are there dangers in normalizing education about religion in the context of predicted trends related to non-belief? In other words, just when a significant proportion of the population is identifying as 'none', what are the specific goals of educating about religion?[15] Will it help, for example, to bridge the gap between the highly religious and those for whom religion is unimportant? Or does it serve to promote the notion that everyone must have a spiritual or religious life? To some extent the WRERU project offers some insight into these questions, providing evidence of benefits that include better understanding and acceptance of religious difference. However, social context regarding this issue is a key variable that forces us to plan our next steps carefully.

Our research in the Immigrant Youth study adds another dimension to this conversation: if people are largely uninformed about their own religions as well as those of others, does this necessarily lead to problems such as conflict, exclusion or 'othering'? Our research would suggest not, although we are unsure of how our participants actually behave. Nonetheless, their mix of friends and relatively casual approach to religion as well as their disdain for any religion that is overtly political suggests that with this group at least there may be another explanation for their approach. In truth, there are likely multiple explanations, but we are left wondering whether Canada's deep commitment to multiculturalism has contributed to a broader sensibility related to diversity that offsets the paucity of knowledge about religion specifically. It is here again that context becomes vital.

Our own experiences along with those of WRERU point to something that may seem self-evident in the current research climate, but that we think bears repeating: interdisciplinary approaches to research issues such as education about religion are not optional. In order to understand the full parameters of both the problems and their solutions they must be examined from a number of perspectives. Discrete disciplines can help us to see issues from a number of angles, while interdisciplinarity can contribute to more robust solutions. In research which is so normatively charged (as this is), particularly when it is carried out with a view to policy reform, it is vital to get it right. Working internationally can also contribute to robustness, although caution must always be exercised in translating research design across contexts.

Acknowledgment

Lori G. Beaman would like to acknowledge the support of the Religion and Diversity Project in the preparation of this chapter as well as the on-going financial support of her research through her Canada Research Chair in the Contextualization of Religion in a Diverse Canada. The authors are grateful to Marianne Abou-Hamad for her editorial assistance.

Notes

1 In a process commonly referred to as 'deconfessionalization', the province of Québec removed Catholic and Protestant religious instruction from all primary and secondary public school curricula in 2008, replacing it with a new programme known as the Ethics and Religious Culture Program (ERC). See Lefebvre (2012); Léroux (2007, 2010); Québec Ministère de l'Éducation, du Loisir et du Sport (n.d.).

2 The term 'public school' in Canada can be a source of confusion when compared to other jurisdictions where distinctions between public (i.e. publicly funded) and private (i.e. privately funded) are more straightforward. Both secular and confessional Catholic schools in Ontario, for example, are entirely funded by the state. In Québec, however, the term public refers exclusively to taxpayer-funded secular education, whereas private institutions can operate with both public and private funding. Education funding policy varies widely from province to province and ranges from very simple to highly complex. For example, only the 'secular public school system' in Prince Edward Island is supported by the state, whereas Alberta offers complete or limited funding to 'six kinds of schools: public, separate, Francophone, charter, alternative, and independent or private' (Bayefsky and Waldman 2007, 11, 5). Leo Van Arragon further clarifies the varying appellation of schools in Ontario, stating that the

designation of schools as 'public' is an extension of the original term 'common' and the idea that the schools thus categorized represent educational interests which Ontarians hold in common. In contrast, 'separate' is a designation which implies that these schools serve narrow sectarian interests while the schools categorized as 'private' are thought to serve a clientele motivated by private rather than public interests.

(Van Arragon 2015, 17)

3 Although our project on religion and education in Canada is in its incipient phase, initial findings show that in Newfoundland and Labrador, for example, religious education courses are offered from kindergarten through high school and aimed at helping 'students to grow religiously, spiritually, and morally and become informed, caring and contributing members of society. Students come to appreciate their own beliefs and values as well as the beliefs and values of others' (Newfoundland and Labrador 2014–2015, 114).

4 In his doctoral dissertation on the history of religious education in Ontario, Michael Perry (2000, 265) notes the use of the term 'Religion Studies' to describe a proposed course which 'was to be a compulsory multifaith, non-indoctrinational and non-sectarian program for all public elementary schools. The focus would be on major world religions.' Currently, in Ontario, that course, an upper secondary school course in 'world religions', is optional and not taught in all public schools (see Van Arragon 2015, 337–338).

5 Arieh Waldman sent his children to a private Jewish school in Ontario, Canada. He asserted that public funding of only one religious tradition's schools infringed his right to the enjoyment of religious freedom and represented a discriminatory financial burden on religious minorities. The UNHRC admonished Canada to 'adopt steps in order to eliminate discrimination on the basis of religion in the funding of schools in Ontario' (UNHRC-CCPR 2006, 21; see also UNHRC 1999).

6 See Anne Bayefsky and Arieh Waldman (2007) for a detailed comparison of public and religious school funding for all provinces and territories in Canada.

7 There exists one commonly overlooked exception to the exclusive funding of (Catholic) separate schools in the province: a small publicly funded Protestant Separate School Board in Penetanguishene, Ontario, operating only one primary school – the Burkevale Protestant Separate School (Protestant Separate School Board Penetanguishene n.d.).

8 Regarding the term 'independent', William Hoverd, Erin LeBrun and Van Arragon indicate that

some privately funded schools prefer to identify themselves as 'independent' both to distance themselves from the elitism associated with 'private' schools and to emphasize their independence of both church and state, thereby distinguishing themselves from Roman Catholic Separate Schools which are church governed and from public schools which are state governed.

(Hoverd et al. n.d., 18)

9 A description of the Religion and Diversity Project is available at http://religionand diversity.ca/en/project-team/.

10 The SSHRC provides federal research funding (see SSHRC n.d.).

11 The rise of the religious nones and those with non-religious worldviews are important trends to consider when discussing the future of education policy and religious diversity in the classroom (see Wallis 2014; Beyer 2015; Beaman and Tomlins 2015; Tomlins 2015). The spiritual but not religious are also a growing segment of the Canadian population; Lori Beaman and Peter Beyer have emphasized this 'unexplored territory of the SBNR group' who 'remain largely absent in the education about religion curricula' (2013, 135).

12 Regarding Canada's indigenous populations, the recent release of an exhaustive report from Canada's Truth and Reconciliation Commission delivers a 'call to action' for education about religious diversity:

The Commission believes that religious diversity courses must be mandatory in all provinces and territories. Any religious school receiving public funding must be required to teach at least one course on comparative religious studies, which must include a segment on Aboriginal spiritual beliefs and practices.

(Truth and Reconciliation Commission of Canada 2015, 294)

13 See *Alberta v. Hutterian Brethren of Wilson Colony*, 2009 SCC 37; *Loyola High School v. Québec (Attorney General)*, 2015 SCC 12; *Mouvement laïque v. Saguenay* (City), 2015 SCC 16; *Multani v. Commission scolaire Marguerite-Bourgeoys*, 2006 SCC 6 [2006], 1 S.C.R. 256; *Syndicat Northcrest v. Amselem*, 2004 SCC 47, [2004] 2 S.C.R. 551; 'Charter of Québec values would ban religious symbols for public workers', available at: http://www.cbc.ca/news/canada/montreal/charter-of-Québec-values-would-ban-religious-symbols-for-public-workers-1.1699315, access date: 23 July 2015; Beaman 2014b.

14 The Westminster Faith Debates brought together leading academics and public figures to debate the latest research on religion and values, each year exploring a different theme. Initially held in central London every spring, the Debates also travelled around the UK to engage with new audiences and issues (see http://faithdebates.org.uk/about/, access date: 23 July 2015; BBC1 'The Big Questions: Nicky Campbell hosts a series of moral, ethical and religious debates', http://www.bbc.co.uk/programmes/b007zpll, access date: 23 July 2015).

15 Robert Jackson addresses the issue of teaching about non-religious convictions and worldviews in *Signposts* (2014, 67–75).

References

Allport, Gordon W. 1954. *The Nature of Prejudice*. New York: Addison-Wesley.

Azmi, Shaheen. 2001. 'Muslim Educational Institutions in Toronto, Canada.' *Journal of Muslim Minority Affairs* 21 (2): 259–272.

Bauer, Julien. 1984. 'Jewish Communities, Jewish Education and Québec Nationalism.' *Social Compass* 31 (4): 391–407.

Bayefsky, Anne F., and Arieh Waldman. 2007. *State Support of Education: Canada versus the United Nations*. Leiden: Martinus Nijhoff.

Beaman, Lori G. 2014a. 'Deep Equality as an Alternative to Accommodation and Tolerance.' *Nordic Journal of Religion and Society* 27 (2): 89–111.

———. 2014b. 'Between the Public and the Private: Governing Religious Expression.' In *Religion in the Public Sphere*, ed. Solange Lefebvre and Lori G. Beaman, 44–65. Toronto: University of Toronto Press.

Beaman, Lori G., and Peter Beyer. 2013. 'Betwixt and Between: A Canadian Perspective on the Challenges of Researching the Spiritual but not Religious.' In *Social Identities: Between the Sacred and the Secular*, ed. Abby Day, Giselle Vincett, and Christopher Cotter, 127–142. Farnham: Ashgate.

Beaman, Lori G., and Steven Tomlins, eds. 2015. *Atheist Identities: Spaces and Social Identities*. Cham: Springer.

Bellah, Robert, Richard Madsen, William M. Sullivan, Ann Swidler, and Steven M. Tipton. 1985. *Habits of the Heart: Individualism and Commitment in American Life*. Berkeley: University of California Press.

Beyer, Peter. 2015. 'From Atheist to Spiritual but not Religious: A Punctuated Continuum of Identities among the Second Generation of Post-1970 Immigrants in Canada.' In *Atheist Identities: Spaces and Social Contexts*, ed. Lori G. Beaman and Steven Tomlins, 137–151. Cham: Springer.

———. 2014. 'Regional Differences and Continuities at the Intersection of Culture and Religion: A Case Study of Immigrant and Second-Generation Young Adults in Canada.' In *Religion in the Public Sphere: Canadian Case Studies*, ed. Solange Lefebvre and Lori G. Beaman, 66–94. Toronto: University of Toronto Press.

Beyer, Peter, and Rubina Ramji, eds. 2013. *Growing up Canadian: Muslims, Hindus, Buddhists*. Kingston: McGill-Queen's University Press.

Canada. 1867. *The Constitution Act*. Section 93: Legislation Respecting Education. 30 & 31 Victoria, c. 3, (U.K.). Available at: http://laws-lois.justice.gc.ca/eng/const/page-4.html#docCont, access date: 23 July 2015.

Clark, Paul, and Bruce MacDougall. 2012. 'The Case for Gay-Straight Alliances (GSAs) in Canada's Public Schools: An Educational Perspective.' *Education Law Journal* 21 (2): 143–165.

Collet, Bruce A. 2007. 'Islam, National Identity and Public Secondary Education: Perspectives from the Somali Diaspora in Toronto, Canada.' *Race, Ethnicity and Education* 10 (2): 131–153.

Dickinson, Gregory M., and Nora M. Findlay. 2014. 'From "Common Christianity" to "Equal Concern and Respect": Working out a New Understanding of Religion's Place in Canada's Schools.' In *International Perspectives on Education, Religion and Law*, ed. Charles J. Russo, 111–133. New York: Routledge.

Duffy, Andrew. 2012. 'Ontario Woman Launches Legal Challenge to Catholic Schools' Taxpayer Funding.' *National Post*, 13 January. Available at: http://news.nationalpost.com/news/canada/ontario-woman-launches-legal-challenge-to-catholic-schools-taxpayer-funding, access date: 23 July 2015.

Gergen, Kenneth J. 2014. 'From Mirroring to World-Making: Research as Future Forming.' *Journal for the Theory of Social Behaviour* 45 (3): 287–310.

Goldbloom, Victor C. 2008. 'La communauté juive et l'accommodement raisonnable.' In *L'accommodement raisonnable et la diversité religieuse à l'école publique*, ed. Marie McAndrew, Micheline Milot, Jean-Sébastien Imbeault, and Paul Eid, 85–90. Québec: Fides.

Goldstein, Tara, Anthony Collins, and Michael Halder. 2007. 'Anti-Homophobia Education in Public Schooling: A Canadian Case Study of Policy Implementation.' *Journal of Gay and Lesbian Studies* 19 (3/4): 47–66.

Guo, Yan. 2011. 'Perspectives of Immigrant Muslim Parents Advocating for Religious Diversity in Canadian Schools.' *Multicultural Education* 18 (2): 55–60.

Hammer, Kate. 2014. 'Catholic Schools Force Students to Study Religion despite Court Order.' *Globe and Mail*, 12 August. Available at: http://www.theglobeandmail.com/news/national/education/catholic-schools-force-students-to-study-religion-despite-court-order/article19998101/, access date: 23 July 2015.

Higgins, Jenny. 2011. 'The Collapse of Denominational Education.' St John's: Heritage Newfoundland & Labrador, Memorial University Newfoundland. Available at: http://www.heritage.nf.ca/articles/society/collapse-denominational-education.php, access date: 23 July 2015.

Hodson, Gordon, and Miles Hewstone, eds. 2013. *Advances in Intergroup Contact*. New York: Psychology Press.

Holtmann, Cathy, and Nancy Nason-Clark. 2012. 'Preparing for Life: Gender, Religiosity and Education amongst Second Generation Hindus in Canada.' *Religion and Gender* 2 (1): 57–79.

Hoverd, William, Erin LeBrun and Leo Van Arragon. n.d. 'Religion and Education in the Provinces of Québec and Ontario.' Available at: http://religionanddiversity.ca/media/uploads/religion_and_education_in_the_provinces_of_Québec_and_ontario_report.pdf, access date: 23 July 2015.

Jackson, Robert. 2014. *Signposts: Policy and Practices for Teaching about Religions and Non-religious World-views in Intercultural Education*. Strasbourg: Council of Europe. Available at: https://book.coe.int/eur/en/human-rights-education-intercultural-education/6101-signposts-policy-and-practice-for-teaching-about-religions-and-non-religious-world-views-in-intercultural-education.html, access date: 23 July 2015.

Lefebvre, Solange. 2012. 'L'approche québecoise, entre laïcité et sécularité.' In *Le programme d'éthique et culture religieuse: de l'exigeante conciliation entre le soi, l'autre soi*, ed. Mireille Estivalèzes and Solange Lefebvre, 85–110. Québec: Les Presses de L'Université Laval.

Lefebvre, Solange, and Amina Triki Yamani. 2011–2012. 'Jeunes adultes immigrés: Dynamiques ethno-religieuses et identitaires.' *Études ethniques canadiennes/Canadian Ethnic Studies* 43–44 (3–1): 183–201.

Léroux, Georges. 2007. *Éthique et culture religieuse: arguments pour un programme.* Montréal: Editions Fides.

———. 2010. 'Culture religieuse et dialogue: les enjeux de l'éducation au pluralisme dans le Québec contemporain.' In *Dialogue des cultures et traditions monotheists,* ed. Dans B. Demers, 183–219. Montréal: Novalis.

McGuire, Meredith B. 2008. *Lived Religion: Faith and Practice in Everyday Life.* Oxford: Oxford University Press.

Newfoundland and Labrador. 2014–2015. 'Religious Education.' In *Program of Studies: Religious Education,* 113–120. St John's: Department of Education and Early Childhood Development. Available at: http://www.ed.gov.nl.ca/edu/k12/curriculum/POS/Program_of_Studies_2014–2015.pdf, access date: 23 July 2015.

Perry, Michael. 2000. 'The Historical and Theological Bases of the Christian Religious Education Program in Ontario Public Schools.' PhD dissertation. Ottawa: University of Ottawa. Available at: http://www.ruor.uottawa.ca/handle/10393/9290, access date: 23 July 2015.

Prince, Jessica, and Grant Bishop. 2014. 'A Principled Ontario Premier Would End Funding for Catholic Schools.' *Globe and Mail,* 9 June. Available at: http://www.theglobeandmail.com/globe-debate/a-principled-ontario-premier-would-end-funding-for-catholic-schools/article19071121/, access date: 23 July 2015.

Protestant Separate School Board Penetanguishene. n.d. 'About us.' Available at: http://pssbp.ca/, access date: 23 July 2015.

Québec Ministère de l'Éducation, du Loisir et du Sport. n.d. 'Ethics and Religious Culture Program.' Available at: http://www.mels.gouv.qc.ca/en/programme-ethique-et-culture-religieuse//, access date: 23 July 2015.

Ramji, Rubina. 2008. 'Being Muslim and Being Canadian: How Second Generation Muslim Women Create Religious Identities in Two Worlds.' In *Women and Religion in the West: Challenging Secularization,* ed. Kristin Aune, Sonya Sharma, and Giselle Vincett, 195–205. Aldershot: Ashgate.

Religion and Diversity Project. n.d. 'Grant Application.' Available at: http://religionanddiversity.ca/media/uploads/project_team/grant_application/, access date: 23 July 2015.

SSHRC. n.d. 'Social Sciences and Humanities Research Council: About SSHRC.' Available at: http://www.sshrc-crsh.gc.ca/about-au_sujet/index-eng.aspx/, access date: 23 July 2015.

Todd, Douglas. 2013. 'World Religions: 4 out of 5 Want Them Taught in B.C. Public Schools.' *Vancouver Sun,* 30 April. Available at: http://blogs.vancouversun.com/2013/04/30/world-religions-8-of-10-want-them-taught-in-b-c-public-schools/, access date: 23 July 2015.

Tomlins, Steven. 2015. 'A Common Godlessness: A Snapshot of a Canadian University Atheist Club, Why Its Members Joined and What the Community Means to Them.' In *Atheist Identities: Spaces and Social Contexts,* ed. Lori G. Beaman and Steven Tomlins, 117–136. Cham: Springer.

Train, Kelly Amanda. 2013. 'Am I that Jew? North African Jewish Experiences in a Toronto Jewish Day School and the Establishment of Or Haemet Sephardic School.' *Diaspora, Indigenous & Minority Education* 7 (1): 6–20.

Truth and Reconciliation Commission of Canada. 2015. *Honouring the Truth, Reconciling for the Future: Summary of the Final Report of The Truth and Reconciliation Commission of Canada.* Winnipeg: Truth and Reconciliation Commission of Canada. Available at: http://www.trc.ca/websites/trcinstitution/File/2015/Exec_Summary_2015_06_25_web_o.pdf, access date: 23 July 2015.

UNHRC. 1999. *Waldman v. Canada*. Communication No. 694/1996: Canada. 11/05/1999. Available at: http://www.unhchr.ch/tbs/doc.nsf/(Symbol)/b3bfc541589cc30f802568690 052e5d6?Opendocument, access date: 23 July 2015.

UNHRC-CCPR. 2006. 'Consideration of Reports Submitted by States Parties under Article 40 of the Covenant: Concluding Observations of the Human Rights Committee.' Available at: http://www.unhchr.ch/tbs/doc.nsf/898586b1dc7b4043c1256a450044f331/ 7616e3478238be01c12570ae00397f5d/$FILE/G0641362.pdf, access date: 23 July 2015.

Van Arragon, Leo. 2015. 'We Educate, They Indoctrinate: Religion and the Politics of Togetherness in Ontario Public Education.' PhD dissertation. Ottawa: University of Ottawa. Available at: http://hdl.handle.net/10393/32206, access date: 23 July 2015.

Wallis, Simeon. 2014. 'Ticking "No Religion": A Case Study amongst "Young Nones".' *Diskus Journal of the British Association for the Study of Religions* 16 (2): 70–87.

Wallner, Jennifer. 2014. *Learning to School*. Toronto: Toronto University Press.

15 A collage of contexts

Young people and religious diversity in the United States

Mary Elizabeth Moore

Introduction

One striking feature of the chapters in this volume is the stunning influence of personal, social and religious contexts on young people and their attitudes to religious diversity. The chapters reveal complex interaction among these many influences. They further reveal that the influences themselves are complex, including history, cultural heritage, country, region, school, curriculum, religious community and family. The studies reported here are qualitative, based on interviews and observations, and quantitative, based on survey instruments; thus, they do not yield cause-and-effect conclusions. On the other hand, they reveal clear relationships between a wide range of contexts and religious attitudes. The result is a finely textured, mixed-method study of young people in the United Kingdom, related to available research in Ireland and other parts of Europe, which discloses a complex collage of contexts that interact with religious attitudes.

The overall effect of this volume is like a painting with rich colors and textures; yet, this painting, as any work of art, leaves much to the imagination. No painting, and no body of studies, can ever give a full picture of human attitudes; however, the studies in this volume represent an enviable body of data and analysis that has not even been attempted in the United States. Thus, a reflection on these studies in relation to the US context will draw upon conversation partners from diverse sectors of scholarship. The present chapter takes the form of an interpretive essay, pointing to connections and potential areas for further engagement.

The sections of this chapter reflect dominant areas of US scholarship in relation to young people, education and religious diversity. The *genres* selected are those that interplay most clearly with the studies of this volume, but they also give a fairly comprehensive aerial view of youth research in the United States. The first major section identifies *genres* of research in religious education and youth, followed by a short suggestive conclusion. The analysis is exploratory, more like a cartoon sketched by an artist in preparation for a more elaborate painting. For the painter, the cartoon provides a way to experiment and eventually to create a full-size drawing in preparation for a larger work. The larger work implicated in this essay is one that will require many researchers working together, as in the Warwick Religions and Education Research Unit (WRERU).

Genres of research topics in religious education

This chapter is an exploratory map of youth educational research in the United States. Though sketched with broad strokes and not exhaustive, the map portrays a landscape with five major *genres* of research, focused on five purposes of religious education with youth. These are personal and interpersonal formation, communal formation, acquisition and analysis of information, engagement with difference and engagement with mystery. Within each *genre* is considerable complexity. For example, many who are concerned with personal, interpersonal or communal formation are focused on forming young people into one religious tradition; others seek to inspire and equip young people to be good citizens in larger public arenas. Some who focus on more informational approaches to education seek to equip young people with skills to explicate their own tradition to others; other researchers focus on the informational-analytic approach to expand young minds as regards religious diversity and the social influences of religion. For some, the explicit accent on diversity is to equip young people with social skills to engage respectfully with diversity or to equip them with a sense of openness to 'the other'. For some, the accent on mystery is to stir a sense of awe; for others, it is to point beyond the limits of cognitive knowing. These research *genres* reveal complexities within complexities.

The mapping of this chapter is a sampling rather than a thorough review of the literature; however, it does give a large view of the landscape and it will hopefully stir conversation across *genres*. People focused on one *genre* or purpose of research are often not in conversation with those focused on other *genres* and purposes. With hope for more conversation about young people and religion within the United States and across the world, I offer this map.

Personal and interpersonal formation

Researchers in the United States give quite a lot attention to the personal and interpersonal formation of young people and to the factors related to that formation, either causally or correlatively. They focus especially on the following: identity or vocational formation (Baker and Mercer 2007; Dean 2010; Mahan, Warren and White 2008; McAdams et al. 2006; Moore 2015; Smith 2005; Smith and Snell 2009); spiritual and human growth (Kress 2013; Mercer 2008; Sandage, Paine and Devor 2014); trust and relationship building (Baker 2005; Bayar and Hirschman 1993; Bischoff 2011; Davis 2001; Moore 2013; Parker 2001); conversion and religious change (Sandage and Moe 2013; Zinnbauer and Pargament 1998); and specialized subjects such as compassion, forgiveness and empathy (Sandage and Jankowski 2011; Sandage and Worthington 2010). This research, viewed as a whole, reveals a collage of contexts that influence young lives.

One recent study gives an aerial view of these contexts. Mary Elizabeth Moore (2015) analyzes the ways a sample of 35 young people told their life stories, including their descriptions of the significant people in their lives (the characters of their stories). The young people described these significant people in ways that could be mapped in circles of nearness. The innermost circle included the most oft-named characters: fathers, mothers, sisters, brothers, God and Jesus (in this largely Christian sample). The second circle included grandmothers, grandfathers, friends, teachers and school leaders, pastors/church leaders and peers. The third circle included cousins, aunts, uncles and public figures. The fourth circle included dogs, bosses, step-family members, saints and a variety of public figures named by one or two young people (Moore 2015, 72–73). This study cannot stand alone, but it points to the diversity of influences on young people. That diversity is even more visible in a recent review of literature on conversion and transformation by Steven Sandage and Shane Moe (2013), describing a wide complex of studies and a wide complex of interacting variables and theoretical explanations.

The complexity of influences is also revealed in the studies of this volume with its focus on the diverse perspectives of young people towards religious diversity. The diversities discovered by Julia Ipgrave reveal the interactive influences of religious traditions, regions, schools and to some extent families. The unique experiences of young people can be seen as one reads comparatively her studies of Muslim students in a Birmingham comprehensive school, young people in an integrated school in Northern Ireland and young people in a Roman Catholic School in Scotland. The studies by Leslie Francis, Gemma Penny and Peter Neil also reveal the complex interaction of diverse factors, pointing beyond schools and communities to issues such as levels of affiliation. Of particular note, they found different attitudes towards religious diversity among young people with diverse levels of affiliation with their own Roman Catholic tradition. Similarly, Francis and Penny found variations in young people's personal and social world-views and concerns as they surveyed young people in three different religious communities of London. They found that variations in these concerns were related to the young people's levels of self-assigned affiliation in their own tra-ditions. These collective studies reveal a pattern that is also found in US-based research, namely that youth's attitudes are predictably related to many factors, including levels of affiliation and the complex world of relationships in which they live.

In the United States, the study of attitudes towards religious diversity is less common, but studies of the personal and interpersonal aspects of young lives abound (e.g. Baker 2005, 2010; Baker and Mercer 2007; Bayar and Hirschman 1993; Bischoff 2011; Davis 2001; Kress 2013; Mercer 2008; Moore 2013, 2015; Parker 2001). This research often focuses on identity formation and on the holistic development of young people. Alongside these studies are biographical and autobiographical reflections that often *do* turn attention to young people's experiences of and attitudes towards religious diversity (Garrod and Kilkenny 2014; Patel 2007, 2012). Methodologically, these biographical studies could be compared with other narrative studies that focus on written life narratives (McAdams et al. 2006), interviews (Moore 2013, 2015) and ethnographies of small storytelling groups (Baker 2005; Baker and Mercer 2007; Bischoff 2011). These combined studies highlight the insights that emerge from young narratives, particularly as regards personal and interpersonal formation. The narrative-oriented studies could be extended in the future to give more attention to attitudes towards religious diversity; that work has only begun.

To conclude this overview of research on personal and interpersonal formation, I turn to research on educational practices. For example, Jeffrey Kress (2013) and his colleagues have studied accents in Jewish education, where the accent often falls on personal and interpersonal formation. Kress describes his own research experience:

> In my years of research, teaching, and consulting, I have continually found that Jewish educators articulate a consistent range of themes when asked about their goals for their students and their biggest hopes for success. [. . . They] frame their goals broadly, envisioning not just a student possessing a particular body of knowledge (though that is an important part of the picture), but a type of person with particular traits and proclivities.
>
> (Kress 2013, ix)

We see here one overview of educators in a particular religious tradition who seek to nourish the full development of whole persons while encouraging an identity with their particular tradition and community. This accent on formation is alive in the studies of educational practice in other religious traditions as well. One example in the Christian tradition is the work of Dori Baker and Joyce Mercer (2007) on the importance of accompanying youth on their vocational quests.

These educational examples within particular traditions reveal a strain of research on personal and interpersonal formation that is more often tradition-oriented than interreligiously focused. The pioneering work of Eboo Patel (2012) promises to draw this *genre* of research into a more interreligious frame. Much of that work is still to be done.

Communal formation

Communal formation is also an important accent in US religious education. The influences of religion and religious communities seem to be strong among youth and young adults in the United States (Commission on Jewish Education in North America 1990; Dean 2010; Sales 2007; Sales, Samuel and Zablotsky 2011; Smith 2005; Smith and Snell 2009), although the variables are many. In the United States, a large portion of the literature on youth and communal formation is religion specific and it often relates closely with the accent on personal and interpersonal formation.

One example of this work was done by Amy Sales, Nicole Samuel and Alexander Zablotsky (2011). Reviewing 20 years of research on youth (especially Jewish youth) and youth professionals, this team identified many influences on Jewish young people, which underscores the theme of this chapter.

The matrix of influences included parents, schools, youth groups, camps, friends, gender factors and engagement with extracurricular activities and technology (Sales, Samuel and Zablotsky 2011, 5–12, 67–72; see also Commission on Jewish Education in North America 1990; Sales 2007). Seeking to understand and respond more astutely to Jewish youth, the study by Sales, Samuel and Zablotsky included three surveys in three populations: youth, their parents and youth professionals. The results reveal a strong accent on communal formation, but with considerable complexity. For example, the young people vary in denominational or secular identity (Sales, Samuel and Zablotsky 2011, 38–39) and these differences interact with others. At the same time, the study concludes:

> Jewish pride runs high among the teens in our study. Their positive feelings about being Jewish are grounded in an appreciation for the sense of community, connection to other Jews, and Jewish tradition and culture, most especially holiday celebrations with family.
>
> (ibid., 66, see also 38–39)

The unfolding picture is complex. The Jewish youth have mixed positive and negative feelings about their Jewish identities, both in relation to external factors, such as anti-Semitism, and internal factors, such as religious services or divisiveness in the Jewish community. They also have mixed valuations of their relationships with Jewish people in general and with Israel. Indeed, their Jewish identity and participation seem to have less influence in their lives than friends and academic achievement and their strongest concerns centre around family and making the world a better place (Sales et al. 2011, 38–45, 66–67). The authors conclude that the youth's concerns seem to be more American than Jewish and 'their outlook is universalistic and not particularistic' (ibid., 66). This study is based on a limited sample – for example, disproportionately affiliated – but it is revealing. Even in this sample in which Jewish identity is relatively high (about half of the sample), the young people weave their Jewish communal identity and their larger public identity in a complicated way. This merits further study, particularly in relation to the WRERU research in this volume. The interplay of Jewish young people with religious diversity would bring other factors of Jewish identity and interreligious attitudes to light.

Research on the formation of an interreligious communal identity is at an earlier stage in the United States than in the studies reflected in the current volume. Some of this work begins within one religious context but opens doors to other contexts. One example of such work is the multifaceted study of Dori Baker and her colleagues. Their research focuses largely on communal formation in Protestant congregations 'where youth and young adults *want* to be' (Baker 2010, 1, emphasis in original). The team concludes from its ethnographic research that congregations that appeal to youth are 'greenhouses of hope'. Some of their collective research attends specifically to the interfaith engagement of the young people and thus points the way towards aspects of interreligious formation that could be studied further.

A review of the *genre* of communal formation is not complete without a glance at educational practice. A scan of Jewish schools and educational programmes reveals a strong interplay between communal and personal formation. One example is the Prozdor programme of the Hebrew College in Newton, Massachusetts. In its programme for youth in secondary school (grades 8–12), Prozdor seeks to provide 'a vibrant community for Jewish youth during their adolescent years' (http://www.hebrewcollege.edu/youth, access date: 30 August 2015). More particularly, its purpose is to 'help students develop strong Jewish identities and prepare them to be future leaders of American Jewry' (ibid.). The accent on Jewish identity is strong here, but the preparation is understood to be for the sake of the Jewish and larger civic communities.

One finds similar accents in Muslim communities concerned with young people. Sadullah Khan (2012) recognizes that Muslim youth are often caught between their culturally Muslim homes and the cultural forces in the larger society, including Islamophobia in many cases. Thus the community needs to give careful attention to the teaching of Muslim children in their homes and madrasahs/schools and to question some of the current practices; communal formation is key. Indeed, some Muslim programmes are already responding to the need to reshape communal formation, focusing on particular issues. One example is the Muslim Youth Project (Advocates for Youth 2015) that was developed in 2008 to respond to the reproductive and sexual health needs of Muslim-identified youth. This project has become a major educational resource for Muslim communities seeking to provide more adequate communal education on sexual health. This project has a particular focus, but it reveals the accent on communal formation and the efforts to challenge and equip communities to respond fully to young people.

To these projects we can add some that are specifically focused on interfaith community building. Some of these projects are documented and analyzed in Patel (2007) and most of these have continued. The research is ongoing, but most publicly available materials are presently in the form of online guidelines, such as the Interfaith Youth Core's 'Interfaith Cooperation at Public Institutions: Promising Practices' (Interfaith Youth Core 2014a). This resource provides a list of promising practices gleaned from the institutions that have been active in building interfaith communities. Another example of these resources is 'Interfaith Communities in Residence Life' (Interfaith Youth Core 2014b), which is similarly oriented to sharing stories and suggestions to cultivate interfaith communal formation. This work is continuing and is focused action and reflection. Further research of the kind being done by WRERU would make an important contribution to this growing body of action-reflection research (or research feeding into action), which has become a major and influential movement in higher education in the United States.

Informational and analytic engagement

In the United States, the distinction between formational approaches to religious education and informational-analytic approaches is fairly sharp, in part because of dichotomous thinking and in part because of wide differences in theological and social perspectives. Some educators do combine formation and critical analysis, however, especially those who seek to equip young people with the art of cultural critique (Mahan, Warren and White 2008; Turpin 2006; White 2005). In interreligious education, the lines between formation and information-analysis are drawn more sharply, fuelled by the traditional separation of religion and state. One of the leading figures in current discussions of interreligious education in public schools and other public venues is Diane L. Moore. Moore (2007) directs the Religious Literacy Project at Harvard University; her research focuses on education that contributes to the public understanding of religion. Her focus, more specifically, is on informational and analytic engagement and she draws particularly on critical theory. For example, she currently leads a collaboration with educators and public leaders to develop open access resources that can enhance public understanding and ethical decision-making in venues where religion intersects with global issues of conflict and human rights (http://rlp.hds.harvard.edu/about; access date: 28 August 2015).

Moore's work builds upon earlier work, especially in the late 1980s and 1990s, which made a case for religion to be taught and taken seriously in public (state) schools (Nord and Haynes 1998). The effort to make that case continues, even as the teaching of religion continues to be controversial. Much of the discussion focuses on the First Amendment of the US Constitution and on interpretations of religious freedom in relation to the teaching of religion in public education (Haynes 2003; Haynes and Thomas 2001; Darden 2006). The efforts to incorporate the study of religion have continued to grow in the United States, yielding new educational decisions across the country and thus yielding a series of publications. In one early example, the state of California decided to introduce a new set of social science textbooks into grades K–8. In response to that action and to the public concerns that emerged, a team (Dorff et al. 1991) developed a guide to accompany the textbooks and to propose ways to teach world religions without proselytizing, neglecting or distorting any of the traditions. Such efforts have not involved empirical research, but they have engaged in historical and philosophical analysis that continues to this day. The impetus behind such efforts is to enhance the teaching of religion for the sake of deeper understandings within the human family and potential contributions to justice, human rights and human flourishing.

Amid those discussions, Diane Moore (2007) describes the central challenge to religious education in public venues as illiteracy, which in turn feeds religious intolerance, bigotry and acts of dehumanization and violence. She is thus a fierce advocate for the teaching of religion in public schools and she has engaged in years of research and action that illumine approaches to teaching, teacher training and the building of learning communities, always with an accent on critical cultural analysis. In addition she has worked with the American Academy of Religion's Task Force on Religion in the Schools to produce guidelines for teaching about religion in the public schools (Moore and the American Academy 2010). The Task Force report is based on three major premises: (1) that illiteracy about religion is prevalent in the United States; (2) that illiteracy has social consequences, such as prejudice, antagonism, diminished respect for diversity and an inability to collaborate across diverse communities; and (3) that one major contributor to literacy can be the non-devotional teaching of religion in the public schools (ibid., 4–6). Moore and the Task Force also identify four major approaches to interreligious teaching: historical, literary, tradition based and cultural studies (ibid., 9–10). The cultural studies approach includes elements of the others and is seen to be the most promising.

One particular note in the cultural studies approach connects to the WRERU chapters of this volume. In this approach, the teaching of religion accents interpretation and its goal is enhanced interreligious understanding. This approach resonates with Robert Jackson's (1997) interpretive approach to religious education. In the Task Force report, the cultural studies approach is in fact described as an interpretive approach:

> A cultural studies approach recognizes that teachers and students (along with the authors and artists being studied) are interpreters of meaning and that conscious and unconscious assumptions about religion profoundly shape the ways that individuals express what they know and interpret what they learn about religion.
>
> (Moore and the American Academy 2010, 10)

This approach is very similar to the interpretive approach expounded in several chapters of the current volume and in the WRERU studies upon which the chapters are based. The potential for future collaborations across the Atlantic is magnified by our parallel interests in the teaching of religion(s) and by the parallel concerns for interpretation and enhanced human relationships.

Engagement with difference

The analysis thus far leads naturally to the fourth *genre* of youth research in the United States: engagement with difference. Some educators and cultural theorists have attended particularly to the dynamics of difference. In the field of religious education, one of the leaders in this work is Gabriel Moran (2008, 2011). For Moran, difference is filled with promise that the very field of religious education can uncover (1994). It is also filled with questions filled with ambiguity, such as the paradox of uniqueness (2008), and with new possibilities for human existence, such as the potential for non-violent language (2011). Two other religious educators – Mary Boys and Sara Lee – have devoted more than two decades of research and action to understand, develop and interpret Jewish-Christian education (Boys and Lee 2006), although their work has focused on adult education.

Other religious educators have focused on the dynamics of difference across gender and culture (Moore 2007; Nishioka 2008; Parker 2001, 2006).

Scholars of religion and the social scientific study of religion also raise questions of education, often developing in-depth accounts of the role and complexities of education (Berling 2004; Seligman 2014; Seligman and Weller 2012). Adam Seligman attends to the interplay of individual selves, civil society, religious traditions, ritual and tolerance. This work has led him, with his colleague Robert Weller, to rethink pluralism, placing a particular emphasis on the importance of ritual and the value of acknowledging ambiguity. Seligman and Weller (2012) argue that the very effort to disambiguate religions leads away from genuine understanding of others. Drawing from rabbinic commentaries, Chinese texts and Greek literature, they make a case instead for the central role of ritual and shared experience in helping people to live with difference. Ritual enables people to permeate boundaries and shared experiences open people to complexities. These same passions have led Seligman (2014) to make connections with religious education in an edited collection that examines education and religious difference across the world and recognizes the importance of education in cultivating understandings and abilities to live with difference. These passions have also led him to found CEDAR (Communities Engaging with Difference and Religion), which engages in active efforts to embody the educational practices that he and Weller describe, collaborating with people involved in contested issues of religion in the public square (see http://www. CEDARnetwork.org, access date: 28 August 2015).

Engagement with mystery

The final theme – engagement with mystery – receives a lighter touch, partly because it is less discussed in the United States, especially in relation to inter-religious encounters. Further, it is not a major feature in the WRERU research. Mystery cannot be ignored, however, as youth yearn to engage with mystery and education always points beyond what is known to the unknown. For Andrew Root and Kenda Creasy Dean (2011), the theological turn in youth ministry is due in part to the significance of mystery and others emphasize the value for youth of engaging the Holy (e.g. Moore 2008). Mystery is also seen in interreligious settings; Seligman and Weller (2012) emphasize the need for ritual when faced with the ambiguities of diversity. All of these signal that religious education needs to include some kind of engagement with mystery. Mystery is particularly important in the face of differences that cannot be reconciled, questions that cannot be answered and moments of awe that break into the flow of life.

Conclusion

The thematic analysis of this chapter has identified five *genres* of youth research, each of which signals new directions for research and educational practice. Future research is suggested in the previous section, so a summary of educational practices will conclude the chapter. The WRERU chapters and this review of research in the United States suggest that religious education is a practice of *opening* – opening persons and communities to new experiences, fresh thinking, critical analysis and imagination. I will thus close with five educational practices that parallel the five *genres* discussed in this chapter: (1) opening to life narratives, (2) opening to communal relationships, (3) opening to information and analysis, (4) opening to the ambiguities of difference and (5) opening to mystery. These educational practices have been briefly exemplified in the presentation of *genres*, but much work is needed to expand them. The largest challenge is to inspire and support educators as they create, venture and participate in an education of openings.

References

Advocates for Youth. 2015. 'The Muslim Youth Project.' Available at: http://www.advocatesforyouth.org/about-us/programs-and-initiatives/345?task=view, access date: 28 August 2015.

Baker, Dori G. 2005. *Doing Girlfriend Theology: God-talk with Young Women.* Cleveland, OH: Pilgrim.

Baker, Dori G., ed. 2010. *Greenhouses of Hope: Congregations Growing Young Leaders who Will Change the World.* Herndon, VA: Alban Institute.

Baker, Dori G., and Joyce Mercer. 2007. *Lives to Offer: Accompanying Youth on their Vocational Quests.* Cleveland, OH: Pilgrim.

Bayar, Steven, and Francine Hirschman. 1993. *Teens and Trust: Building Bridges in Jewish Education.* Los Angeles, CA: Torah Aura Productions.

Berling, Judith A. 2004. *Understanding Other Religious Worlds: A Guide for Interreligious Education.* Maryknoll, NY: Orbis.

Boys, Mary, and Sara Lee. 2006. *Christians and Jews in Dialogue: Learning in the Presence of the Other.* Woodstock, VT: Skylight.

Bischoff, Claire. 2011. *Toward Tensegrity: Young Women, Narrative Agency, and Religious Education.* Dissertation. Emory University, Atlanta, GA.

Commission on Jewish Education in North America. 1990. *A Time to Act: The Report of the Commission on Jewish Education in North America.* Lanham, MD: University Press of America.

Darden, Edwin C. 2006. 'Religion and Public Schools.' Alexandria, VA: Center for Public Education. Available at: http://www.centerforpubliceducation.org/Main-Menu/Public-education/The-law-and-its-influence-on-public-school-districts-An-overview/Religion-and-Public-Schools.html, access date: 30 August 2015.

Davis, Patricia H. 2001. *Beyond Nice: The Spiritual Wisdom of Adolescent Women.* Minneapolis, MN: Augsburg.

Dean, Kenda Creasy. 2010. *Almost Christian: What the Faith of our Teenagers Is Telling the American Church.* Oxford: Oxford University Press.

Dorff, Elliot N., Robert Ellwood, Fathi Osman, and Mary Elizabeth Moore. 1991. *Teaching about World Religions: A Teacher's Supplement.* Boston: Houghton Mifflin.

Garrod, Andrew, and Robert Kilkenny. 2014. *Growing up Muslim in America: Muslim College Students in America Tell their Life Stories.* Ithaca, NY: Cornell University.

Haynes, Charles C. 2003. *The First Amendment in Schools.* Alexandria, VA: Association for Supervision and Curriculum Development.

Haynes, Charles C., and Oliver Thomas. 2001. *Finding Common Ground: A First Amendment Guide to Religion and Public Education.* Nashville, TN: First Amendment Center. Available at: http://www.centerforpubliceducation.org/Main-Menu/Public-education/The-law-and-its-influence-on-public-school-districts-An-overview/Religion-and-Public-Schools. html#sthash.L8HsybE2.dpuf, access date: 28 August 2015.

Interfaith Youth Core. 2014a. 'Interfaith Cooperation at Public Institutions: Promising Practices.' Available at: https://www.ifyc.org/sites/default/files/u4/InterfaithPublicSchools. pdf, access date: 28 August 2015.

———. 2014b. 'Interfaith Communities in Residence Life.' Available at: https://www.ifyc. org/sites/default/files/u4/ResLife.pdf, access date: 28 August 2015.

Jackson, Robert. 1997. *Religious Education: An Interpretive Approach.* London: Hodder and Stoughton.

Khan, Sadullah. 2012. 'The Dilemma of Teaching Islam to Contemporary Youth.' Available at: http://www.islamicity.org/8522/the-dilemma-of-teaching-islam-to-contemporary-youth/, access date: 27 August 2015.

Kress, Jeffrey S., ed. 2013. *Growing Jewish Minds, Growing Jewish Souls: Promoting Spiritual, Social, and Emotional Grown in Jewish Education.* New York: URJ Press.

Mahan, Brian J., Michael Warren, and David F. White. 2008. *Awakening Youth Discipleship: Christian Resistance in a Consumer Culture.* Eugene, OR: Wipf and Stock.

McAdams, Dan P., Jack J. Bauer, April R. Sakaeda, Nana Akua Anyidoho, Mary Anne Machado, Katie Magrino-Faila, Katie W. White, and Jennifer L. Pals. 2006. 'Continuity and Change in the Life Story: A Longitudinal Study of Autobiographical Memories in Emerging Adulthood.' *Journal of Personality* 74 (5): 1371–1400.

Mercer, Joyce Ann. 2008. *Girltalk/Godtalk: Why Faith Matters to Teenage Girls . . . and their Parents.* San Francisco: Jossey-Bass.

Moore, Diane L. 2007. *Overcoming Religious Illiteracy: A Cultural Studies Approach to the Study of Religion in Secondary Education.* New York: Palgrave McMillan.

Moore, Diane L., and the American Academy of Religion's Task Force on Religion in the Schools. 2010. *Guidelines for Teaching about Religion in K-12 Public Schools in the United States.* Atlanta, GA: American Academy of Religion.

Moore, Mary Elizabeth. 2007. 'Dynamics of Religious Culture: Ethogenic Method.' In *International Handbook of the Religious, Moral and Spiritual Dimensions in Education. Vol 1.* eds. Marian de Souza, Kath Engebretson, Gloria Durka, Robert Jackson and Andrew McGrady, 415–431. Dordrecht: Springer.

———. 2008. 'Yearnings, Hopes, and Visions: Youth Dreams and Ministry Futures.' In *Children, Youth, and Spirituality in a Troubling World*, eds. Mary Elizabeth Moore and Almeda Wright, 108–122. St Louis, MO: Chalice.

———. 2013. 'Desires of the Young.' In *City of Desires: A Place for God?*, eds. R. Ruard Ganzevoort, Rein Brouwer and Bonnie Miller-McLemore, 101–110. Zurich: LIT Verlag.

———. 2015. 'Youth Navigating Identities: Charting the Waters through Narrative.' In *Complex Identities in a Shifting World: Practical Theological Perspectives*, eds. Pamela Couture, Robert Mager, Pamela McCarroll and Natalie Wigg-Stevenson, 65–76. Zurich: LIT Verlag.

Moran, Gabriel. 1994. *Religious Education as a Second Language.* Birmingham, AL: Religious Education Press.

———. 2008. *Uniqueness: Problem or Paradox in Jewish and Christian Traditions.* Eugene, OR: Wipf and Stock.

———. 2011. *Living Non-Violently: Language for Resisting Violence.* Lanham, MD: Lexington Books, Rowman & Littlefield.

Nishioka, Rodger. 2008. 'Violence, Boy Code, and Schools.' In *Children, Youth, and Spirituality in a Troubling World*, eds. Mary Elizabeth Moore and Almeda Wright, 62–77. St Louis, MO: Chalice.

Nord, Warren A., and Charles C. Haynes. 1998. *Taking Religion Seriously across the Curriculum*. Alexandria, VA: Association for Supervision and Curriculum Development.

Parker, Evelyn L. 2001. 'Hungry for Honor: Children in Violent Youth Gangs.' *Interpretation* 55 (2): 148–160.

———. ed. 2006. *The Sacred Selves of Adolescent Girls: Hard Stories of Race, Class, and Gender*. Cleveland, OH: Pilgrim.

Patel, Eboo. 2007. *Acts of Faith: The Story of an American Muslim, the Struggle for the Soul of a Generation*. Boston: Beacon.

———. 2012. *Sacred Ground: Pluralism, Prejudice, and the Promise of America*. Boston: Beacon.

Root, Andrew, and Kenda Creasy Dean. 2011. *The Theological Turn in Youth Ministry*. Downers Grove, IL: InterVarsity.

Sales, Amy L. 2007. *Lessons from Mapping Jewish Education*. Waltham, MA: Brandeis University, Fisher-Bernstein Institute for Jewish Philanthropy and Leadership.

Sales, Amy L., Nicole Samuel, and Alexander Zablotsky. 2011. *Engaging Jewish Teens: A Study of New York Teens, Parents, and Practitioners*. Waltham, MA: Brandeis University, Maurice and Marilyn Cohen Center for Modern Jewish Studies. Available at: http://www.jewished project.org/sites/default/files/uploaded/EngagingJewishTeens111011.pdf, access date: 30 August 2015.

Sandage, Steven J., and Peter J. Jankowski. 2011. 'Forgiveness, Differentiation of Self, and Mental Health.' In *A Journey through Forgiveness*, eds. M. M. Maamri, N. Nevin and E. L. Worthington, Jr., 87–98. Oxford: Inter-Disciplinary Press.

Sandage, Steven J., and Shane Moe. 2013. 'Spiritual Experience: Conversion and Transformation.' In *APA Handbook of Psychology, Religion, and Spirituality. Vol. 1*, eds. Kenneth I. Pargament, J. J. Exline and J. W. Jones, 407–422. Washington, DC: American Psychological Association.

Sandage, Steven J., David R. Paine, and Nancy Gieseler Devor. 2014. 'Psychology and Spiritual Formation: Emerging Prospects for Differentiated Integration.' *Journal of Spiritual Formation and Soul Care* 7 (2): 229–247.

Sandage, Steven J., and Everett L. Worthington, Jr. 2010. 'Comparison of Two Group Interventions to Promote Forgiveness: Empathy as a Mediator of Change.' *Journal of Mental Health Counseling* 32 (1): 35–57.

Seligman, Adam B., ed. 2014. *Religious Education and the Challenge of Pluralism*. Oxford: Oxford University Press.

Seligman, Adam B., and Robert P. Weller. 2012. *Rethinking Pluralism: Ritual, Experience, and Ambiguity*. Oxford: Oxford University Press.

Smith, Christian. 2005. *Soul Searching: The Religious and Spiritual Lives of American Teenagers*. New York: Oxford University Press.

Smith, Christian, and Patricia Snell. 2009. *Souls in Transition: The Religious and Spiritual Lives of Emerging Adults*. New York: Oxford University Press.

Turpin, Katherine. 2006. *Branded: Adolescents Converting from Consumer Faith*. Cleveland, OH: Pilgrim.

White, David F. 2005. *Practicing Discernment with Youth: A Transformative Youth Ministry Approach*. Cleveland, OH: Pilgrim.

Zinnbauer, Brian J., and Kenneth I. Pargament. 1998. 'Spiritual Conversion: A Study of Religious Change among College Students.' *Journal for the Scientific Study of Religion* 37 (1): 161–180.

16 Young people and religious diversity

A European perspective, with particular reference to Germany

Alexander Yendell

Introduction

In this chapter I focus on young people's attitudes towards religious diversity in five selected European countries. In this context I also discuss the impact of direct and indirect contact with members of different religions and attitudes towards them. I mainly focus on views of Muslims, as views of Islam and Muslims are particularly negative in comparison with other religions and their members. The reason for this interest is that one of the most important and interesting results of the Young People's Attitudes to Religious Diversity project is the relevance of direct and indirect contact with people of different religions and religious views. The project revealed that contact with members of other religious groups, and knowledge about other religions, can shape attitudes towards religious diversity in a positive way. The interviews with young people in particular show that contact with members of other religions, as well as knowledge about the range of religions, break down stereotypes and stereotyping. Religious diversity is viewed as a fact of life which young people accept. The interviews also show that multicultural and interreligious contact plays an even more important role as the media concentrate on the 'bad news'. The young people interviewed in England and Wales were often aware that the media produce negative images of religions, thus encouraging stereotypes and generalizations. Young people were also media savvy, without prejudice and tolerant. One of the key findings is that knowledge of religions and religious people mitigates the (mis)representation of religion(s) in the media. The results of the interviews are in line with the so-called contact hypothesis, which I will briefly describe, as it is important for the following analysis. The contact hypothesis assumes that individual personal contact with members of an outgroup reduces stereotyping (Allport 1954). However, not every type of contact automatically reduces stereotyping. According to Susanne Rippl (1995, 277–278), the degree of stereotyping depends on both the type of relationship (e.g. contact with colleagues, acquaintances, friends or relatives) and the quality of the contact. Certain conditions such as equal status, cooperative activity, continuity and meeting in person may improve interpersonal attitudes between in- and outgroups (Pettigrew and Tropp 2000). Also, the transmission of knowledge about the respective outgroup can reduce stereotyping (Smith and Mackie 2000). In this context, the type of mediation of knowledge plays an important role. What matters is whether the transfer of knowledge is considered credible or not (Cialdini 1997). A problem of the validation of the contact hypothesis is whether contact actually reduces stereotyping or whether individual openness to strangers makes frequent contact with them more likely. In this context, the meta-analysis of Thomas Pettigrew and Linda Tropp is revealing (2006, 757–758). It shows that the average strength of the negative effect of contact with strangers on stereotyping is greater in studies in which respondents had no contact options, compared to studies in which respondents had to choose whether they would like contact with strangers or not. Thus, according to these research results, contact does have a stereotype-reducing effect. The classical contact hypothesis is broadened by the para-social contact hypothesis (Horton and Wohl 1956); it postulates that mass media such as radio, TV and films can produce the illusion of direct contact and influence the attitudes towards a social group which is perceived as foreign or strange. Especially regarding Islam there is a strong 'bad news' bias as the media concentrate on reports of terrorist attacks by Islamists (Schiffer 2005; Hafez 2010). It can be assumed that indirect contact with Islam is mainly negative and can produce stereotyping, especially if direct contact with Muslims is infrequent. On the contrary, direct contact with Muslims could mitigate the negatively biased information on Islam and Muslims, as revealed in some of the interviews in the Young People's Attitudes to Religious Diversity project. It is possible that younger people are more likely to be tolerant compared to elderly people, as they have more direct contact due to increasing numbers of young people with migration background through their schools, universities, neighbourhoods, workplaces and so forth. Increased contact is probably more frequent than among the older generations. The considerations regarding the contact hypothesis lead to the following research questions: What attitudes do young people have towards religious plurality in general? How do young people perceive religions and their members? Which attitudes do young people have regarding religious practices, especially Islamic religious practices? What explains the attitudes towards members of religious groups, and which role does contact play in the context of a complex explanatory model?

Data and methods

The following quantitative analysis is based on data from the survey 'The Legitimacy of Religious Pluralism: Perception and Acceptance of Religious Diversity among the European Population' (PARD). The survey was conducted between July and August 2010 in the Netherlands, Denmark, France, Germany and Portugal by the University of Münster, Germany. The questionnaire included questions about the acceptance of religious pluralism and about attitudes towards different religious groups. Its emphasis focused on views of Islam and Muslims. The questionnaire also included items on contact with members of different religious groups and engagement with different religions. In addition, it asked questions about religiosity, attitudes towards democracy, value orientations, social position, membership in voluntary organizations and socio-demographic characteristics such as age, sex, educational background, income and occupational status. The same questionnaire was used in all countries, but the German questionnaire included additional questions. These were detailed items on contact with members of different religious groups, as opposed to the questionnaire used in the other countries which only asked about the frequency of contact. Based on a sample derived from the selection system of the *Arbeitsgemeinschaft deutscher Marktforschungsinstitute* (ADM), 1,041 computer-assisted personal interviews (CAPI) were conducted in pre-1990 Western Germany and 1,002 interviews in pre-1990 Eastern Germany. In Denmark, 1,014 computer-assisted telephone interviews (CATI) were conducted; 1,001 were conducted in France and 1,000 each in the Netherlands and Portugal. The data were weighted based on standard sample distortion which includes age, sex and educational background.

Attitudes towards religious diversity

In the following section, I discuss general attitudes towards religious diversity in the population of the five selected countries and details regarding tolerance in relation to religious practices and members of non-Christian religions. I am particularly interested in the attitudes of young people in comparison to older age groups. The pluralism of lifestyles, the different education systems in each of the surveyed countries and individual levels of maturation make it difficult to categorize youth. That is why the following categorization of age groups follows a pragmatic approach, so that enough cases in each age group exist. Young people are here defined as being part of the 18–24 age group. At first sight, it seems as if the majority of people in all countries are interested in positive interactions with all religions. Figure 16.1 shows that the majority believe that all religions deserve respect.

In Germany, about 80 per cent of the population think that all religions deserve respect, and in the other countries the percentage is even higher. There

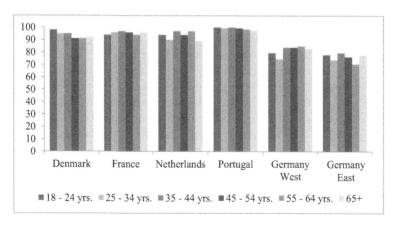

Figure 16.1 Respect for all religions by country and age groups.

Source: PARD 2010; own calculations; respect all religion: 'How do you personally judge the situation?'; scale from 1 to 4 (agree strongly, agree somewhat, disagree somewhat, disagree strongly); percentage of those who strongly or somewhat agree that we must respect all religions.

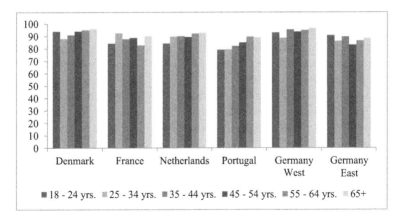

Figure 16.2 Support of freedom of religious belief by country and age groups.

Source: PARD 2010; own calculations; freedom of belief: 'Please specify how important the following aspects of political life are to you.'; scale from 1 to 4 (very important, somewhat important, somewhat unimportant, very unimportant); percentage of those who find freedom of religious beliefs very or somewhat important.

are no noticeable differences between the age groups regarding respect towards all religions. The high acceptance of religious diversity is also expressed in the broad agreement on the principle of freedom of belief.

Between 80 and 90 per cent of the population of the five countries find freedom of religious belief very important or somewhat important (see Figure 16.2). It seems that the majority support the liberal values of democratic society. Age does not matter in this context, except in Portugal where freedom of belief seems to be more important to the elderly.

If respect towards all religions and freedom of belief is regarded as an important value, one could assume that the majority believe that all religious groups have equal rights. As expected, this is the case in Denmark, France, the Netherlands and Portugal, but paradoxically not in Germany (see Figure 16.3). Only about 50 per cent of the population in Germany agree that all religious groups should have equal rights, whereas in the other countries the percentage lies between 70 and 80 per cent. It is notable that in all countries younger people are more in favour of equal rights for all religious groups than older people. The biggest difference between the oldest group (65+) and the youngest (18- to 24-year-olds) can be found in Denmark (15 percentage points) and Germany (9 percentage points). In the other countries the differences are lower. However, there seems to be a contradiction in Germany: on the one hand, the German population believes in freedom of belief and agrees that all religions should be respected, but on the other hand, about half the population does not believe that all religious groups should be granted equal rights.

Further, unlike the population in Denmark, France, the Netherlands and Portugal, the population in Germany seems to be sceptical about religious diversity: only

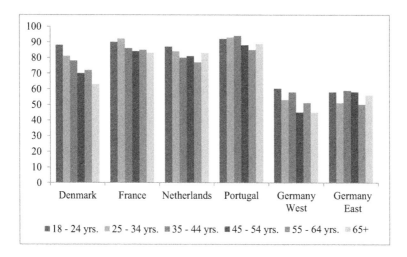

Figure 16.3 Granting rights for all religious groups by country and age groups.

Source: PARD 2010; own calculations; religious rights: 'How do you personally judge the situation?'; scale from 1 to 4 (agree strongly, agree somewhat, disagree somewhat, disagree strongly); percentage of those who strongly or somewhat agree that all religious groups (in the country) should have equal rights.

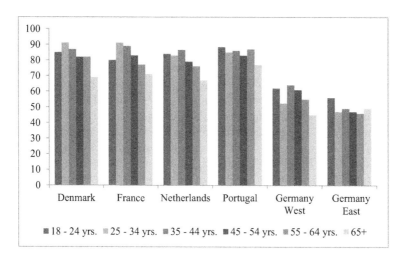

Figure 16.4 Religious diversity as cultural enrichment by country and age groups.

Source: PARD 2010; own calculations; religious rights: 'How do you personally judge the situation?'; scale from 1 to 4 (agree strongly, agree somewhat, disagree somewhat, disagree strongly); percentage of those who strongly or somewhat agree that the increasing variety of religious groups is a source of cultural enrichment.

slightly over 50 per cent believe that the increasing variety of religious groups is a source of cultural enrichment, whereas in the other countries more than three-quarters of the population find religious diversity enriching (see Figure 16.4).

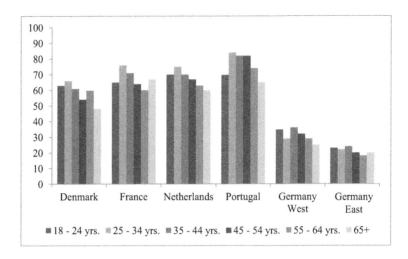

Figure 16.5 Support for building mosques by country and age groups.

Source: PARD 2010; own calculations; support for building mosques: 'Generally speaking, do you approve the building of mosques in [country]?'; percentage of those who support building mosques.

Again the differences between the youngest group (18- to 24-year-olds) and the oldest respondents are significant: the former seem to have fewer problems with an increasing variety of religious groups than the latter. Generally speaking, in all countries, the age groups over 54 are less positive towards an increasing variety of religious groups than the youngest group (18- to 24-year-olds).

If many people in Germany are sceptical about an increasing variety of religious groups, and if many people there do not believe that all religious groups should have equal rights, how does this attitude express itself in the discussion of religious practice? Regarding the building of mosques, Germans show a restrictive attitude. Only about 28 per cent of the population in Western Germany and only about 20 per cent of the population in Eastern Germany support the building of mosques (see Figure 16.5). In Denmark, France, the Netherlands and Portugal, over half of the population approves the building of mosques. In all five countries except Portugal, the groups under the age of 45 are more in favour of building mosques than the older age groups.

The impression that the German population specifically refuses Islam equal rights is confirmed when people are asked about restrictions of the Islamic faith. In Western Germany, 42 per cent and over 50 per cent in Eastern Germany agree that practising the Islamic faith should be severely restricted. The level of agreement is also high in France, which is not surprising as the French principle of *laïcité* bans religion from the public sphere. Figure 16.6 also reveals that again the younger respondents show less of a restrictive attitude whereas agreement with restricting Islamic practice is higher among the older age groups.

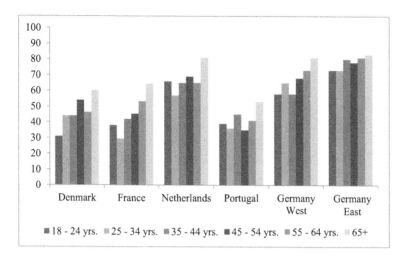

Figure 16.6 Restriction of Islamic faith by country and age groups.

Source: PARD 2010; religious rights: 'What is your opinion on the following statement?'; scale from 1 to 4 (agree strongly, agree somewhat, disagree somewhat, disagree strongly); percentage of those who strongly or somewhat agree that practising the Islamic faith in [country] must be severely restricted.

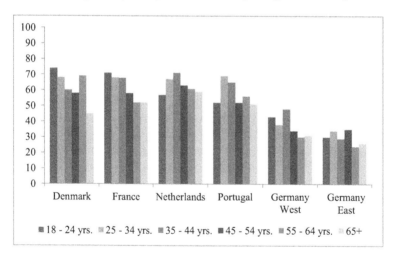

Figure 16.7 Positive attitudes towards Muslims by country and age groups.

Source: PARD 2010; own calculations; attitudes towards Muslims: 'What is your personal attitude towards members of the following religious groups?'; percentage of those who have a positive or somewhat positive attitude of Muslims.

Regarding attitudes towards Muslims, the question is whether these too are more negative in Germany and whether younger people are less negative about Muslims than older age groups. Figure 16.7 shows that in Denmark, France, the Netherlands and Portugal the majority of respondents have a positive attitude

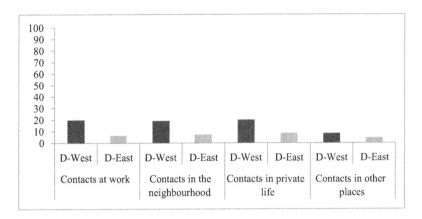

Figure 16.8 Contact with Muslims by age groups.

Source: PARD 2010; own calculations; contacts with Muslims: 'Do you personally have contact with members of the following religious groups?'; percentage of those who have a lot of or some contact with Muslims.

towards Muslims, whereas in Germany most people have negative attitudes towards Muslims. There are significant but weak correlations between age and attitude towards Muslims in Denmark, France, Portugal and Western Germany.[1] In the Netherlands, as in Eastern Germany, there are no such correlations. The younger the people in Denmark, France, Portugal and Western Germany, the more likely they are to have positive attitudes.

There are also significant correlations between age and the frequency of contact in Germany, Denmark, France and the Netherlands (see Figure 16.8). In Portugal, a country with only a very small Muslim population, there is no such correlation. In the other countries, age significantly correlates with contact. It is especially the age groups over 54 who have the least contact with Muslims. It is very likely that not age itself, but contact with Muslims has an impact on attitudes. The multivariate model discussed later will reveal which factor is crucial regarding attitudes towards Muslims.

Factors determining negative attitudes towards Muslims in Western and Eastern Germany, with particular focus on the contact hypothesis

In this section I will analyze the factors which have an impact on attitudes towards Muslims in Western and Eastern Germany. I will focus on the contact hypothesis but also consider factors which derive from other prominent theories in order to estimate the strength of the impact of contact in comparison with other factors. The structural equation models in Table 16.1 contain only manifest variables. The dependent indicator in the model is the question regarding attitude towards Muslims. The model includes a fairly high number

Table 16.1 Results of the structural equation model: attitudes towards Muslims

	Western Germany	*Eastern Germany*
Frequency of contact with Muslims	.284★★★	.190
Contacts with Muslims in private life	.114★★	n.s.d.e.
Contacts with Muslims in the neighbourhood	n.s.d.e.	n.s.d.e.
Contacts with Muslims at work	n.s.d.e.	n.s.d.e.
Contacts with Muslims at other places	n.s.d.e	n.s.d.e.
Occupation with Islam	n.s.d.e.	n.s.d.e.
Frequency of church attendance	.131★★★	.149
Religious dogmatism	−.168★★★	−.120
Authoritarianism	n.s.d.e.	n.s.d.e.
National pride	n.s.d.e.	−.075
Religions lead to conflicts	−.142★★★	−.159
Political attitude	−.109★★★	−.180
Relative deprivation	−.103★★★	−.109
Position on social ladder	n.s.d.e.	n.s.d.e.
Unemployment	n.s.d.e.	n.s.d.e.
Net household income	n.s.d.e.	n.s.d.e.
Age	n.s.d.e.	n.s.d.e.
Sex	n.s.d.e.	n.s.d.e.
Educational level	n.s.d.e.	.090
Urban vs. rural area	n.s.d.e.	n.s.d.e.
R^2	.212	.169
E	.788	.831
RMSEA	.000	.050
PCLOSE	1.000	.554

Source: PARD 2010; own calculations; standardized regression coefficient; significance: ★★★ $p < .001$; ★★ $p < .01$; ★ $p < .05$; n.s.d.e.: no significant direct effect on the dependent variable; *dependent variable*: 'What is your personal attitude towards members of the following religious groups?' (here: Muslims); 4-point scale (1 = very negative, 2 = somewhat negative, 3 = somewhat positive, 4 = very positive); *independent variables*: see Appendix.

of indicators which may potentially explain the attitude towards Muslims. The test of the contact hypothesis includes six items. The first five are the number of contacts with Muslims, contacts with Muslims in private life, in the neighbourhood, at work and in other areas. Since it is also assumed that knowledge about religions can reduce stereotyping different religious groups, I added an additional item, that is how much a person has engaged with Islam.

In addition to the contact items, the model contains indicators which measure the influence of objective deprivation, such as household income and unemployment. Deprivation is measured in relative terms: exclusive categories of getting a fair share, more than a fair share, somewhat less or very much less than a fair share. Additionally, individual position on the social ladder was included as well as political attitude (here the scale runs from left to right), national pride, authoritarianism, religious dogmatism and frequency of church attendance. Also, social structural variables such as region (urban vs. rural), educational level, gender and age were included. Unlike a conventional regression analysis, path models with simple causal structure for Western and Eastern Germany have the advantage that the correlations between explanatory factors are sufficiently taken into account, which reduces the likelihood of biased regression weights and consequent misinterpretations (see Weiber and Mühlhaus 2010, 25). Such models may be presumed to yield more precise parameter estimates. They also offer the advantage of distinguishing between direct and indirect factors – those which are directly related to the dependent variable and those which are mediated by one or more other factors related to the dependent variable. Furthermore, path analysis, being a special type of structural equation modelling, provides the possibility of considering measurement errors, reducing the bias of statements regarding the relationships between theoretical constructs.

Model fit and correlations between the independent variables

Model fit for Western Germany was excellent in terms of the root mean square error of approximation (RMSEA) (Browne and Cudeck 1992, 239). Among the significant correlations between the independent indicators in both models, some of the more important relations showed a strong correlation between the different areas in which people can have contact with Muslims. That is, if a person has contact at work or in the neighbourhood or in other areas, s/he is likely also to have contact in his/her private life. The number of contacts is also significantly connected to the study of Islam. As expected, another fairly strong correlation exists between church attendance and religious dogmatism.

Factors in Western Germany

The strongest direct effect regarding attitude towards Muslims in the model for Western Germany is the frequency of contact. The types of contact, such contact at work, in the neighbourhood or elsewhere, are less important for attitude towards Muslims; only private contact has a direct positive effect on attitudes towards Muslims. This probably means that frequent contact leads to a differentiated view of Muslims so that they are perceived as a heterogeneous group. Engagement with Islam has no significant direct effect on attitudes towards Muslims. I assume that the item does not measure religious knowledge as intended because it is astonishing that the majority of respondents answered that they had engaged with Islam. A better idea is probably to ask detailed questions about the Qur'an and Islamic practices. Furthermore, religious dogmatism is relevant. People who believe that there is only one true religion are very likely to have a negative stance towards Muslims. Religious dogmatism in turn is highly correlated with frequency of church attendance which has a positive effect on attitude towards Muslims. The effect of the interaction between religious dogmatism and church attendance can indeed have a very positive effect on attitude towards Muslims. In addition, the model for Western Germany reveals that viewing the increasing religious diversity as a cause of conflict has a negative effect on attitude towards Muslims. As expected, political attitude correlates with attitude towards Muslims: the more right-wing a person is, the more likely s/he is to have a negative attitude towards Muslims. National pride and authoritarianism have no direct influence: both factors correlate with religious dogmatism. There are also interesting findings regarding the concept of deprivation. While unemployment, household income and self-assessed position on the social ladder are not related with attitude towards Muslims, there is a correlation between feeling socially disadvantaged and attitude towards Muslims. Thus relative deprivation proves to be crucial in this model. Indicators of objective deprivation – which are associated with the indicator of relative deprivation – do not play a role as direct influences. Social statistical characteristics such as sex, region (urban vs. rural) and age are insignificant.

Factors in Eastern Germany

As in the Western German model, the strongest factor in the model for Eastern Germany is frequency of contact, although this factor is weaker than in the Western German model. The contact types are – unlike in the Western German model – completely insignificant. In Eastern Germany, only frequency of contact with Muslims plays a role; whether they occur privately, professionally, in the neighbourhood or on other occasions is not important. Moreover, political attitude seems to play an important role for the Eastern German population: those who state to be politically right-wing are more likely to have negative attitudes towards Muslims than those who are left-wing. As in Western Germany, those who see a potential for conflict in religious diversity are more likely to have negative attitudes towards Muslims. The same applies to religious dogmatism which also has a negative effect on attitude towards Muslims, while frequency of church attendance in Eastern Germany has a positive effect on attitude towards Muslims. Like in Western Germany, indicators of objective socio-economic disadvantage play no role in Eastern Germany, while relative deprivation has a negative effect on attitude towards Muslims. Another significant but weak indicator is the level of education. National pride has a slightly negative effect on attitude towards Muslims. Not recognizable as direct influences are social statistical characteristics such as age, sex and region (urban vs. rural). Whether people live in the country or in the city makes no difference regarding their acceptance or rejection of Muslims in Eastern Germany. It should however be noted that in Eastern Germany – in contrast to Western Germany – small significant associations exist between possibilities of contact and region: those who live in the country have little contact with the Muslim population and are therefore more prone towards prejudice against Muslims. In the Western part of Germany, such a correlation is not evident in the structural equation models.

Frequency of contact with Muslims in Germany and possible periodical effects and media influence

The multivariate models reveal that frequency of contact plays the most important role in explaining attitudes towards Muslims. It can be assumed that one reason for the differences in the results regarding attitude towards Muslims in Eastern and Western Germany is the frequency of distribution of this variable. Regarding contact with Muslims, the following can be stated: the population in Eastern Germany has much less contact with Muslims than the population of Western Germany. This applies to all areas where opportunities may arise to meet Muslims. At work, in the neighbourhood, in private life as well as in other areas, people in Eastern Germany meet Muslims less often than people in Western Germany (see Table 16.2).

What role do the media play in this context? The PARD survey did not ask respondents about their media consumption, which is why it is not possible to correlate the consumption of TV, the Internet, radio or print media with attitudes towards Muslims. One way to measure the 'bad news' effect on attitudes towards Muslims is to analyze discrimination against Muslims over time to see if an incident such as 9/11 has an effect on attitudes towards Muslims. The analysis of the 'neighbourhood question' in the European Values Survey (EVS) shows that in the 1990s the rejection of Muslims as neighbours reduced in Eastern and Western Germany, but after 2000 more and more people did not want to have Muslims as neighbours, especially in Eastern Germany. The analysis of the data of the EVS wave of 2008–2010 (Figure 16.9) reveals that 34 per cent of the population in Eastern Germany do not want to live next to a Muslim, which is an increase of 20 percentage points since the EVS wave of 1999–2000.

It seems that the terror attacks of 9/11 mark a turning point regarding attitudes towards Muslims. The high rate of rejection in Eastern Germany is especially astonishing because only 2 per cent of the Muslim population of Germany (about 61,000 people) live in this part of Germany and because contact with Muslims is very rare. It seems that the majority of the population in Germany has mainly indirect contact through the media and that many people are not

Table 16.2 Frequency of contacts with Muslims

	Western Germany	Eastern Germany
yes, a lot	7.2	3.9
yes, somewhat	32.9	12.2
no, rather not	25.9	20.7
no, not at all	33.3	62.5
don't know	0.3	0.4
no answer	0.3	0.3
Total	100.0	100.0

Source: PARD 2010; own calculations; 'Do you personally have contact with members of the following religious groups?'; 4-point scale (1 = yes, a lot; 2 = yes, somewhat; 3 = no, rather not; 4 = no, not at all).

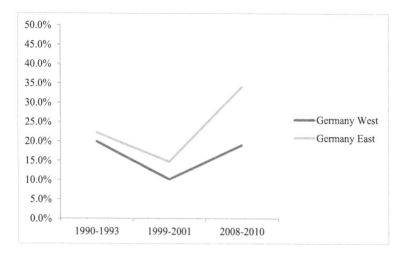

Figure 16.9 Rejection of Muslims as neighbours.

Source: EVS; own calculations; Muslims as neighbours: 'Could you indicate any people that you would not like as neighbours?'; percentage of those who would not like Muslims as neighbours.

able to develop a complex and differentiated picture of Islam and its members as they have no direct contact with Muslims. In Eastern Germany, the negative effect of 'bad news' is stronger than in Western Germany, as people there have less stereotype-reducing contact with the Muslim population.

Conclusion

No matter whether young or old, the majority of the populations in Denmark, France, the Netherlands, Germany and Portugal believe that all religions must be respected. At the same time there is scepticism about the increasing religious plurality and especially Islam, and its members are viewed critically and often encounter rejection. Compared with the population of Denmark, France, the Netherlands and Portugal, the population in Germany is the most sceptical about Islam and Muslims, and unlike the population of the other countries the majority of the population in Germany do not support the building of mosques. Regarding tolerance towards Islam and Muslims in all the countries surveyed, the youngest respondents are more likely to be open-minded than the oldest respondents, but not necessarily more so than the middle-aged groups. This is also because the oldest respondents have less contact with Muslims than the younger respondents. The multivariate analysis for Western and Eastern Germany reveals that frequency of contact is the most important factor in explaining attitude towards Muslims. It is more important than the place where people meet Muslims, such as the workplace, private life or the neighbourhood, and it is also more important that other factors such as deprivation or age. It seems that the more frequent the contact the more differentiated the image of Muslims, and that the influence of 'bad news' about Islam diminishes. The results of the this quantitative analysis match the results of the qualitative study of the Young People's Attitudes to Religious Diversity project: contact with Muslims reduces stereotypes and makes (young) people immune to the negative image of Islam and Muslims projected by the media.

Note

1   Correlations between age and attitude towards Muslims: Denmark Kendall tau-b = 0.113 (p = 0.000); France Kendall Tau-b = 0.115 (p = 0.000); Portugal Kendall tau-b = 0.065 (p = 0.014); Western Germany Kendall tau-b = 0.087 (p = 0.000).

References

Allport, G. W. 1954. *The Nature of Prejudice.* Cambridge, MA: Perseus Books.

Browne, M., and R. Cudeck. 1992. 'Alternative Ways of Assessing Model Fit.' *Sociological Methods and Research* 21 (2): 230–258.

Cialdini, R. B. 1997. *Psychologie des Überzeugens.* Bern: Huber.

Hafez, K. 2010. 'Mediengesellschaft – Wissensgesellschaft? Gesellschaftliche Entstehungsbedingungen des Islambilds deutscher Medien.' In *Islamfeindlichkeit. Wenn die Grenzen verschwimmen* (2nd ed.), ed. T. G. Schneiders, 101–210, Wiesbaden: VS Verlag.

Horton, D., and R. R. Wohl. 1956. 'Mass Communication and Para-social Interaction: Observations on Intimacy at a Distance.' *Psychiatry* 19 (3): 215–229.

Pettigrew, T. F., and L. R. Tropp. 2000. 'Does Intergroup Contact Reduce Prejudice? Recent Meta-analytic Findings.' In *Reducing Prejudice and Discrimination: Social Psychological Perspectives*, ed. S. Oskamp, 93–114. Mahwah, NJ: Psychology Press.

———. 2006. 'A Meta-analytic Test of Intergroup Contact Theory.' *Journal of Personality and Social Psychology* 90 (5): 751–783.

Rippl, S. 1995. 'Vorurteile und persönliche Beziehungen zwischen Ost- und Westdeutschen.' *Zeitschrift für Soziologie* 24 (4): 273–283.

Schiffer, S. 2005. 'Der Islam in deutschen Medien.' *Aus Politik und Zeitgeschichte* 55 (20): 23–30.

Smith, E. R., and D. M. Mackie. 2000. *Social Psychology.* Philadelphia: Psychology Press.

Weiber, R., and D. Mühlhaus. 2010. *Strukturgleichungsmodellierung: Eine anwendungsorientierte Einführung in die Kausalanalyse mit Hilfe von AMOS, SmartPLS und SPSS.* Berlin: Springer.

Appendix

Independent variables in Table 16.1

frequency of contact with Muslims: 'Do you personally have contact with members of the following religious groups?'; 4-point scale (1 = yes, a lot; 2 = yes, somewhat; 3 = no, rather not; 4 = no, not at all).

contact with Muslims (places): 'Where do these contacts take place?' (at work; in the neighbourhood; in private life; in other places).

occupation with Islam: 'Have you ever busied yourself with the following religions?' (here: Islam); 4-point scale (1 = no, not at all; 2 = no, rather not; 3 = yes, somewhat; 4 = no, not at all).

frequency of church attendance: 'How often do you attend religious services?' (never, less than once a year, several times a year, about once a month, 2–3 times a month, every week or more often).

religious dogmatism: 'There is only one true religion'; 4-point scale (1 = disagree strongly; 2 = disagree somewhat; 3 = agree somewhat; 4 = agree strongly).

authoritarianism: 'We should be grateful for leaders who can tell us exactly what to do and how to do it'; 4-point scale (1 = disagree strongly; 2 = disagree somewhat; 3 = agree somewhat; 4 = agree strongly).

national pride: 'I am proud of my nationality'; 4-point scale (1 = disagree strongly; 2 = disagree somewhat; 3 = agree somewhat; 4 = agree strongly).

religion leads to conflicts: 'Looking around the world, religions bring more conflict than peace'; 4-point scale (1 = disagree strongly; 2 = disagree somewhat; 3 = agree somewhat; 4 = agree strongly).

political attitudes: 'Some people are talking of "left" and "right" when trying to describe different political attitudes. Where would you place your own political attitudes on a scale from 1 to 10, where 1 means "left" and 10 means "right"?'; 10-point scale (1 = left; 10 = right).

relative deprivation: 'Compared with how others live in (country): Do you think you get your fair share, more than your fair share, somewhat less or very much less than your fair share?'; 4-point scale (1 = more than fair share; 2 = fair share; 3 = somewhat less; 4 = very much less).

position on social ladder: 'Some people believe that they belong to high society, whereas others believe they belong to the underclass. Please try to imagine a ladder with seven steps and each of them stands for a social status. Where would you and your family stand on such a ladder? 7 means "on top" and 1 means "at the bottom".'

educational background: not completed school, German *Volks-/ Hauptschule*; German *Realschule*; polytechnic high school (Year 8 or 9); polytechnic high school (Year 10); German *Fachhochschulreife*; German *Abitur*; degree at university of applied sciences; university degree.

List of contributors

Tania ap Siôn is Associate Professor in Education and the Social Significance of Religion in the Warwick Religions and Education Research Unit (WRERU) in the Centre for Education Studies at the University of Warwick and Director of the St Mary's Centre, Wales, for research and curriculum development in religion and education. Her recent research and publications have focused on community cohesion and religious diversity in Wales, young people and education in faith-related contexts and studies in the prayer and sacred space. She serves on the Executive Committee of the Wales Association of SACREs (Standing Advisory Council for Religious Education), holding the position of Chair 2013–2015.

Elisabeth Arweck PhD is Principal Research Fellow in WRERU, Centre for Education Studies, University of Warwick, and Editor of the *Journal of Contemporary Religion*. Her recent research has focused on young people's attitudes to religious diversity and the religious socialization and nurture of young people. Recent publications include a number of co-authored articles (with Eleanor Nesbitt) and co-edited volumes, such as *Religion and Knowledge* (with Mathew Guest, Ashgate 2012), *Exploring Religion and the Sacred in a Media Age* (with Chris Deacy, Ashgate 2009) and *Reading Religion in Text and Context* (with Peter Collins, Ashgate 2006). She is the author of several book chapters and of *Researching New Religious Movements in the West* (Routledge 2007) and co-author (with Peter Clarke) of *New Religious Movements in Western Europe: An Annotated Bibliography* (Greenwood Press 1997).

L. Philip Barnes is Emeritus Reader in Religious and Theological Education at King's College London. He has published widely in the related areas of religious studies, theology and education. Recent research has focused on the challenge of diversity to religious education in schools. He is the (co-) editor of a number of standard introductory texts for teachers of religious education: *Learning to Teach Religious Education in the Secondary School* (with Andrew Wright and Ann-Marie Brandom, Routledge 2008) and *Debates in Religious Education* (Routledge 2012). His most recent co-authored publications include *Does Religious Education Work?* (Bloomsbury 2012) and *Religious*

Education: Educating for Diversity (Bloomsbury 2015) as well as *Education, Religion and Diversity: Developing a New Model of Religious Education* (Routledge 2014) which provides an analysis and critique of post-confessional religious education in Britain. He is currently working on a book titled *Morality, Religion and Education: The Continuing Travail of Post-confessional Religious Education*, the second volume in a planned trilogy on theory and practice in British religious education.

Lori G. Beaman PhD is the Canada Research Chair in the Contextualization of Religion in a Diverse Canada, Professor in the Department of Classics and Religious Studies at the University of Ottawa, and the Principal Investigator of the Religion and Diversity Project, a 37-member international research team whose focus is religion and diversity (see http://www.religionanddiversity.ca). Recent publications include: 'Deep Equality as an Alternative to Accommodation and Tolerance', *Nordic Journal of Religion and Society* 27 (2) 2014; 'Opposing Polygamy: A Matter of Equality or Patriarchy?', in M.-P. Robert, D. Koussens and S. Bernatchez, eds., *Of Crime and Religion: Polygamy in Canadian Law* (Éditions Revue de droit de l'Université de Sherbrooke 2014); 'Reframing Understandings of Religion: Lessons from India', in S. Sikka, B. Puri and L.G. Beaman, eds., *Living with Religious Diversity* (Routledge India 2016); and 'Woven Together: Advocacy and Research as Complementary', *Religion* 44 (2) 2014.

James A. Beckford, a Fellow of the British Academy, is Professor Emeritus of Sociology at the University of Warwick and a former President of the Association for the Sociology of Religion, the International Society for the Sociology of Religion and the Society for the Scientific Study of Religion. His main research interests are chaplaincies and relations between religion and the state. His principal publications include *The Trumpet of Prophecy. A Sociological Study of Jehovah's Witnesses* (1975), *Cult Controversies* (1985), *Religion and Advanced Industrial Society* (1989), *Religion in Prison. Equal Rites in a Multi-Faith Society* (1998, with Sophie Gilliat), *Social Theory and Religion* (2003), *Muslims in Prison: Challenge and Change in Britain and France* (2005, with D. Joly and F. Khosrokhavar), and *The SAGE Handbook of the Sociology of Religion* (2007, edited with N.J. Demerath III) and *Migration and Religion* (2 edited volumes, 2015).

Peter Beyer is Professor of Religious Studies at the University of Ottawa, Canada. His work has focused primarily on religion in Canada and on developing sociological theory concerning religion and globalization. His publications include *Religion and Globalization* (Sage 1994), *Religions in Global Society* (Routledge 2006) and *Religion in the Context of Globalization* (Routledge 2013). Since 2001 he has been conducting research on religious diversity in Canada. From this research, he is principal author and editor, along with Rubina Ramji, of *Growing Up Canadian: Muslims, Hindus, Buddhists* (McGill-Queen's 2013).

Christine L. Cusack holds an MA in Communication and is pursuing a PhD in Religious Studies at the University of Ottawa. Her doctoral dissertation is focused on religious literacy and public education, and her other research interests include feminism and the intersections of gender, religion and the media. Her most recent publication (with L. G. Beaman and L. G. Forbes) is titled 'Law's Entanglements: Resolving Questions of Religion and Education', in *Issues in Religion and Education: Whose Religion?*, edited by L. G. Beaman and L. Van Arragon (Brill 2015).

Leslie J. Francis PhD, ScD, DLitt, DD is Professor of Religions and Education and Director of the WRERU within the Centre for Education Studies at the University of Warwick. He also serves as Canon Theologian at Bangor Cathedral. He holds visiting chairs at York St John University and Glyndŵr University and a visiting position at Pretoria University, South Africa. He is Editor of *Rural Theology* and Associate Editor of *Journal of Beliefs and Values*. His research interests embrace religious education, practical theology, psychology of religion and empirical theology. His most recent books are *History, Remembrance and Religious Education* (edited with Stephen Parker and Rob Freathy, Peter Lang 2015) and *Anglican Cathedrals in Modern Life: The Science of Cathedral Studies* (Palgrave Macmillan 2015).

Julia Ipgrave PhD was, at the time of writing, Senior Research Fellow in the WRERU at the University of Warwick and is now Senior Research Fellow in the Department of Humanities (Ministerial Theology) at the University of Roehampton. She is the principal investigator for the London strand of the Religion and Dialogue in Modern Society project of the World Academy of Religions at the University of Hamburg, Germany. Her research interests include religion in education, young people's religious understanding, inter-religious engagement at community level, and religion and political thought in the seventeenth century – fields in which she has published widely.

Robert Jackson PhD DLitt FAcSS was Director of the WRERU (1994–2012) and is Emeritus Professor of Religions and Education at the University of Warwick and Visiting Professor in Humanities and Social Sciences Education at Stockholm University. He has been involved since 2002 in the Council of Europe's work on the place of religions and non-religious convictions in inter-cultural education and was Special Adviser to the European Wergeland Centre 2009–2014, holding a Visiting Professorship at Oslo University College. He contributed to the European Commission-funded REDCo (Religion, Education, Dialogue, Conflict) project and directed the Young People's Attitudes to Religious Diversity project in the Religion and Society Programme in the UK, on which he served as a member of the Steering Committee. He was Editor of the *British Journal of Religious Education* (1996–2011). In 2013 he received the William Rainey Harper Award from the Religious Education Association of the USA and Canada, presented to 'outstanding leaders whose work in other fields has had a profound impact upon religious education'. His publications include 26 books, including *Signposts: Policy and Practice for Teaching about Religions and Non-religious Worldviews in Intercultural Education* (Council of Europe 2014). *Signposts* provides ideas for policy makers, schools and teacher educators across Europe for implementing the 2008 Council of Europe Recommendation on teaching about religions and non-religious convictions.

Ursula McKenna PhD is a research fellow in the WRERU based in the Centre for Education Studies at the University of Warwick. She is currently working on the project titled Ten Leading Schools: The Spiritual Influence of Christian-Ethos Secondary Education. Her most recent book (with Joyce Miller and Kevin O'Grady) is *Religion in Education: Innovation in International Research* (Routledge 2013).

Mary Elizabeth Moore is Dean of the School of Theology and Professor of Theology and Education at Boston University. Drawing on theological and cultural analysis, she focuses much of her research on youth and on religious practices for justice, peace and sustainability. In addition to numerous articles on youth and the co-edited volume *Children, Youth, and Spirituality in a Troubling World* (with Almeda M. Wright, Chalice Press 2008), her recent books include *Teaching as a Sacramental Act* (Pilgrim 2004), *Ministering with the Earth* (Chalice Press 1998), *Teaching from the Heart* (Trinity 1998), *A Living Tradition: Critical Recovery and Reconstruction of the Wesleyan Heritage* (edited, Kingswood Books 2013) and *Practical Theology and Hermeneutics* (co-edited, Brill 2005).

Rev Canon Professor **Peter Neil** PhD is Vice Chancellor of Bishop Grosseteste University and visiting professor at Glyndŵr University. He has held various positions in universities in the four jurisdictions in the UK in education (Queen's, Belfast, Aberystwyth and the University of the West of Scotland). He is an international trustee on the Board of the Colleges and Universities of the Anglican Communion and Vice Chair of the Cathedrals Group of universities. He is an ordained Anglican priest and Canon of Lincoln Cathedral. He has conducted research into various aspects of education. His research in theology focused on the beliefs and practices of churchgoers in mid-Wales and is currently on the experiences of lay members of churches who have engaged in the study of theology in higher education. The findings of both projects are presented in recent editions of *Rural Theology*. While in Scotland he was engaged in supporting the research project in Scottish schools.

Dr Gemma Penny is an associate research fellow in the WRERU, Centre for Education Studies, University of Warwick. Her recent research has focused on individual differences in young people's attitudes towards religion and the connection between attendance in schools with a religious character and young people's values. Recent publications have appeared in *Research in the Social Scientific Study of Religion*, *Scottish Educational Review* and *Contemporary Religion*.

Mandy Robbins is a reader in the psychology of religion at Glyndŵr University, Wrexham, Wales, and an Honorary Research Fellow at the WRERU at University of Warwick. She received her PhD from the University of Wales and her Post-graduate Diploma in Psychology from the Open University. Her recent publications include 'Life in the Church' with Greg Smith, published in *21st Century Evangelicals* (edited by Greg Smith, Evangelical Alliance 2015) and 'Subjective Well-Being and Psychological Type among Australian Clergy' with Nicole Hancock, published in *Mental Health, Religion and Culture* (2015).

Alexander Yendell is a research fellow in the Department of the Sociology of Religion and Church in the Institute of Practical Theology at Leipzig University, Germany. Before joining the Institute in Leipzig, he was a Research Fellow in the Cluster of Excellence 'Religion and Politics' at the University of Münster, Germany, where he began his research on 'Attitudes towards Religious Diversity', using quantitative methods. Besides book chapters and articles, recent publications include two co-authored books: *Grenzen der Toleranz* (with Detlef Pollack, Olaf Müller, Gergely Rosta and Nils Friedrichs) (Springer VS 2014) and *Der Deutsche Evangelische Kirchentag: Religiöses Bekenntnis, politische Veranstaltung oder doch nur ein Event?* (with Gert Pickel and Yvonne Jaeckel) (Nomos 2015).

Index

Note: Page numbers in italics indicate figures and tables.

AHRC *see* Arts and Humanities Research
  Council (AHRC)
AHRC/ESRC Religion and Society
  Programme 155
Allport, Gordon 61
Alves, Colin 154
American Academy of Religion 270; Task
  Force on Religion in the Schools 270
American Psychologist 170
ap Siôn, Tania 38
*Arbeitsgemeinschaft deutscher
  Marktforschungsinstitute* (ADM) 277
Archive for the Psychology of Religion 32
Argyle, Michael 31–2, 36–7
Arts and Humanities Research Council
  (AHRC) 4, 10
Arweck, Elisabeth 12, 21, 22, 251
aspiration, integrated education in
  Northern Ireland and 63–4
Astley-Francis Scale of Attitude toward
  Theistic Faith 34–5
attitudes: diversity, in London multicultural
  school 140–2; to diversity and context
  in Wales 107–12, 117–21; frequency
  of contact and, towards Muslims
  286–7, *286–7*; towards Catholics in
  Northern Ireland 177, *177*; towards
  cultural diversity in England 165–6,
  166; towards Protestants in Northern
  Ireland 176–7, *177*; towards religion
  in Northern Ireland 176, *176*; towards
  religions in England *164,* 164–5; towards
  religions in London 234–5, *235*; towards
  religions in Wales 214, *214*; towards
  religions/religious diversity in Wales
  213–17; towards religious distinctiveness
  in England *166,* 166–7; towards religious

plurality in England 165, *165*; towards
  youth and religious diversity in Europe
  277–8, 277–82, 279, 280, 281, 282
Attitudes toward Religion project 33
Attitude toward Muslim Proximity
  Index 35
Attitude toward Religious Diversity
  Index 39
authenticity 78
authority: Muslims and reliance on external
  53–6; of non-Muslim RE teachers 55–6

Baker, Dori 266, 267
Barlow, Anne 187, 225
Barnes, Philip 38
Beit-Hallahmi, Ben 36–7
Bellah, Robert 253
belonging 78
Big Questions, The (BBC1) 248
Bloody Sunday Report 66–8
Bobrow, Martin 225
Boys, Mary 270
British and Foreign Schools Society 153,
  206
British North America Act 246
British Social Attitudes Survey 187, 224,
  225, 239
British Values *vs.* extremist influences 23
Brockett, Adrian 35
Brown, Gordon 77
Brown, Millward 63

Cairns, Ed 170
Canada, religion and education in 246–7;
  current research status 248–50
Canada, youth and religious diversity
  in 245–57; conflict and 252; context

and 251; introduction to 245–6; RE
contribution to 252–3; Religion and
Diversity Project 247–8; religion and
education in Canada 246–7; religious/
cultural identities and 253–6; WRERU
project and 250–1
Cartledge, Mark 32
Catholic and Protestant schools in
Northern Ireland research 170–84;
attitudes towards Catholics results 177,
177; attitudes towards Protestants results
176–7, *177*; attitudes towards religion
results 176, *176*; Greer and 171–2;
introduction to 170–4; living with
cultural diversity results 180–1, *181*;
living with religious plurality results 180,
180; method used in 175–6; Murray and
171; 1998 survey 172–3; past research
170–2; religious clothing acceptance
results 182, *183*; religious education
in schools results 181–2, *182*; religious
plurality acceptance results *179*, 179–80;
research question 174–5; results for
176–83; shaping views about Catholics
results 178, *179*; shaping views about
Protestants results 178, *178*; Teenage
Religion and Values Survey and 173–4;
Turner and 171
Catholic identities 189
Catholic Poor School Committee 153, 206
Catholics in secular Scotland 77–95;
see also growing up Catholic in Scotland
research; St. Albert's RC High School
perspectives; Church of Scotland census
statistics 79; disconnection of 78–9;
memory and 77–8; Roman Catholic
education and 79–80; St. Albert's RC
High School perspectives on 80–93
Census White Paper 204
Chadwick, Priscilla 206
Charter for Catholic Schools in Scotland 80
Charter of Québec Values 248
Children and Worldviews Project 154
Children's Spirituality Project 154
Christian country 120–1
Christie, Ian 225
Clery, Elizabeth 225
collective memory in religion 77
Collins-Mayo, Sylvia 58, 78, 85, 90
Committee of Enquiry 206, 207
communal validation 78
Communities Engaging with Difference
and Religion (CEDAR) 271

community 25
community relations, impact of integrated
education on 64
Conroy, James 39, 47; 'Does Religious
Education Work?' project 155–6
Constitution Act of 1867 246
constitutive religion, Islam as 48–9
contact hypothesis 61, 116, 120, 275–6,
282–3
Cox, Edwin 154
Croft, Jennifer 12
Cruickshank, Marjorie 206
cultural diversity: in England, attitudes
towards 165–6, *166*; in London, living
with 236–7, *237*; in Northern Ireland,
living with 180–1, *181*; in Scotland,
living with 198–9, *199*; in Wales, living
with *216*, 216–17

Darby, John 170
Davie, Grace 78
Day, Abby 78
Dean, Kenda Creasy 271
Death of Christian Britain, The (Brown) 222
Department for Children, Schools and
Families (DCSF) project 4–5; case study
research included in 5; strands of 5
discovery/exploration of Islam 51–3
diversity: attitudes in London multicultural
school 140–2; value in London
multicultural school 142–7
diversity and context in Wales 97–123;
attitudes to 107–12, 117–21; differences
and 103–7, 112–17; focus groups
overview 101–2; geographical/social
contexts influence on pupils' attitudes/
outlooks 102–21; introduction to 97;
school profiles 97–101
Diversity project *see* Young People's
Attitudes to Religious Diversity project
Dixie, John 223
Dowds, Lizanne 64, 65, 73
Dummett, Ann 207
Duncan, Simon 187

Economic and Social Research Council
(ESRC) 3, 10
Education for All (Swann Report) 207
Egan, Josephine 189
Elgenius, Gabriella 225
empirical theology 32–3
*Empirical Theology in Texts and Tables:
Qualitative, Quantitative and Comparative*

Perspectives (Francis, Robbins and Astley) 32

ESRC *see* Economic and Social Research Council (ESRC)

Ethics and Religious Culture (ERC) programme 249

ethos theory 156–7

Europe, youth and religious diversity in 275–88; *see also* PARD religions survey; attitudes towards *277–8, 277–82, 279, 280, 281, 282*; attitude towards Muslims 282–4, *283*; data and survey methods used 276–7; Eastern Germany factors 285; frequency of contact and attitudes towards Muslims of 286–7, *286–7*; introduction to 275–6; knowledge transfer and 275–6; model fit for Western Germany 284; Western Germany factors 284–5

European Values Survey (EVS) 286

Exley, Sonia 225

experience, integrated education in Northern Ireland and 64

Eysenck, Hans 36–8

Eysenck Personality Questionnaire 37

Eysenck Personality Questionnaire Revised 37

Faith in Education (Welsh Government) 205–6

Faith of Generation Y, The (Collins-Mayo) 58

family validation, St. Albert's RC High School perspectives on 87–91

Finch, Stewart 154

formation: communal 266–8; of young people, personal/interpersonal 264–6

Fox News Network 45

Francis, Leslie 11–12, 78, 173, 174, 183, 209, 239, 265; Catholic identities and 189; ethos theory and 156–7; quantitative research expertise of 4, 32–40; religious affiliation in London and 225–7; Teenage Religion and Values Survey 187–9

Francis Scale of Attitude toward Christianity 34

Gearon, Liam 7–9

Gergen, Kenneth J. 252

Getting on Together: A Community Cohesion Strategy for Wales (Welsh Assembly Government) 205

Gibson, H. M. 189

Gill, Robin 187

Goldman, Ronald 154

Gould, Arthur 225

Greer, John E. 171–2, 183

growing up Catholic in Scotland research 186–202; Catholic identities and 189; Christian beliefs results 193, *193*; conclusions drawn from 200–2; introduction to 186–7; living with cultural diversity results 198–9, *199*; living with religious plurality results 198, *198*; method used in 190; non-conventional beliefs results 194–5, *195*; question 189; religion and education results *195*, 195–6; religion and society results *196*, 196–7; religious affect results 194, *194*; religious and life results 192, *193*; religious conversation results 191–2, *192*; religious differences acceptance results 199–200, *200*; religious identity results 190–1, *191*; religious plurality acceptance results 197, *197*; results for 190–200; Teenage Religion and Values Survey 187–9

Harvey, T. J. 154

Hayes, Bernadette 64, 65, 73, 225

Heath, Anthony 225

Hegy, Pierre 33

Hervieu-Léger, Danièle 77–8, 82, 91

Hill, Peter 32

Hood, Ralph 32

horizontal validation 83

Hull, John 46

Humanist Association 248

Hyde, Kenneth 154

identities: Catholic 189; Catholic, in Scotland 189; integrated 64; religious/cultural, youth in Canada 253–6; religiously-based ethnonationalist 62; shared, in Northern Ireland 71–3

Imagining God (Ziebertz) 33

individual differences psychology 23

informational-analytic engagement, in United States 269–70

institutional validation 78; interconnected aspects of 84; St. Albert's RC High School perspectives on 84–7

instruments of measurement, quantitative research 36–8

Integrated Education, Northern Ireland 61–74; *see also* Woodside Integrated College; aspiration and 63–4; attitudes

and 62; context of 61–6; criticism of 64–6; experience and 64; impact of, on community relations 64; migration and 63; Nicie movement and 61–3; pupil perspectives of 66–73; residential separation and 62–3; Roman Catholic Church and 65–6; shared identity and 71–3; social change and 62; socio-economic divide and 65; at Woodside Integrated College 61–2
integrated identity 64
'Interfaith Communities in Residence Life' (Interfaith Youth Core) 268
'Interfaith Cooperation at Public Institutions: Promising Practices' (Interfaith Youth Core) 268
Interfaith Youth Core 268
International Journal for the Psychology of Religion 32
International Society for Empirical Research in Theology 32
Ipgrave, Julia 12, 21, 22, 251, 252, 265

Jackson, Robert 11, 31, 207–8, 270
James, Grace 187
Journal of Beliefs and Values (Cartledge) 32
Journal of Empirical Theology 32, 33
Journal of Psychology and Theology 33
Junior Eysenck Personality Questionnaire 37
Junior Eysenck Personality Questionnaire Revised 37

Katz-Francis Scale of Attitude toward Judaism 34
Kay, William 34
Khan, Sadullah 268
Kress, Jeffrey 266

Lee, Lois 225
Lee, Sara 270
'Legitimacy of Religious Pluralism, The: Perception and Acceptance of Religious Diversity among the European Population' (PARD) 276; *see also* PARD religions survey
levels of measurement, quantitative survey 35–6
Leverhulme Trust 3
Lewis, E. O. 154
Likert, Rensis 36
Likert scaling 36
Ling, Rodney 225

London *see* multicultural school impressions in London; religious affiliation in London study
Loukes, Harold 154

Madge, Violet 154
Making of Post-Christian Britain, The (Gilbert) 222
Marangudakis, Manussos 225
Marteau, Theresa 225
Martin, Jean 225
McAllister, Ian 64, 65, 73
McKenna, Ursula 12
McLean, Sheila 225
McNeal, Julia 207
media influence 24
Mental Health 32
Mercer, Joyce 266
Moe, Shane 265
Moore, Diane L. 269–70
Moore, Mary Elizabeth 264
Moran, Gabriel 270
Mori, Ipsos 63
multicultural school impressions in London 125–48; difference question responses 129–34; diversity attitudes 140–2; diversity value 142–7; ethos of school researched 127–9; focus groups in school researched 129; introduction to 125; religion conversations 134–6; school profile 126–7; values and, questions of 136–40
Murphy, James 206
Murray, D. 39, 171
Muslims in Birmingham, attitude to religion of 45–59; authority and 53–6; constitutive religion and 48–9; discovery and 51–3; modernity and 46–8; obedience and 49–51; ontological security and 58–9; relations with other religions and 56–8; study overview 45–6
Muslim Youth Project 268
mutual validation 78; defined 83; St. Albert's RC High School perspectives on 91–3

National Society 153, 206
Neil, Peter 38, 265
NICIE *see* Northern Ireland Council for Integrated Education (NICIE) movement
Northern Ireland, Catholic and Protestant schools in *see* Catholic and Protestant schools in Northern Ireland research

Northern Ireland Council for Integrated
    Education (NICIE) movement 61–3;
    see also Integrated Education, Northern
    Ireland

obedience to God 49–51
Office for National Statistics (ONS) 223
Office of Democratic Institutions and
    Human Rights (ODHIR) 61
ontological security 78, 85
Outgroup Prejudice project 33, 35
own religion *vs.* non-religious
    perspectives 26

PARD religions survey: contact with
    Muslims by age groups *282*; granting
    rights for religious groups by country
    and age groups *279*; positive attitudes
    towards Muslims by country and age
    groups *281*; religious diversity as cultural
    enrichment by country and age groups
    279; respect for religions by country and
    age groups *277*; restriction of Islamic
    faith by country and age groups *281*;
    support for building mosques by country
    and age groups *280*; support of freedom
    of religious belief by country and age
    groups *277*
Park, Alison 187, 225
Patel, Eboo 266
Penny, Gemma 21, 156–7, 209, 265
personality, dimensional model of 36–7
Pettigrew, Thomas 276
Phillips, Miranda 225
policy makers, Diversity project
    implications for 26–7
Practical Theology 33
Protestant schools in Northern Ireland
    see Catholic and Protestant schools in
    Northern Ireland research
Psychology of Religion and Spirituality 32
Public Significance of Religion, The (Francis
    and Ziebertz) 32
Pyke, Alice 12

qualitative strand, Diversity project 19–30;
    characteristics of religious context
    found in 20–1; community and 25;
    contextualizations of 23; diversity
    attitudes and 22–3; exploratory nature
    of 21–2; implications drawn from
    26–8; influences/insights from 24–6;
    introduction to 19; local dynamics of
    28–30; media influence and 24; overview
    of 19–20; own religion *vs.* non-religious
    perspectives and 26; policy makers,
    implications for 26–7; religiosity attitudes
    and 22–3; religious diversity and 24–5;
    RE teachers/departments, implications
    for 27–8; school influence and 24; school
    managers, implications for 26–7; schools
    visited for 20
quantitative strand, Diversity project
    31–40; designing/conducting survey for
    38–9; empirical research traditions used
    in 33–5; instruments of measurement
    for 36–8; introduction to 31; levels of
    measurement for 35–6; present volume
    layout 39–40; theory sources for 31–3

Race and Church Schools (Dummett and
    McNeal) 207, 208
REDCo (Religion, Education, Dialogue,
    Conflict) project 4, 5–9; aims of 5–6;
    critical feedback on 7–9; Diversity
    project reinforcement of 10, 13–14;
    findings of 6–7; as innovative 6;
    WRERU's participation in 5
Rees, Reginald 154
relations with other religions, Muslims and
    56–8
Religion and Culture 32
Religion and Diversity Project 247–8
Religion and Society Programme 10; youth
    call 10–11
*Religion Inside and Outside Traditional
    Institutions* (Streib) 32
religious affiliation, described 222–4
religious affiliation in London study
    222–39; attitudes towards religions results
    234–5, *235*; attitude towards religious
    plurality results *235*, 235–6; conclusions
    drawn from 238–9; introduction to
    222–4; living with cultural diversity
    results 236–7, *237*; living with religious
    differences results 237–8, *238*; living
    with religious plurality results 236,
    236; overview of 224; personal/
    social correlates of 225–7; personal
    wellbeing results 233, *233*; personal
    worldview and experience theme
    229–34; religious beliefs results *232*,
    232–3; religious conversation results 231,
    231; religious identity results 229, *229*;
    religious importance results 230, *230*;
    religious influence results 231–2, *232*;

religious self-assessment results *230,* 230–1; research method overview 228–9; research question 227–8; social wellbeing results 233–4, *234*; social worldview theme 234–8
Religious Affiliation Sub-Group of Census Content Working Group 223
Religious Behaviour (Argyle) 31–2
religious clothing acceptance: in Northern Ireland 182, *183*; in Wales 217, *217*
religious conversations in London multicultural school 134–6
religious diversity 24–5; as personal/ social value (*see* multicultural school impressions in London); question responses concerning, in London school 129–34; in Wales (*see* religious diversity in Wales study); youth and, in Canada (*see* Canada, youth and religious diversity in)
religious diversity and education studies (WRERU) 3–4
Religious Diversity and Young People survey 158, 175, 190, 210, 228
religious diversity in Wales study 204–21; attitudes towards religions/religious diversity theme 213–17; attitudes towards religions results 214, *214*; community cohesion and 204–6; conclusions drawn from 220; influence sources results *218*, 218–19; living with cultural diversity results *216*, 216–17; living with religious plurality results *215*, 215–16; religion in schools results 213, *213*; religious beliefs results *212*, 212–13; religious clothing acceptance results 217, *217*; religious discussion results *211*, 211–12; religious identity results 211, *211*; religious plurality acceptance results 214–15, *215*; religious self-assessment results 212, *212*; religious worldview of students theme 210–13; research aim 209; research method overview 209–10; shaping attitudes towards religions/religious diversity theme 218–19; state-maintained schools and 206–9; studying religion at school results 219, *219*
religious education (RE); *see also* religious education (RE) in England study: in Canada 245–6 (*see also* Canada, religion and education in); Education Act of 1870 and 153; Education Act of 1944 and 153–4; Education Reform Act of

1988 and 154; equality concept and, in Northern Ireland 68–9; in London multicultural school 127; multi-faith 57–8; Ofsted report on 47; role of 46–7; in Wales schools 99
Religious Education Council (REC) 47
religious education (RE) in England study 153–68; attitudes towards cultural diversity results 165–6, *166*; attitudes towards religions results *164,* 164–5; attitudes towards religious distinctiveness results *166,* 166–7; attitudes towards religious plurality results 165, *165*; Conroy's investigation into 155–6; distinctive place of 153; Education Act of 1944 and 153–4; ethos theory and 156–7; experiencing RE theme 161–4; locally agreed syllabus and 153–4; main influences results 162, *162*; religious affect results 159–60, *160*; religious beliefs results 159, *159*; religious discussion results 161, *161*; religious diversity theme 164–7; religious environment results *160,* 160–1; religious studies at school results 162–3, *163*; religious worldview theme 159–61; research method overview 158–9; research question overview 157–8; student responses to, past studies of 154–7; understanding religious/cultural difference results *163,* 163–4
religious education teachers/departments, Diversity project implications for 27–8
religious identity: growing up Catholic in Scotland research 190–1, *191*; religious affiliation in London study 229, *229*; religious diversity in Wales study 211, *211*
Religious Identity and National Heritage (Anthony and Ziebertz) 32
religious plurality: acceptance in Wales 214–15, *215*; acceptance results in Northern Ireland *179,* 179–80; attitudes towards, in England 165, *165*; attitude towards, in London *235,* 235–6; living with, in London 236, *236*; living with, in Northern Ireland 180, *180*; living with, in Wales *215,* 215–16
Respect and Resilience-Developing Community Cohesion: A Common Understanding for Schools and Their Communities (Welsh Assembly Government) 205, 206
Review of Religious Research 33

Rhead, Rebecca 187, 225
Right to Divide? Faith Schools and Community Cohesion (Berkeley) 40, 208–9, 220
Rippl, Susanne 275
Robbins, Mandy 12, 78, 173, 174–5, 183, 227, 239
Robinson, Peter 62
Roman Catholic Church: educational situation for, in Scotland 79–80 (*see also* St. Albert's RC High School perspectives); integrated education and 65–6
Root, Andrew 271
Rose, L. D. 171
Royal Lancasterian Society 206
Runnymede Trust 40, 206–7, 208, 220

Sahin-Francis Scale of Attitude toward Islam 34
St. Albert's RC High School perspectives 80–93; on family validation 87–91; on institutional validation 84–7; on mutual validation 83, 91–3; research overview 80–1; on secular society religion 81–3; on self-validation 83–4
Sales, Amy 266–7
Samuel, Nicole 266–7
Sandage, Steven 265
Santosh-Francis Scale of Attitude toward Hinduism 34
Savage, Mike 225
school influence 24
school managers, Diversity project implications for 26–7
Schools for the Future: Funding, Strategy, Sharing (Bain) 65
Scotland, growing up Catholic in *see* growing up Catholic in Scotland research
secular society religion: St. Albert's RC High School perspectives on 81–3
self-validation 78; St. Albert's RC High School perspectives on 83–4
Seligman, Adam 47, 49, 271
Senior, Nicki 225
Shared Education Programme,The (SEP) 65
Sheilaism concept 253
'Should the State Fund Faith Based Schools?' (Jackson) 207–8
Signposts (Council of Europe) 61
Social Sciences and Humanities Research Council (SSHRC) 247
sociology/social psychology 23
Spilka, Bernard 32

state-maintained system of education, England and Wales 206–9
Stratford, Nina 225
Sturgis, Patrick 225
Surridge, Paula 225
Swann Report 46–7

Taylor, Charles 21–2, 50, 78
Teenage Religion and Values (Francis and Kay) 33
Teenage Religion and Values project 13, 33–4, 173
Teenage Religion and Values Survey 173, 174, 187–9, 224, 225
Teenagers and the Church (Francis) 33
theological context 23
Toledo Guiding Principles 61
Trojan Horse affair 45, 46
Tropp, Linda 276
Turner, E. B. 171

United Nations Human Rights Committee 246
United States, youth and religious diversity in 263–72; communal formation and 266–8; engagement with difference and 270–1; engagement with mystery and 271; *genres* of RE research for 264–71; informational-analytic engagement and 269–70; introduction to 263; personal/interpersonal formation and 264–6
Urban Hope and Spiritual Health (Francis and Robbins) 33

validation 78; communal 78; family, St. Albert's RC High School perspectives on 87–91; horizontal 83; institutional 78; mutual 78, 83; self 78
validation regimes 78
values, questions of, in London multicultural school 136–40
Values Debate, The (Francis) 33, 188
Van Arragon, Leo 249
van der Ven, Hans 32
Village, Andrew 33, 35, 225
Voas, David 79, 225

Waldman v. Canada 246
Wales *see* diversity and context in Wales; religious diversity in Wales study
Wallner, Jennifer 247
Warwick Religions and Education Research Unit (WRERU) 154; Attitudes toward

Religion project 33; Department for
Children, Schools and Families project
4–5; Diversity project 10–14, 31, 34–5;
further project involvement of 14–15;
Outgroup Prejudice project 33, 35;
qualitative research at 4, 5; quantitative
research at 4, 5; REDCo project 5–9;
religious diversity and education studies
of 3–4; Teenage Religion and Values
project 13, 33–4
Weller, Robert 271
Westminster Faith Debates 248
What Do We Imagine God to Be? (Hegy) 33
Williams, Emyr 225
Williams, Roma 154
Woodhead, Linda 10, 83
Woodside Integrated College; *see also*
Integrated Education, Northern Ireland:
Bloody Sunday Report and 66–8;
equality concept and 68–9; establishment
of 61; NICIE movement and 61–2;
population of 67; pupil perspectives of
66–73; religiously-based ethnonationalist
identities and 62; shared identity at 71–3

'worlds apart' thesis in Northern Ireland
see Catholic and Protestant schools in
Northern Ireland research
WRERU *see* Warwick Religions and
Education Research Unit (WRERU)

Young People's Attitudes to Religious
Diversity project 7, 10–14; *see also*
Catholic and Protestant schools in
Northern Ireland research; funding
for 10; London as special case within
224; overview of 10; proposal 10–12;
qualitative research overview 12 (*see also*
qualitative strand, Diversity project);
quantitative research overview 12–13
(*see also* quantitative strand, Diversity
project); REDCo findings and 10, 13–14;
research questions 11; roots of 34; scope
of 34–5; team members of 11–12;
themes 10–11
Youth in Transit (Francis) 33

Zablotsky, Alexander 266–7
Ziebertz, Hans-Georg 33